Confluence of Computer Vision and Computer Graphics

T0225997

NATO Science Series

A Series presenting the results of activities sponsored by the NATO Science Committee. The Series is published by IOS Press and Kluwer Academic Publishers, in conjunction with the NATO Scientific Affairs Division.

A. Life Sciences	IOS Press
B. Physics	Kluwer Academic Publishers
C. Mathematical and Physical Sciences	Kluwer Academic Publishers
D. Behavioural and Social Sciences	Kluwer Academic Publishers
E. Applied Sciences	Kluwer Academic Publishers
F. Computer and Systems Sciences	IOS Press

1. Disarmament Technologies	Kluwer Academic Publishers
2. Environmental Security	Kluwer Academic Publishers
3. High Technology	Kluwer Academic Publishers
4. Science and Technology Policy	IOS Press
5. Computer Networking	IOS Press

NATO-PCO-DATA BASE

The NATO Science Series continues the series of books published formerly in the NATO ASI Series. An electronic index to the NATO ASI Series provides full bibliographical references (with keywords and/or abstracts) to more than 50000 contributions from international scientists published in all sections of the NATO ASI Series.
Access to the NATO-PCO-DATA BASE is possible via CD-ROM "NATO-PCO-DATA BASE" with user-friendly retrieval software in English, French and German (WTV GmbH and DATAWARE Technologies Inc. 1989).

The CD-ROM of the NATO ASI Series can be ordered from: PCO, Overijse, Belgium

Series 3. High Technology – Vol. 84

Confluence of Computer Vision and Computer Graphics

edited by

Aleš Leonardis
Franc Solina
University of Ljubljana,
Ljubljana,
Republic of Slovenia

and

Ruzena Bajcsy
University of Pennsylvania,
Philadelphia, U.S.A.
and
National Science Foundation,
Washington, U.S.A.

Kluwer Academic Publishers

Dordrecht / Boston / London

Published in cooperation with NATO Scientific Affairs Division

Proceedings of the NATO Advanced Research Workshop on
Confluence of Computer Vision and Computer Graphics
Ljubljana, Republic of Slovenia
29–31 August 1999

A C.I.P. Catalogue record for this book is available from the Library of Congress.

ISBN 0-7923-6611-5 (HB)
ISBN 0-7923-6612-3 (PB)

Published by Kluwer Academic Publishers,
P.O. Box 17, 3300 AA Dordrecht, The Netherlands.

Sold and distributed in North, Central and South America
by Kluwer Academic Publishers,
101 Philip Drive, Norwell, MA 02061, U.S.A.

In all other countries, sold and distributed
by Kluwer Academic Publishers,
P.O. Box 322, 3300 AH Dordrecht, The Netherlands.

Printed on acid-free paper

Contents

List of Figures

List of Tables

Preface

This volume is a collection of original contributions from a new field which lies at the intersection of computer vision and computer graphics. Recently, great effort has been made towards the integration of computer vision and computer graphics techniques in the areas of realistic modeling of objects and scenes, interactive computer graphics, and augmented reality.

General issues and numerous specific applications are discussed which demonstrate the close relationships between computer vision, computer graphics, and communication technologies. These include urban and archeological site modeling, modeling dressed humans, medical visualisation, figure and facial animation, real-time 3D-teleimmersion and telecollaboration, augmented reality as a new user interface concept, and augmented reality for underwater scene understanding.

The contributions collected in this volume are extensively revised versions of papers which were initially presented at the NATO Advanced Research Workshop which was held in Ljubljana, Slovenia, on 29–31 August 1999. The workshop was funded by the NATO Scientific & Environmental Affairs Division: High Technology Priority Area. Additional support was provided by the Ministry of Science and Technology of the Republic of Slovenia, University of Ljubljana, Faculty of Computer and Information Science, IEEE Slovenia Section, and Hermes SoftLab.

Aleš Leonardis, Franc Solina, Ruzena Bajcsy

Contributing Authors

Caroline Baillard is a Research Assistant in the Visual Geometry Group of the Department of Engineering Science in Oxford University. She received a Dipl.Ing. (1994) and Ph.D. degree (1997) in signal and image processing, both from ENST (Ecole Nationale Superieure des telecommunications), Paris. Her main research interests in computer vision are image matching, stereovision, segmentation and 3D image analysis.

Department of Engineering Science, University of Oxford, 19 Parks Road, Oxford, OX1 3PJ, United Kingdom.
caroline@robots.ox.ac.uk

Ruzena Bajcsy is currently the Assistant Director of the Directorate for Computer and Information Science and Engineering (CISE) at the National Science Foundation. She is the founder and director of the General Robotics Automation Sensing and Perception (GRASP) Laboratory at the University of Pennsylvania. Ruzena Bajcsy received her first Ph.D. in EE from Slovak University (Czechoslovakia) in 1967 and her second Ph.D. in 1972 from Stanford University under John McCarthy. She then joined the faculty at University of Pennsylvania—chairing the department from 1985 through 1990. She has served on numerous National Research Council and National Science Foundation advisory boards and committees. She was elected a fellow of IEEE (1992) and of ACM (1995), elected member in the National Institute of Medicine, member of National Academy of Engineering (1997). She is also a founding fellow of AAAI and has served for 3 years on the CRA Board. Her contributions are in computer vision, robotics, and integration of sensory information.

University of Pennsylvania, GRASP Laboratory, Department of Computer and Information Science, Philadelphia, PA 19104-6389, USA.
bajcsy@central.cis.upenn.edu

Igor R. Belousov is a Senior Researcher in the Keldysh Institute of Applied Mathematics, Russian Academy of Sciences and a Visiting Fellow at De Montfort University. He graduated in Mechanics from Lomonosov Moscow State University, from where he was also awarded his Ph.D. in Theoretical Mechanics. His research interests include space robotics, remote robot control over the Internet, robot manipulator kinematics and dynamics, fast integration algorithms, automatic robot interaction with fast moving objects, man-machine interfaces, 3D graphic simulation and virtual reality. He was awarded a State Scientific Fellowship of the Russian Academy of Sciences in 1998 and an INTAS Fellowship Award for Young Scientists in 1999. He is a member of the UK-VRSIG.

Department of Computer & Information Sciences, De Montfort University, United Kingdom.

Marie-Odile Berger is an INRIA research scientist working with the Image Synthesis and Analysis group (ISA) of the Laboratoire lorrain de recherche en informatique et ses applications (LORIA), Nancy, France. Her research interests include augmented reality, computer vision and medical imaging. Dr. Berger received a Agrégation of Mathematics (1986) and a Ph.D. in Computer Science (1991) from the Institut National Polytechnique de Lorraine.

LORIA-INRIA Lorraine, BP 239, 54506 Vandoeuvre-les-Nancy, France.
berger@loria.fr

Gordon J. Clapworthy is Reader in Computer Graphics in the Department of Computer & Information Sciences, De Montfort University, Milton Keynes, United Kingdom. His interests are medical visualisation, computer animation, biomechanics, virtual reality, surface modeling and fundamental graphics algorithms. He was awarded a B.Sc. in Mathematics and a Ph.D. in Aeronautical Engineering from the University of London, and an M.Sc. in Computer Science from The City University, London. He is a member of ACM, ACM Siggraph, Eurographics and the UK-VRSIG, and Secretary of the ACM British Chapter.

Department of Computer & Information Sciences, De Montfort University, United Kingdom.
gc@dmu.ac.uk

Geoffrey Cross is a DPhil student in the Visual Geometry Group of the Department of Engineering Science, University of Oxford. He received a B.A. and M.Eng. from the University of Cambridge in 1996 in Electrical and Information Science. His particular interests are in surface reconstruction from uncalibrated image sequences.

Department of Engineering Science, University of Oxford, 19 Parks Road, Oxford, OX1 3PJ, United Kingdom.
geoff@robots.ox.ac.uk

Kostas Daniilidis is an Assistant Professor of Computer and Information Science at the University of Pennsylvania since March 1998. Previously, he was with the Computer Science Institute at Kiel University. He received his Ph.D. in Computer Science at the University of Karlsruhe in 1992 and his M.Sc. in Electrical Engineering at the National Technical University of Athens. His contributions are geometric results in scene and motion recovery and calibration. Nowadays, his research centers on omnidirectional vision and immersive environments.

University of Pennsylvania, GRASP Laboratory, Department of Computer and Information Science, Philadelphia, PA 19104-6389, USA.
kostas@grip.cis.upenn.edu

Filip Defoort, Katholieke Universiteit Leuven, ESAT-PSI/VISICS, Kardinaal Mercierlaan 94, B-3001 Leuven, Belgium.
filip.defoort@esat.kuleuven.ac.be

Charles R. Dyer is Professor of Computer Sciences at the University of Wisconsin–Madison. He received the B.S. degree in mathematical sciences from Stanford University in 1973, the M.S. degree in computer science from the University of California at Los Angeles in 1974, and the Ph.D. degree in computer science from the University of Maryland in 1979. His research interests include image-based view synthesis, multi-view representations, and motion analysis.

University of Wisconsin, Department of Computer Sciences, 1210 W. Dayton Street, Madison, WI 53706, USA.
dyer@cs.wisc.edu

Andrew Fitzgibbon is a Royal Society University Research Fellow in the Information Engineering group, University of Oxford. His research topic is computer vision from multiple views, particularly the recovery of 3D information from video sequences. He received his Ph.D. in Artificial Intelligence (Edinburgh) in 1997, investigating object recognition and automatic model extraction from range images, with excursions into nonparametric statistics and 2D curve representation.

Department of Engineering Science, University of Oxford, 19 Parks Road, Oxford, OX1 3PJ, United Kingdom.
awf@robots.ox.ac.uk

Andrea Fusiello is a Research Associate at the University of Verona. He received his Laurea (M.Sc.) degree in Computer Science from the Università di Udine in 1994 and his Ph.D. in Information Engineering from the Università di Trieste in 1999. He has published papers on autonomous vehicles navigation, stereo, feature tracking, autocalibration and 3-D vision. His present research is focused on 3-D computer vision, with applications to underwater robotics.

Dipartimento Scientifico e Tecnologico, Universita' degli Studi di Verona, Ca' Vignal 2, Strada Le Grazie 15, I-37134 Verona, Italy.
fusiello@sci.univr.it

André Gagalowicz is a research director at INRIA, France. He is the creator of the first laboratory involved in image analysis/synthesis collaboration techniques. He graduated from Ecole Superieure d'Electricite in 1971 (engineer in Electrical Engineering), obtained his Ph.D. in Automatic Control from the University of Paris XI, Orsay, in 1973, and his state doctorate in Mathematics (doctorat d'Etat es Sciences) from the University of Paris VI (1983). He is fluent in english, german, russian and polish and got a bachelor degree in chinese from the University of Paris IX, INALOCO in 1983. His research interests are in 3D approaches for computer vision, computer graphics, and their cooperation and also in digital image processing and pattern recognition. He received the prices of the best scientific communication and the best technical slide at the Eurographics'85 conference. He was awarded the second price of the Seymour Cray competition in 1991 and one of his papers was selected by the Computers and Graphics journal as one of the three best publications of this journal from the last ten years.

INRIA – Rocquencourt, Domaine de Voluceau, 78153 Le Chesnay, CEDEX, France.
Andre.Gagalowicz@inria.fr

Philippe Gérard received his engineer graduation from the Conservatoire National Des Arts et Metiers in 1996 at the EEC department. He is currently a Ph.D. student at INRIA and at the University Paris VI. At the INRIA, he is taking part in the European project Nemesis, dealing with 3D model-based tracking for video-production purposes. His main interests are: tracking, 3D reconstruction and special effects in video-production.

INRIA – Rocquencourt, Domaine de Voluceau, 78153 Le Chesnay, CEDEX, France.
Philippe.Gerard@inria.fr

Václav Hlaváč is a professor at the Department of Cybernetics, Faculty of Electrical Engineering, Czech Technical University in Prague, Czech Republic. He received M.Sc. (1981) and Ph.D. (1987), and became an Associate Professor (1992) and a Professor (1998), all at the Czech Technical University in Prague. Since 1996 he has become the head of the Center for Machine Perception. His main research interests include 3D computer vision, omnidirectional vision, pattern recognition, and industrial applications of machine vision.

Czech Technical University in Prague, Faculty of Electrical Engineering, Dept. of Cybernetics, Center for Machine Perception, Karlovo nám. 13, 121-35 Prague, Czech Republic.
hlavac@cmp.felk.cvut.cz

Thomas S. Huang is the William L. Everitt Distinguished Professor of Electrical and Computer Engineering at the University of Illinois at Urbana-Champaign (UIUC), a Research Professor in Coordinated Science Laboratory at UIUC and the Head of the Image Formation and Processing Laboratory at the Beckman Institute for Advanced Science and Technology. Dr. Huang also held professorships at Purdue University and MIT and served as a consultant for numerous industrial firms and government agencies both in the U.S. and abroad. He has published 12 books, and over 300 papers in Network Theory, Digital Filtering, Image Processing, and Computer Vision. He is a Fellow of the International Association of Pattern Recognition, IEEE, and the Optical Society of America; and has received a Guggenheim Fellowship, an A.V. Humboldt Foundation Senior U.S. Scientist Award, and a Fellowship from the Japan Association for the Promotion of Science. He received the IEEE Acoustics, Speech, and Signal Processing Society's Technical Achievement Award in 1987, and the Society Award in 1991.

Image Processing and Formation Laboratory, Beckman Institute, University of Illinois at Urbana-Champaign, Urbana, IL 61801, USA.
huang@ifp.uiuc.edu

Johannes Hug, ETH Zürich, Computer Vision Group BIWI, Gloriastrasse 35, CH-8092 Zürich, Switzerland.
hug@vision.ee.ethz.ch

Nebojša Jojić is a Ph.D. candidate at the University of Illinois, Urbana-Champaign (UIUC). He was awarded a Microsoft Graduate Fellowship in 1999 and the Robert T. Chien award for excellence in research by Electrical and Computer Engineering Department at UIUC in 2000. He has published papers in the areas of image processing, computer vision, computer graphics and machine learning.

Image Processing and Formation Laboratory, Beckman Institute, University of Illinois at Urbana-Champaign, Urbana, IL 61801, USA.

Gregor Kalberer, ETH Zürich, Computer Vision Group BIWI, Gloriastrasse 35, CH-8092 Zürich, Switzerland.
kalberer@vision.ee.ethz.ch

Gerda Kamberova is an Assistant Professor in Computer Science at Hofstra University since September 1999. During 1998-1999 she was visiting the Computer Science Department at Washington University in St. Louis. Previously, she was with the GRASP Laboratory at the University of Pennsylvania where she received her Ph.D. in Computer Science in 1992. She has an M.S. in Mathematics from Sofia State University, Bulgaria. Her contributions are in robust minimax estimation with applications to sensor fusion and stereo vision and recently in surface deformations and reconstruction.

University of Pennsylvania, GRASP Laboratory, Department of Computer and Information Science, Philadelphia, PA 19104-6389, USA.

Konrad Karner is a software engineer at Vexcel Corporation in Boulder, Colorado, with responsibility for the automated extraction of 3D-objects from stereo photographs. He holds a Dipl.-Ing. (1991) and Dr. techn. degree (1996) from Graz University of Technology, Graz, Austria.

Vexcel Corp., 4909 Nautilus Ct., Boulder, Co. 80301, USA.
Karner@vexcel.com

Gudrun Klinker received a Ph.D. in computer vision from Carnegie Mellon University in 1988, promoting and demonstrating a physical approach towards color image understanding. At Digital Equipment Corporation, she then explored the use of scientific visualization environments as workbenches for computer vision tasks, as well as for tele-collaborative data exploration applications. In 1994, she joined the User Interaction and Visualization group at the European Computer-industry Research Center (ECRC) in Munich, focusing on Augmented Reality issues with particular emphasis on vision-based approaches. Dr. Klinker has continued this line of research as the leader of the Project Group for Augmented Reality at the Fraunhofer Institute for Computer Graphics and is now professor for Augmented Reality at the Technical University of Munich.

Technische Universität München, Fachbereich für Informatik (H1), Lehrstuhl Applied Software Engineering, Arcisstr. 21, D-80333 München, Germany.
klinker@in.tum.de

Reinhard Koch, Katholieke Universiteit Leuven, ESAT-PSI/VISICS, Kardinaal Mercierlaan 94, B-3001 Leuven, Belgium.
reinhard.koch@esat.kuleuven.ac.be

Franz W. Leberl is professor of Computer Graphics and Vision at Graz University of Technology, and directs the University's Institute of the same name. He founded Vexcel Corporation in Boulder, Co in 1985. He spent 1998/9 there and helped in the development of Vexcel's building modeling capability.

Institute for Computer Graphics and Vision, Graz University of Technology, Inffeldgasse 16, 8010 Graz, Austria.
Franz@vexcel.com

Aleš Leonardis is an associate professor of computer and information science at the Faculty of Computer and Information Science of the University of Ljubljana in Ljubljana, Slovenia. He received a Dipl.Ing. (1985) and a M.Sc. (1988) degrees in electrical engineering and a Ph.D. degree (1993) in computer science, all from the University of Ljubljana. His main research interests in computer vision are object and scene modeling, robust recognition and segmentation.

University of Ljubljana, Faculty of Computer and Information Science, Tržaška 25, SI-1000 Ljubljana, Slovenia.
ales.leonardis@fri.uni-lj.si

Vincent Lepetit is a Ph.D. candidate working with the Image Synthesis and Analysis group (ISA) of the Laboratoire Lorrain de recherche en informatique et ses applications (LORIA), Nancy, France. His work focuses on detecting occlusions in a context of augmented reality. Vincent Lepetit received a Diplôme d'études approfondies in Computer Science in 1996 and expects to complete his Ph.D. in 2000.

LORIA-INRIA Lorraine, BP 239, 54506 Vandoeuvre-les-Nancy, France.
lepetit@loria.fr

Russell A. Manning is a graduate student in the Department of Computer Sciences at the University of Wisconsin–Madison. He received the B.S. degree in engineering and applied sciences from the California Institute of Technology in 1991 and the M.S. degree in computer science from the University of Wisconsin–Madison in 1997. His research interests include image-based rendering, auto calibration, and scene reconstruction, particularly in the context of dynamic scenes.

University of Wisconsin, Department of Computer Sciences, 1210 W. Dayton Street, Madison, WI 53706, USA.
rmanning@cs.wisc.edu

Markus Maresch is a software engineer at Vexcel Corporation in Boulder, Colorado, with responsibility for automating the photogrammetic set up of photographs. He holds a Dipl.Ing. (1991) and Dr. techn. degree (1997) from Graz University of Technology, Graz, Austria.

Vexcel Corp., 4909 Nautilus Ct., Boulder, CO 80301, USA.
Maresch@vexcel.com

Danny Martens, Katholieke Universiteit Leuven, ESAT-PSI/VISICS, Kardinaal Mercierlaan 94, B-3001 Leuven, Belgium.
danny.martens@esat.kuleuven.ac.be

Raymond McKendall is an independent computing professional currently affiliated with the GRASP Lab at the University of Pennsylvania. He consults broadly in scientific computing for both academic and commercial R&D projects. His experience includes tele-immersion, image processing, parallel computing, statistical sensor fusion, financial modeling, and teaching. He holds a Ph.D. in Systems Engineering from the University of Pennsylvania, an M.S. in Applied Mathematics from Carnegie-Mellon University, and a B.S. in Applied Mathematics from Brown University.

University of Pennsylvania, GRASP Laboratory, Department of Computer and Information Science, Philadelphia, PA 19104-6389, USA.

Jane Mulligan received her M.Sc. and Ph.D. from the University of British Columbia in Vancouver, Canada, where she worked with Alan Mackworth on vision based manipulator position sensing and empirical analysis of robotic part manipulation tasks. Currently she is a Post-doctoral Fellow in the Grasp Laboratory at the University of Pennsylvania, working with Kostas Daniilidis and Ruzena Bajcsy on the National Tele-immersion Initiative and real-time stereo.

University of Pennsylvania, GRASP Laboratory, Department of Computer and Information Science, Philadelphia, PA 19104-6389, USA.

Vittorio Murino is an Associate Professor at the University of Verona, Italy. His main research interests include: computer vision and pattern recognition, acoustic and optical underwater vision, probabilistic techniques for image processing, and neural networks. Recently, he has become interested in the integration of image analysis and synthesis methodologies for object recognition and virtual reality modeling. Dr. Murino is also associate editor of the Pattern Recognition and IEEE Systems, Man, and Cybernetics journals.

Dipartimento Scientifico e Tecnologico, Universita' degli Studi di Verona, Ca' Vignal 2, Strada Le Grazie 15, I-37134 Verona, Italy.
murino@sci.univr.it

Tomáš Pajdla is an assistant professor at the Department of Cybernetics, Faculty of Electrical Engineering, Czech Technical University in Prague, Czech Republic. He received M.Sc. from the Czech Technical University in Prague in 1992. His research interests include camera systems calibration, scene reconstruction from images, 3D data acquisition and processing, and omnidirectional vision. He is a co-founder of the company Neovision specialized in industrial and medical applications of computer vision and image processing.

Czech Technical University in Prague, Faculty of Electrical Engineering, Dept. of Cybernetics, Center for Machine Perception, Karlovo nám. 13, 121-35 Prague, Czech Republic.
pajdla@cmp.felk.cvut.cz

Marc Pollefeys, Katholieke Universiteit Leuven, ESAT-PSI/VISICS, Kardinaal Mercierlaan 94, B-3001 Leuven, Belgium.
marc.pollefeys@esat.kuleuven.ac.be

Marc Proesmans, Katholieke Universiteit Leuven, ESAT-PSI/VISICS, Kardinaal Mercierlaan 94, B-3001 Leuven, Belgium.
marc.proesmans@esat.kuleuven.ac.be

Gerhard Roth is a Senior Research Officer in the Visual Information Technology Group of the National Research Council of Canada. He received an Honours B.Math degree (1976) from the University of Waterloo, a Masters in Computer Science from Carleton University (1985), and Ph.D. in Electrical Engineering from McGill (1993). He has published papers in the areas of robust statistics applied to computer vision, genetic algorithms, reverse engineering, mesh creation, projective vision, and model building in general. He is a Senior member of the IEEE.

Visual Information Technology Group, National Research Council of Canada, Ottawa, Canada K1A OR6.
Gerhard.Roth@nrc.ca

Radim Šára is a research fellow in the Center for Machine Perception at the Faculty of Electrical Engineering of the Czech Technical University in Prague, Czech Republic. He received his Dipl.Ing. degree in electrical engineering from the Czech Technical University in 1987 and Ph.D. degree from the Johannes Kepler University in Linz, Austria in 1994. His main research interest is computer vision, namely 3D model reconstruction, polynocular stereo vision, shape from shading and other photometric methods for obtaining information about 3D shape and intrinsic texture.

Czech Technical University, Faculty of Electrical Engineering, Technická 2, CZ–16627 Prague, Czech Republic.
sara@cmp.felk.cvut.cz

Alexander Savenko is a research student in the Department of Computer and Information Sciences at De Montfort University. He received an M.Sc. in Computer Science from the Department of Calculus, Mathematics & Cybernetics of Moscow State University in 1998. His research interests include computer graphics and computer animation, in particular character animation, and photorealistic rendering.

Department of Computer & Information Sciences, De Montfort University, United Kingdom.

David Schmid is a Consultant working for American Management Systems since August 1999. He graduated at the University of Pennsylvania with a B.S.E. in Computer Science. He contributed to the real-time image processing aspects of the tele-immersion project.

University of Pennsylvania, GRASP Laboratory, Department of Computer and Information Science, Philadelphia, PA 19104-6389, USA.

Gilles Simon is a research assistant working with the Visual Geometry group at the Department of Engineering Science of the University of Oxford, UK. He also worked with the Image Synthesis and Analysis group (ISA) of the Laboratoire lorrain de recherche en informatique et ses applications (LORIA), Nancy, France, where he accomplished his Ph.D. His research interests include augmented reality and computer vision. Dr. Simon received a Diplôme d'Ingénieur in computer Science (1995) and a Ph.D. in Computer Science (1999) from the Université Henri Poincaré, Nancy 1.

Dept of Engineering Science, University of Oxford, 19 Parks Road, OX1 3PJ, United Kingdom.
gs@robots.ox.ac.uk

Danijel Skočaj is a Ph.D. student and research assistant at the Faculty of Computer and Information Science of the University of Ljubljana in Ljubljana, Slovenia. He received Dipl.Ing. and M.Sc. in computer science from the University of Ljubljana in 1996 and 1999, respectively. His main research interests in computer vision are acquisition of range images and construction of 3-D models from range data.

University of Ljubljana, Faculty of Computer and Information Science, Tržaška 25, SI-1000 Ljubljana, Slovenia.
danijel.skocaj@fri.uni-lj.si

Franc Solina is a professor of computer and information science at the Faculty of Computer and Information Science of the University of Ljubljana in Ljubljana, Slovenia where is also the head of the Computer Vision Laboratory. He received a Dipl.Ing. (1979) and a M.Sc. degrees (1982) in electrical engineering from the University of Ljubljana and a Ph.D. degree (1987) in computer science from the University of Pennsylvania. His main research interests in computer vision are segmentation and part-level object representation.

University of Ljubljana, Faculty of Computer and Information Science, Tržaška 25, SI-1000 Ljubljana, Slovenia.
franc.solina@fri.uni-lj.si

Wei Sun is a Research Fellow in the 3D group at the University of Surrey, United Kingdom. He received a B.Sc. and M.Sc. in Mathematics from Harbin Technical University, China. He was a Mathematics lecturer in China for over 8 years before registering as a Ph.D. student at De Montfort University. He is about to submit his Ph.D. thesis which relates to wavelet modeling of biped locomotion. His current research is concerned with building layered animation models from 3D captured data.

Department of Computer & Information Sciences, De Montfort University, United Kingdom.

JiaCheng Tan is a Ph.D. student in the Department of Computer Sciences of De Montfort University. He received a B.Eng. in Mechanical Engineering from Jilin University of Technology, China and an M.Sc. in Mechanical Engineering from Xidian University, China. His research interests include teleoperation, virtual environments, computer graphics, human-computer interfaces, robotics and dynamic systems.

Department of Computer & Information Sciences, De Montfort University, United Kingdom.

Hai Tao received his B.S. and M.S. Degrees from Tsinghua University, Beijing, China, in 1991 and 1993, respectively. He received his M.S. degree from the Mississippi State University in 1994. In 1998, he received his Ph.D. degree in Electrical Engineering from the University of Illinois at Urbana-Champaign. Dr. Tao's professional interests lie in the broad area of image and video processing, especially on video processing, computer vision, and computer graphics. He has published more than 20 technical papers and one book chapter, and he holds three patents. He is a member of the IEEE Computer Society.

Media Vision Group, Vision Technologies Laboratory, Sarnoff Corporation, 201 Washington Rd. CN 5300, Princeton, NJ 08543, USA.
htao@sarnoff.com

Martin Urban is a researcher at the Center for Machine Perception, Department of Cybernetics, Faculty of Electrical Engineering, Czech Technical University in Prague, Czech Republic where he received his M.Sc. degree in 1995. His main research interest is 3D scene reconstruction from images.

Czech Technical University in Prague, Faculty of Electrical Engineering, Dept. of Cybernetics, Center for Machine Perception, Karlovo nám. 13, 121-35 Prague, Czech Republic.
urbanm@cmp.felk.cvut.cz

Luc Van Gool is professor at the University of Leuven in Belgium and the ETH Zürich in Switzerland. At both places he leads a computer vision group. His main research interests are object recognition, grouping, the link between perception and machine vision, the analysis and synthesis of textures, and 3D acquisition and visualisation. With his teams he received several prizes, including a David Marr Prize, two TechArt prizes, a Golden Eye Award, and a Henry Ford European Conservation Award. He is co-founder of the company Eyetronics, which is active in new-generation 3D acquisition and modeling. He is a member of the program committees of several major international conferences in his field. He co-authored over 100 publications and has served as computer vision consultant to several companies. He has coordinated several European projects.

ETH Zürich, Computer Vision Group BIWI, Gloriastrasse 35, CH-8092 Zürich, Switzerland.
vangool@vision.ee.ethz.ch

Katholieke Universiteit Leuven, ESAT-PSI/VISICS Kardinaal Mercierlaan 94 B-3001 Leuven, Belgium.
luc.vangool@esat.kuleuven.ac.be

Serge L. Van Sint Jan is a Lecturer in Anatomy at the University of Brussels (ULB). He was Research Fellow at De Montfort University for 2 years, 1998-99. His interests are computer graphics simulation, medical imaging, image processing and joint kinematics. He has obtained an M.Sc. and Ph.D. in Physiotherapy and a degree in Biomechanics from ULB, and a B.Sc. in Computer Science from the Institute of Commercial Carers (Brussels). He is a member of the Belgian Society for Medical Informatics, IEEE Computer Society, IEEE Engineering in Medicine & Biological Sciences Society and the International Society for Orthopaedic Research & Traumatology.

Maarten Vergauwen, Katholieke Universiteit Leuven, ESAT-PSI/VISICS, Kardinaal Mercierlaan 94, B-3001 Leuven, Belgium.
maarten.vergauwen@esat.kuleuven.ac.be

Andrew Wojdala graduated with a M.S. in Computer Sciences from the Technical University of Warsaw, Poland. For several years, he worked with Japanese Integra, Inc. as the project leader of the lighting simulation and rendering software. Since 1993, Dr. Wojdala is involved in the development of the virtual studio technology. Formerly with Accom, Inc., he is currently the manager of Virtual Set Division at Orad Hi-Tec Systems. Dr. Wojdala published several white papers on realistic image synthesis and virtual studio. His scientific and academic background includes research and teaching computer graphics and software engineering at the Technical Universities of Warsaw and Szczecin, Poland.

Accom Poland, ul. Szczerkowa 10, 71-751 Szczecin, Poland.
aw.accom@inet.com.pl

Alexey Zalesny, ETH Zürich, Computer Vision Group BIWI, Gloriastrasse 35, CH-8092 Zürich, Switzerland.
zalesny@vision.ee.ethz.ch

Andrew Zisserman is a professor at the Department of Engineering Science. He joined the department in 1987, and leads the Visual Geometry Group there. He has authored over 90 papers in Photogrammetry and Computer Vision, and is on the editorial board of two international Computer Vision journals.

Department of Engineering Science, University of Oxford, Parks Road, Oxford, OX1 3PJ, United Kingdom.
az@robots.ox.ac.uk

Introduction

Aleš Leonardis, Franc Solina, Ruzena Bajcsy

In the past, the fields of computer vision and computer graphics have been considered as tackling the inverse problems. Traditionally, computer vision starts with input images and process them for the purpose of understanding geometric and physical properties of objects and scenes, and to build appropriate models. On the other hand, traditional computer graphics starts with geometric models and then generates, manipulates, and displays virtual representations in the form of images. In the recent years, we have seen great efforts towards the integration of computer vision and computer graphics techniques, in particular, in the areas of realistic modeling of objects and scenes, interactive computer graphics, and augmented reality.

Which are the main reasons that have brought the researchers of computer vision and computer graphics closer together? Computer graphics community has been active in inventing increasingly better, faster, and more complex methods of animation for creating virtual 3D synthetic environments. This paradigm has been successfully demonstrated in the constantly expanding series of complex digital animations. Yet, even though these animations have been successful (also commercially), it is clear that in order to create even more realistic virtual environments and on a much larger scale, the cost and time involvement have to be lowered. Such a leap in cost and quality is possible by incorporating sensor data of actual physical objects and environments, that can later be modified and extended with synthetic data. For example, it should be less costly to make a 3D model of a complex geometric object directly from images, than to have an animator construct such a model by hand.

Sensor data, which are crucial for an efficient creation of larger and more realistic virtual(ized) environments, need to be properly interpreted, processed, and modeled—and this is precisely what computer vision does. In other words, computer vision provides the tools needed

A. Leonardis et al. (eds.), Confluence of Computer Vision and Computer Graphics, xxxiii-xl.
© 2000 Kluwer Academic Publishers. Printed in the Netherlands.

to transform the real world back into the virtual. The marriage of computer graphics and computer vision techniques is further facilitated by increasingly lower costs of hardware for image capture and processing.

Some of the most critical issues in this emerging field are:

- generation of highly realistic 3D graphical models from a collection of calibrated or non-calibrated images obtained with multiple cameras, stereo-rigs, or video cameras;

- building of dynamic deformation models using the motions captured from real video sequences;

- dynamic image-based rendering;

- role of computer vision in interactive computer graphics;

- tracking, ego-motion estimation, and registration techniques for harmonious integration of real worlds and computer generated objects;

- virtual studio techniques.

The key element for the successful merger of computer graphics and computer vision technique are appropriate models. The models provide the information describing the geometry, the dynamics, and many other attributes of objects and scenes that represent the prior knowledge and impose a set of constraints for analysis, and later for rendering the virtual environments.

The Book at a Glance

The book focuses on the integration of computer vision and computer graphics techniques in the areas of realistic modeling of objects and scenes, interactive computer graphics, and augmented reality. Each chapter of the book presents recent results within this emerging domain. The results encompass both theoretical formulations and derivations, as well as numerous examples of applications. These include urban and archeological site modeling, modeling dressed humans, medical visualisation, figure and facial animation, real-time 3D-teleimmersion and telecollaboration, augmented reality as a new user interface concept, and augmented reality for underwater scene understanding. The chapters have been designed to serve as technical overviews with extensive references to related work. We hope that this will enable researches working in individual fields to quickly get acquainted with the main common integration issues, while providing the experts with in-depth technical details.

The book starts with a chapter that describes a method to completely automatically recover a 3D scene structure from a sequence of images acquired by an unknown camera undergoing unknown motion. *Zisserman et al.* argue that, in contrast to previous approaches, which have used calibration objects or landmarks, their approach is far more general since no other information than images themselves is required. The automatic process can be thought of, at its simplest, as converting a camcoder to a sparse range sensor. Together with more graphical post-processing, such as triangulation and texture mapping, the system becomes a "VHS to VRML" converter. The authors demonstrate two applications of their method: the first is the construction of 3D graphical models of a piecewise planar scene, and the second is the insertion of virtual objects into the original image sequence, which is of use for post-production in the film industry.

The next chapter by *Cross* and *Zisserman* describes a novel approach to reconstructing the complete surface of an object from multiple views, where the camera circumnavigates the object. To achieve the goal, the approach combines two sources of information, namely, the apparent contour and the imaged surface texture. The authors argue that the proposed approach has significant advantages over using either the contour or texture alone: in particular, the geometric constraints available are complementary, so that the deficiencies of one source can be overcome by the strengths of the other. In addition, the novelty lies also in an implementation which uses different surface representations as appropriate for accuracy and efficiency. Numerous examples of automatically generated texture-mapped graphical models demonstrate that the approach is successful for various objects and camera motions. The objects may contain concavities and have non-trivial topology.

The subsequent chapter by *Urban et al.* also addresses the problem of scene reconstruction from multiple views. The authors, in particular, concentrate on consistent projective reconstruction which involves a set of more than four views. The method is based on concatenation of trifocal constraints and requires only linear estimates. The accuracy and stability of the method have been analyzed, and the projective reconstruction from seven real images has been successfully demonstrated.

Šára explores a bottom-up approach to precise and accurate 3D surface model reconstruction. The focus is on acquiring 3D models of natural objects for medical applications, augmented reality, and telepresence. The author proposes performing several successive steps in which more complex models are inferred from simpler models. The model at the lowest level consists of a set of unorganized points in 3D space obtained from polynocular stereo system which utilizes five fully-calibrated cameras and an uncalibrated infrared texture projector. The intermediate-level model consists of local geometric primitives, called "fish-scales". By linking together close and compatibly oriented fish-scales, a discrete pseudo-surface is obtained, which presents the high-level model. Throughout the chapter, the approach is demonstrated on a textured 3D geometric model reconstruction of a human face.

The contribution by *Roth* brings a systematic review of the problem of model building from sensor data, which stands at the interface between computer vision and computer graphics. The author first describes the basic steps in the model building pipeline; calibration, acquisition, registration, point creation, model creation, model compression, and texture creation. After which he systematically discusses open research questions that remain in each step and describes several overall research themes that he believes should further guide work in this area. Among the most important open problems in model building, the author lists: automation of the entire model building pipeline, incremental construction of the models, the role of active versus passive sensors, image-based versus model-based rendering, and environment modeling versus object modeling.

Skočaj and *Leonardis* address the problem of 3D reconstruction of objects of non-uniform reflectance using a structured light sensor. Namely, standard approaches using structured light sensors assume that the reflectance properties of the objects are uniform. The authors illustrate the need to devise an approach that overcomes this constraint, which means that objects consisting of both high and low reflective surfaces should reliably be reconstructed. They propose to systematically vary the illumination intensity of the light projector and to form high dynamic scale radiance maps. The authors report experiments on objects which have surfaces of very different reflectance properties, and demonstrate that range images obtained from high dynamic scale radiance maps are of much better quality than those obtained by the standard approach.

While the previous chapters have explored in particular the 3D reconstruction of objects and scenes, which can subsequently be used in computer graphics applications, this chapter, by *Manning* and *Dyer*, addresses the view-interpolation as a means of creating virtual views of scenes without explicit scene reconstruction. The authors present a technique, called "dynamic view morphing", for view interpolation between two reference views of a dynamic scene captured at different times. The interpolations produced portray one possible physically-valid version of what transpired in the scene between the time points when the two reference views were taken. The presented method works with widely-separated, uncalibrated cameras and sparse point correspondences, and does not involve finding the camera-to-camera transformation.

Tao and *Huang* address the problem of building deformation models of faces and facial expressions using the motions captured from real video sequences, which is an excellent example that demonstrates the close relationship between computer graphics and vision technologies. The authors propose an explanation-based facial motion tracking algorithm based on a piecewise Bézier volume deformation model (PBVD), which is a suitable model both for the synthesis and the analysis of facial images. With the PBVD model, which is linear and independent of the facial mesh structure, basic facial movements, or action units, are interactively defined. By changing the magnitudes of these action units, a variety of different animated facial images can be generated. The magnitudes of these action units can be computed (learned) from real video sequences using a model-based tracking algorithm. The authors present experimental results on PBVD-based animation, model-based tracking, and explanation-based tracking.

The subsequent chapter by *Van Gool et al.* brings together many different techniques for realistic object, scene, and event modeling from image data, to realize a system for visits to a virtual 3D archeological site. To model the landscape and buildings at the site, the authors propose a shape-from-video system that turns multiple, uncalibrated images into realistic 3D models. The texture that covers the 3D models of the landscape is synthesized from images of the natural surfaces which results in a compact, yet effective texture model. To model smaller pieces, like statues and ornaments, they use an active, one-shot range sensor which exploits the projections of a special pattern onto the object under observation to yield high resolution 3D models. Once the model of the site is built, one can navigate through this virtual environment accompanied by a virtual guide. The virtual guide responds through head movements and facial expressions. The authors also developed a technique for learning natural lip motions from observed 3D face dynamics which will be used to animate the virtual guide in the future versions of the system.

Jojić and *Huang* present another application which demonstrates how computer vision techniques can be exploited in conjunction with computer graphics for modeling dressed humans. They combine computer vision based approaches such as 3D reconstruction of a human body and analysis-by-synthesis of the behavior of cloth material with the computer graphics approaches for realistic rendering of complex objects. The experimental results presented in the chapter include building textured 3D models of humans from multiple images, dressing these models into virtual garment, and joint estimation of cloth draping parameters and the underlying object's geometry in range images of dressed objects.

The next chapter by *Leberl et al.* describes urban site modeling. The authors argue that while 3D models of buildings have long been produced based on photogrammetric technology, the focus today has shifted towards producing 3D computer models of urban areas on a large scale, with perhaps half a million buildings of one metropolitan area. Thus, they discuss various issues related to the creation of such large data sets, with verified accuracy and detail, in a reasonable time and at a moderate cost.

Clapworthy et al. have identified a number of relatively-unconnected areas where computer graphics aspects i.e., visualization and animation, are influenced by the use of computer vision techniques. These techniques include 3D scene and object reconstruction, motion capture, and segmentation. The authors present various examples from diverse areas such as medical visualization, biomechanics, figure animation, and robot teleoperation.

In his chapter, *Wojdala* presents an exciting new technology, called "Virtual Studio", whose main goal is to combine two separate images or video streams. A typical example is to merge a foreground, filmed with a camera, with a computer-generated background, so well, that the composite looks as if it was shot together, in one environment. To answer the basic question, namely, how realistic virtual sets can appear, the author discusses various techniques involved into this very interdisciplinary technology. These techniques are related to computer graphics, graphics hardware, chroma keying, lighting, video camera parameters, camera tracking, and interaction between real and virtual worlds. While some problems still remain, the current level of visual realism has reached the point where more and more broadcasters are using this technology, even for complex, live-to-air productions.

The contribution by *Daniilidis et al.* presents an application which demonstrates the confluence of computer vision, computer graphics, and communication. In particular, they implemented a new medium for telecollaboration, which was realized in the form of two tele–cubicles connected at two Internet nodes. At each telecubicle a stereo-rig is used to provide an accurate dense 3D reconstruction of a person in action. The two real dynamic worlds are transmitted over the network and visualized stereoscopically. The full 3D information facilitates interaction with any virtual object. The remote communication and the dynamic nature of telecollaboration offers the challenge of optimal representation for graphics and vision. Thus, the authors treat the issues of limited bandwidth, latency, and processing power with a tunable 3D representation, where the user can select the trade-off between delay and 3D resolution by tuning the spatial resolution, the size of the working volume, and the uncertainty of reconstruction.

The last four chapters deal with Augmented Reality—a technology by which a user's view of the real world is augmented with additional information from a computer model. In her chapter, *Klinker* gives an overview of this new technology which shows great promise as a new user interface concept for many applications. Namely, users can work with and examine real 3D objects, while receiving additional information about these objects or the task at hand. Yet, augmented reality applications require fast and accurate solutions to several very complex problems, such as tracking the user and the real object, handling the occlusions and reflections, as well as the motion of the virtual user. Klinker discusses computer vision based solutions which are currently considered to be among the most promising approaches towards solving these issues.

Simon et al. focus on one of the most crucial problems in augmented reality, namely, how to achieve a harmonious integration of real world and computer generated objects. They propose a robust and accurate registration method which performs pose computation over the sequence of images in a completely autonomous manner. The accuracy of the pose computation is achieved by combining model-image correspondences of tracked curves in an image and 2D keypoint correspondences matched in the consecutive frames. The authors demonstrate the seamless integration of the real and virtual worlds by integrating a virtual car into a real-world video sequence.

In the next chapter by *Gagalowicz* and *Gérard*, the authors also tackle the problem of tracking in images. The approach is model-based and proceeds as a two-step process. After the interactive calibration session, the geometric model of the object is automatically rendered with texture. Then, a 3D predictor gives the position of the object model in the next image and the fine tuning of the position is obtained by minimizing the error between the textured model and the real image of the object. The robustness of the approach has been verified by creating an augmented reality sequence.

In the last chapter, a specific application of augmented reality is presented by *Murino* and *Fusiello*. They describe how to integrate visual and acoustic 3D data to enhance the perception of an underwater environment during teleoperation tasks.

The chapters in this book present only a selection of some of the representative approaches that have emerged in the recent years. In fact, the problems have mainly been observed from the point-of-view of computer vision researchers. A similar book, but more from the point-of-view of computer graphics researchers, would nicely complement this volume and shed additional light on this exciting new research domain. Many challenges are waiting in this interdisciplinary research field. One of the ultimate challenges is to bring these exciting ideas, in the form of easy to use tools, into the hands of all computer users.

Chapter 1

FROM IMAGES TO VIRTUAL AND AUGMENTED REALITY

Andrew Zisserman, Andrew Fitzgibbon, Caroline Baillard, Geoffrey Cross

Abstract   We describe a method to completely automatically recover 3D scene structure together with a camera for each frame from a sequence of images acquired by an unknown camera undergoing unknown movement. Previous approaches have used calibration objects or landmarks to recover this information, and are therefore often limited to a particular scale. The approach of this paper is far more general, since the "landmarks" are derived directly from the imaged scene texture. The method can be applied to a large class of scenes and motions, and is demonstrated here for sequences of interior and exterior scenes using both controlled-motion and hand-held cameras.

We demonstrate two applications of this technology. The first is the automatic construction of a 3D graphical model of a piecewise planar scene; the second is the insertion of virtual objects into the original image sequence.

1.   INTRODUCTION

The goal of this work is to obtain 3D scene structure and camera projection matrices from an uncalibrated sequence of images. The structure and cameras form the basis for a number of applications and two of these will be illustrated in this paper. The first application is building 3D graphical models from an image sequence acquired by a hand-held camcorder. This enables texture mapped models of isolated objects, building interiors, building exteriors etc. to be obtained simply by videoing the scene, even though with a camcorder the motion is unlikely to be smooth, and is unknown *a priori*. The second application is to use the camera which is estimated for each frame of the sequence in order to insert virtual objects into the original real image sequence [14]. An 'augmented reality' facility of this type is of use for post-production in the film industry.

1

A. Leonardis et al. (eds.), Confluence of Computer Vision and Computer Graphics, 1–23.
© *2000 Kluwer Academic Publishers. Printed in the Netherlands.*

To obtain the structure and cameras we employ Structure and Motion recovery results from the photogrammetry and computer vision literature, where it has been shown that there is sufficient information in the perspective projections of a static cloud of 3D points and lines to determine the 3D structure as well as the camera positions *from image measurements alone*. In our approach these points and lines are obtained automatically from features in the scene, and their correspondence established across multiple views. Establishing this correspondence is a significant part of the problem.

The core of the system is shown in figure 1.1. This automatic process can be thought of, at its simplest, as converting a camcorder to a sparse range sensor. Together with more standard graphical post-processing such as triangulation of sparse 3D point and line sets, and texture mapping from images, the system becomes a "VHS to VRML" converter.

The key advantage of the approach we adopt is that no information other than the images themselves is required *a priori*: more conventional photogrammetry techniques require calibration objects or 3D control points to be visible in every frame.

1.1   BACKGROUND

Although the general framework for uncalibrated structure from motion has been in place for some time [3, 10, 13] only recently have general acquisition systems come near to becoming a reality. This is because a combination of image processing, projective geometry for multiple views [8, 21, 23], and robust statistical estimation [26, 29] has been required in order to succeed at automating structure and motion algorithms [2, 12]. Tomasi and Kanade [24] demonstrated that 3D models could be built from an uncalibrated sequence, but employed a simplified camera which does not model perspective effects (those that give rise to vanishing points etc.).

1.2   THE SCOPE OF THE APPROACH

The limitations of the approach of this paper are: first, that the images must be sufficiently "interesting"—if the scene has no significant texture (to be defined more precisely later), then the feature based methods we use will have too few 2D measurements to work with; and second, that the camera motion between images needs to be relatively small, in particular rotation about the optical axis should be limited—otherwise the cross-correlation techniques used to match the features between images will fail. Happily, this restricted motion is the typical motion between frames of a video sequence, and the system is tuned for such data. We

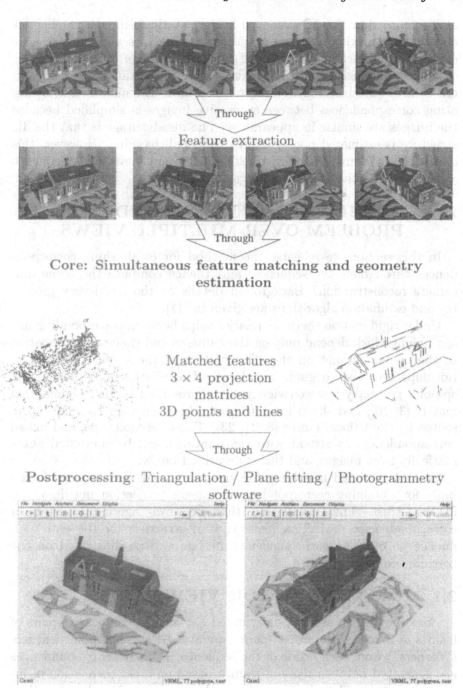

Figure 1.1 Overview of the system. Four frames from the 32-frame input video sequence are shown at the top; views of the automatically acquired VRML model are shown at the bottom.

also require that the 3D scene be largely static, although smaller independently moving objects—shadows, passing cars and the like—are excised automatically by the use of robust estimation techniques.

The advantage of a video sequence, where the distance between camera centres (the baseline) for successive frames is small, is that evaluating correspondences between successive images is simplified because the images are similar in appearance. The disadvantage is that the 3D structure is estimated poorly due to the small baseline. However, this disadvantage is ameliorated by tracking over many views in the sequence so that the effective baseline is large.

2. REVIEW: THE CORRESPONDENCE PROBLEM OVER MULTIPLE VIEWS

In this section we rehearse the method for establishing correspondences throughout the sequence, and thence compute the scene and camera reconstruction. Background details on the multi-view geometry and estimation algorithms are given in [11].

Under rigid motion there are relationships between corresponding image points which depend only on the cameras and their motion relative to the scene, but not on the 3D structure of the scene. These relationships are used to guide matching. The relationships include the epipolar geometry between view pairs, represented by the fundamental matrix [3, 10]; and the trifocal geometry between view triplets, represented by the trifocal tensor [8, 21, 23]. These relationships, and image correspondences consistent with the relations, can be computed automatically from images, and this is described below.

Geometry guided matching, for view pairs and view triplets, is the basis for obtaining correspondences, camera projection matrices and 3D structure. The triplets may then be sewn together to establish correspondences, projection matrices and structure for the entire sequence [2, 6]. The correspondence method will be illustrated on the corridor sequence of figure 1.2.

2.1 MATCHING FOR VIEW PAIRS

Correspondences are first determined between all consecutive pairs of frames as follows. An interest-point operator [7] extracts point features ("corners") from each frame of the sequence. Putative correspondences are generated between pairs of frames based on cross-correlation of interest point neighbourhoods and search windows. Matches are then established from this set of putative correspondences by simultaneously estimating epipolar geometry and matches consistent with this estimated geometry. The estimation algorithm is robust to mismatches and is described in detail in [25, 27, 29]. This basic level of tracking is termed the F-Based Tracker ("F" for fundamental matrix).

Typical results. Typically the number of corners used in a 768×576 image of an indoor scene is about 500, the number of seed matches is about 200, and the final number of matches is about 250. Using corners computed to sub-pixel accuracy, the average distance of a point from its epipolar line is ~ 0.2 pixels.

The robust nature of the estimation algorithms means that it is not necessary to restrict putative correspondences to nearest neighbours or even the highest cross-correlation match, as the rigidity constraint can be used to select the best match from a set of candidates. Typically the radius of the search window for candidate matches is 10–20% of the image size, which adequately covers image point motion for most sequences.

2.2 MATCHING FOR VIEW TRIPLETS

Correspondences are then determined between all consecutive triplets of frames. The 3-view matches are drawn from the 2-view matches provided by the F-Based Tracker. Although a proportion of these 2-view matches are erroneous (outliers), many of these mismatches are removed during the simultaneous robust estimation of the trifocal tensor and consistent matches [26]. The trifocal geometry provides a more powerful disambiguation constraint than epipolar geometry because image position is completely determined in a third view, given a match in the other two views, whereas image position is only restricted to a line by the epipolar geometry between two views.

The output at this stage of matching consists of sets of overlapping image triplets. Each triplet has an associated trifocal tensor and 3-view point matches. The camera matrices for the 3-views may be instantiated from the trifocal tensor [9], and 3D points instantiated for each 3-view point match by minimizing reprojection error over the triplet.

Typical results. Typically the number of seed matches over a triplet is about 100 corners. The final number of matches is about 180. Using corners computed to sub-pixel accuracy, the typical distance of a corner from its transferred position is ~ 0.2 pixels. An example is shown in figure 1.2.

2.3   MATCHING LINES OVER VIEW TRIPLETS

Line matching is notoriously difficult over image pairs as there is no geometric constraint equivalent to the fundamental matrix for point correspondences. However, over 3 views a geometric constraint is provided by the trifocal tensor computed as above from point correspondences.

Line segments are matched over the triplet in two stages. First, given the trifocal tensor and putatively corresponding lines in two images, the corresponding line in the third image is determined. A line segment should be detected at the predicted position in the third image for a match to be instantiated. Second, the match is verified by a photometric test based on correlation of the line's intensity neighbourhood. The point to point correspondence for this correlation is provided by the computed epipolar geometry. Details are given in [19].

Typical results. Typically there are 200 lines in each image and a third of these are matched over the triplet. The line transfer error is generally less than a pixel. In practice the two stages of verification eliminate all but a couple of mismatches. An example is shown in figure 1.2.

2.4   MATCHING FOR SEQUENCES

Correspondences are extended over many frames by merging 3-view point matches for overlapping triplets [6, 12]. For example a correspondence which exists across the triplet 1-2-3 and also across the triplet 2-3-4 may be extended to the frames 1-2-3-4, since the pair 2-3 overlaps for the triplets. The camera matrices and 3D structure are then computed for the frames 1-2-3-4. This process is extended by merging neighbouring groups of frames until camera matrices and correspondences are established throughout the sequence. At any stage the available cameras and structure can be used to guide matching over any frame of the sequence. The initial estimate of 3D points and cameras for a sequence is refined by a hierarchical bundle adjustment [6, 22]. Finally, the projective coordinate system is transformed to Euclidean (less overall scale) by autocalibration [4, 17].

In this manner structure and cameras may be computed automatically for sequences consisting of hundreds of frames. Examples are given in the following section.

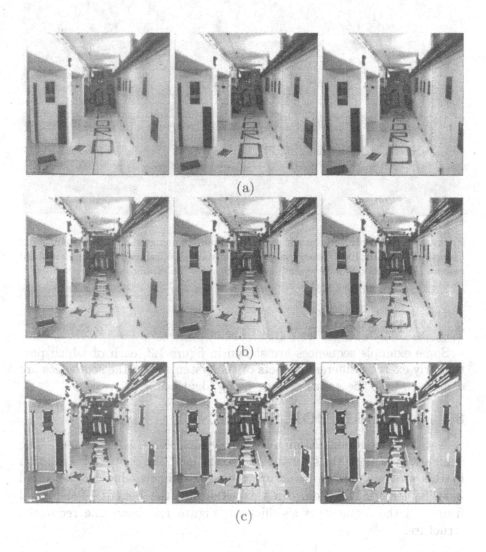

Figure 1.2 **Image triplet processing**: The workhorse of the system, converting a passive, uncalibrated, camera into a sparse range sensor. (a) The first three images of the corridor sequence. (b) Point (white) and line (grey) features extracted from the sequence. (c) features matched across these three views.

Figure 1.3 **Example sequences**: **Corridor**, camera mounted on indoor vehicle (12 frames); **Dinosaur**, fixed camera, object on turntable (36 frames); **Castle**, hand-held camera (25 frames); **Wilshire**, camera in helicopter (350 frames).

3.   RESULTS

Some example sequences are shown in figure 1.3, each of which particularly exercise different aspects of the system. First the sequences are discussed, with the points of note being identified.

3.1   CORRIDOR SEQUENCE

A camera is mounted on a mobile vehicle for this sequence. The vehicle moves along the floor turning to the left. The forward translation in this sequence makes structure recovery difficult, due to the small baseline for triangulation. In this situation, the benefit of using all frames in the sequence is significant. Figure 1.4 shows the recovered structure.

3.2   DINOSAUR SEQUENCE

In this sequence, the model dinosaur is rotated on a turntable so that effectively the camera circumnavigates the object. Feature extraction is performed on the luminance component of the colour signal. No reliable lines are extracted on this object so only points are used. In this case, the additional constraint that the motion is known to be circular is applied [5], resulting in improved structure fidelity. Although the angle

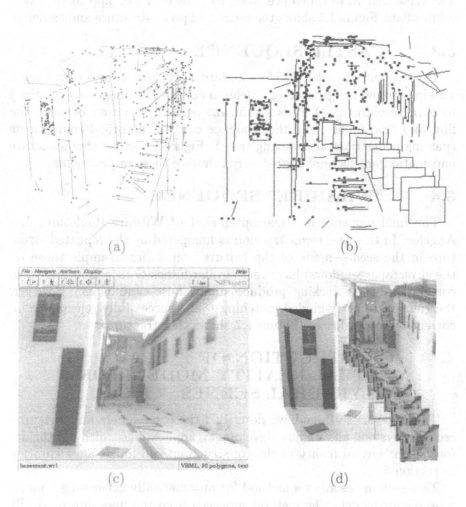

Figure 1.4 **Corridor sequence.** (a) A three dimensional reconstruction of points and lines in the scene, and (b) cameras (represented by their image planes) computed automatically from the images. A texture mapped triangulated graphical model is then constructed as described in section 4. (c) A rendering of the scene from a novel viewpoint, different from any in the sequence. (d) VRML model of the scene with the cameras represented by their image planes (texture mapped with the original images from the sequence).

of rotation was known to be precisely $10° \pm 0.005°$, this information was not supplied to the system in order to gain a measure of accuracy. The recovered RMS difference from $10°$ was $0.04°$, or approximately 1 milliradian. Figure 1.5 shows the recovered point structure and cameras.

3.3   CASTLE SEQUENCE

This sequence is taken with a standard SLR camera, by a cameraman walking around the grounds of a Belgian castle. The images are digitized to PAL resolution. There is significant lighting variation between the first and final frames, and the sequence contains non-rigid components (passing pedestrians and moving trees). Figure 1.6 shows that structure and motion are successfully recovered despite these impediments.

3.4   "WILSHIRE" SEQUENCE

The final sequence is a helicopter shot of Wilshire Boulevard, Los Angeles. In this case reconstruction is hampered by the repeated structure in the scene—many of the feature points (for example those on the skyscraper windows) have very similar intensity neighbourhoods, so correlation-based tracking produces many false candidates. However, the robust geometry-guided matching (§2.1) successfully rejects the incorrect correspondences. Figure 1.7 shows the structure.

4.   CONSTRUCTION OF VIRTUAL-REALITY MODELS FOR POLYHEDRAL SCENES

The previous sections have described the core camera-and-structure recovery system, and we now develop two applications which use this information: virtual reality model construction; and image augmentation in section 5.

This section describes a method for automatically generating a piecewise planar model. The method proceeds from the lines automatically matched using the trifocal tensor over 3 views. Consequently it must cope with the shortcomings of that process and the earlier line detection: missing lines, fragmented lines, and the occasional mis-match.

The method is based on searching for planes by sweeping through a one-parameter family. There are three main stages, which will be illustrated on the building shown in figure 1.11(a), which is a detail from figure 1.8.

Figure 1.5 **Dinosaur:** 3D point structure and camera positions for the Dinosaur sequence. The automatic computation of a 3D graphical model for this sequence is described in Chapter 2 of this volume, and also in [5].

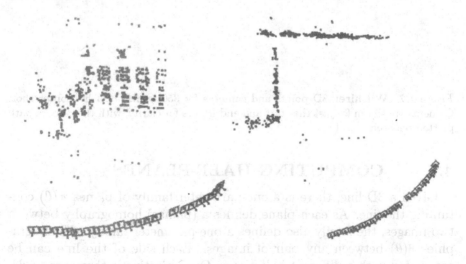

Figure 1.6 **Castle:** Computed cameras and 3D point structure. The plan view shows the accuracy of the self calibration.

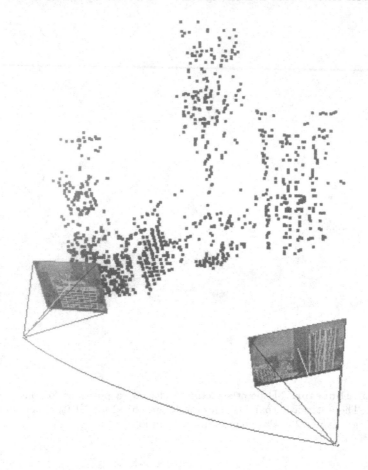

Figure 1.7 **Wilshire:** 3D points and cameras for 350 frames of a helicopter shot. Cameras are shown for just the start and end frames for clarity, with the camera path plotted between.

4.1   COMPUTING HALF-PLANES

Given a 3D line, there is a one-parameter family of planes $\pi(\theta)$ containing the line. As each plane defines a (planar) homography between two images, the family also defines a one-parameter family of homographies $H(\theta)$ between any pair of images. Each side of the line can be associated with a different half-plane. Our objective is therefore to determine for each line side whether there is an attached half-plane or not, and if there is we want to compute a best estimate of θ. We wish to

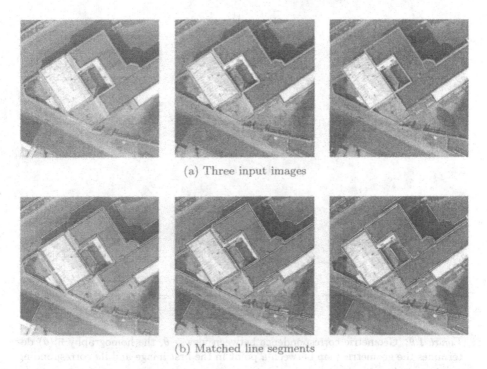

(a) Three input images

(b) Matched line segments

Figure 1.8 **Aerial views.** The input images are 600 × 600 pixels. There are 248/236/212 detected line segments and 88 lines are matched over 3 views using the trifocal tensor, with only one erroneous match.

employ only the minimal information of a single 3D line and its image neighbourhood. Essentially we are hypothesizing a planar facet attached to the line, and verifying or refuting this model hypothesis using image support over multiple views.

The existence of an attached half-plane and a best estimate of its angle is determined by measuring image similarity over multiple views. The geometry is illustrated in figure 1.9. Given θ, the plane $\pi(\theta)$ defines a point to point homography map $H(\theta)$ between the images. If the plane is correct then the intensities at corresponding pixels will be highly correlated. The similarity as a function of θ, $Sim(\theta)$, is computed by measuring the normalized cross-correlation between all image pairs, with the point to point map $H(\theta)$. Figure 1.10 shows two typical examples of similarity functions.

Results of half-plane detection. Figure 1.12 shows all the half-planes which are hypothesised on the example building. All parts of the roof of the main building are detected, whereas no valid planes are detected for the walls within the considered angle interval (we are not aiming to

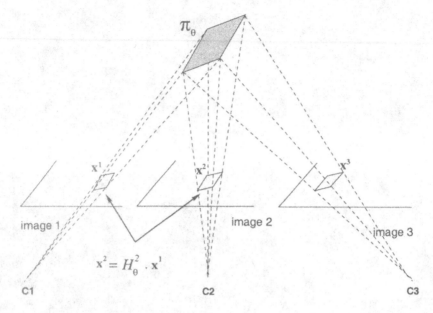

Figure 1.9 Geometric correspondence between views. θ, the homography $\mathtt{H}^i(\theta)$ determines the geometric map between a point in the first image and its corresponding point in image i.

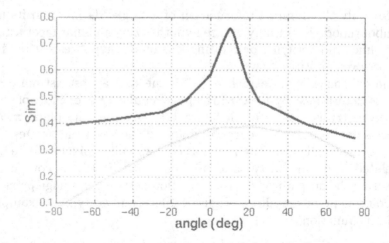

Figure 1.10 Example of similarity score functions $Sim(\theta)$. The black curve corresponds to a valid plane, whereas the grey one is rejected.

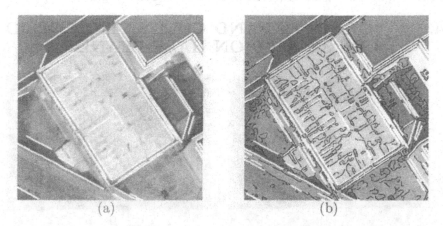

(a)   (b)

Figure 1.11 (a) Detail of figure 1.8(a) with projected 3D lines (white). This building is used to illustrate the reconstruction method. The correct reconstruction is a four plane hip roof. (b) Detected edges (black) after applying an edge detector with a very low threshold on gradient. The similarity function is computed at points on these edges.

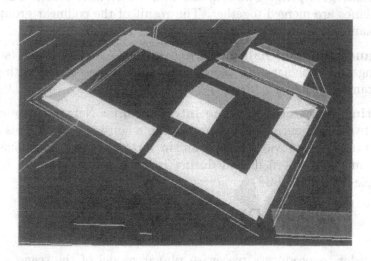

Figure 1.12 Detected half-planes over the interval $[-75°; +75°]$.

reconstruct vertical walls). Occasionally erroneous half-planes arise at shadows, but these are removed in the subsequent stages.

4.2   GROUPING AND COMPLETION OF 3D LINES BASED ON HALF-PLANES

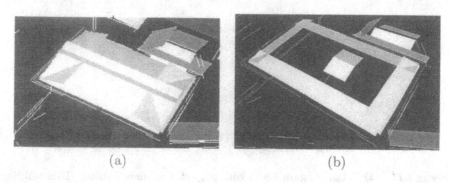

(a)   (b)

Figure 1.13   3D line grouping. (a) Collinear grouping reduces the 9 planes prior to grouping to only 6. (b) Coplanar grouping and plane merging reduces the number of planes further so that only 4 remain. These are the correct four planes which define the roof, but at this stage the plane boundaries are not delineated.

The computed half-planes are now used to support line grouping and the creation of new lines.

Collinear grouping: Two collinear lines which have attached coplanar half-planes are merged together. The result of the collinear grouping of half-planes of figure 1.12 is shown in figure 1.13a.

Coplanar line and half-plane grouping: Any line which is neighbouring and coplanar with the current plane is associated with it (see the example of figure 1.13(b)).

Creating new lines by plane intersections: New lines are created when two neighbouring planes intersect in a consistent way. This is very important as it provides a mechanism for generating additional lines which may have been missed during image feature detection (see the example of figure 1.14(a).

4.3   PLANE DELINEATION AND VERIFICATION

In order to produce a piecewise planar model of the scene a closed delineation is required for each plane. A closed delineation can then be computed by using heuristic grouping rules based on polygonal shapes and convex hulls [15, 16, 28].

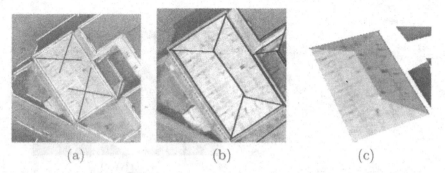

(a)   (b)   (c)

Figure 1.14 (a) New lines (black) created by plane intersection; (b) Delineation of the verified roofs projected onto the first image; (c) 3D view with texture mapping.

Each delineated 3D face so produced is then verified by assessing intensity similarity over the complete image set, at corresponding points within the projected delineation. This verification step removes fallacious planes, for example those which erroneously bridge two buildings. Figure 1.14 shows both the 2D delineation and a 3D view of the roof produced for the building of figure 1.11(a). Finally, occlusion prediction is used to signal and resolve conflicts between inconsistent plane hypotheses. A conflict occurs between two facet hypotheses when their projections onto an image substantially overlap, i.e. when one of them is occluded by the other.

4.4   RESULTS OF MODEL BUILDING

Figure 1.15 shows the 3D reconstruction of the full scene of figure 1.8a. Figure 1.16 shows the result on much larger and more complicated images. Note that intricate and unusual roofs (for example the factory in the upper part of the image) have been completely recovered. This also demonstrates how little photometric texture is required by the method, since roofs with virtually homogeneous intensity are retrieved. Only two roofs are missed in the entire scene.

5.   AUGMENTED REALITY

Because the system automatically determines the camera position for each view, it is possible to render computer-generated objects as if they are part of the scene. Figures 1.17 and 1.18 demonstrate this process on two of the example sequences. In figure 1.17, planar surfaces are identified in the 3D structure, and then an image is transformed via the implied 2D perspective transformation such that it appears to be

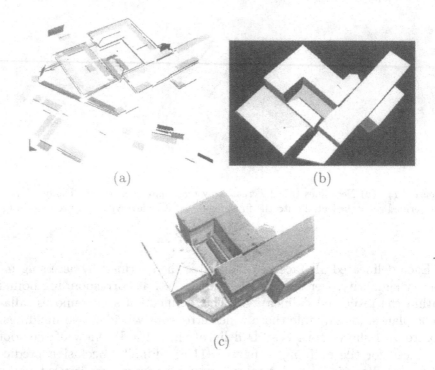

(a)

(b)

(c)

Figure 1.15 Model reconstruction results on the full example scene of figure 1.8. (a) 49 detected half-planes from 137 3D lines. (b) 3D model of the scene (12 roof planes). The vertical walls are produced by extruding the roof's borders to the ground plane. (c) 3D model of the scene with texture mapping.

attached to the plane. Figure 1.18 demonstrates the use of the recovered 3D structure of the scene for depth-keying. The cage around the object is rendered into a Z-buffer which is initialized using the 3D model, so that the bars behind the object are correctly occluded, and those in front correctly occlude the object.

6. FUTURE DEVELOPMENTS

We have presented a system that will take sequences of images from an uncalibrated camera or cameras, and will automatically recover camera positions and 3D point and line structure from these sequences. We are currently extending the core system to include space curves [20], and cope with wide baselines between frames [18]. More details of the plane sweeping method for generating 3D models of piecewise planar scenes are given in [1].

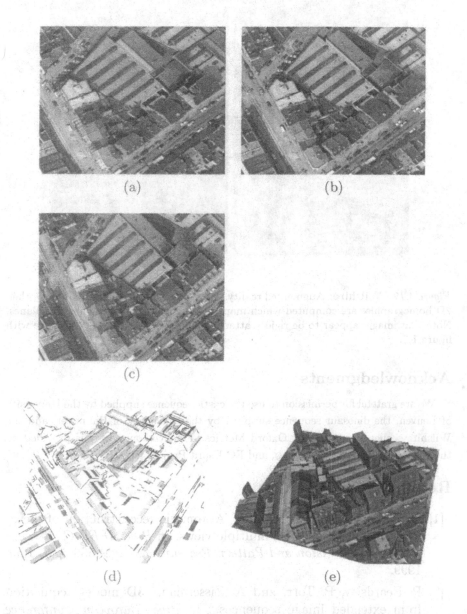

Figure 1.16 (a)–(c) Three of six overlapping aerial views. The images are about 1200 × 1200 pixels, one pixel corresponding to a ground length of 8.5cm. (d) The 452 reconstructed 3D lines and the 267 detected half-planes. (e) A view of the 3D model of the scene, with texture mapping (180 roof planes).

Figure 1.17 **Wilshire**: Augmented reality. Planar surfaces are identified in 3D, then 2D homographies are computed which map the augmenting images onto the planes. Note that images appear to be rigidly attached onto two skyscrapers. Compare with figure 1.3.

Acknowledgments

We are grateful for permission to use the castle sequence supplied by the University of Leuven, the dinosaur sequence supplied by the University of Hannover, and the Wilshire sequence supplied by Oxford Metrics. Financial support was provided by the EC ACTS project VANGUARD, and EC Esprit Project IMPACT.

References

[1] C. Baillard and A. Zisserman. Automatic reconstruction of piece-wise planar models from multiple views. In *Proc. IEEE Conference on Computer Vision and Pattern Recognition*, pages 559–565, June 1999.

[2] P. Beardsley, P. Torr, and A. Zisserman. 3D model acquisition from extended image sequences. In *Proc. European Conference on Computer Vision*, LNCS 1064/1065, pages 683–695. Springer-Verlag, 1996.

[3] O. Faugeras. What can be seen in three dimensions with an uncalibrated stereo rig? In *Proc. European Conference on Computer Vision*, LNCS 588, pages 563–578. Springer-Verlag, 1992.

Figure 1.18 **Dinosaur**: Augmented reality. The recovered 3D structure is used to depth-key the cage, which then correctly occludes the model. Compare with figure 1.3.

[4] O. D. Faugeras, Q. Luong, and S. Maybank. Camera self-calibration: Theory and experiments. In *Proc. European Conference on Computer Vision*, LNCS 588, pages 321–334. Springer-Verlag, 1992.

[5] A. W. Fitzgibbon, G. Cross, and A. Zisserman. Automatic 3D model construction for turn-table sequences. In R. Koch and L. Van Gool, editors, *3D Structure from Multiple Images of Large-Scale Environments, LNCS 1506*, pages 155–170. Springer-Verlag, June 1998.

[6] A. W. Fitzgibbon and A. Zisserman. Automatic camera recovery for closed or open image sequences. In *Proc. European Conference on Computer Vision*, pages 311–326. Springer-Verlag, June 1998.

[7] C. J. Harris and M. Stephens. A combined corner and edge detector. In *Proc. 4th Alvey Vision Conference, Manchester*, pages 147–151, 1988.

[8] R. I. Hartley. A linear method for reconstruction from lines and points. In *Proc. International Conference on Computer Vision*, pages 882–887, 1995.

[9] R. I. Hartley. Lines and points in three views and the trifocal tensor. *International Journal of Computer Vision*, 22(2):125–140, 1997.

[10] R. I. Hartley, R. Gupta, and T. Chang. Stereo from uncalibrated cameras. In *Proc. IEEE Conference on Computer Vision and Pattern Recognition*, 1992.

[11] R. I. Hartley and A. Zisserman. *Multiple View Geometry in Computer Vision*. Cambridge University Press, 2000. (to appear).

[12] S. Laveau. *Géométrie d'un système de N caméras. Théorie, estimation et applications*. PhD thesis, INRIA, 1996.

[13] H. C. Longuet-Higgins. A computer algorithm for reconstructing a scene from two projections. *Nature*, 293:133–135, September 1981.

[14] P. Milgram, S. Shumin, D. Drascic, and J. Grodski. Applications of augmented reality for human-robot communication. In *International Conference on Intelligent Robots and Systems Proceedings, Yokohama, Japan*, pages 1467–1472, 1993.

[15] T. Moons, D. Frère, J. Vandekerckhove, and L. Van Gool. Automatic modelling and 3D reconstruction of urban house roofs from high resolution aerial imagery. In *Proc. 5th European Conference on Computer Vision, Freiburg, Germany*, pages 410–425, 1998.

[16] S. Noronha and R. Nevatia. Detection and description of buildings from multiple images. In *Proc. IEEE Conference on Computer Vision and Pattern Recognition, Puerto Rico*, pages 588–594, 1997.

[17] M. Pollefeys, R. Koch, and L. Van Gool. Self calibration and metric reconstruction in spite of varying and unknown internal camera parameters. In *Proc. 6th International Conference on Computer Vision, Bombay, India*, pages 90–96, 1998.

[18] P. Pritchett and A. Zisserman. Wide baseline stereo matching. In *Proc. 6th International Conference on Computer Vision, Bombay, India*, pages 754–760, January 1998.

[19] C. Schmid and A. Zisserman. Automatic line matching across views. In *Proc. IEEE Conference on Computer Vision and Pattern Recognition*, pages 666–671, 1997.

[20] C. Schmid and A. Zisserman. The geometry and matching of curves in multiple views. In *Proc. European Conference on Computer Vision*, pages 394–409. Springer-Verlag, June 1998.

[21] A. Shashua. Trilinearity in visual recognition by alignment. In *Proc. 3rd European Conference on Computer Vision, Stockholm*, volume 1, pages 479–484, May 1994.

[22] C. Slama. *Manual of Photogrammetry*. American Society of Photogrammetry, Falls Church, VA, USA, 4th edition, 1980.

[23] M. E. Spetsakis and J. Aloimonos. Structure from motion using line correspondences. *International Journal of Computer Vision*, 4(3):171–183, 1990.

[24] C. Tomasi and T. Kanade. Shape and motion from image streams under orthography: A factorization approach. *International Journal of Computer Vision*, 9(2):137–154, November 1992.

[25] P. H. S. Torr and D. W. Murray. Statistical detection of independent movement from a moving camera. *Image and Vision Computing*, 1(4):180–187, May 1993.

[26] P. H. S. Torr and A. Zisserman. Robust parameterization and computation of the trifocal tensor. *Image and Vision Computing*, 15:591–605, 1997.

[27] P. H. S. Torr and A. Zisserman. Robust computation and parameterization of multiple view relations. In *Proc. 6th International Conference on Computer Vision, Bombay, India*, pages 727–732, January 1998.

[28] U. Weidner and W. Förstner. Towards automatic building extraction from high-resolution digital elevation models. *ISPRS j. of Photogrammetry and Remote Sensing*, 50(4):38–49, August 1995.

[29] Z. Zhang, R. Deriche, O. D. Faugeras, and Q. Luong. A robust technique for matching two uncalibrated images through the recovery of the unknown epipolar geometry. *Artificial Intelligence*, 78:87–119, 1995.

Chapter 2

SURFACE RECONSTRUCTION FROM MULTIPLE VIEWS USING APPARENT CONTOURS AND SURFACE TEXTURE

Geoffrey Cross, Andrew Zisserman

Abstract   We describe a novel approach to reconstructing the complete surface of an object from multiple views, where the camera circumnavigates the object. The approach combines the information available from the apparent contour with the information available from the imaged surface texture.

It is demonstrated that this approach of combining two information sources has significant advantages over using either the contour or texture alone: first, the geometric constraints available are complementary, so that the deficiencies of one source can be overcome by the strengths of the other; second, judicious use of the two sources enables an efficient automatic reconstruction algorithm to be developed.

In particular we make the following contributions: it is shown that the set of epipolar tangencies generates an *epipolar net* at which the visual hull coincides with the surface; a statistical cost function is defined which incorporates terms for error in image intensity similarity and geometric error in the apparent contour; and, an improved photo-consistency constraint is developed for space carving.

Examples of automatically generated texture-mapped graphical models are given for various objects and camera motions. The objects may contain concavities, and have non-trivial topology.

1. INTRODUCTION

Surface reconstruction from images has been extensively investigated over the past three decades. The methods that have been developed can broadly be categorized into four classes: reconstruction from the apparent contour [5, 7, 13, 15, 18, 30, 32, 33] where the *visual hull* [21] is computed; texture correlation [2, 10, 14, 16] where a dense reconstruction is computed based on a measure of intensity similarity; feature

25

A. Leonardis et al. (eds.), Confluence of Computer Vision and Computer Graphics, 25–47.
© 2000 *Kluwer Academic Publishers. Printed in the Netherlands.*

based matching, e.g. [1, 24] which produces only a sparse surface map; and, more recently, space carving [20, 27] which is a variant on texture correlation, where voxels are progressively carved from an occupancy representation based on the principle of "photo-consistency" between images.

A secondary issue, but of considerable importance in implementations, is how the surface is represented. The choice is broadly either a parameterized surface, for example a triangulated mesh or tensor product surface; or voxel occupancy. A recent elegant addition is representation by a level set of a hyper-surface in 4D [28]. This representation was the basis of the texture correlation method described in [10], and has the advantage of being able to represent surfaces with various topologies.

The objective of this paper is the automatic reconstruction of a surface from multiple views, where the camera may circumnavigate an object (Fig. 2.1). This means that methods which build a depth-map reconstruction from a particular view are not appropriate. The novelty here lies in combining elements from the various classes of reconstruction method, and also in an implementation which uses different surface representations as appropriate for accuracy and efficiency, such that all views contribute equally.

We start in section 2.1 by rehearsing and extending the geometry of the visual hull, which is the surface bound computed by back-projecting apparent contours. In particular we introduce the "epipolar net" which is the collection of surface point constraints provided by the apparent contours over a set of view points. The computation of the visual hull is then described in section 2.3. Section 3 introduces space carving and the photo-consistency test which is central to the algorithm. We then develop and implement an extension to the standard photo-consistency test [19]. The extension enables sub-pixel registration and greater invariance to photometric variations. Section 4 then describes a statistical cost function which is an extension of that proposed and implemented by Faugeras and Keriven in [10]. The extension is to include a geometric error based on conformity to the measured apparent contour.

These three developments (visual hull, photo-consistency, and statistical optimization of the surface) form the elements of an efficient and 'optimal' automatic surface reconstruction algorithm in which space carving proceeds from the visual hull, rather than the much looser bound usually used in [20], and the statistical optimization proceeds from the space carved surface. Because the cost function includes both texture and apparent contour terms, regions of the surface may be reconstructed even in the absence of adequate texture for correlation.

Figure 2.1 Six images (*top* image set) from a sequence of a toy dinosaur. The figure demonstrates that the apparent contours (*middle* image set) are a rich source of information for reconstruction. Corner matches (*lower* image set) also provide further information on the surface structure.

It is assumed that the camera matrices are known for each view. For all the example sequences included here the objects are rotated on an (uncalibrated) turn table, and the camera matrices are computed automatically from the image sequence using the method described in [11]. Other methods for generating the cameras from corner features, e.g. [3, 12, 34], or from the apparent contour and other image features [4, 6, 8, 25] could equally well be used.

2. RECONSTRUCTION FROM APPARENT CONTOURS

In this section we first review the geometric constraints on surface reconstruction provided by the apparent contour over multiple images. Then we describe a surface reconstruction algorithm using the apparent contours.

2.1 GEOMETRY

The image outline of a smooth surface S results from surface points at which the imaging rays are tangent to the surface, as shown in figure 2.2. The *contour generator* on S is the set of points $\mathbf{X}$ on S for which rays are tangent to S. The corresponding image *apparent contour* is the set of points $\mathbf{x}$ which are the image of $\mathbf{X}$, i.e. the apparent contour is the image of the contour generator. Image points on the apparent contour back-project to rays tangent to the surface, and image lines tangent to

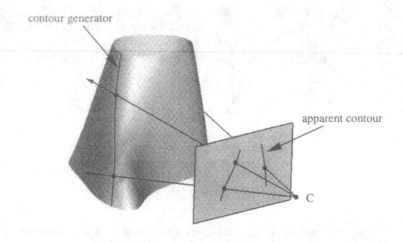

Figure 2.2   The apparent contour is the image of the contour generator. The surface tangent plane at any point on the contour generator passes through the camera centre **C**.

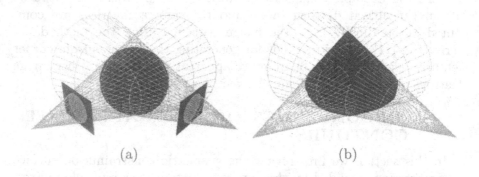

(a)   (b)

Figure 2.3   (a) Back-projecting the apparent contour gives a cone tangent to the surface along the contour generator. (b) The visual hull is given by the intersection of the cones, one for each view. It encloses the original surface and is tangent to this surface along the contour generators.

the apparent contour back-project to planes which are tangent planes to the surface.

Back-projecting apparent contours.   For known cameras, the apparent contour generates a set of tangency constraints and a bound for surface reconstruction. Each apparent contour back-projects to a "cone"

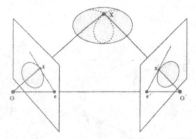

Figure 2.4 At an epipolar tangent point **X** on the surface, the surface tangent plane passes through both camera centres.

as shown in figure 2.3(a). The surface is tangent to this cone at the contour generator, and all points on the surface must lie on or within this semi-infinite cone.

If two or more images of the surface are available, the cones intersect to enclose the surface [17]. The closed surface as reconstructed from these cones is referred to as the *visual hull* (see figure 2.3(b)). The visual hull is guaranteed to fully enclose the surface (as each of the generating cones enclose the surface). The surface will be coincident with and tangent to the visual hull along each of the contour generators but not elsewhere. As can be seen in figure 2.6(a), the visual hull does not, however, penetrate concavities of the surface, and only reconstructs the convex elliptic and hyperbolic parts of the surface.

Epipolar tangents. Consider two views. In general the cones back projected from apparent contours intersect in a space curve which does not lie on the surface. However, as shown in figure 2.4, at a point where the epipolar plane is tangent to the surface the space curve is coincident (and tangent to) the surface. Such points arise where the apparent contour is tangent to the epipolar lines, and are termed *epipolar tangencies* [25, 26] or *frontier points* [6].

Epipolar nets. Since an epipolar tangent point on the surface arises from contact with an epipolar plane, it is a property of view pairs. If one of the camera centres changes position then the epipolar tangent points will also move in general[1]. For three views there are epipolar tangencies for each pair of images of the triplet, and over a set of views

---

[1]Epipolar tangent points are the same over multiple views if the cameras share an epipolar plane, e.g. in the case of three views with collinear camera centres.

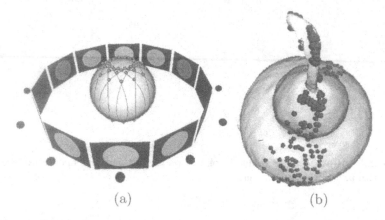

(a)   (b)

Figure 2.5   The epipolar net. (a) The intersections of each pair of contour generators
are epipolar tangent points for the associated pair of images. The epipolar tangent
points combine to create an epipolar net of points through which both the surface
and the visual hull must pass. The camera centres and image planes are shown. (b)
The model from the gourd sequence of figure 2.15 with all epipolar tangent points
superimposed demonstrates that a significant part of the surface is covered by the
epipolar net. The net is for 30 images covering a 180 degree sweep.

an *epipolar net* of such points is built up (see figure 2.5). Each point of
the net arising at the intersection of two contour generators for a view
pair. However, since not all contour generators actually intersect with
each other, some image pairs will not provide epipolar tangent points.

Each point (node) on the epipolar net is a 3D point which can be
found directly from the apparent contour. The visual hull is coincident
with the viewed surface at each of the 3D points of the net. Therefore
in areas with a dense epipolar net the visual hull models a surface more
closely than elsewhere.

2.2   DEFICIENCIES IN RECONSTRUCTING FROM THE VISUAL HULL

As shown above, reconstruction from apparent contours alone provides the visual hull which is a bound on the surface, but does not fully
reconstruct the surface. There are two types of deficiencies: first, concavities are not reconstructed since they do not contribute to the apparent
contour, see figure 2.6(a); second, even for a convex surface the visual
hull is not coincident with the surface, see figure 2.6(b). This difference
between the visual hull and surface depends on the surface shape, and
the number and position of the views.

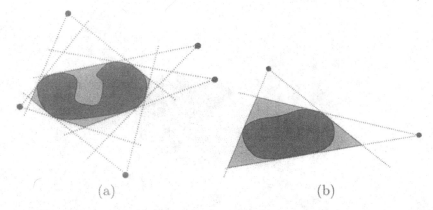

Figure 2.6 2D schematic of the difference between the 'surface' and the visual hull computed from image 'outlines'. (a) The visual hull does not 'capture' surface concavities; (b) Even if there are no concavities, the visual hull computed from a finite number of images may not coincide with the surface.

On the other hand, surface points (e.g. texture), viewed over multiple images and reconstructed by triangulation, "probe" the surface at all visible points including concavities, see figure 2.7. So, triangulating on surface features does reconstruct concavities, but provides no constraints at texture-less surface patches; and, the visual hull does not reconstruct surface concavities, but does reconstruct surface regions even in the absence of any surface features. Consequently, triangulating on surface texture features complements the tangency constraints provided by the apparent contour. We return to triangulation on surface texture in section 3.

2.3   COMPUTING THE VISUAL HULL

If no assumptions are made about the surface shape, the visual hull must simply be reconstructed as the intersections of the back-projected cones as in figure 2.8(a). However, an approach used by several authors [5, 7, 15] is to assume a local quadric form of the surface which is fitted generally to three apparent contours (see figure 2.8(b)). This hull surface is then parameterized by a net formed by the contour generator for each view linked by epipolar curves. The problem with this parameterization is that it is singular at epipolar tangencies, and reconstruction errors result. An alternative approach is a volumetric computation where the visual hull is computed and represented by voxel occupancy. This idea dates back to [22].

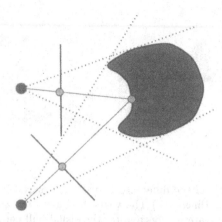

Figure 2.7 Two views of a surface provide information from both the apparent contours in the form of a tangent constraint and a point match which provides a surface point constraint. Both reconstruction methods complement each other, and will be used together to provide complete models.

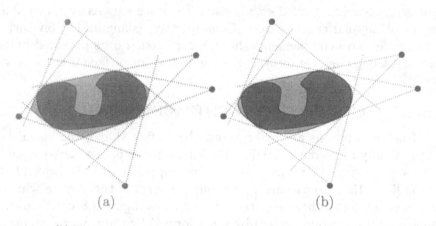

(a)   (b)

Figure 2.8 (a) The visual hull can be reconstructed as the intersection of the cones generated by back-projecting the apparent contour in each image. (b) If assumptions are made about the smoothness of the surface, the visual hull can be reconstructed by locally fitting quadratic or Bezier patches.

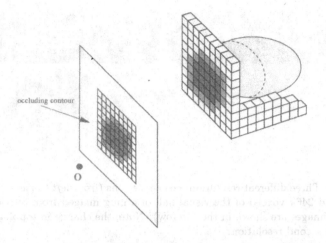

occluding contour

O

Figure 2.9 A region of space is sampled, and each voxel is assigned one of three values. Light cubes are known to lie outside the visual hull, and dark cubes are known to lie inside the visual hull (from this single image). Gray cubes lie on the surface and can be sub-sampled for greater resolution.

2.3.1 Volumetric model generation.

A region of space, known to enclose the surface, is subdivided volumetrically at a given (but not necessarily uniform) resolution. Each sub-region is then classified according to whether it lies inside the visual hull, outside the visual hull or spans the surface of the visual hull (figure 2.9). This classification is achieved by observing the projection of the sub-region, or *voxel*, onto each image plane: if the projected voxel lies outside any of the apparent contours, it must also lie outside the visual hull. The algorithm is close to that presented by Szeliski in [31].

Octree representation. An implementation based on octrees has significant speed advantages. A region of space is subdivided into a set of cubes at a low resolution. Each cube is then classified with respect to the visual hull as above. If a higher resolution is required, each cube is subdivided into 8 equal sized cubes and the classification is repeated. However, cubes which are known to lie completely outside or completely inside the visual hull do not need to be subdivided, as the classification of their 'children' will be the same as that of their parents.

Using this approach, an arbitrary volumetric resolution can be achieved. A trade-off is required at this point: at a low resolution, important topological features of the visual hull may be missed, whilst high resolution models take longer to generate and are more difficult to manipulate. Figure 2.10 demonstrates this trade-off.

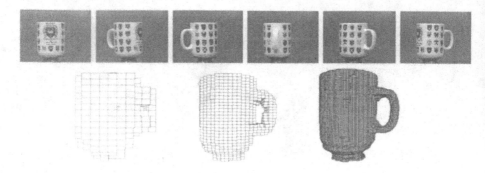

Figure 2.10   Three different resolution reconstructions (from *left* to *right*: 728 voxels, 4k voxels and 246k voxels) of the visual hull of a mug imaged from 36 views (six of the original images are shown in the top row). Note, the change in topology between the first and second resolution.

3.   COMPUTING THE SURFACE FROM TEXTURE INFORMATION

It has been shown that the apparent contour does not give any information about concavities of the viewed surface. In order to accurately reconstruct such surface regions, it is necessary to make use of other information such as texture.

Dense stereo algorithms, e.g. [16], make good use of texture information, but to date have only been extended from two views to many by merging surface patches — an approach that does not generalize well to circumnavigation of the object.

It is also possible to obtain surface shape information from features such as corners or curves in the image. However, this data is sparse and generally a parameterized surface model must subsequently be fitted, e.g. [14], in order to obtain a dense reconstruction.

3.1   SPACE CARVING

Space carving [20, 27] does not suffer from either of these limitations. It provides a successive algorithm for removing voxels in a voxmap with the aim of creating a 3D shape which reproduces the input images.

In brief, the idea of space carving is to project each voxel on the surface into the set of images. The projected voxel defines a correspondence between image points, and the intensity at the corresponding points is evaluated to determine if it is "photo-consistent" (see below), ensuring the voxel is only compared with pixel values in images in which it is not occluded. If the voxel is not photo-consistent it is removed (carved) from the occupancy space, and the algorithm repeats. If it is photo-consistent then the voxel can be coloured with the corresponding pixel value. The final result is a set of voxels which closely reproduce the original images.

There are 2 main drawbacks to the original implementation described in [19]. The first concerns initialization, and the second the photo-consistency test. The following sections describe improvements in these two areas.

3.2   SURFACE DIRECTED INITIALIZATION

It is often necessary to initialize the algorithm with a very large voxmapped space in order to ensure that it completely encloses the surface. Each voxel must then be tested in turn for consistency with the images which results in a high computational load. As has been shown in section 2.1, the visual hull completely encloses the generating surface, and can be efficiently constructed using octrees. It follows naturally that the visual hull should be used as a starting point for the space carving algorithm.

3.3   IMPROVED PHOTO-CONSISTENCY CONSTRAINT

In the original implementation of space carving [19], the photo-consistency test proceeded as follows: project a voxel centroid into each image, and compare the intensities of the corresponding pixels. If the intensities differ by less than a threshold then the voxel is photo-consistent. Unfortunately this test is prone to errors from image intensity noise and from the spatial sampling noise inherent in the voxelation of space. A "shift transform" was introduced in [20] to solve the second of these problems. However, it can be shown that a bias is introduced such that the model is larger than the original object and hence misses certain small concavities.

If the threshold on the photo-consistency test is too low, the result is false protrusions on the surface. Conversely, (and more serious here), if the test is too conservative (i.e. points are not considered consistent even when they are) the result is indentations or holes in the final surface. The photo-consistency test must therefore be robust to image noise.

Here we improve the photo-consistency test so that it is more robust in two ways: first, a smooth surface fit is used to provide an image to image map (see figure 2.11). This enables registration to sub-pixel accuracy. Interpolation is now required because pixels from one image will not in general coincide with pixel positions in the other image; second, the comparison of intensities uses normalized cross-correlation so is invariant

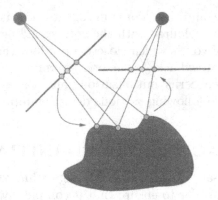

Figure 2.11 Surface-induced transfer. Any image point back-projects to a ray in space. Given the local geometry of a surface, this ray can be intersected with the surface to give a 3D point, which in turn can be projected into a second image. This process defines a point to point mapping between the images induced by the surface.

to a local affine transformation in brightness $(I \rightarrow \alpha I + \beta)$. The photo-consistency test defines a binary valued *indicator function* for voxels.

3.3.1   Photo-consistency constraint—implementation.

In order to provide an accurate and smooth surface-induced mapping, it is necessary to fit a local surface patch to the voxelated surface. This is achieved by locally fitting a quadratic patch to a set of surface points. Each patch can then be represented as a quadric surface in the form

$$\mathbf{x}^\top Q \mathbf{x} = 0 \ ,$$

where $\mathbf{x} = (X, Y, Z, 1)^\top$ is a 3D point on the surface patch, and Q is a 4×4 symmetric matrix representing the quadric. It can be shown [9, 29] that the quadric induces an algebraic mapping, $\mathbf{x}_i = \mathbf{f}(\mathbf{x}_j)$ between any two images, i and j, where $\mathbf{x}_i$ and $\mathbf{x}_j$ are corresponding points in images i and j respectively.

The photo-consistent indicator function is then computed as follows for each voxel: fit a quadric patch to the voxel neighbourhood, and project the voxel centroid into each image. The projected centroid defines corresponding points between the images. Starting from the most fronto-parallel image measure the normalized cross-correlation with corresponding image neighbourhoods, where the map between images is defined by the fitted quadric patch. If the cross-correlations are above a threshold (here 0.8) then the voxel is photo-consistent.

3.4 SPACE CARVING IMPLEMENTATION

The starting point for the space carving algorithm is the voxel representation of the visual hull produced from the apparent contours. Often, and in particular when many views of a single object are available, the visual hull is close to the final surface. Incorrectly modeled regions (the two deficiencies illustrated in figure 2.6) are identified using the indicator function, and only these regions are a candidate for space carving. Voxels are successively removed in these regions until the surface is photo-consistent with the images.

3.5 RESULTS

Figure 2.12 shows six images from a sequence of 36 images of a skull, and the computed visual hull. The eye and nose areas are not accurately modeled by the visual hull. However, areas around the back of the head which are convex and smooth are accurately reconstructed in the visual hull. These two types of regions are identified by the photo-consistency indicator function. Figure 2.13 shows the number of voxels remaining in the model through iterations of the algorithm in section 3.4.

Figures 2.14 and 2.15 shows further examples of using the voxel based algorithm. In each case the VRML models generated have in the order of 50k faces which allows them to be rendered in reasonable speeds on a workstation.

4. MINIMISING REPROJECTION ERRORS USING A SURFACE REPRESENTATION

Although the results from the space carving algorithm are subjectively good, and objectively accurate to within one voxel, they are limited by the resolution of the voxels (which is often limited by computation time and available memory). This limitation is illustrated in figure 2.16(a).

To overcome this limitation a parameterized surface representation may be used instead of voxel occupancy. In [10] a parameterized surface fit was obtained using a cost function based on image correlation. Here we extend the cost function to also enforce the geometric constraints arising from the apparent contour.

Intensity correlation. The cost function used in [10] has the form

$$C_t = \frac{1}{4pq} \int_{-p}^{+p} \int_{-q}^{+q} \left(I_1(m_1 + m) - \bar{I}_1(m_1) \right) \left(I_2(K(m_1 + m)) - \bar{I}_2(K(m_1)) \right) dm \ ,$$

$$(2.1)$$

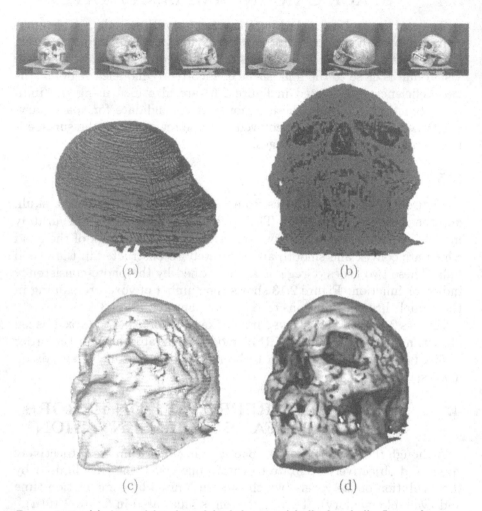

Figure 2.12 (a) A voxelelated model of the visual hull of a skull. It can be seen that the visual hull "smoothes over" concavities such as the nose and eye sockets. (b) An indicator function (section 3.3) is applied to the surface of the visual hull, and regions with high score are shown in *gray* and those with low score are shown in *black*. A high score indicates that the reprojection of the surface is consistent with the input images. It can be seen that the eyes and nose regions have been marked as "incorrect". (c) The final model after applying the space carving algorithm as described in section 3.4. After space carving, areas such as the eye socket and nose region are correctly reconstructed. A simple mesh smoothing algorithm has been applied to the surface to highlight these areas, but the model is stored as 128^3 voxels. (d) A textured-mapped model using intensities from the original images.

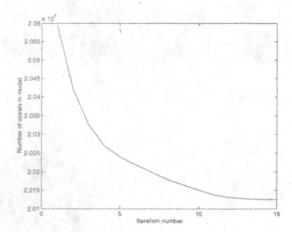

Figure 2.13   Number of voxels remaining in model (figure 2.12) as the space-carving algorithm converges.

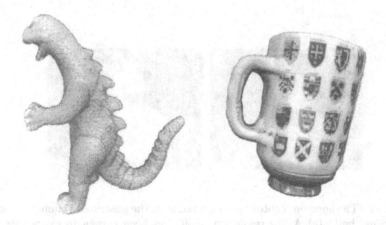

Figure 2.14   Texture-mapped 3D models of the dinosaur from sequence in figure 2.1 and the cup from the sequence in figure 2.10

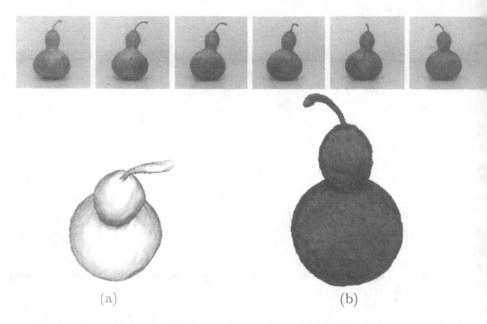

(a)   (b)

Figure 2.15   (*top*) Six images from a sequence (30 images) of a gourd. (a) An untextured model and (b) a textured model.

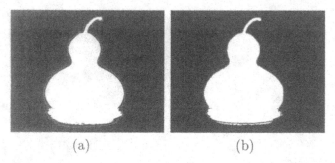

(a)   (b)

Figure 2.16   The apparent contour as projected from the generated volumetric model of the visual hull. (a) A low resolution model has been chosen to exaggerate the re-projection errors. This model has approximately 8000 polygons and gives an approximate reprojection error of 5–7 pixels. (b) The errors are reduced to sub-pixel if the cost function of equation (2.2) is used in a minimization over the surface.

Figure 2.17 Six images (*top*) from a sequence of 100 images of a plasticine object with a single large concavity. The plane common to the cameras is intersected with each image plane and the 1D intensity image corresponding to the line of intersection (*bottom*) taken as an example in section 4.1.

thus correlating a texture patch, centred around image point m_1 in a first image, $I_1(m)$ with the surface-mapped patch in a second image, $I_2(m)$. The function $K(m)$ maps points between the two images given a hypothesized surface shape (the optimization parameter), S. The mean patch intensities, $\bar{I}_1$ and $\bar{I}_2$, allow for an affine scaling of intensities.

Here, we extend the cost function by introducing an extra distance term to minimise errors in the reprojected surface:

$$\mathcal{C}_a = \int d(\mathbf{P}(S)(s), \mathbf{c}(s)) ds \ . \tag{2.2}$$

The distance function, d, measures the distance between the projected apparent contour, $\mathbf{P}(S)$ from the apparent contour detected in the original images, $\mathbf{c}$.

The overall cost function balances these two terms according to variance of the noise probability distributions, σ_t (of intensity cross-correlation) and σ_a (of pixel localization error), on each one of the cost terms:

$$\mathcal{C} = \frac{\mathcal{C}_t}{\sigma_t^2} + \frac{\mathcal{C}_a}{\sigma_a^2} \ . \tag{2.3}$$

The importance of including this term is that the surface is now constrained (by the apparent contour) at regions at which there is no texture. This information is unused in the original work [10] because the cost is not included.

4.1   TWO DIMENSIONAL EXAMPLE—IMPLEMENTATION

Figure 2.17(*top*) shows a turn-table image sequence of a plasticine object with a large concavity. As an example, we will consider a cross-section of the object by considering the images along a set of corresponding epipolar lines (figure 2.17(*bottom*)).

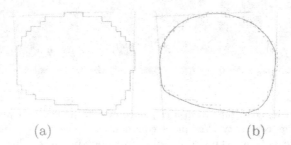

Figure 2.18 (a) A voxel model of the visual hull. Due to sampling errors, it does not accurately obey the apparent contour constraints. (b) Applying the cost function of equation (2.2) (minimizing errors in the reprojected apparent contour along), the model is significantly improved from the voxelated visual hull.

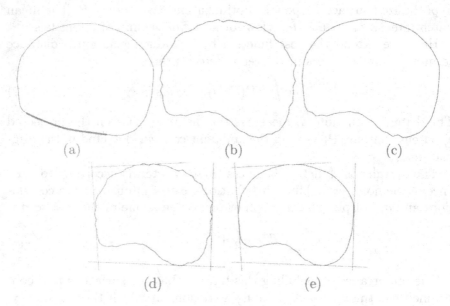

Figure 2.19 (a) The cost function (2.3) is applied to the surface of the visual hull. Areas with high cost (incorrectly modeled regions such as the concavity) are marked. (b) A model generated by minimising the cost function of equation (2.1) is shown. The concavity is now more accurately modeled, but if the full cost function (equation (2.3)) is used the convex regions are further constrained by the apparent contour constraint (c). (d) and (e) show the results of (b) and (c) with two of the back-projected apparent contours superimposed. (d) clearly shows that the model does not obey the apparent contour constraint if cost (2.2) is not directly included in the cost function (as is the case in (e)).

The visual hull (figure 2.18) is used as the starting point for the optimization (computed using the algorithm outlined in section "Volumetric model generation" on page 31). By applying a similar indicator function to that used in section 3.3, the correctly reconstructed regions of the curve are located and held constant during the optimization (figure 2.19(a)).

For the purposes of this example (see discussion below), the curve is represented as a piecewise linear spline, with approximately 150 line segments. The vertices are restricted to move along the curve normals. The cost function (2.3) is minimized by moving the vertex positions of the curve using a Levenberg-Marquardt algorithm. A Z-buffer is maintained during the optimization to compute the reprojected apparent contour, and to ensure that occluded regions are not included in the correlations. Figure 2.19(b) shows the results of this optimization if the texture term alone is used (it is clear that the algorithm has only converged to a local minimum, and is far from the correct solution), whilst figure 2.19(c) shows how the apparent contour term improves the model considerably. In the concave region, results (b) and (c) are identical as the apparent contour provides no information. It is clear that the texture does not provide sufficient information alone (indeed, figure 2.19(d) violates the visual hull constraint) and is augmented by the apparent contour constraint in the convex regions.

The gourd sequence of figure 2.15 is used as a 3D example using the cost function of equation (2.2). Figure 2.16 demonstrates how the reprojection errors of the apparent contour reduce from 5–7 pixels to subpixel.

5.   SUMMARY

The algorithm presented here enables an accurate and complete model of a surface to be built automatically from multiple images, and we now discuss limitations and possible extensions to this approach.

Apparent contours. This contribution to the cost function involves a geometric image error minimization. The error makes minimal assumptions about the world (cf. the photo-consistency constraint discussed below). Its use requires that the apparent contour is correctly segmented from the image (here this is achieved by 'blue-screening') and this is the point at which errors can occur. There are two failure modes: first, under segmentation (where parts of the contour are missed). This failure is not particularly serious because the surface can still be carved away from other views where the contour is detected; the second type of failure, over segmentation, is serious because parts of the actual object will then be removed.

Photo-consistency.   This requires assumptions about the photo-metric properties of the surface, i.e. about the BRDF, which is generally assumed to be Lambertian. A serious problem is with specularities where the assumed properties are strongly violated. The naive use of the space carving algorithm is inappropriate in such cases. Unfortunately, specularities do commonly occur, e.g. for metallic and shiny surfaces. However, it is possible to verify the consistency of the BRDF assumptions: at the epipolar net points the visual hull generates surface points (and the surface normal), and the brightness of these points can be used to assess, for example, the Lambertian assumption.

Extensions.   The presence of specularities can also be turned to an advantage if the position of the light source is known. In this case, based on the standard geometry of mirror reflection, the surface (position and normal) can be reconstructed up to a one parameter family. Shadows may also be used to provide geometric constraints.

In the current implementation, it has been assumed that the visual hull correctly captures the topology, and the topology does not subsequently change in the optimization stage. We are currently investigating other parameterizations of the surface, such as the level sets used in [10] and the T-snakes developed in [23] which will enable changes in surface topology within the optimization.

Acknowledgments

Figure 2.2 was provided by Roberto Cipolla and Peter Giblin. The dinosaur image sequence of figure 2.1 was provided by the University of Hannover. The gourd sequence (figure 2.15) was provided by Edmond Boyer of INRIA, Grenoble. Funding for this work was provided by the Engineering Physical Sciences Research Council (EPSRC).

References

[1] N. Ayache and O. D. Faugeras. Building a consistent 3D representation of a mobile robot environment by combining multiple stereo views. In *Proc. International Joint Conference on Artificial Intelligence*, pages 808–810, 1987.

[2] H. H. Baker and T. O. Binford. Depth from edge and intensity based stereo. In *IJCAI81*, pages 631–636, 1981.

[3] P. Beardsley, P. Torr, and A. Zisserman. 3D model acquisition from extended image sequences. In *Proc. European Conference on Computer Vision*, LNCS 1064/1065, pages 683–695. Springer-Verlag, 1996.

[4] R. Berthilsson and K. Åström. Reconstruction of 3-D curves from 2-D images using affine shape methods for curves. In *Proc. IEEE Conference on Computer Vision and Pattern Recognition*, 1997.

[5] E. Boyer and M.O. Berger. 3D surface reconstruction using occluding contours. *International Journal of Computer Vision*, 22(3):219–233, March 1997.

[6] R. Cipolla, K. Åström, and P. Giblin. Motion from the frontier of curved surfaces. In *Proc. 5th International Conference on Computer Vision, Boston*, pages 269–275, 1995.

[7] R. Cipolla and A. Blake. Surface shape from the deformation of apparent contours. *International Journal of Computer Vision*, 9(2):83–112, 1992.

[8] G. Cross, A. W. Fitzgibbon, and A. Zisserman. Parallax geometry of smooth surfaces in multiple views. In *Proc. 7th International Conference on Computer Vision, Kerkyra, Greece*, pages 323–329, September 1999.

[9] G. Cross and A. Zisserman. Quadric surface reconstruction from dual-space geometry. In *Proc. 6th International Conference on Computer Vision, Bombay, India*, pages 25–31, January 1998.

[10] O. Faugeras and R. Keriven. Complete dense stereovision using level set methods. In *Proc. 5th European Conference on Computer Vision, Freiburg, Germany*, pages 379–393, 1998.

[11] A. W. Fitzgibbon, G. Cross, and A. Zisserman. Automatic 3D model construction for turn-table sequences. In R. Koch and L. Van Gool, editors, *3D Structure from Multiple Images of Large-Scale Environments, LNCS 1506*, pages 155–170. Springer-Verlag, June 1998.

[12] A. W. Fitzgibbon and A. Zisserman. Automatic camera recovery for closed or open image sequences. In *Proc. European Conference on Computer Vision*, pages 311–326. Springer-Verlag, June 1998.

[13] P. Giblin and R. Weiss. Reconstruction of surfaces from profiles. In *Proc. 1st International Conference on Computer Vision, London*, pages 136–144, London, 1987.

[14] W. E. L. Grimson. *From Images to Surfaces: A Computational Study of the Human Early Visual System*. MIT Press, 1981.

[15] T. Joshi, N. Ahuja, and J. Ponce. Structure and motion estimation from dynamic silhouettes under perspective projection. In *Proc. 5th International Conference on Computer Vision, Boston*, pages 290–295, 1995.

[16] R. Koch. 3D surface reconstruction from stereoscopic image sequences. In *Proc. 5th International Conference on Computer Vision, Boston*, pages 109–114, 1995.

[17] J. J. Koenderink. What does the occluding contour tell us about solid shape? *Perception*, 13:321–330, 1984.

[18] K. Kutulakos. Affine surface reconstruction by purposive viewpoint control. In *Proc. 5th International Conference on Computer Vision, Boston*, pages 894–901, 1995.

[19] K. Kutulakos and S. Seitz. What do N photographs tell us about 3D shape? Technical Report 680, University of Rochester, January 1998.

[20] K. Kutulakos and S. Seitz. A theory of shape by space carving. In *Proc. 7th International Conference on Computer Vision, Kerkyra, Greece*, pages 307–314, 1999.

[21] A. Laurentini. The visual hull concept for silhouette-based image understanding. *IEEE Transactions on Pattern Analysis and Machine Intelligence*, 16(2):150–162, February 1994.

[22] W. N. Martin and J. K. Aggarwal. Volumetric description of objects from multiple views. *IEEE Transactions on Pattern Analysis and Machine Intelligence*, 5(2):150–158, March 1983.

[23] T. McInerney and D. Terzopoulos. Topologically adaptable snakes. In *Proc. 5th International Conference on Computer Vision, Boston*, pages 840–845, 1995.

[24] S. B. Pollard, J. E. W. Mayhew, and J. P. Frisby. PMF: A stereo correspondence algorithm using a disparity gradient limit. *Perception*, 14:449–470, 1985.

[25] J. Porrill and S. B. Pollard. Curve matching and stereo calibration. *Image and Vision Computing*, 9(1):45–50, 1991.

[26] J. H. Rieger. Three dimensional motion from fixed points of a deforming profile curve. *Optics Letters*, 9(1):123–125, 1986.

[27] S.M. Seitz and C.R. Dyer. Photorealistic scene reconstruction by voxel coloring. In *Proc. IEEE Conference on Computer Vision and Pattern Recognition, Puerto Rico*, pages 1067–1073, 1997.

[28] J. A. Sethian. *Level Set Methods*. Cambridge University Press, Cambridge, 1998.

[29] A. Shashua and S. Toelg. The quadric reference surface: Theory and applications. In *Proc. International Conference on Computer Vision*, 1997.

[30] S. Sullivan and J. Ponce. Automatic model construction and pose estimation from photographs using triangular splines. *IEEE Transactions on Pattern Analysis and Machine Intelligence*, 20(10):1091–1096, October 1998.

[31] R. Szeliski. Rapid octree construction from image sequences. *CVGIP*, 58(1):23–32, July 1993.

[32] R. Szeliski and R. Weiss. Robust shape recovery from occluding contours using a linear smoother. *International Journal of Computer Vision*, 28(1):27–44, June 1998.

[33] R. Vaillant and O. D. Faugeras. Using extremal boundaries for 3-D object modeling. *IEEE Transactions on Pattern Analysis and Machine Intelligence*, 14(2):157–173, February 1992.

[34] Z. Zhang, R. Deriche, O. D. Faugeras, and Q. Luong. A robust technique for matching two uncalibrated images through the recovery of the unknown epipolar geometry. *Artificial Intelligence*, 78:87–119, 1995.

Chapter 3

CONSISTENT PROJECTIVE RECONSTRUCTION FROM MULTIPLE VIEWS

Martin Urban, Tomáš Pajdla, Václav Hlaváč

Abstract   Projective reconstruction recovers 3-D points in projective space $\mathcal{P}^3$ from their several projections to 2-D images. Applications of projective reconstruction include algorithms for selecting point correspondences, algorithms for camera self-calibration, and algorithms for 3D shape recovery. We introduce a method for the projective reconstruction from n views. The method is based on concatenation of trifocal constraints and relies on linear estimates only. The method is not symmetrical with respect to input data. One of the captured images is selected as a reference image which plays a special role during the computation. The proposed algorithm requires that all the points involved be visible in the reference image. Accuracy and stability of the proposed algorithm with respect to pixel errors were tested. Experimental results are presented too.

1.   INTRODUCTION

The second half of nineties witnessed a qualitative move from stereovision that remained for a long time in photogrammetric framework providing relation between two views only. Information from more views was not acquired simultaneously as the multi-image geometric constraints were not commonly applied. A precise elaboration of multiple view geometry led to a new view on stereovision. Partial contributions for two, three, and four images followed. The unified treatment of the subject is provided in [6, 7, 4]. The new theoretical tools open the door to processing of large number of images and, subsequently, to qualitatively better results than before.

We present a method which applies trifocal relations to obtain projective reconstruction from $n > 4$ views. The proposed method comes

A. Leonardis et al. (eds.), Confluence of Computer Vision and Computer Graphics, 49–67.
© 2000 *Kluwer Academic Publishers. Printed in the Netherlands.*

from the algorithm for the projective reconstruction from three views introduced by Hartley [5]. Since it is necessary for the proper insight, Hartley's algorithm is reviewed in Section 3 after basic preliminaries (Sections 1 and 2). The very method is described in Section 4.

1.1   PROJECTIVE RECONSTRUCTION

Let us consider that a camera is modeled by a projection from a projective space $\mathcal{P}^3$ to $\mathcal{P}^2$. The homogeneous coordinates of points in the i-th image are denoted by $\tilde{\mathbf{u}}^{(i)} \in \mathcal{P}^2$ and homogeneous coordinates of a point from $\mathcal{P}^3$ are denoted by $\tilde{\mathbf{x}}$.

Then, the projections of a set of m points by n cameras can be expressed as

$$s_j^{(i)} \tilde{\mathbf{u}}_j^{(i)} = \tilde{\mathbf{P}}^{(i)} \tilde{\mathbf{x}}_j, \ i = 1, \dots, n, \ j = 1, \dots, m, \tag{3.1}$$

where 3×4 real matrix $\tilde{\mathbf{P}}^{(i)} \in \mathcal{M}^{3,4}$ is so-called camera projection matrix, $s_j^{(i)} \in \mathcal{R} \backslash \{0\}$ are scale factors.

The goal of a projective reconstruction is to find camera matrices $\tilde{\mathbf{P}}^{(i)}$ and homogeneous coordinates $\tilde{\mathbf{x}}_j$ so that Eq. (3.1) is satisfied for all image points $\tilde{\mathbf{u}}_j^{(i)}$, $i = 1, \dots, n$, $j = 1, \dots, m$.

Since both $\tilde{\mathbf{P}}^{(i)}$ and $\tilde{\mathbf{x}}_j$ are unknown, it is obvious that they can be recovered up to a choice of a coordinate system in $\mathcal{P}^3$, i.e., up to a homography. Having camera matrices $\tilde{\mathbf{P}}^{(i)}$, the consequent recovery of points $\tilde{\mathbf{x}}_j$ is trivial (and vice versa). Therefore, the following definition of projective reconstruction is introduced:

Definition 1 (Projective reconstruction) *The recovery of the equivalence class P*

$$P = \left\{ \left(\mathbf{P}^{(1)}, \dots, \mathbf{P}^{(n)} \right) \mid \left(\mathbf{P}^{(1)}, \dots, \mathbf{P}^{(n)} \right) = \left(\tilde{\mathbf{P}}^{(1)} \mathbf{H}, \dots, \tilde{\mathbf{P}}^{(n)} \mathbf{H} \right), \right.$$
$$\left. \mathbf{H} \in \mathcal{M}^{4,4}, \ \det(\mathbf{H}) \neq 0 \right\}$$

from a set of points $\tilde{\mathbf{u}}_j^{(i)}$ $i = 1, \dots, n$, $j = 1, \dots, m$, such that there exists a corresponding set of points $\tilde{\mathbf{x}}_j \in \mathcal{P}^3$ so that $s_j^{(i)} \tilde{\mathbf{u}}_j^{(i)} = \tilde{\mathbf{P}}^{(i)} \tilde{\mathbf{x}}_j$, is called the **projective reconstruction**.

1.2   MULTIFOCAL CONSTRAINTS

The projective reconstruction is based on the so-called multifocal constraints. The multifocal constraints are equations constraining the image points and projection matrices. They are derived from (3.1) by eliminating $s_j^{(i)}$ and $\tilde{\mathbf{x}}_j$.

Scale factors $s_j^{(i)}$ in (3.1) can be eliminated by introducing matrix

$$\mathbf{L}_j^{(i)} = \begin{bmatrix} 0 & -\tilde{u}_j^{(i)3} & \tilde{u}_j^{(i)2} \\ \tilde{u}_j^{(i)3} & 0 & -\tilde{u}_j^{(i)1} \\ -\tilde{u}_j^{(i)2} & \tilde{u}_j^{(i)1} & 0 \end{bmatrix} .$$

Then, the image equations (3.1) can be transformed to the equivalent system

$$\begin{bmatrix} \mathbf{L}_j^{(1)} \tilde{\mathbf{P}}^{(1)} \\ \vdots \\ \mathbf{L}_j^{(n)} \tilde{\mathbf{P}}^{(n)} \end{bmatrix} \tilde{\mathbf{x}}_j = \mathbf{M}_j \tilde{\mathbf{x}}_j = 0, \ j = 1, \ldots, m .$$

The constraints between $\tilde{\mathbf{P}}^{(i)}$ and $\tilde{\mathbf{u}}_j^{(i)}$, assuring the existence of $\tilde{\mathbf{x}}_j \in \mathcal{P}^3$, $\tilde{\mathbf{x}}_j \neq 0$, can be expressed as

$$\det(\mathbf{M}_j^{\iota\kappa\lambda\mu}) = 0 , \ \forall \, \mathbf{M}_j^{\iota\kappa\lambda\mu}, \ j = 1 \ldots, m , \qquad (3.2)$$

where $\mathbf{M}_j^{\iota\kappa\lambda\mu}$ stands for the minor of $\mathbf{M}_j$ consisting of rows $\iota, \kappa, \lambda, \mu$. It is seen from the size of $\mathbf{M}_j$ that $m\binom{3n}{4}$ such constraints can be constructed. Since rank $\mathbf{L}^{(i)} = 2$, it follows that at most $\binom{2n}{4}$ of them are linearly independent.

Depending on the chosen rows, the minor $\mathbf{M}_j^{\iota\kappa\lambda\mu}$ can comprise coordinates of points from two, three, or four images. They are called bifocal, trifocal, or quadrifocal constraints.

It was shown [10] that the solution of a projective reconstruction from m points projected to n views is described by a system of $m\binom{3n}{4}$ polynomial equations (3.2) of degree four. To solve such a system appears to be an overwhelming problem.[1] In addition, the measured data $\tilde{\mathbf{u}}_j^{(i)}$ involve errors in real situations and thus this overconstrained system (3.2) need not have any non-trivial solution. Therefore, some optimization technique should be applied.

1.3   OPTIMIZATION METHODS FOR PROJECTIVE RECONSTRUCTION

The ideal technique for a projective reconstruction minimizes the distances between original and reconstructed image points. Due to the

---

[1]In this context, we shall mention the paper from Bondyfalat, Mourrain, Pan [1]. They present a method for resolving overconstrained polynomial systems. However, the full comprehension requires rather deep knowledge from elimination algebra and from the cursory view we are not sure if this approach is applicable for the systems of our dimension.

non-linearity and complexity of the problem, this can be solved only by a numerical search (e.g. by the gradient descent) which considers an initial estimate and a minimal parameterization of P, see [2, 6]. For all those considerations, the recovery of the global minimum is not guaranteed.

Instead, a *linearization* of the problem is often used. It means that a non-linear task is decomposed to several subtasks which can be solved by a least-square solution of a linear system. The approaches based on the linearization are not ideal in the previously mentioned sense, i.e., they minimize imaginary algebraic distances instead of image discrepancies. However, these algorithms are efficient and the results are mostly sufficiently correct. The results can be used also as initial estimates for the numerical search in the ideal optimization technique.

At present, the methods based on the linearization are known only for bifocal, trifocal, or quadrifocal constraints. Thus, they can be used for the projective reconstruction either from two or three or four images. For a detailed description see [3, 4, 5, 11].

Naturally, it is tempting to use already existing effective algorithms for projective reconstruction from two, three, or four views at first and then only join the obtained classes somehow. However, this method fails due to inaccuracies in measured data and in numerical computations.

In this paper, we introduce a technique for an estimation of class P from n views. The presented method is based on a concatenation of the trifocal constraints of different triplets of views. The constraints are bound together so that a single optimization task can be constructed.

2.   PROBLEM OF JOINING TWO INDEPENDENT PROJECTIVE RECONSTRUCTIONS

Let us consider n views. Let P_1 is the equivalence class describing a projective reconstruction from views $\langle 1, \ldots, k \rangle$ and P_2 is the class corresponding to the reconstruction from views $\langle l, \ldots, n \rangle$, where $l \leq k$. We study now, how to join classes P_1 and P_2 and create a class P describing the projective reconstruction from all n views.

Consider the representative $\left(\tilde{\mathbf{P}}_{P_1}^{(1)}, \ldots, \tilde{\mathbf{P}}_{P_1}^{(k)} \right) \in P_1$. Let us select $\left(\tilde{\mathbf{P}}_{P_2}^{(l)}, \ldots, \tilde{\mathbf{P}}_{P_2}^{(n)} \right) \in P_2$ such that

$$\tilde{\mathbf{P}}_{P_1}^{(i)} = \tilde{\mathbf{P}}_{P_2}^{(i)} \, , \quad i = l, \ldots, k \, . \tag{3.3}$$

If $l < k$, then the representative of P_2 is constrained uniquely by (3.3) and the representative of P can be expressed as

$$\left(\tilde{\mathbf{P}}_{P_1}^{(1)}, \ldots, \tilde{\mathbf{P}}_{P_1}^{(k)}, \tilde{\mathbf{P}}_{P_2}^{(k+1)}, \ldots, \tilde{\mathbf{P}}_{P_2}^{(n)}\right) \in P \ . \tag{3.4}$$

This is based on the fact that if $l < k$, the classes P_1, P_2 have at least two common views and so the appropriate representative of P_2 is fixed uniquely by (3.3). Otherwise, if P_1, P_2 have not at least two common views then the appropriate representative of P_2 is not determined uniquely by (3.3) and the representative of P cannot be expressed by the n-tuple (3.4).

2.1   THE INCONSISTENCY OF P_1, P_2 IN REAL SITUATIONS

Image data involve errors in real situations and therefore the results of projective reconstructions are only approximations of P_1 and P_2. The problem of numerical inconsistency of P_1 and P_2 arises. It means that it may be impossible to select the elements of P_1 and P_2 such that (3.3) holds. Consequently, the previous approach fails. We propose a method overcoming this problem. The idea is to concatenate the projective reconstructions from multiple triplets of images. The trick is that the estimates of the classes P_i are not performed independently. The computations (Hartley's approach, see Section 3.3) of all the classes P_i are bound together and a representative of P is then recovered directly from image data. The method can also be viewed as an extension of Hartley's algorithm [5] from three views to n views.

Binding the computations of P_i requires a special grouping of view triplets to a configuration which we call the *cake configuration* and which is described in Section 4.

3.   PROJECTIVE RECONSTRUCTION FROM THREE VIEWS

Notation.   In the next paragraph, the following notation is used. The element in i-th column and j-th row of a matrix $\mathbf{A}$ is denoted by a_i^j. The i-th column of $\mathbf{A}$ is denoted by $\mathbf{a}_i$. Einstein summation convention is used. An index that appears as a subscript and superscript is summed over. The matrix $\mathbf{A}^{(i)}$ is used to denote the matrix of the first three columns of the projection matrix $\tilde{\mathbf{P}}^{(i)}$, $\mathbf{e}^{(i)}$ denotes the fourth column of $\tilde{\mathbf{P}}^{(i)}$, i.e., $\tilde{\mathbf{P}}^{(i)} = [\mathbf{A}^{(i)}, \mathbf{e}^{(i)}]$. Matrix $\mathbf{T}_i$ signifies 3×3 matrix consisted of nine elements $j, k = 1, 2, 3$ of the tensor T_i^{jk}. Sometimes a matrix or a tensor has to be rearranged to a vector of an appropriate length. Then, the following expression is used: $\mathbf{t} = \text{vector}_{mn}(\mathbf{T})$, $\mathbf{t} \in \mathcal{R}^{mn}$, $\mathbf{T} \in \mathcal{M}^{m,n}$. The way of arrangements follows from the context.

3.1   THE TRIFOCAL CONSTRAINTS AND THE TRIFOCAL TENSOR

The trifocal constraints are equations (3.2) where $\mathbf{M}_j^{\iota\kappa\lambda\mu}$ comprises the coordinates of three views. Consider the minors consisting of two rows coming from the first view and one row from the second and the third view. Without loss of generality, one of the camera matrices, say $\tilde{\mathbf{P}}^{(1)}$, may be chosen as $\tilde{\mathbf{P}}^{(1)} = [\mathbf{I}, \mathbf{0}]$, where $\mathbf{I}$ is the 3×3 identity matrix and $\mathbf{0}$ zero vector.

Then, the expanded form of the corresponding determinants (3.2) can be written (see Appendix A) as

$$\tilde{u}^{(1)\lambda}\tilde{u}^{(1)i}l_j^{(2)\iota}l_k^{(3)\kappa}(e^{(3)k}a_i^{(2)j} - e^{(2)j}a_i^{(3)k}) = 0 , \quad \iota,\kappa,\lambda = 1,2,3 , \quad (3.5)$$

where $\lambda, \iota, \kappa = 1, 2, 3$ are free indices (i.e., system (3.5) represents 27 equations) and i, j, k are the indices it is summed over. Since at least one $\tilde{u}^{(1)\lambda} \neq 0$, system (3.5) is equivalent to

$$\tilde{u}^{(1)i}l_j^{(2)\iota}l_k^{(3)\kappa}(e^{(3)k}a_i^{(2)j} - e^{(2)j}a_i^{(3)k}) = 0 , \quad \iota,\kappa = 1,2,3 . \quad (3.6)$$

Naturally, the term in the parenthesis can be written as a $3 \times 3 \times 3$ tensor

$$T_i^{jk} = e^{(3)k}a_i^{(2)j} - e^{(2)j}a_i^{(3)k} , \quad i,j,k = 1,2,3 . \quad (3.7)$$

This $3 \times 3 \times 3$ tensor is called the *trifocal tensor*. Likewise, (3.5) can be written using tensorial notation as

$$\tilde{u}^{(1)i}l_j^{(2)\iota}l_k^{(3)\kappa}T_i^{jk} = 0 , \quad \iota,\kappa = 1,2,3 . \quad (3.8)$$

Definition 2 (Hartley) *Suppose we have three distinct views described by projective matrices $\tilde{\mathbf{P}}^{(1)}$, $\tilde{\mathbf{P}}^{(2)}$, $\tilde{\mathbf{P}}^{(3)}$. Let us choose the basis of projective space $\mathcal{P}^3$ such as the projective matrix of the reference view is $\tilde{\mathbf{P}}^{(1)} = [\mathbf{I}, \mathbf{0}]$. Consider that $\tilde{\mathbf{P}}^{(i)} = [\mathbf{A}^{(i)}, \mathbf{e}^{(i)}]$, $i = 2, 3$, where $\mathbf{A}^{(i)}$ is a 3×3 matrix composed from the first three columns; $\mathbf{e}^{(i)}$ is the fourth column of $\tilde{\mathbf{P}}^{(i)}$. Then, the trivalent tensor formed as*

$$T_i^{jk} = e^{(3)k}a_i^{(2)j} - e^{(2)j}a_i^{(3)k} , \quad i,j,k = 1,2,3 , \quad (3.9)$$

*is called the **trifocal tensor**.*

One triplet of corresponding points $\tilde{\mathbf{u}}^{(1)}, \tilde{\mathbf{u}}^{(2)}, \tilde{\mathbf{u}}^{(3)}$ gives 9 linear equations (3.8) in elements of T_i^{jk} but only four of them are linearly independent (due to rank $\mathbf{L}^{(i)} = 2$). Thus, at least seven point correspondences are necessary so that T_i^{jk} can be computed as a least-squares solution of the linear system (3.8). It should be noticed that the least-squares estimate is only an approximation of the ideal solution and thus the obtained tensor does not fulfill the definition of the trifocal tensor.

In the next paragraphs, we will use the matrix form of relation (3.9)

$$\mathbf{T}_i = \mathbf{a}_i^{(2)} \mathbf{e}^{(3)\top} - \mathbf{e}^{(2)} \mathbf{a}_i^{(3)\top} \, , \quad i = 1, 2, 3 \, . \tag{3.10}$$

3.2   DECOMPOSITION OF THE TRIFOCAL TENSOR INTO CAMERA MATRICES

Special configurations occur when the equivalence class P is not determined uniquely by the trifocal tensor, see [9]. Here, we focus only on the cases when $\dim(\operatorname{Ker} \mathbf{T}_i) = 1$, $i = 1, 2, 3$. Then, P is determined uniquely and the method of the tensor decomposition to $\left(\tilde{\mathbf{P}}^{(1)}, \tilde{\mathbf{P}}^{(2)}, \tilde{\mathbf{P}}^{(3)} \right)$ consists of the following steps :

1. **Recovery of $\mathbf{e}^{(2)}$ and $\mathbf{e}^{(3)}$ from $\mathcal{T}$.**

   Vector $\mathbf{e}^{(2)}$ can be computed as the common normal to the kernels of matrices $\mathbf{T}_i^\top$, $i = 1, 2, 3$ and vector $\mathbf{e}^{(3)}$ as the common normal to kernels of $\mathbf{T}_i$, $i = 1, 2, 3$.

2. **Recovery of $\mathbf{A}^{(2)}, \mathbf{A}^{(3)}$ from $\mathcal{T}$, $\mathbf{e}^{(2)}$ and $\mathbf{e}^{(3)}$.**

   For each i, the matrix equation (3.10) represents 9 linear equations in six elements of vectors $\mathbf{a}_i^{(2)}$ and $\mathbf{a}_i^{(3)}$. We can write this system of equations in a matrix form as:

   $$\operatorname{vector}_9 (\mathbf{T}_i) = \mathbf{F} \begin{bmatrix} \mathbf{a}_i^{(2)} \\ \mathbf{a}_i^{(3)} \end{bmatrix} \, , \tag{3.11}$$

   where $\mathbf{F}$ is a matrix composed from the elements of $\mathbf{e}^{(2)}, \mathbf{e}^{(3)}$:

   $$\mathbf{F} = \begin{bmatrix} e_1^{(3)} \mathbf{I} & -\mathbf{e}^{(2)} & \mathbf{0} & \mathbf{0} \\ e_2^{(3)} \mathbf{I} & \mathbf{0} & -\mathbf{e}^{(2)} & \mathbf{0} \\ e_3^{(3)} \mathbf{I} & \mathbf{0} & \mathbf{0} & -\mathbf{e}^{(2)} \end{bmatrix} \, . \tag{3.12}$$

Except for the critical configurations[2], $\dim(\mathrm{Ker}\,\mathbf{F}) = 1$,

$$\mathrm{Ker}\,\mathbf{F} = \left\{ \omega \begin{bmatrix} \mathbf{e}^{(2)} \\ \mathbf{e}^{(3)} \end{bmatrix}, \quad \omega \in \mathcal{R} \right\}$$

and hence, just 5 equations from 9 is linearly independent. Therefore, the solution of (3.11) is a set of dimension one in $\mathcal{R}^6$:

$$\begin{bmatrix} \mathbf{a}_i^{(2)} \\ \mathbf{a}_i^{(3)} \end{bmatrix} \in \left\{ \begin{bmatrix} \mathbf{y}_i^{(2)} \\ \mathbf{y}_i^{(3)} \end{bmatrix} + \omega_i \begin{bmatrix} \mathbf{e}^{(2)} \\ \mathbf{e}^{(3)} \end{bmatrix} \;\middle|\; \omega_i \in \mathcal{R} \right\}, \tag{3.13}$$

where $\begin{bmatrix} \mathbf{y}_i^{(2)} \\ \mathbf{y}_i^{(3)} \end{bmatrix}$ is a particular solution of (3.11) different from $\omega_i \begin{bmatrix} \mathbf{e}^{(2)} \\ \mathbf{e}^{(3)} \end{bmatrix}$.

Selecting any element of the set (3.13) (for all $i = 1, 2, 3$), we obtain a representative of P

$$\left(\tilde{\mathbf{P}}^{(1)},\ \tilde{\mathbf{P}}^{(2)},\ \tilde{\mathbf{P}}^{(3)} \right) \in P,$$

where

$$\tilde{\mathbf{P}}^{(1)} = [\mathbf{I}, \mathbf{0}], \; \tilde{\mathbf{P}}^{(2)} = [\mathbf{a}_1^{(2)}, \mathbf{a}_2^{(2)}, \mathbf{a}_3^{(2)}, \mathbf{e}^{(2)}], \; \tilde{\mathbf{P}}^{(3)} = [\mathbf{a}_1^{(3)}, \mathbf{a}_2^{(3)}, \mathbf{a}_3^{(3)}, \mathbf{e}^{(3)}].$$

3.3   ALGORITHM FOR PROJECTIVE RECONSTRUCTION FROM THREE VIEWS

It is possible to estimate the trifocal tensor from image data and to decompose tensor to projective matrices as was described in Section 3.2. However, this method is not optimal from the numerical point of view. The estimated tensor is only an approximation of the trifocal tensor, it does not have to satisfy (3.10). The consecutive decomposition to projective matrices can lead to incorrect results.

Therefore, the following method is preferred:

1. Estimate $\mathcal{T}$ from image data and then recover $\mathbf{e}^{(2)}, \mathbf{e}^{(3)}$ from $\mathcal{T}$.

2. Using $\mathbf{e}^{(2)}, \mathbf{e}^{(3)}$, formulate one optimization task for the estimation of remaining columns $\mathbf{a}_i^{(2)}, \mathbf{a}_i^{(3)}$, $i = 1, 2, 3$, directly from image data.

---

[2] when $\exists i : \dim(\mathrm{Ker}\,\mathbf{T}_i) > 1$.

This method was first presented by Hartley in [5]. In the following paragraph, we detail the algorithm only for the case, when $\dim(\text{Ker } \mathbf{T}_i) = 1$. The other cases mentioned in [9] have to be treated individually.

Algorithm:

1. Construct a matrix $\mathbf{C}$ from image data according to (3.8) so that $\mathcal{T}$ can be estimated as a LS solution of the following optimization problem:

   $$minimize\ \|\mathbf{Ct}\|\ subject\ to\ \|\mathbf{t}\| = 1,\ \mathbf{t} = vector_{27}(\mathcal{T})$$

2. From $\mathcal{T}$, estimate the fourth columns $\mathbf{e}^{(2)}$ and $\mathbf{e}^{(3)}$ of $\tilde{\mathbf{P}}^{(2)}, \tilde{\mathbf{P}}^{(3)}$. Perform SVD on $\mathbf{T}_i$:

   $$\mathbf{T}_i = \mathbf{U}_i \mathbf{D}_i \mathbf{V}_i^\top ,$$

   where $\mathbf{U}_i, \mathbf{V}_i$ are orthogonal matrices, $\mathbf{D}_i \in \mathcal{M}^{3,3}$ is a diagonal matrix of singular values in decreasing order.

   Concatenate the third columns of $\mathbf{U}_i$, $i = 1, 2, 3$, to matrix $\mathbf{W}_L$ and the third columns of $\mathbf{V}_i$, $i = 1, 2, 3$, to matrix $\mathbf{W}_R$:

   $$\mathbf{W}_L = (\mathbf{u}_3^{(1)}, \mathbf{u}_3^{(2)}, \mathbf{u}_3^{(3)}) , \qquad (3.14)$$
   $$\mathbf{W}_R = (\mathbf{v}_3^{(1)}, \mathbf{v}_3^{(2)}, \mathbf{v}_3^{(3)}) , \qquad (3.15)$$

   where $\mathbf{u}_3^{(i)}$ denotes the third column of $\mathbf{U}_i$ and $\mathbf{v}_3^{(i)}$ denotes the third column of $\mathbf{V}_i$.
   Compute $\mathbf{e}^{(2)}, \mathbf{e}^{(3)}$ so that

   $$\mathbf{e}^{(2)}\ minimizes\quad \|\mathbf{W}_L^\top \mathbf{e}^{(2)}\|\quad subject\ to\ \|\mathbf{e}^{(2)}\| = 1 \ (3.16)$$
   $$\mathbf{e}^{(3)}\ minimizes\quad \|\mathbf{W}_R^\top \mathbf{e}^{(3)}\|\quad subject\ to\ \|\mathbf{e}^{(3)}\| = 1 \ (3.17)$$

   (e.g., using SVD compute $\mathbf{e}^{(2)}$ as the third singular vector of $\mathbf{W}_L$ and $\mathbf{e}^{(3)}$ as the third singular vector of $\mathbf{W}_R$.)

3. From $\mathbf{C}$ and $\mathbf{e}^{(2)}$, $\mathbf{e}^{(3)}$ estimate $\mathbf{a}_i^{(2)}$, $\mathbf{a}_i^{(3)}$, $i = 1, 2, 3$.
   The estimate is based on the tensor decomposition described in Section 3.2. Having $\mathcal{T}$ and $\mathbf{e}^{(2)}$, $\mathbf{e}^{(3)}$, $\mathcal{T}$ can be decomposed to $\mathbf{a}_i^{(2)}$, $\mathbf{a}_i^{(3)}$ by solving (3.11). The solution is one dimensional set

   $$\begin{bmatrix} \mathbf{a}_i^{(2)} \\ \mathbf{a}_i^{(3)} \end{bmatrix} \in \left\{ \begin{bmatrix} \mathbf{y}_i^{(2)} \\ \mathbf{y}_i^{(3)} \end{bmatrix} + \omega_i \begin{bmatrix} \mathbf{e}^{(2)} \\ \mathbf{e}^{(3)} \end{bmatrix} \ \Big|\ \omega_i \in \mathcal{R} \right\}, \ i = 1, 2, 3 .$$

   Let us select one solution, e.g. $\begin{bmatrix} \mathbf{a}_i^{(2)} \\ \mathbf{a}_i^{(3)} \end{bmatrix}$ orthogonal to $\begin{bmatrix} \mathbf{e}_i^{(2)} \\ \mathbf{e}^{(3)} \end{bmatrix}$. This solution can be expressed as

   $$\begin{bmatrix} \mathbf{a}_i^{(2)} \\ \mathbf{a}_i^{(3)} \end{bmatrix} = \mathbf{V}^0 \mathbf{z}_i , \quad i = 1, 2, 3 , \qquad (3.18)$$

where $\mathbf{V}^0$, $\mathbf{V}^0 \in \mathcal{M}^{6,5}$, is a matrix which columns form a basis of five-dimensional subspace of $\mathcal{R}^6$ and are orthogonal to vector

$$\begin{bmatrix} \mathbf{e}_i^{(2)} \\ \mathbf{e}^{(3)} \end{bmatrix}.$$

Having substituted (3.18) to (3.11), we obtain

$$\text{vector}_9(\mathbf{T}_i) = \mathbf{F}\mathbf{V}^0\mathbf{z}_i \,, \quad i = 1,2,3 \,, \qquad (3.19)$$

and we can formulate one optimization task for $\mathbf{z}_i$, $i = 1,2,3$, directly from image data:

$$minimize \left\| \hat{\mathbf{C}} \begin{bmatrix} \mathbf{F}\mathbf{V}^0 & 0 & 0 \\ 0 & \mathbf{F}\mathbf{V}^0 & 0 \\ 0 & 0 & \mathbf{F}\mathbf{V}^0 \end{bmatrix} \begin{bmatrix} \mathbf{z}_1 \\ \mathbf{z}_2 \\ \mathbf{z}_3 \end{bmatrix} \right\| \; subject\ to \; \left\| \begin{bmatrix} \mathbf{z}_1 \\ \mathbf{z}_2 \\ \mathbf{z}_3 \end{bmatrix} \right\| = 1 \,.$$

Sought $\mathbf{a}_i^{(2)}$ and $\mathbf{a}_i^{(3)}$ we then obtain simply by the back projection

$$\begin{bmatrix} \mathbf{a}_i^{(2)} \\ \mathbf{a}_i^{(3)} \end{bmatrix} = \mathbf{V}_0\mathbf{z}_i \,, i = 1,2,3 \,.$$

4.   PROJECTIVE RECONSTRUCTION FROM N VIEWS BASED ON CONCATENATION OF TRIFOCAL CONSTRAINTS

4.1   CAKE CONFIGURATION

The method requires the following configuration of view triplets: consider n views $\langle 1, 2, 3, 4, \ldots, n \rangle$ are grouped into $n - 1$ triplets $\langle 1, 2, 3 \rangle$, $\langle 1, 3, 4 \rangle$, $\ldots$, $\langle 1, n, 2 \rangle$. It means that view $\langle 1 \rangle$ is common to all the triplets and the others are common to a pair of triplets, for an illustration see Figure 3.1.

Consider we have performed the projective reconstruction from each triplet, and we have obtained

$$\left(\tilde{\mathbf{P}}_{P_1}^{(1)}, \tilde{\mathbf{P}}_{P_1}^{(2)}, \tilde{\mathbf{P}}_{P_1}^{(3)} \right) \in P_1 \quad \text{from the triplet} \quad \langle 1, 2, 3 \rangle \,,$$

$$\left(\tilde{\mathbf{P}}_{P_2}^{(1)}, \tilde{\mathbf{P}}_{P_2}^{(3)}, \tilde{\mathbf{P}}_{P_2}^{(4)} \right) \in P_2 \quad \text{from} \quad \langle 1, 3, 4 \rangle \,,$$

$$\vdots$$

$$\left(\tilde{\mathbf{P}}_{P_{n-1}}^{(1)}, \tilde{\mathbf{P}}_{P_{n-1}}^{(n)}, \tilde{\mathbf{P}}_{P_{n-1}}^{(2)} \right) \in P_{n-1} \quad \text{from} \quad \langle 1, n, 2 \rangle \,.$$

Furthermore, we can assume without lost of generality that

$$\tilde{\mathbf{P}}_{P_1}^{(1)} = \tilde{\mathbf{P}}_{P_2}^{(1)} = \ldots = \tilde{\mathbf{P}}_{P_{n-1}}^{(1)} = [\mathbf{I}, \mathbf{0}] \,.$$

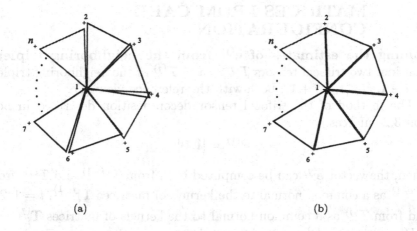

Figure 3.1 Cake configuration of n-1 triplets of views. (a) Inconsistent state, (b) consistent state.

Then in the ideal case, when the errors are not taken into account, it should hold

$$\tilde{\mathbf{P}}^{(2)}_{P_{n-1}} \simeq \tilde{\mathbf{P}}^{(2)}_{P_1}\mathbf{H}^{(1)} ,$$

$$\vdots$$

$$\tilde{\mathbf{P}}^{(n)}_{P_{n-2}} \simeq \tilde{\mathbf{P}}^{(n)}_{P_{n-1}}\mathbf{H}^{(n-1)} , \qquad\qquad (3.20)$$

where $\mathbf{H}^{(i)}$ is from

$$\left\{ \begin{bmatrix} 1 & 0 & 0 & 0 \\ 0 & 1 & 0 & 0 \\ 0 & 0 & 1 & 0 \\ \omega_1 & \omega_2 & \omega_3 & \omega_4 \end{bmatrix} \mid \omega_j \in \mathcal{R},\ i = 1,\ldots,3,\ \omega_4 \neq 0 \right\} .$$

That implies

$$\mathbf{e}^{(3)}_{P_1} \simeq \mathbf{e}^{(3)}_{P_2},\ldots,\mathbf{e}^{(2)}_{P_{n-1}} \simeq \mathbf{e}^{(2)}_{P_1} .$$

With regard to the algorithm of trifocal tensor decomposition in Section 3.2, one can see, that the estimates of $\mathbf{e}^{(i)}$ from trifocal tensors of the neighboring triplets $\langle 1, i-1, i \rangle$, $\langle 1, i, i+1 \rangle$ can simply be joined together.

Furthermore, this configuration allows to formulate one optimization task for estimating all $\mathbf{A}^{(i)}$, $i = 2,\ldots,n$ from image data and $\mathbf{e}^{(i)}$, $i = 2,\ldots,n$.

4.2   RECOVERY OF PROJECTION MATRICES FROM CAKE CONFIGURATION

Joining the estimates of $e^{(j)}$ from the neighboring triplets.
Consider two trifocal tensors $\mathcal{T}^{(j-1)}$ and $\mathcal{T}^{(j)}$ of the neighboring triplets $\langle 1, j-1, j \rangle$, $\langle 1, j, j+1 \rangle$, both with the reference view $\langle 1 \rangle$.

The method of the trifocal tensor decomposition described in Section 3.2 enforces

$$\tilde{\mathbf{P}}^{(1)} = [\mathbf{I}, \mathbf{0}] .$$

Then, the vector $e^{(j)}$ can be computed both from $\mathcal{T}^{(j-1)}$ and $\mathcal{T}^{(j)}$, from $\mathcal{T}^{(j-1)}$ as a common normal to the kernels of matrices $\mathbf{T}_i^{(j-1)}$, $i = 1, 2, 3$ and from $\mathcal{T}^{(j)}$ as a common normal to the kernels of matrices $\mathbf{T}_i^{(j)\top}$.

Hence, vector $e^{(j)}$ can be recovered at once as the common normal to the kernels of six matrices $\mathbf{T}_i^{(j-1)}, \mathbf{T}_i^{(j)\top}$, $i = 1, 2, 3$.

Recovery of $\mathbf{A}^{(j)}$ from the tensors of Cake configuration. Consider $n-1$ tensors $\mathcal{T}^{(1)}, \ldots, \mathcal{T}^{(n-1)}$ of the triplets $\langle 1, 2, 3 \rangle, \ldots, \langle 1, n, 2 \rangle$. Assume we have already performed the estimates of $e^{(j)}$, $j = 2, \ldots, n$.

The method for determination of $\mathbf{A}^{(j)}$ is based on the relation (3.11) for decomposition of the trifocal tensor; see Section 3.2. Let us write the equations analogical to (3.11) for all the tensors $\mathcal{T}^{(j)}$:

$$
\begin{aligned}
\mathrm{vector}_9(\mathbf{T}_i^{(1)}) &= \mathbf{F}^{(1)} \begin{bmatrix} \mathbf{a}_i^{(2)} \\ \mathbf{a}_i^{(3)} \end{bmatrix}, \\[2mm]
\mathrm{vector}_9(\mathbf{T}_i^{(2)}) &= \mathbf{F}^{(2)} \begin{bmatrix} \mathbf{a}_i^{(3)} \\ \mathbf{a}_i^{(4)} \end{bmatrix}, \\[2mm]
&\vdots \\[2mm]
\mathrm{vector}_9(\mathbf{T}_i^{(n-1)}) &= \mathbf{F}^{(n-1)} \begin{bmatrix} \mathbf{a}_i^{(n)} \\ \mathbf{a}_i^{(2)} \end{bmatrix}, \quad i = 1, 2, 3,
\end{aligned}
\tag{3.21}
$$

where

$$
\mathbf{F}^{(1)} = \begin{bmatrix} e_1^{(3)}\mathbf{I} & -e^{(2)} & \mathbf{0} & \mathbf{0} \\ e_2^{(3)}\mathbf{I} & \mathbf{0} & -e^{(2)} & \mathbf{0} \\ e_3^{(3)}\mathbf{I} & \mathbf{0} & \mathbf{0} & -e^{(2)} \end{bmatrix},
$$

$$
\mathbf{F}^{(2)} = \begin{bmatrix} e_1^{(4)}\mathbf{I} & -e^{(3)} & \mathbf{0} & \mathbf{0} \\ e_2^{(4)}\mathbf{I} & \mathbf{0} & -e^{(3)} & \mathbf{0} \\ e_3^{(4)}\mathbf{I} & \mathbf{0} & \mathbf{0} & -e^{(3)} \end{bmatrix},
$$

$$\vdots$$

$$
\mathbf{F}^{(n)} \;=\; \begin{bmatrix} e_1^{(2)}\mathbf{I} & -\mathbf{e}^{(n)} & 0 & 0 \\ e_2^{(2)}\mathbf{I} & 0 & -\mathbf{e}^{(n)} & 0 \\ e_3^{(2)}\mathbf{I} & 0 & 0 & -\mathbf{e}^{(n)} \end{bmatrix}.
$$

The set of equations (3.21) can be rewritten in the matrix form

$$
\begin{bmatrix} \mathrm{vector}_9(\mathbf{T}_i^{(1)}) \\ \vdots \\ \mathrm{vector}_9(\mathbf{T}_i^{(n-1)}) \end{bmatrix} = \mathbf{G} \begin{bmatrix} \mathbf{a}_i^{(2)} \\ \vdots \\ \mathbf{a}_i^{(n)} \end{bmatrix}, \quad i = 1,2,3, \tag{3.22}
$$

where $\mathbf{G}$ is $9(n-1) \times 3(n-1)$ matrix. The structure of $\mathbf{G}$ is described in Appendix B. The kernel of $\mathbf{G}$ has dimension one and is generated by the vector

$$
\begin{bmatrix} \mathbf{e}^{(2)} \\ \vdots \\ \mathbf{e}^{(n)} \end{bmatrix}.
$$

Therefore, the solution of (3.22) is a set of dimension one in $\mathcal{R}^{3(n-1)}$

$$
\begin{bmatrix} \mathbf{a}_i^{(2)} \\ \vdots \\ \mathbf{a}_i^{(n)} \end{bmatrix} \in \left\{ \begin{bmatrix} \mathbf{y}_i^{(2)} \\ \vdots \\ \mathbf{y}_i^{(n)} \end{bmatrix} + \omega_i \begin{bmatrix} \mathbf{e}_i^{(2)} \\ \vdots \\ \mathbf{e}_i^{(n)} \end{bmatrix}, \quad \omega_i \in \mathcal{R} \right\},
$$

where $\begin{bmatrix} \mathbf{y}_i^{(2)} \\ \vdots \\ \mathbf{y}_i^{(n)} \end{bmatrix}$ is a particular solution of (3.22) different from $\begin{bmatrix} \mathbf{e}^{(2)} \\ \vdots \\ \mathbf{e}^{(n)} \end{bmatrix}$.

Having performed this decomposition of all $n-1$ tensors $\mathcal{T}^{(j)}$, we obtain directly the representative of the projective reconstruction from n views:

$$
\left([\mathbf{I},\mathbf{0}], [\mathbf{A}^{(2)}, \mathbf{e}^{(2)}], \ldots, [\mathbf{A}^{(n)}, \mathbf{e}^{(n)}] \right) \in P.
$$

4.3 ALGORITHM FOR PROJECTIVE RECONSTRUCTION FROM N VIEWS

Here, an algorithm for a projective reconstruction from the Cake configuration is outlined. The algorithm has two parts: the estimation of the fourth columns $\mathbf{e}^{(j)}$ of $\tilde{\mathbf{P}}^{(j)}$ and the consecutive estimation of $\mathbf{A}^{(j)}$, $j = 2, \ldots, n$, from image data.

Algorithm for the estimation of $\mathbf{e}^{(j)}$, $j = 2, \ldots, n$:

1. From image data of $n-1$ triplets $\langle 1,2,3 \rangle$, $\langle 1,3,4 \rangle$, $\ldots$, $\langle 1,n,2 \rangle$ construct matrices $\mathbf{C}^{(1)}$, $\mathbf{C}^{(2)}, \ldots$, $\mathbf{C}^{(n-1)}$ according to (3.8) and estimate independently tensors $\mathcal{T}^{(1)}, \mathcal{T}^{(2)} \ldots, \mathcal{T}^{(n-1)}$.

2. Partition the tensors $\mathcal{T}^{(l)}$ to matrices $\mathbf{T}_i^{(l)}$,
   $i = 1, 2, 3$, $l = 1, \ldots, n - 1$.

3. Perform SVD on $\mathbf{T}_i^{(l)}$:

$$\mathbf{T}_i^{(l)} = \mathbf{U}^{(l,i)} \mathbf{D}^{(l,i)} \mathbf{V}^{(l,i)^\top} ,$$

   where $\mathbf{U}^{(l,i)}, \mathbf{V}^{(l,i)}$ are orthogonal matrices, $\mathbf{D}^{(l,i)} \in \mathcal{R}^{3\times3}$ is a diagonal matrix of singular values in decreasing order.

4. Concatenate the third right singular vectors of matrices $\mathbf{T}_i^{(k)}$, $i = 1, 2, 3$ and the third left singular vectors of matrices $\mathbf{T}_i^{(j)}$, $i = 1, 2, 3$, to matrix $\mathbf{W}^{(j)}$

$$\mathbf{W}^{(j)} = [\mathbf{v}_3^{(k,1)}, \mathbf{v}_3^{(k,2)}, \mathbf{v}_3^{(k,3)}, \mathbf{u}_3^{(j,1)}, \mathbf{u}_3^{(j,2)}, \mathbf{u}_3^{(j,3)}] , \qquad (3.23)$$

   where $k = \mod(j - 3, n - 1) + 2$, $j = 2, 3, \ldots, n$.

5. Compute $\mathbf{e}^{(j)}$, $j = 2, \ldots, n$ so that

$$\mathbf{e}^{(j)} \text{ minimizes } \|\mathbf{W}^{(j)^\top} \mathbf{e}^{(j)}\| \text{ subject to } \|\mathbf{e}^{(j)}\| = 1 , \; j = 2, \ldots, n .$$

   (The third singular vector of $\mathbf{W}^{(j)^\top}$.)

Algorithm for the estimation of $\mathbf{A}^{(j)}$, $j = 2, \ldots, n$:

1. The algorithm is based on the decomposition of $\mathcal{T}^{(1)}, \ldots, \mathcal{T}^{(n-1)}$ to $\mathbf{A}^{(j)}$, $j = 2, \ldots, n$, described in Section 4.2. Having $\mathcal{T}^{(1)}, \ldots, \mathcal{T}^{(n-1)}$ and $\mathbf{e}^{(j)}$, $j = 2, \ldots, n$, then $\mathbf{A}^{(j)}$, $j = 2, \ldots, n$ can be obtained by solving (3.22). As it was shown in Section 4.2, the solution of (3.22) is a set of dimension one

$$\begin{bmatrix} \mathbf{a}_i^{(2)} \\ \vdots \\ \mathbf{a}_i^{(n)} \end{bmatrix} \in \left\{ \begin{bmatrix} \mathbf{y}_i^{(2)} \\ \vdots \\ \mathbf{y}_i^{(n)} \end{bmatrix} + \omega_i \begin{bmatrix} \mathbf{e}_i^{(2)} \\ \vdots \\ \mathbf{e}_i^{(n)} \end{bmatrix} , \; \omega_i \in \mathcal{R} \right\} , \; i = 1, 2, 3.$$

2. Let us select one of the solutions, e.g., one orthogonal to

$$\mathbf{f} = \begin{bmatrix} \mathbf{e}^{(2)} \\ \vdots \\ \mathbf{e}^{(n)} \end{bmatrix} .$$

Let $\mathbf{V}^0$, $\mathbf{V}^0 \in \mathcal{M}^{3(n-1),3(n-1)-1}$, is a matrix whose columns form a basis of the space orthogonal to vector $\mathbf{f}$ and let $\mathbf{z}_i \in \mathcal{R}^{3(n-1)-1}$, then the selected solution can be expressed as

$$\begin{bmatrix} \mathbf{a}_i^{(2)} \\ \vdots \\ \mathbf{a}_i^{(n)} \end{bmatrix} = \mathbf{V}^0 \mathbf{z}_i , \; i = 1, 2, 3 . \qquad (3.24)$$

3. Substituting (3.22), (3.24) to

$$\mathbf{C}^{(j)}\mathbf{t}^{(j)} = 0 \,, \quad \mathbf{t}^{(j)} = \text{vector}_{27}(\mathcal{T}^{(j)}), \quad j = 1, \ldots, n-1 \,,$$

we can formulate the optimization task directly for $\mathbf{z}_i$, $i = 1, 2, 3$,

$$\text{minimize } \left\| \mathbf{D} \begin{bmatrix} \mathbf{GV}^0 & 0 & 0 \\ 0 & \mathbf{GV}^0 & 0 \\ 0 & 0 & \mathbf{GV}^0 \end{bmatrix} \begin{bmatrix} \mathbf{z}_1 \\ \mathbf{z}_2 \\ \mathbf{z}_3 \end{bmatrix} \right\| \text{ subject to } \left\| \begin{bmatrix} \mathbf{z}_1 \\ \mathbf{z}_2 \\ \mathbf{z}_3 \end{bmatrix} \right\| = 1 \,,$$

where matrix $\mathbf{D}$ is composed from matrices $\mathbf{C}^{(1)}$, $\mathbf{C}^{(2)}, \ldots, \mathbf{C}^{(n-1)}$.

4. The columns $\mathbf{a}_i^{(2)}, \ldots, \mathbf{a}_i^{(n)}$, $i = 1, 2, 3$, can easily be obtained by the back projection

$$\begin{bmatrix} \mathbf{a}_i^{(2)} \\ \vdots \\ \mathbf{a}_i^{(n)} \end{bmatrix} = \mathbf{V}_0 \mathbf{z}_i \,, i = 1, 2, 3 \,.$$

5.   EXPERIMENTS

The accuracy and the stability of the algorithm with respect to noise in image data was tested on simulated experiments with synthetic data. The point coordinates in artificial images were perturbed by Gaussian noise. The standard deviation of the noise increases gradually from 0.5% to 2% of the image size. The projective reconstruction was obtained from the sets of three and five images. The results were then reprojected back to the images and the discrepancy was measured (the discrepancy between the original points without the noise and reprojected image points). Two hundred of such experiments were done for a given value of the deviation of noise.

It was observed that a higher number of views stabilizes the process and improves the accuracy of the results. In other words, a larger number of images are used for projective reconstruction, the more the results correspond to reality.

In other experiment, we demonstrate one of possible applications of the proposed algorithm. A projective reconstruction from 7 real uncalibrated images is computed using the proposed algorithm. Then, it is used as the input for Pollefeys' algorithm [8] which performs Euclidean reconstruction[3]. The texture was mapped using the hand-marked polygons. The input images and the obtained model is in Figure 3.2.

---

[3] Pollefeys algorithm assumes a simpler structure of the matrices $\mathbf{K}^{(i)}$. This allows to estimate $\mathbf{K}^{(i)}$ from the class P and then compute the Euclidean model of an observed scene (up to a scale) using information from all n images.

Figure 3.2   Seven input images were used to compute a projective reconstruction P. A 3D Euclidean model was then recovered by upgrading P by Pollefeys' algorithm [8].

6.   SUMMARY

We have presented a new approach for consistent projective reconstruction from a set of n views even if $n > 4$. The views are grouped by triplets to the Cake configuration. The knowledge of point correspondences across the triplets is assumed. The Cake configuration is not symmetrical with respect to the views. The reference view has an exceptional position. It is common to all the triplets and only points visible in the reference view can be involved in computations.

All used estimations are linear, none of them requires a numerical search. A huge number of point correspondences can be employed. The solution is determined uniquely except for critical configurations. The occurrence of the critical configurations is very improbable in practical situations and can be detected numerically [9].

The properties of the algorithm were verified in two experiments both on synthetic and real data. In the first experiment, the stability of the algorithm was tested on projective reconstructions from sets of three and five synthetic images. In the second experiment, the projective reconstruction from 7 real images was successfully demonstrated.

The main contribution of this approach is that it makes possible to estimate the consistent projective structure of n views even if $n > 4$.

Acknowledgments

This research is supported by the Grant Agency of the Czech Republic under the grants 102/97/0480, 102/97/0855, and 201/97/0437, and by the Czech Ministry of Education under the grant VS 96049 and the grant OCAMS.

Appendix A: Trifocal constraints

One group (from three) of the trifocal constraints can be expressed as

$$
\begin{vmatrix}
-\bar{u}^{(1)3}, & 0, & \bar{u}^{(1)1}, & 0 \\
0, & -\bar{u}^{(1)3}, & \bar{u}^{(1)2}, & 0 \\
& 1^{(2)\iota} \mathbf{A}^{(2)}, & & 1^{(2)\iota} \mathbf{e}^{(2)} \\
& 1^{(3)\kappa} \mathbf{A}^{(3)}, & & 1^{(3)\kappa} \mathbf{e}^{(3)}
\end{vmatrix} = 0 , \quad \iota, \kappa = 1, 2, 3 , \qquad (3.25)
$$

$$
\begin{vmatrix}
-\bar{u}^{(1)3}, & 0, & \bar{u}^{(1)1}, & 0 \\
-\bar{u}^{(1)2}, & \bar{u}^{(1)1}, & 0 & 0 \\
& 1^{(2)\iota} \mathbf{A}^{(2)}, & & 1^{(2)\iota} \mathbf{e}^{(2)} \\
& 1^{(3)\kappa} \mathbf{A}^{(3)}, & & 1^{(3)\kappa} \mathbf{e}^{(3)}
\end{vmatrix} = 0 , \quad \iota, \kappa = 1, 2, 3 , \qquad (3.26)
$$

$$\begin{vmatrix} -\bar{u}^{(1)2}, \bar{u}^{(1)1}, 0 & 0 \\ 0, -\bar{u}^{(1)3}, \bar{u}^{(1)2}, & 0 \\ 1^{(2)\iota}\mathbf{A}^{(2)}, & 1^{(2)\iota}\mathbf{e}^{(2)} \\ 1^{(3)\kappa}\mathbf{A}^{(3)}, & 1^{(3)\kappa}\mathbf{e}^{(3)} \end{vmatrix} = 0 , \quad \iota, \kappa = 1, 2, 3 , \qquad (3.27)$$

where $1^{(i)\iota}$ is ι-th row of $\mathbf{L}^{(i)}$. Expanding the determinant we obtain

$$\bar{u}^{(1)3}\bar{u}^{(1)i} \left((l_j^{(2)\iota}a_i^{(2)j})(l_k^{(3)\kappa}e^{(3)k}) - (l_j^{(2)\iota}e^{(2)j})(l_k^{(3)\kappa}a_i^{(3)k}) \right) = 0$$

$$\bar{u}^{(1)1}\bar{u}^{(1)i} \left((l_j^{(2)\iota}a_i^{(2)j})(l_k^{(3)\kappa}e^{(3)k}) - (l_j^{(2)\iota}e^{(2)j})(l_k^{(3)\kappa}a_i^{(3)k}) \right) = 0$$

$$\bar{u}^{(1)2}\bar{u}^{(1)i} \left((l_j^{(2)\iota}a_i^{(2)j})(l_k^{(3)\kappa}e^{(3)k}) - (l_j^{(2)\iota}e^{(2)j})(l_k^{(3)\kappa}a_i^{(3)k}) \right) = 0 ,$$

$$\iota, \kappa = 1, 2, 3 ,$$

and after grouping the common terms

$$\bar{u}^{(1)\lambda}\bar{u}^{(1)i}l_j^{(2)\iota}l_k^{(3)\kappa}(e^{(3)k}a_i^{(2)j} - e^{(2)j}a_i^{(3)k}) = 0 , \quad \iota, \kappa, \lambda = 1, 2, 3 , \quad (3.28)$$

where $\lambda, \iota, \kappa = 1, 2, 3$ are free indices (i.e., system (3.28) represents 27 equations). Since at least one $u^{(1)\lambda} \neq 0$, system (3.28) is equivalent to

$$\bar{u}^{(1)i}l_j^{(2)\iota}l_k^{(3)\kappa}(e^{(3)k}a_i^{(2)j} - e^{(2)j}a_i^{(3)k}) = 0 , \quad \iota, \kappa = 1, 2, 3 . \qquad (3.29)$$

Appendix B: The structure of matrix G

$$\mathbf{G} = \begin{bmatrix} \begin{bmatrix} e_1^{(3)}\mathbf{I} \\ e_2^{(3)}\mathbf{I} \\ e_3^{(3)}\mathbf{I} \end{bmatrix} & \begin{bmatrix} -e^{(2)} & 0 & 0 \\ 0 & -e^{(2)} & 0 \\ 0 & 0 & -e^{(2)} \end{bmatrix} & \begin{bmatrix} 0 & 0 & 0 \\ 0 & 0 & 0 \\ 0 & 0 & 0 \end{bmatrix} & \cdots \\ \begin{bmatrix} 0 & 0 & 0 \\ 0 & 0 & 0 \\ 0 & 0 & 0 \end{bmatrix} & \begin{bmatrix} e_1^{(4)}\mathbf{I} \\ e_2^{(4)}\mathbf{I} \\ e_3^{(4)}\mathbf{I} \end{bmatrix} & \begin{bmatrix} -e^{(3)} & 0 & 0 \\ 0 & -e^{(3)} & 0 \\ 0 & 0 & -e^{(3)} \end{bmatrix} & \cdots \\ \vdots & \vdots & & \ddots \\ \begin{bmatrix} -e^{(n)} & 0 & 0 \\ 0 & -e^{(n)} & 0 \\ 0 & 0 & -e^{(n)} \end{bmatrix} & \begin{bmatrix} 0 & 0 & 0 \\ 0 & 0 & 0 \\ 0 & 0 & 0 \end{bmatrix} & \cdots & \begin{bmatrix} e_1^{(2)}\mathbf{I} \\ e_2^{(2)}\mathbf{I} \\ e_3^{(2)}\mathbf{I} \end{bmatrix} \end{bmatrix}$$

Considering $\mathbf{e}^{(i)} \neq \mathbf{0}$ the kernel of $9(n-1) \times 3(n-1)$ matrix $\mathbf{G}$ has also dimension one and is generated by vector $\begin{bmatrix} \mathbf{e}^{(2)} \\ \vdots \\ \mathbf{e}^{(n)} \end{bmatrix}$.

References

[1] D. Bondyfalat, B. Mourrain, and V. Y. Pan. Controlled iterative methods for solving polynomials systems. Proceedings ISSAC'98, pages 252–259. ACM Press, 1998.

[2] O. Faugeras and T. Papadopoulo. Grassmann-Cayley algebra for modeling systems of cameras and the algebraic equations of the manifold of trifocal tensors. Technical Report 3225, INRIA, July 1997.

[3] O. D. Faugeras. What can be seen in three dimensions with an uncalibrated stereo rig? In *Proceedings ECCV-92*, pages 563–578. Springer-Verlag, LNCS 588, 1992.

[4] R. I. Hartley. Computation of the quadrifocal tensor. In *Proceedings ECCV-98*, volume I, pages 20–35. Springer Verlag, 1998.

[5] R. I. Hartley. Lines and points in three views and the trifocal tensor. *International Journal of Computer Vision*, 22(2):125–140, March 1997.

[6] A. Heyden. A common framework for multiple view tensors. In *Proceedings ECCV-98*, volume I, pages 3–19. Springer Verlag, 1998.

[7] A. Heyden. Reduced multilinear constraints - theory and experiments. *International Journal of Computer Vision*, 30:5–26, 1998.

[8] M. Pollefeys, R. Koch, and L. VanGool. Self-calibration and metric reconstruction in spite of varying and unknown internal camera parameters. In *Proceedings ICCV98*, pages 90–95, 1998.

[9] M. Urban, T. Pajdla, and V. Hlaváč. Projective reconstruction from multiple views. Technical Report CTU-CMP-1999-5, CMP, FEL ČVUT, Karlovo náměstí 13, Praha, Czech Republic, December 1999.

[10] M. Urban. *Uncalibrated 3D Vision: Contributions to Projective Reconstruction and Camera Self-Calibration*. PhD thesis, Czech Technical University, Faculty of Electrical Engineering, Department of Cybernetics, Karlovo náměstí 13, Prague, Czech Republic, 1999.

[11] Z. Zhang. Determining the epipolar geometry and its uncertainty: A review. *International Journal of Computer Vision*, 27(2):161–195, 1998.

Chapter 4

ACCURATE NATURAL SURFACE RECONSTRUCTION FROM POLYNOCULAR STEREO

Radim Šára

Abstract   We show in this chapter that the bottom-up approach to 3D surface model reconstruction is feasible and may be used in applications requiring precision and accuracy. We focus on acquiring 3D models of natural objects for medical applications, augmented reality, and telepresence. The reconstruction consists of several successive steps in which more complex models are inferred from simpler models. The low-level model we use is a set of unorganized points in 3-space obtained from polynocular stereo. The intermediate-level model consists of local geometric primitives which we call fish-scales. Fish-scales are reconstructed from the unorganized point model by local PCA. The high-level model is a discrete pseudo-surface. It is reconstructed by linking together close and orientation-compatible fish-scales. The ungrouped isolated points and the unlinked fish-scales remain unexplained by the higher-level models. The approach is demonstrated on textured 3D geometric model reconstruction of a human face.

1.   INTRODUCTION

Our long-term project of building a system for reconstructing textured 3D surface models of unknown objects from a set of its images is introduced in this paper. The system is scalable up or down according to the particular application needs. The stress is on accuracy and geometric precision of the model reconstruction process. By accuracy we mean the ability to reliably infer artefact-free structures that have strong support in input data. The recovered structure must not be sensitive to small calibration error or sensor noise.

The system we describe below in detail solves the stereo problem first to obtain primary 3D data in the form of unorganized isolated points

A. Leonardis et al. (eds.), Confluence of Computer Vision and Computer Graphics, 69–86.
© 2000 *Kluwer Academic Publishers. Printed in the Netherlands.*

in Euclidean space. The cloud of points is subsequently verified in the input images (or in a new set of images from another view) and pruned, based on propagated image error.

The verified set of accurate points is then locally grouped to form disk-like local geometric primitives which we call fish-scales. They are represented by fuzzy sets of infinite extent and ellipsoidal kernel. Subsequently, the fish-scale model is verified in the images (or in a new set of images) and, optionally, it is refined based on the mutual congruence of sub-images onto which each primitive projects. The verified fish-scales are linked to a pseudo-surface structure in the final reconstruction step.

In this paper, the whole image interpretation procedure is demonstrated on accurate reconstruction of 3D human face models with the aim of capturing the geometry of facial expression as accurately as possible. We focus solely on the vision part of the problem and omit any high-level surface modeling.

The paper is organized as follows. Section 2 describes in greater detail the problem of point set reconstruction from stereo images. Section 3 focuses on local fish-scale model reconstruction from the point set. The surface reconstruction problem is discussed in Section 4 and some related open questions are posed. Finally, in Section 5, the whole procedure is demonstrated on an example of human face geometric 3D model reconstruction.

2.   THE POINT-SET MODEL RECONSTRUCTION

Unlike the standard structured-light range-finders, a calibrated polynocular camera system together with a set of uncalibrated texture projectors is a robust setup that can be easily extended to make a system of more complete visual field without any interference between the multiple cameras/projectors. This is the reason why we use stereo vision for data acquisition.

In this section, our approach to polynocular stereo matching and disparity map fusion is described. It allows artefact-free, high-precision wide-baseline stereo.

The stereo setup   The input data device we use consists of five cameras; four are used for stereo and the fifth for texture acquisition, see Fig. 4.1(a). Cameras are fully calibrated using a special flat calibration target that is moved towards the cameras in known distance steps, see Fig. 4.1(b). Usually, 189 calibration points (63 per target position) filling the stereo-rig workspace are used. Off-the-shelf progressive-scan digital

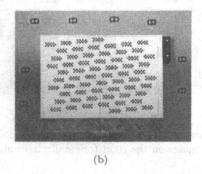

(a)   (b)

Figure 4.1 (a) Stereo rig used in our experiments. The color texture camera is not shown. (b) One of the calibration images as viewed by the first camera.

cameras are used (Pulnix TM-9701) with good but inexpensive 25mm lenses (Tamron, 23FM25L, not shown in Fig. 4.1(a)). The lens has a negligible radial distortion. All camera shutters are triggered simultaneously from the frame-grabber. After the 20ms exposure interval, the images are transferred one by one from each camera internal memory to the host computer via a digital frame-grabber. The progressive-scan cameras and the synchronized camera exposure enable capturing consistent stereo image sets that do not violate the global epipolar constraint even if the objects move in the scene. This is very important for a precise capture of time-variant geometry.

To enforce surface texture on textureless objects, uncalibrated infrared texture projector is used (not shown in Fig. 4.1(a)). The IR cutoff filter is substituted for an IR long-pass filter in a standard commercial slide projector. The projected pattern is invisible to the human eye and to the texture camera equipped with an IR cutoff filter. A long-pass IR filter is used in the stereo cameras. The texture effect is visible in the images shown in Fig. 4.2.

Stereo matching Stereo matching establishes consistent pixelwise correspondence among the images in a stereo set. We match pixels per image pairs, which speeds up the processing time and allows to paral-

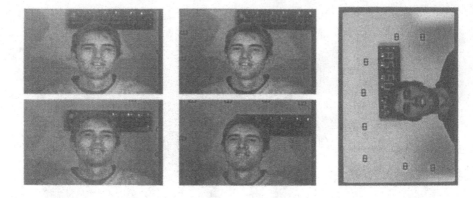

Figure 4.2 The input images. Only the four on the left are used for stereo matching. The image on the right (originally color slide) is used for texture projection.

lelize the computation. The consistency is enforced in a fusion step that follows matching.

Epipolar image rectification is done to simplify stereo matching. The matching then compares 5×5 centered image windows X and Y using the modified normalized cross-correlation (MNCC) [12]

$$c(X, Y) = \frac{2 \operatorname{cov}(X, Y)}{\operatorname{var} X + \operatorname{var} Y}. \qquad (4.1)$$

The advantage of this correlation measure over a standard normalized cross-correlation coefficient (NCC) is that it tends to zero when there is a significant difference in variance between the variables X and Y, while it approximates the NCC closely for equivariant X and Y. This property reduces the likelihood of a mismatch between similarly textured areas of very different contrast.

In our current implementation, we use the Stable Monotonic Matching Algorithm [14]. It searches for the largest set of stable pixel assignments complying with the ordering constraint. Each pair of epipolar lines is matched independently. We briefly sketch the stability principle on which the matching is based. Precise definitions, the existence and uniqueness theorem, and the implementation details can be found in [14].

Let I and J be two sets that index pixels on the corresponding epipolar image lines. A *matching* M is a subset of $I \times J$ in which each $i \in I$ and each $j \in J$ is represented at most once. Let $(i, j) \in M$ be a pair of corresponding pixels (an assigned pair), let $c(i, j)$ be the correlation measure computed between the neighborhoods of i and j using (4.1).

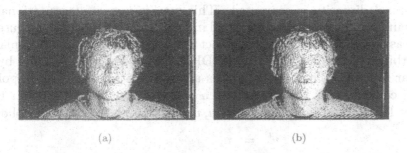

(a)   (b)

Figure 4.3 (a) Grey-encoded binocular disparity map computed for the top image pair from Fig. 4.2. Unmatched pixels are black. (b) The result of fusion of all binocular disparity maps shown in the disparity space of the same image pair.

If there is a unassigned pair $(i, l) \in I \times J$ such that $c(i, l) > c(i, j)$ the assigned pair $(i, j) \in M$ will be *unstable* iff there is no assigned pair $(k, l) \in M$ such that $c(k, l) > c(i, l)$. Clearly, the pixel l is a better candidate than j to be assigned to i. Symmetrically, if there is an unassigned pair $(m, j) \in I \times J$ such that $c(m, j) > c(i, j)$ the pair $(i, j) \in M$ will be unstable iff there is no pair $(m, n) \in M$ such that $c(m, n) > c(m, j)$.

A matching is stable if none of its pairs is unstable. A matching is complete if it has maximum possible cardinality. A matching M is monotonic iff for each two pairs $(i, j) \in M$ and $(k, l) \in M$ it holds that $k > i$ implies $l > j$ (the 'ordering' property holds). It can be shown that stable monotonic matching is a subset of stable complete matching. A stable complete matching is found by a simple $O(N^2)$ algorithm, where N is the epipolar line length in pixels. Its largest monotonic subset is found by a modification of dynamic programming algorithm.

Unlike most of the standard algorithms, this approach to binocular stereo matching does not use any matching cost functional and is completely parameter-free. It does not suffer from most of the usual matching artefacts (jagged contours, streaks) that appear in functional-based matching when applied to a wide-baseline stereo pair. The regions where pixelwise correspondence cannot be established reliably, like when the surface texture is locally weak or repetitive, remain unmatched. These properties of the matching algorithm increase the precision of the final 3D reconstruction result considerably.

An example of a binocular disparity map computed for the top pair of the image set from Fig. 4.2 is shown in Fig. 4.3(a). Matching window of 5×5 pixels was used and the entire disparity range was searched.

Sub-pixel disparity   After pixel correspondences are established, the sub-pixel disparity is computed. This step is not so computationally demanding, therefore a more general image formation model can be used. It is assumed that the observed object is locally approximated by a plane of arbitrary orientation and its BRDF is first-order approximated by a linear function. Then, if the images are rectified so that their epipolar lines coincide with the image lines $u = $ const, it is known [3] that the affine left-to-right image mapping $(u, v) \mapsto (u', v')$ is expressed as follows

$$
\begin{aligned}
u' &= u, \\
v' &= c_1 u + c_2 v + d_\varepsilon,
\end{aligned}
\tag{4.2}
$$

where the constants c_1 and c_2 are related to local surface orientation and d_ε is the sub-pixel disparity update to be found. In addition to the above three parameters, we use two more to linearly approximate the relation between the left- and the right-image values

$$
I_{\text{right}}(u', v') = c_3\, I_{\text{left}}(u, v) + c_4.
\tag{4.3}
$$

A least-squares procedure is used to find the parameters $c_1, c_2, c_3, c_4, d_\varepsilon$ and their variance. Details are found in [15]. Only d_ε is used in subsequent processing together with its relative variance estimate. The variance is computed under the assumption of unit standard deviation i.i.d. Gaussian image noise.

Point reconstruction and error propagation   Point reconstruction from binocular disparity is a simple quasi-linear procedure. The disparity error is propagated through this step and is used to compute the variance of the z-coordinate (which is most sensitive to error) [10]. Reconstructed points whose z-error exceeds a given threshold are filtered out. We use the threshold of $0.5\,\text{mm}/\sigma$, where σ is the image noise standard deviation. We assume the value of $\sigma = 1.0$, which is valid for standard 8-bit cameras [8].

The point set verification   The point set verification is a procedure of re-projecting all the reconstructed points to the disparity space of all camera pairs, re-computing the correlation and re-running the matching procedure. The verification can be also considered disparity map fusion.

   This step *considerably* reduces the percentage of mismatches and thus *fuses* the binocular point sets by preserving only those points that have strong support in more than just two images. The fusion is performed by the stable monotonic matching algorithm discussed above. See [14] for the implementation details. The result of verification is shown in Fig. 4.3(b) in the form of a fused disparity map.

Open problems The geometric accuracy of the reconstructed point set is most affected by the accuracy of sub-pixel disparity estimates. Currently, the ordering constraint is not employed in the estimation procedure. Our experience shows that the local ordering is violated quite frequently in the subpixel-resolution disparity map. Whether the use of the constraint would improve the quality of the estimates remains a question left for further research.

3. THE FISH-SCALE MODEL RECONSTRUCTION

The set of unorganized (unstructured, isolated) reconstructed points in 3-space that results from polynocular stereo is typically highly redundant with respect to the noise level (cf. Fig. 4.8). If the object is a surface, the reconstructed points will form a layer of non-uniform density. If the object is a curve, the points will form a non-uniform density string. We seek a mean manifold (or a set of them) but do not want to assume closedness, orientability, or other global constraints. Since we may be observing a set of curves, surfaces, or both, we do not want to restrict the class of models too early. The structure is therefore inferred in a bottom-up way. First, the point-cloud structure is *locally* modeled by means of simple geometric primitives. This is described in this section. Second, the primitives are linked under sufficient evidence to form larger structures. This will be described in the next section.

Fuzzy fish-scales from unorganized point set The point cloud is locally interpolated by partially overlapping round geometric primitives of prescribed diameter. We call them *fish-scales*. The concept is similar to the oriented particles of Szeliski and Tonnessen [17]. An example of a fish-scale set is shown in Fig. 4.9. For the sake of clarity, we restrict the following discussion to fish-scales representing two-dimensional surface patches in three-dimensional space. With only slight alterations in wording, the reasoning is valid for other space or fish-scale dimensions as well.

Fish-scales are recovered by local principal component analysis (PCA) as follows. The 3-space is divided into non-overlapping cubic cells of given size. The covariance structure of each non-empty cell contents is computed. The result is a set of fish-scales $S_i = (\bar{\mathbf{x}}_i, \mathbf{S}_i)$, $i = 1, 2, \ldots, n$, where $\bar{\mathbf{x}}_i$ are location estimates representing the fish-scale *position* and $\mathbf{S}_i$ are covariance matrix estimates representing the fish-scale *structure*. The direction of minimum covariance is called the fish-scale *orientation* (it is known up to a sign) and the plane perpendicular to this direction and containing the center is called the *principal plane*.

A fuzzy-set fish-scale representation is then constructed by selecting a scalar influence function $f(\cdot)$ that takes a scalar argument:

$$\mu(\mathcal{S}) = f(\frac{1}{2}(\mathbf{x} - \bar{\mathbf{x}})^\mathsf{T}\mathbf{S}^{-1}(\mathbf{x} - \bar{\mathbf{x}})), \tag{4.4}$$

where $\mu(\mathcal{S})$ is the fuzzy membership function for the fish-scale $\mathcal{S} = (\bar{\mathbf{x}}, \mathbf{S})$. It is important for f to have infinite domain, to be strictly positive and smaller than or equal to 1, to be square-integrable, and such that $f(0) = 1$. We have selected $f(t) = e^{-t}$.

The fuzzy fish-scale collection properties   With the help of the fish-scale *size*

$$\|\mu(\mathcal{S})\| = \int_{\mathbb{R}^3} \mu(\mathbf{x}|\mathcal{S})\, d\mathbf{x} < \infty \tag{4.5}$$

we define the *relative intersection* of two fish-scales as the ratio of the size of their intersection over the size of their union:

$$\omega(\mathcal{S}_1, \mathcal{S}_2) = \frac{\|\mu(\mathcal{S}_1 \cap \mathcal{S}_2)\|}{\|\mu(\mathcal{S}_1 \cup \mathcal{S}_2)\|}, \tag{4.6}$$

where $\cap$ and $\cup$ are the fuzzy-set-theoretic intersection and union, respectively. More details on how to compute the intersection is found in [16].

The relative intersection captures both proximity and compatibility of orientation: close fish-scales have larger relative intersection over the more distant ones, so have collinear fish-scales over the non-collinear ones, see Fig. 4.4 for an example in 2-D.

Note that from (4.4), (4.5) and (4.6) it follows that the relative intersection is invariant under affine transformation of $\mathbf{x}$ (this means that a small camera calibration error will not affect the recovery of global structure based on ω). Note also that the relative intersection is defined for any space dimension other than or equal to 3.

Fish-scale verification   Fish-scale verification is a process of elimination of local models that are unlikely to correspond to real surface patches. This is not a procedure redundant to the verification described in Section 2, since we verify whether the local primitives reconstructed in the previous step do indeed have the *orientation* that has been recovered at the predetermined diameter. Verification is more important for large fish-scales as opposed to small ones, since a large fish-scale is much more likely to be biased in orientation by outliers from the stereo matching

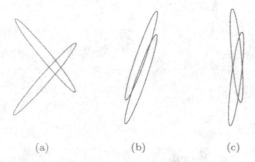

(a)   (b)   (c)

Figure 4.4 Close fish-scales that are (a) perpendicular or (b) parallel but non-collinear intersect much less than those that are (c) (almost) collinear. The degree of their intersection is measured by ω.

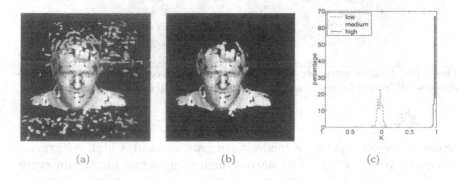

(a)   (b)   (c)

Figure 4.5 Fish-scale verification. (a) The set of fish-scales recovered for the size parameter of 15mm. (b) The set after verification. (c) The histograms correspond to three types of fish-scales according to their image congruence.

process. The likelihood stems from the sole fact that a large fish-scale is born out of points within a larger spatial region, which may include more residuals of the matching artefacts. The verification process effectively removes outliers created by a non-robust (but fast) fish-scale fitting process and thus improves the performance of the global 3D model reconstruction. The effect of verification is demonstrated in Figure 4.5.

Fish-scales are verified by re-projecting n points randomly selected from their principal plane to a (new) set of m camera retinas and by computing the mutual congruence of their (cubicly interpolated) images, see Fig. 4.6. The image congruence is computed in k trials and a histogram of the values is obtained. Three typical histograms for the fish-scales from Fig 4.5(a) are shown in Fig. 4.5(c): from left to right they rep-

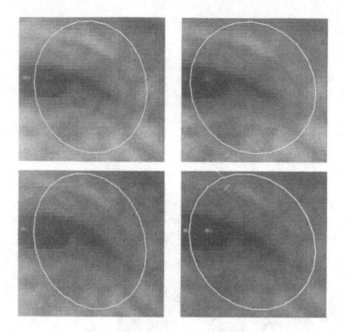

Figure 4.6 Image congruence is used for fish-scale verification. Fish-scales are projected to all images (ellipses) and the mutual image congruence is computed.

resent a low-congruence, a medium-congruence, and a high-congruence fish-scale, respectively. The narrow high-congruence histogram corresponds to a fish-scale of correct pose visible to all cameras. Note that the low-congruence histogram is relatively narrow as well; it corresponds to a fish-scale of incorrect pose. The wide histogram in-between corresponds to a fish-scale of correct pose located close to the occluding boundary and invisible to one or two cameras.

The fish-scale is accepted based on statistical test at a given confidence level using the computed image congruence value histogram: If the cumulative histogram value K_α corresponding to the given confidence level α exceeds the *prior* image congruence value K_p, the fish-scale is accepted, otherwise it is rejected. The K_p is a parameter to the rejection procedure and is chosen individually for each application. The value is not critical, however. In the example in Fig. 4.5 we used $K_p = 0.7$ at the confidence level of $\alpha = 0.1$ (lower decile). This approach avoids the need for the prior knowledge of the congruence measure statistical distribution required for the verification decision. Such a distribution would be difficult to obtain under hypotheses other than independence, which would clearly not be useful here when testing statistical dependence.

The image congruence is measured by Spearman coefficient of concordance K among m vectors of length n [11]

$$K = \frac{12}{m(m-1)n(n^2-1)} \sum_{i=1}^{n} \left(\sum_{j=1}^{m} r_{ij} \right)^2 - \frac{3m(n+1)-n+1}{(m-1)(n-1)}, \quad (4.7)$$

where $r_{ij} \in \{1, 2, \ldots, n\}$ is the rank of the i-th point projected to j-th image. The ranks are assigned based on image values in image j. The index i ranges from 1 to n and the index j ranges from 1 to m. If the images are all congruent, $K = 1$. If they are statistically independent, $K = 0$.

Although other normalized concordance measures can be used as well in the rejection procedure, we use a rank method for two reasons:

1. To weaken the influence of surface reflectance angular anisotropy on the rejection decision.

   The underlying assumption is that images of the same surface patch taken from different viewpoints have the same image value up to an unknown *monotonic* transformation.

2. To relieve the influence of image texture statistical distribution on the congruence measure distribution.

   Note that, under the hypothesis of independence, the statistical distribution of K is invariant to the statistical distribution of image values [11]. Under hypotheses other than independence, this is no longer true, but the sensitivity of K to the distribution is small. This is important given the enormous variability of real-world textures.

The original (unrectified) images are used in the verification test in order to eliminate any possible systematic errors due to epipolar image rectification. The verification thus uses *the most general imaging model* and avoids any preprocessing artefacts. As to the surface, local planarity is assumed, although this constraint can be easily relaxed (one can work with curved fish-scales).

For the fish-scales verification, at least three images taken from a general position are required. We use up to four images to make the verification more reliable.

We have observed that the verification rejects only gross outliers, not the slightly biased fish-scales that are very near to the true surface. However, because of the discrete image nature small fish-scales cover only a few pixels and the rejection decision becomes based on too little evidence which may results in rejecting many good models when the rejection threshold K_p is set too high.

Open problems Currently, to recover a collection of fish-scales, the size parameter must be selected. Large values result in surface over-smoothing, small values increase the number of fish-scales in the model. Ideally, the size parameter should adapt to the local surface curvature. This is the subject of our ongoing work.

4.   THE DISCRETE MANIFOLD MODEL RECONSTRUCTION

The last step in image interpretation we discuss here is the reconstruction of a pseudo-surface (or a set of pseudo-surfaces) from the collection of verified fish-scales. Discrete pseudo-surface (with boundary) is a simplicial complex in which each edge is incident to at most two faces [5].

The previous attempt to interconnect a set of local geometric primitives to form a larger structure has been made by Fua [6]. He used 2-D Delaunay triangulation over a projection of local primitive centers. This restricts the application to surfaces that can be globally mapped on a plane by a one-to-one projection.

We pose the 3D model reconstruction problem in full generality with respect to space dimension, manifold genus, its orientability or structure. The following discussion, however, deals with fish-scale model representing a set of continuous (orientable or unorientable) surfaces. Generalizations are straightforward.

Pseudo-surface reconstruction from unorganized fish-scales
Given a collection $(S_1, S_2, \ldots, S_n)$ of fish-scales, let T be a tetrahedralization defined over the fish-scale centers $\bar{x}_1, \bar{x}_2, \ldots, \bar{x}_n$. It is a complex in which every tetrahedron has four triangular faces and every face is bounded by three edges. The function ω defined in (4.6) acts on the edges of this structure. If we select a subset of triangles from T and a subset of edges such that any selected edge is incident to exactly two selected triangles, the result is a closed pseudo-surface. We choose the pseudo-surface of maximum aggregated compatibility by maximizing the sum of selected edge costs ω_j:

$$\sum_{j=1}^{e} \varepsilon_j \, \omega_j, \tag{4.8}$$

where ε_j, $j = 1, 2, \ldots, e$ are the binary edge selection variables. The edge-triangle incidence constraints are formalized as follows:

$$\sum_{j=1}^{e} \kappa_{ij} - 3\,\tau_i = 0, \qquad i = 1, 2, \ldots, t, \tag{4.9}$$

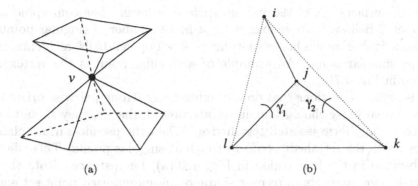

(a)   (b)

Figure 4.7 (a) Singular point v of a closed pseudo-surface. (b) Edge-triangle compatibility.

$$\sum_{i=1}^{t} \kappa_{ij} - 2\,\varepsilon_j = 0, \qquad j = 1, 2, \ldots, e, \tag{4.10}$$

where τ_i, $i = 1, 2, \ldots, t$ are the binary triangle selection variables, ε_j are the edge selection variables as above, and κ_{ij} are the binary triangle-edge incidence variables. The constraint (4.9) requires each selected triangle to be incident to three selected edges and the constraint (4.10) requires each selected edge to be incident to two selected triangles. The (4.8)–(4.10) is a Boolean programming problem. The solution consists of triangles, for which $\tau_i = 1$ and edges for which $\varepsilon_j = 1$.

We are not aware of a polynomially bound algorithm for this problem. Our implementation uses a heuristic approach. First, the Delaunay tetrahedralization is computed over the fish-scale centers. A local constraint is then applied in an edge elimination process implemented as a greedy procedure. The edge pruning process starts with removing all edges of very low compatibility. This step introduces a boundary to the resulting pseudo-surface. From the remaining edges, the lowest-cost edge violating a local constraint is removed. The constraint states that an edge (i, j) is incompatible with a triangle (j, k, l) if both angles $\gamma_1 = \angle\{(j, l, i), (j, k, l)\}$ and $\gamma_2 = \angle\{(i, k, j), (j, k, l)\}$ are smaller than $\frac{2}{3}\pi$, see Fig. 4.7(b). The algorithm then continues in the edge elimination process by proceeding to higher-cost edges violating the constraint.

The computational complexity of this procedure is $O(n^2 \log n)$, which is the complexity of 3-D Delaunay tetrahedralization. The algorithm finds a sub-optimal solution to the original optimization problem (4.8)–(4.10). More details on the reconstruction procedure are given in [16].

Open problems   The class of pseudo-surfaces is much wider than the class of surfaces. A closed pseudo-surface is locally homeomorphic to an open 2-ball everywhere except for a finite number of singular points whose neighborhood is homeomorphic to $k > 1$ open 2-balls, all identified to the singular point. An example of a singular point is the vertex v shown in Fig. 4.7(a).

Fish-scale collections that do not exhibit any strong pairwise orientation compatibility should remain uninterpreted, that is, they should be linked to only form isolated tetrahedra. When the pseudo-surface class is assumed, the tetrahedra tend to touch at singular points. This effect is observed in the hair region in Fig. 4.10(a), for instance. Note that other known attempts to recover shape of an unorganized point set end up with either a set of orientable closed surfaces (top-down approaches, e.g. [13, 2, 7]) or with a pseudo-surface (bottom-up approaches [9, 4, 1]). It seems that bottom-up surface reconstruction is a more difficult problem than the bottom-up pseudo-surface reconstruction.

Our ongoing work focuses on formalizing the necessary local manifold conditions forbidding the singular points. It is clear that the conditions will have to include vertex properties in addition to edge and triangle properties. We find that complexes are not a suitable representation for this purpose.

5.   HUMAN FACE 3D MODEL RECONSTRUCTION

We have built two similar stereo setups, one in our laboratory, and the other at the Neuropsychiatry Department at the University of Pennsylvania Medical Center. The former is used for experiments and the latter is used to capture 3D textured models of human faces on a routine basis in a study of facial expression, which is motivated by neuropsychological research. The following example shows the results of the individual processing steps as described in this paper. The input data consists of 481×768, 8-bit images captured by the calibrated stereo cameras and of a high-resolution scanned color slide captured by a still photographic camera, which is calibrated as well (the markings on the background visible in Figs. 4.1(b) and 4.2 are used to register the scanned slides). The photographic images are also used in other psychological experiments. The stereo rig is placed at about 1.2m distance from the subject. The cameras verge so that pairwise disparity is approximately zero for a point on the rig's axis at this distance. Large-screen soft-light illuminants are used to reduce the specular surface effect. Infrared pattern projected from two uncalibrated random-texture projectors enforces surface tex-

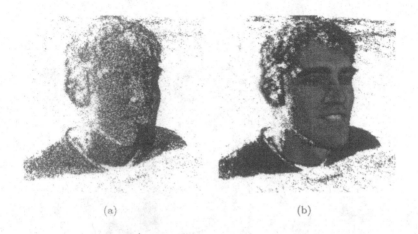

(a)   (b)

Figure 4.8 The point set reconstructed from stereo. (a) Only 20% of randomly selected points are shown. (b) The full set of colored points.

ture. The infrared texture is invisible to the photographic camera. The input data set from this rig is shown in Fig. 4.2.

Stereo matching is run for all six camera pairs independently. The images are rectified and passed to the subsequent stereo matching as standard left-right pairs. The set of all space points that results from stereo matching, point reconstruction, verification, and pruning based on propagated error, is shown in Fig. 4.8.

The set of fish-scales recovered from the point set is shown in Fig. 4.9, the verified subset is light-gray and the rejected fish-scales are dark-gray. The size parameter was chosen to be 4mm (uniformly for all fish-scales). The verification procedure uses the four input images. The rejected primitives are located in hair, along self-occluding boundaries, and on highly non-Lambertian surface patches (such as the eyes or teeth).

The final surface reconstruction is shown in Fig. 4.10(a) and its textured version in Fig. 4.10(b).

6.   SUMMARY

In this paper we dealt with the problem of 3D surface reconstruction from the images of an unknown scene. We took the bottom-up approach. It works in successive steps in which the model constraints are progressively more restrictive. The low-level model is a set of unorganized points in 3-space. The intermediate-level model consists of local geometric primitives which we call fish-scales. Fish-scales are reconstructed from the unorganized point model by local PCA. The high-level model

Figure 4.9 Fish-scales reconstructed from the point set

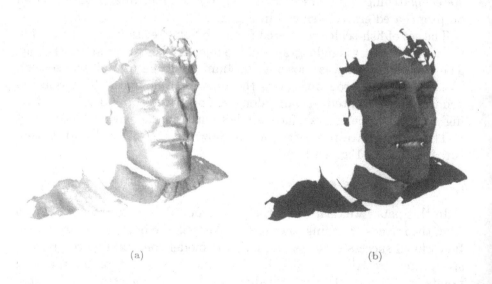

(a)   (b)

Figure 4.10 Surface reconstructed from the verified fish-scale set

is a discrete pseudo-surface. It is reconstructed by linking together close and orientation-compatible fish-scales. The unlinked fish-scales and the ungrouped isolated points remain unexplained by the higher-level models.

The approach presented here relies on strong support in input data when a higher-order model is inferred. This is motivated by the accuracy requirement: no structure should be inferred unless it is observed reliably. This is the reason why no strong prior models are used.

We believe the approach can be applied in areas like augmented reality, telepresence, and medical imaging, where accuracy is of concern.

The work described in this paper is an ongoing effort. An array of smaller problems are still not satisfactorily solved, they have been discussed at the end of each section.

Acknowledgments

The initial stages of this project were conducted in GRASP Lab at the University of Pennsylvania. I wish to thank Ruzena Bajcsy who directed the project and to Gerda Kamberova who did the work on error modeling and propagation. I also want to thank Ruben C. Gur from the Medical School at UPenn who made the facial expression project possible and to Oren Marom and Michael Hagendoorn, who suffered a lot during its early stages. My thanks also go to Brian Klimas who put a lot of his time in the project.

The author was supported by the Czech Ministry of Education under the grant VS96049 and by the Grant Agency of the Czech Republic under the grants GAČR 102/97/0855 and GAČR 102/97/0480.

References

[1] N. Amenta, M. Bern, and M. Kamvysselis. A new Voronoi-based surface reconstruction algorithm. In *Proc. SIGGRAPH'98*, Computer Graphics Proceedings, Annual Conference Series, pages 415–421, July 1998.

[2] V. Caselles, R. Kimmel, G. Sapiro, and C. Sbert. Three dimensional object modeling via minimal surfaces. In *Proc. European Conference on Computer Vision*, volume 1, pages 97–106. Springer, April 1996.

[3] F. Devernay. Computing differential properties of 3-D shapes from stereoscopic images without 3-D models. Research Report RR-2304, INRIA, Sophia Antipolis, 1994.

[4] H. Edelsbrunner and E. P. Mücke. Three-dimensional alpha shapes. *ACM Transaction on Graphics*, 13(1):43–72, January 1994.

[5] P. A. Firby and C. F. Gardiner. *Surface Topology*. Ellis Horwood Ltd., 1982.

[6] P. Fua and P. Sander. Reconstructing surfaces from unstructured 3D points. In *Proc. ARPA Image Understanding Workshop*, pages 615–625, January 1992.

[7] G. Guy and G. Medioni. Inference of surfaces, 3D curves, and junctions from sparse, noisy 3D data. *IEEE Trans. PAMI*, 19(11):1265–1277, November 1997.

[8] G. E. Healey and R. Kondepudy. Radiometric CCD camera calibration and noise estimation. *IEEE Trans. PAMI*, 16(3):267–276, March 1994.

[9] H. Hoppe, T. DeRose, T. Duchamp, J. McDonald, and W. Stuetzle. Surface reconstruction from unorganized points. *Computer Graphics (SIGGRAPH '92)*, 26(2):71–78, July 1992.

[10] G. Kamberova and R. Bajcsy. Sensor errors and the uncertainties in stereo reconstruction. In K. Bowyer and P. J. Phillips, editors, *Empirical Evaluation Techniques in Computer Vision*, pages 96–116. IEEE Computer Society Press, 1998.

[11] M. Kendall and J. D. Gibbons. *Rank Correlation Methods*. Edward Arnold, 1990.

[12] H. P. Moravec. Towards automatic visual obstacle avoidance. In *Proc. 5th Int. Joint Conf. Artifficial Intell.*, page 584, 1977.

[13] R. Poli, G. Coppini, and G. Valli. Recovery of 3D closed surfaces from sparse data. *Computer Vision, Graphics, and Image Processing: Image Understanding*, 60(1):1–25, July 1994.

[14] R. Šára. The class of stable matchings for computational stereo. Research Report CTU–CMP–1999–22, Center for Machine Perception, Czech Technical University, November 1999.

[15] R. Šára. On the differential refinement of binocular disparity map. Research Report CTU–CMP–2000–01, Center for Machine Perception, Czech Technical University, January 2000.

[16] R. Šára and R. Bajcsy. Fish-scales: Representing fuzzy manifolds. In *Proc. 6th International Conference on Computer Vision*, pages 811–817, January 1998.

[17] R. Szeliski and D. Tonnesen. Surface modeling with oriented particle systems. *Computer Graphics (SIGGRAPH '92)*, 26(2):185–194, July 1992.

Chapter 5

BUILDING MODELS FROM SENSOR DATA: AN APPLICATION SHARED BY THE COMPUTER VISION AND THE COMPUTER GRAPHICS COMMUNITY

Gerhard Roth

Abstract   The problem of building virtual models from sensor data increases in importance as powerful graphics rendering hardware becomes widespread. Model building stands at the interface between computer vision and computer graphics, and researchers from both areas have made contributions. We believe that only by a systematic review of the remaining open research question can further progress be made. This paper is an attempt at providing such a review. First, we describe the basic steps in the model building pipeline. Then we discuss the open problems that remain in each step. Finally, we describe some overall research themes that we believe should guide further work in this area.

1.   INTRODUCTION

In the past the fields of computer graphics and computer vision have been considered to be at opposite ends of the spectrum. The graphics field involves the display of virtual representations, and their manipulation [18]. The vision field involves the processing of sensor data for the purpose of image understanding [2]. A number of recent changes have occurred that make this dichotomy less accurate.

First, the basic technology of 3D graphics display systems as embodied by the applications interfaces like OpenGL, Direct3D, etc. have been widely distributed commercially. The graphics community has been very successful industrially in terms of creating the necessary infrastructure for the display of 3D models. It is now possible to display complex simulations of reality on inexpensive personal computer systems. For this

A. Leonardis et al. (eds.), Confluence of Computer Vision and Computer Graphics, 87–103.

reason the question of realistic content, that is what should be displayed on the graphics hardware, is becoming a more important issue.

Traditionally the graphics community has subscribed to the idea that an animator using a complex piece of animation software should create the 3D content synthetically. This paradigm has been successfully demonstrated in the ever-increasing series of complex digital animations. Yet, even though these animations have been successful commercially, it is clear that in order to create more realistic virtual environments it will be necessary to incorporate sensor data of actual physical environments, not simply to use only synthetic environments.

There are a number of reasons for this. First of all, people are familiar with their current physical world. Even if some of the 3D content is synthetic, they relate better if the virtual environment has a connection to the physical world. This is not in complete contradiction to the traditional graphics path of using only synthetic content. It simply says that to widen the impact of a virtual experience it is desirable to use sensor data of an actual physical environment. Second, it is less costly to make a 3D model of a complex geometric object directly from sensor data than to have an animator construct such a model by hand.

In order to create more realistic virtual environments it will be necessary to use sensor data. This problem of model building has long been a topic of research by some members of the vision community. However, it is a relatively small part of a much broader effort that has been directed towards the general problem of image understanding [20]. In the vision community this is beginning to change, and more vision researchers are working directly on the problem of model building [16, 35]. One of the reasons is that the investment in basic vision research has lead to a broader understanding of images and their geometric relationships [50, 27, 45]. The results are a suite of vastly improved algorithms for dealing with such basic vision problems as correspondence, stereo, and structure from motion. It seems that the capacity to obtain 3D structure from image sequences does exist. While this is a significant step in the model building process, it is, as we shall see, only one step.

There has also been ongoing work in model building by those who use active projection techniques to obtain 3D data. In the past few years these research activities have focused on both the problems of model building and inspection. Model building goes under many names, and is sometimes called reverse engineering [28, 37, 41, 30, 17]. The work done by many groups in this field has resulted in a more complete understanding of the basic steps in the model building sequence.

For the above reasons building 3D models from sensor data is an activity that is pursued by both the graphics and vision community. For example, there has recently been an effort to make models of some of the statues of Michelangelo [29], and to build models of environments [34]; both by researchers from the graphics community. In this paper we discuss the problem of model building and suggest some future research directions. One caveat is that because of space limitations our reference list is far from being complete.

Our thesis is that only by understanding and improving the entire model building process is it possible to make significant further progress. We believe that to accomplish this goal it will be necessary to have more interaction between the computer vision and computer graphics community.

2. MODEL BUILDING PIPELINE

In this section we will list the steps in the model building process. Regardless of the type of sensor used the model building pipeline proceeds in a number of distinct steps, where the output of one step is the input of the next step. We will describe each of these steps in a quick survey, which is not meant to be exhaustive. For each step we will also discuss some open problems, along with their importance and difficulty.

The input to the model building process is some sensor data, and the output is a geometric model. In practice, 3D triangles are the most commonly used geometric data representation in the graphics world. The current generation of graphics hardware has been optimized to display such textured triangles efficiently. For this reason the output of a model creation process is normally a set of possibly textured 3D triangles.

The model building process consists of the following sequential steps.

1. Calibration: the sensor characteristics and configuration are determined.

2. Acquisition: the sensor is moved to a number of different viewpoints and the data is acquired.

3. Registration: the data from different sensor positions is registered to be in the same co-ordinate frame.

4. Point Creation: a set of 3D data points are created from the sensor data.

5. Model Creation: a geometric model consisting of a number of triangular meshes is created from the 3D data points.

6. Model Compression: this triangular mesh model may be compressed to a more manageable size.

7. Texture creation: if possible 2D textures are mapped onto the 3D triangles of the mesh model.

We will now describe each of these steps in more detail, concentrating on what we think are the open problems that still remain to be solved.

2.1   CALIBRATION

There are many different sensors and sensor geometries used during the data acquisition process. A calibration step is necessary in order to accurately find the sensor parameters. For a single camera the standard calibration parameters are the intrinsic (or internal) parameters, or the extrinsic (or external parameters).

In many model building systems there are often multiple sensors, and even different types of sensors (i.e. active sensors and passive sensors). This means that the calibration process is necessary more complex than with a single passive sensor. However, a good calibration is essential if an accurate geometric model is to be produced. There are still open problems in terms of creating simple and efficient calibration processes, but progress has been made [5].

Note also that while traditionally calibration is done once, in a laboratory, it may be necessary to do the calibration on-site. The reason is that the sensors may be disassembled during transit, and only reassambled in their final configuration at the acquisition site. On-site calibration is an area in which little work has been done. However, there has been considerable progress in self calibration for standard cameras [21, 38], so it may be that research in this area will have further applications to the problem of on-site calibration.

2.2   ACQUISITION

A sensor must be moved to different locations in order to acquire data. This is currently done manually in a rather ad-hoc process. In certain situations, where a sensor is mounted on a programmable motion device such as a co-ordinate measuring machine (CMM) or robot there is also the added issue of avoiding collisions with obstacles. There has been work done in the automation of the acquisition process [31, 39, 36], but some basic questions remain:

- Can we perform both view planning and obstacle avoidance at the same time? This is important when dealing with sensors that have a very small field of view. They must be close to the object in order to obtain 3D data, but must still avoid collisions.

- Can we integrate knowledge of the sensor accuracy into the planning process?

- For the registration step we would like to maintain a certain minimum overlap in the sensor data. Can we incorporate this goal into a viewpoint-planning algorithm?

2.3   REGISTRATION

Here the goal is to place all the sensor data into a common co-ordinate reference frame. This process is currently performed manually by choosing corresponding feature points [19], or by accurate sensor motion devices such as turntables or CMMs. Manual registration of the sensor data is time consuming, and automatic registration using accurate positioning devices is expensive. An alternative is to use the 3D data itself to perform data-based registration. In practice there are two kinds of data-based registration algorithms. Those which refine an already approximately known registration are called pose refinement algorithms. They are usually based on an iterative closest point (ICP) strategy [9, 4]. While these algorithms work, there are still some open questions:

- What is the best way to perform a multi-image ICP, where we must register multiple sets of 3D points at once?

- Assuming that each data point has an uncertainty estimate, we would like these estimates to be used by the registration algorithm. What is the best way of propagating such uncertainty estimates into the registration process?

If there is no prior estimate of the registration available we face the more difficult problem of pose determination. There has been less progress on the problem of data-based pose determination since it is computationally difficult [6, 1, 12]. There are many open questions:

- To what degree can the process of pose determination be automated?

- Which approach to the problem of pose determination is computationally tractable?

- Can the problem of pose determination be solved using only the sensor data itself, or must targets be manually placed to aid in the registration process?

The problem of pose determination is strongly related to the traditional vision problem of finding correspondence. As we have stated, a manual registration process requires that the corresponding points be chosen by the user in the different sensor views [50, 45]. This manual process can take a number of hours for a significant number of images, and therefore needs to be automated. Attempting to automate pose determination is equivalent to attempting to solve the correspondence problem.

2.4   3D POINT CREATION

Assuming that the sensor data has been acquired, it is then necessary to extract 3D points from this data. In practice, there are two types of sensors used in model building. Active sensors project light onto the object using a source such as a laser beam. There are a number of different technologies for active sensors: time of flight, triangulation and structured light being the most common [8]. For any type of active sensor 3D points are acquired efficiently and reliably by the sensing process.

Passive sensors, which do not project an illumination pattern, rely totally on the texture of the object. Traditionally depth from passive sensors is extracted using stereo algorithms [27]. However, these algorithms assume that the epipolar geometry of the two cameras is known. When a sensor is moved around an object this epipolar geometry is not known beforehand. Finding the epipolar geometry requires that we find correspondences between features in different sensor views so that again the correspondence problem is at the core. There are a number of important issues that need further study.

- When using passive sensors it is necessary to find corresponding points among many different 3D views in order to obtain the epipolar geometry and the 3D data points. Can this correspondence process be efficiently automated?

- Is it necessary to use active sensors to get 3D data, or are passive sensors sufficient? If not, what type of active projection technology should be used?

2.5   MESH CREATION

From the 3D data points a triangular mesh must be created. There are many mesh creation algorithms, which work with different types of 3D data [47, 24, 14, 41, 7]. When very dense 3D data is available the mesh creation process is simplified. This is because the topology of the mesh can be found easily with dense 3D data, but as the data becomes sparser, this is more difficult. Passive sensors tend to produce a much sparser set of 3D data points than active sensors. This implies that mesh creation using data from a passive sensor is likely to be more difficult than with data from an active sensor.

There are still some open problems in mesh creation.

- How dense does the 3D data have to be in order to get good results? At some point the 3D data will not be dense enough to make a good model.

- How can these algorithms handle data with significantly different accuracy. This again requires that these methods incorporate estimates of uncertainty into the mesh creation process.

- How should these algorithms deal with very large amounts of data? This situation occurs when making models of large objects or environments.

2.6 MESH COMPRESSION

Active sensors produce a very dense sampling of the surface geometry. If all of these points are used to create a 3D mesh then the resulting mesh is often very large. For this reason a mesh created from active sensor data needs to be compressed for efficient viewing. This is not difficult to do when the final compressed mesh is at a single resolution. If we wish to display the data at multiple resolutions then we will need a different compression scheme, one based on a continuous compression of the mesh [23].

A multi-resolution, continuous compression scheme is especially useful when a large number of triangles are to be displayed. There are a number of competing continuous compression methods, and little systematic work has been done in terms of comparing them [23, 13, 49].

2.7 TEXTURE MAPPING

In order to make realistic models it is desirable to add texture to the 3D mesh triangles. This is normally done by using the data from a set of 2D images [33, 15]. This is a difficult problem, which encompasses a number of issues. First of all, the images from the 2D camera must be registered with the 3D data. This is trivial if the 3D data were created from the same set of 2D images, as is the case when a single passive sensor is used for the entire process. However, if a separate active sensor was used to get the 3D data, then it is necessary that the 2D and 3D sensors data be registered accurately [25].

Before the 2D data is textured mapped onto the 3D triangles the 2D images must be pre-processed. The goal is to remove the effect of the local lighting, and also to remove any artifacts produced by surface specularity. The textures that we map on the geometric model should be as free as possible of shadows, highlights, specularities, and colour distortions. Removing such artifacts is a difficult problem. It requires both a knowledge of the lighting conditions, and the surface characteristics. No general solution has been found, but under specific conditions it has been shown to be possible to remove certain types of specularities and ambient lighting affects [3, 42]. Once pre-processed the 2D images are mapped onto the 3D mesh by a projection process.

3.   RESEARCH THEMES

In the previous sections we described the model building process, and some of the basic open problems in each step of this process. In this section we will discuss the following research themes that we believe are among the most important open problems in model building:

1. Automation of the entire model building pipeline.

2. Constructing models incrementally.

3. The role of active versus passive sensors.

4. Image-based rendering versus model-based rendering.

5. Environment modeling versus object modeling.

3.1   AUTOMATION OF THE ENTIRE PROCESS

There are available some commercial systems for building geometric models from dense 3D data. For certain applications, such as scanning human bodies the model building process is automated. However, for model building in general one of the problems with current systems is the lack of automation. A number of steps in the 3D model building process are currently very laborious, and require a rather high degree of skill. The goal is to make the model building process more automatic. This way we can decrease the time necessary to build such models, and decrease the required skill level.

Currently the acquisition process and the subsequent registration steps are the most time consuming part of the pipeline. Therefore these steps in the model building pipeline would gain the most from automation. However, automating these two steps is difficult. Planning the acquisition process is equivalent to viewpoint planning. This is a high dimensional search for which no general solutions have been found.

Automating registration is equivalent to solving the correspondence problem. While traditionally this has been considered to be an intractable problem, recent computer vision research gives hope that the correspondence problem can be solved for certain situations. First of all, there has been some success in solving the correspondence problem for 2D images if they are not too far apart in viewpoint [46, 50]. For 3D data we believe that it is much easier to automate the correspondence problem than for 2D data [40]. This is because in 3D Euclidean distances are an invariant under a rigid transformation. Finally, faster computers make it more likely that both model planning and correspondence computation can be automated because these problems are computationally difficult.

3.2   INCREMENTAL MODEL CONSTRUCTION

A second requirement that must be met in order for 3D models to be built efficiently is to make the model building process incremental. Currently, all the data is acquired at once, then it is registered, etc. in a sequential pipeline as we have described. This means that if there are errors in the data, or there is missing data, this will not be realized till late in the process. By this time the acquisition system may be dismantled, which means that collecting more data is impossible.

A better way is to build the models incrementally, that is to perform all the steps in the process but only on a subset of the sensor data. Then by looking at the partial model we get valuable feedback which we can use to adjust the acquisition and building process. We may notice that we need to change some of the parameters of the sensor, or may need to move closer, or to scan some area again.

To incorporate feedback into the process it is necessary to build models incrementally and to save the intermediate results. This is not trivial for some steps in the process such as mesh creation. The reason is that this step requires, for example, that the current mesh model be updated incrementally as new 3D data is acquired while still keeping the old model [41].

3.3   ACTIVE VERSUS PASSIVE SENSORS

Active sensors use a light source such as a laser to project texture onto an object. The 3D data is only obtained where this light source strikes the surface of the object [8]. Passive sensors do not use artificial light, but instead extract 3D points using natural texture. Both approaches have advantages and disadvantages.

Since active sensors supply their own illumination they are not affected by the ambient illumination. They can therefore successfully obtain 3D data under a wide variety of ambient lighting conditions. They project their own texture—they do not require any texture on the objects being scanned. Active sensors also produce dense 3D data, which we have argued simplifies the mesh creation process.

However, active sensors are significantly more costly than passive sensors. There is also a safety issue with active sensors because the active projection system itself is sometimes powerful enough to harm the human eye (i.e. a strong laser).

Passive systems are generally less expensive than active sensors, and there are no safety issues involved in their use. However, they have all the disadvantages for which active systems have an advantage. They are intolerant to changes in the ambient illumination, they require textures on the objects being scanned, and they produce only sparse 3D data.

We believe that active projection technology will continue to be used in many model building applications. When building geometric models there may or may not be enough texture to compute detailed 3D structure using only passive sensors. This means that we cannot really predict beforehand how well a passive system will work for a given situation. By contrast active sensors produce accurate 3D data for a wide variety of ambient lighting conditions and object texture.

There are still a number of open questions in the use of active sensors. The cost of an active sensor is dependent strongly on the speed of data acquisition. This in turn impacts the density of the data that can be acquired. What density of 3D data is sufficient to make a good model? If we can still create good quality models from sparser 3D data, then this is preferable. Active sensors that produce sparser data will be less expensive, and the data acquisition process will not take as long.

Another question is what active sensor technology is best suited for a particular application? The major technologies are time of flight, triangulation and structured light. It seems that triangulation technology is very accurate, but is useful only for distances of ten meters or less. Time of flight technology is more expensive, but is useful for longer distances. Structured light systems tend to be less accurate, and produce fewer 3D data points than either time of flight or triangulation systems. However, structured light systems are the least expensive of the three. There has been a systematic survey of active sensors [8], but there has been little experience regarding the merits of different active sensor technology for the specific application of model building.

3.4   IMAGE-BASED VERSUS MODEL-BASED TECHNOLOGY

Traditionally only model-based technology has been used in rendering virtual worlds. In this approach the goal is to have a geometric model that can be displayed on standardized commercially available rendering hardware. Recently the field of image-based rendering has matured sufficiently to provide some competition to the model-based paradigm. The idea is to not create a geometric model, but instead to use the images directly, and therefore bypass the model creation step [22, 11, 26].

The most common image-based rendering methods use image mosaics. The technology of image mosaics has matured to the point where they can be built easily with passive sensors. Mosaic acquisition, creation and display are possible without having any 3D representation of the object [43, 44]. However, mosaics do not handle viewpoint translation unless it is the case that only a planar surface is being observed.

In order for an image based rendering system to deal with translation it is necessary to have depth data. If scaled depth is available for each 2D image then that image can be rendered from a different viewpoint using image-based rendering [32]. It has also been shown that for some type of depth data, even projective depth is sufficient for performing image extrapolation [48], which is somewhere between traditional 3D reconstruction, and image interpolation [10]. So for image-based rendering systems, other than mosaics, it will still be a requirement that 3D be available, at least in projective form. What will not be necessary is the creation of a 3D model from this data. This implies that steps 4, 5 and 6 of the model creation process will be eliminated with an image-based rendering system. While this is advantageous the effectiveness of image based rendering systems relative to traditional 3D graphics systems is not yet clear. They have advantages for rendering very large models, but their practical creation and display has not yet been demonstrated. The requirement that dense depth data be available makes image-based rendering systems, other than mosaics, difficult to implement in practice.

3.5   ENVIRONMENT MODELING VERSUS OBJECT MODELING

In the past there has been a concentration of work on building models of objects. Here an object is loosely defined as a blob that we view from the outside and can walk around. Objects have the following characteristics:

- You can walk around an object, it does not enclose you.

- You can move as close as you want to any part of the object.

- You can often control the lighting conditions around the object.

Recently there has been an increase in interest in building models of environments [15, 33, 34]. For environments the situation is different than for objects:

- The environment encloses you, since you are on the inside.

- You cannot necessarily move as close as you want to certain parts of the environment (i.e. there may be a high ceiling).

- It is difficult to control the lighting for the entire environment.

These differences have significant implications when building models. Basically, the problem of making and rendering object models is much simpler than for environment models for the following reasons:

- The fact that you cannot move as close as you want to a part of the environment means that the sensor data will always be at different resolutions. This is not the case for objects. We usually have the ability to scan an object at a single stand off distance. This means that the sensor data for objects tends to all be at approximately the same resolution.

- There is likely to be much more sensor data for environments than for objects. This is because environments are large and open ended, while objects are usually smaller and are closed. It is also more likely that a number of different sensors will be used for creating environment models.

- Models of environments are more likely to require multi-resolution compression and visualization methods due to their large model sizes.

- The accuracy and the quality of the data is likely to be much worse for environments than for objects. This is because the lighting conditions, and the specular characteristics of the environment are much harder to control than is the case for objects.

4.   CONCLUSION

In this short discussion paper we have described the problem of building models from sensor data. We believe that this application is one of the main drivers in an ongoing process that will create a much closer relationship between the fields of computer vision and computer graphics.

We have listed what we believe are the basic model building steps, along with the open problems in each step. The graphics community tends to concentrate more efforts on the last steps in this process, and the vision community on the first steps. In the mesh creation step, which is the middle step, there has been an equal amount of work done by both communities.

We believe that to make faster progress there should be more interaction between the graphics and vision research communities. Researchers in image based rendering are clearly dealing with many vision problems, and have initiated a wider dialogue between the two communities. This paper is an attempt to encourage more such interaction on the problem of model building in order to define the open problems and future research directions.

References

[1] A. P. Ashbrook, R. B. Fisher, C. Robertson, and N. Werghi. Finding surface correspondence for object recognition using pairwise geometric histograms. In *Computer Vision-ECCV'98*, pages 674–686, Freiburg, Germany, June 1998.

[2] D. Ballard and C. Brown. *Computer vision.* Prentice Hall, 1982.

[3] R. Baribeau, M. Rioux, and G. Godin. Color reflectance modeling using a polychromatic laser sensor. *IEEE Transactions on Pattern Analysis and Machine Intelligence*, 14(2):263–269, 1992.

[4] R. Benjemaa and F. Schmitt. A solution for the registration of multiple 3D point sets using unit quaternions. In *Computer Vision-ECCV'98*, pages 34–50, 1998.

[5] J. Beraldin, F. Blais, J. Cournoyer, M. Rioux, F. Blais, S.F. El-Hakim, and G. Godin. Object model creation from multiple range images: acquisition, calibration, model building and verification. In *International Conference on Recent Advances in 3-D Digital Imaging and Modelling*, pages 326–333, Ottawa, Canada, 1997.

[6] R. Bergevin, D. Laurendeau, and D. Poussart. Registering range views of multipart objects. *Computer Vision and Image Understanding*, 61(1):1–16, January 1995.

[7] F. Bernardini, C. Bajaj, J. Chen, and D. Schikore. Automatic reconstruction of CAD models from digital scans. *International Journal of Computational Geometry and Applications*, 9(4):327–330, August 1999.

[8] P. J. Besl. Active, optical range imaging sensors. *Machine Vision and Applications*, 1(1):127–152, 1988.

[9] P. J. Besl and N. D. McKay. A method for registration of 3-D shapes. *IEEE Trans. on Pattern Analysis and Machine Intelligence*, 14(2):239–256, Feb. 1992.

[10] E. Chen and L. Williams. View interpolation for image synthesis. In *Computer Graphics: Siggraph*, pages 279–288, 1993.

[11] Y. Chen and G. Medioni. Description of complex objects from multiple range images using an inflating balloon model. *Computer Vision and Image Understanding*, 61(3):325–334, May 1995.

[12] C-S. Cheng, Y-P. Hung, and J-B. Chung. A fast automatic method for registration of partially overlapping range images. In *International Conference on Computer Vision*, pages 242–248, Bombay, India, 1998.

[13] A. Ciampalini, P. Cignoni, C. Montani, and R. Scopigno. Multiresolution decimation based on global error. *Visual Computer*, 13:228–246, 1997.

[14] B. Curless and M. Levoy. A volumetric method for building complex models from range images. In *Computer Graphics: Siggraph'96 Proceedings*, pages 221–227, 1996.

[15] S. F. El-Hakim, C. Brenner, and G. Roth. A multi-sensor approach to creating accurate virtual environments. *ISPRS Journal of Photogrammetry and Remote Sensing*, 53(6):379–391, December 1998.

[16] O. Faugeras. *Three-dimensional computer vision*. The MIT Press, 1996.

[17] R. Fisher, A. Fitzgibbon, and D. Eggert. Extracting surface patches from complete range descriptions. In *International Conference on Recent Advances in 3-D Digital Imaging and Modelling*, pages 148–157, Ottawa, Canada, May 1997. IEEE Press.

[18] J. D. Foley and A. Van Dam. *Fundamentals of Interactive Computer Graphics*. Addison-Wesley, Reading, Mass., 1982.

[19] E. Gagnon, J.-F. Rivest, M. Greenspan, and N. Burtnyk. A computer assisted range image registration system for nuclear waste cleanup. In *IEEE Instrumentation and Measurement Conference*, pages 224–229, Brussels, Belgium, June 1996.

[20] W. Grimson and J. Mundy. Computer vision applications. *Communications of the ACM*, 37(3):45–51, Mar. 1994.

[21] R. I. Hartley. Self-calibration of stationary cameras. *International Journal of Computer Vision*, 22(1):5–23, February 1997.

[22] M. Hirose. Image-based virtual world generation. *IEEE Multi-Media*, pages 27–33, Jan. 1997.

[23] H. Hoppe. Progressive meshes. In *Computer Graphics: Siggraph'96 Proceedings*, pages 225–235, 1996.

[24] H. Hoppe, T. DeRose, T. Duchamp, J. McDonald, and W. Stuetzle. Surface reconstruction from unorganized data points. In *Computer Graphics 26: Siggraph'92 Conference Proceedings*, volume 26, pages 71–78, July 1992.

[25] P. Jasiobedski. Fusing and guiding range measurements with colour video images. In *Proceedings International Conference on Recent Advances in 3-D Digital Imaging and Modelling*, pages 339–347, Ottawa, Ontario, 1997. IEEE Computer Society Press.

[26] S. B. Kang. A survey of image-based rendering techniques. Technical Report CRL 97/4, Digital Equipment Corporation, Cambridge Research Lab., Cambridge, MA, 1997.

[27] R. Klette, K. Schluns, and A. Koschan. *Computer Vision: three-dimensional data from images*. Springer, 1996.

[28] V. Koivunen and R. Bajcsy. Geometric methods for building CAD models from range data. In *Geometric Methods in Computer Vision II*, volume 2031, pages 205–216. SPIE, The International Society for Optical Engineering, July 1993.

[29] M. Levoy. The digital Michelangelo project. Technical Report (see http://graphics.stanford.firenze.it/projects/mich/), Stanford University, Computer Graphics Laboratory, 1998.

[30] A. D. Marshall and R. R. Martin. *Computer vision, models and inspection*. World Scientific, 1992.

[31] J. Maver and R. Bajcsy. Occlusion as a guide for planning the next best view. *IEEE Transactions on Pattern Analysis and Machine Intelligence*, 15(5):417–433, May 1993.

[32] L. McMillan. *An image-based approach to three-dimensional computer graphics*. PhD thesis, Univ. of North Carolina at Chapel Hill, 1997.

[33] K. Ng, V. Sequeira, S. Butterfield, D. Hogg, and J. G. M. Goncalves. An integrated multi-sensory system for photo-realistic 3D scene reconstruction. In *ISPRS Commission V Symposium: Real-Time Imaging and Dynamic Analysis*, volume XXXII, pages 356–363, 1998.

[34] L. Nyland and D. McAllister. The impact of dense range data on computer graphics. In *Proceedings of multi-view analysis and modelling workshop*, Fort Collins, June 1999.

[35] M. Petrov, A. Talapov, and T. Robertson. Optical 3D digitizers: bringing life to the virtual world. *IEEE Computer Graphics and Applications*, pages 28–37, May/June 1998.

[36] R. Pito and R. Bajcsy. A solution to the next best view problem for automated CAD model acquisition. In *SPIE*, volume 2596, pages 78–89, 1995.

[37] R. Pito and R. Bajcsy. Data acquisition and representation of mechanical parts and interfaces to manufacturing devices. In *International Conference on Recent Advances in 3-D Digital Imaging and Modelling*, pages 2–9, Ottawa, Ontario, Canada, 1997.

[38] M. Pollefeys, R. Koch, M. Vergauwen, and L. VanGool. Automatic generation of 3D models from photographs. In *Proceedings Virtual Systems and MultiMedia*, 1998.

[39] M. Reed, P. Allen, and S. Stamos. 3-D modelling from range imagery: an incremental method with a planning component. In *International Conference on Recent Advances in 3-D Digital Imaging and Modelling*, pages 76–83. IEEE Press, 1997.

[40] G. Roth. An automatic registration algorithm for two overlapping range images. In F. Solina and A. Leonardis, editors, *Computer Analysis of Images and Patterns, 8th International Conference CAIP'99, Ljubljana, Slovenia, September 1999*, volume 1689 of *Lecture Notes in Computer Science*, pages 329–338. Springer, 1999.

[41] G. Roth and E. Wibowo. An efficient volumetric method for building closed triangular meshes from 3-D image and point data. In *Graphics Interface 97*, pages 173–180, Kelowna, BC, Canada, May 1997.

[42] Y. Sato and K. Ikeuchi. Reflectance analysis for 3d computer graphics model generation. *Graphical models and image processing*, 58(5):437–451, September 1996.

[43] H.-Y. Shum and R. Szeliski. Panoramic image mosaics. Technical Report MSR-TR-97-23, Microsoft Research, Redmond, WA, 1997.

[44] R. Szeliski. Video mosaics for virtual environments. *IEEE Computer Graphics and Applications*, pages 22–30, March 1996.

[45] P. Torr. *Motion segmentation and outlier detection*. PhD thesis, University of Oxford, 1995.

[46] P. Torr and D. Murray. Outlier detection and motion segmentation. In *Sensor Fusion VI*, volume 2059, pages 432–443, 1993.

[47] G. Turk and M. Levoy. Zippered polygon meshes from range images. In *Computer Graphics (Siggraph '94)*, volume 26, pages 311–318, 1994.

[48] T. Werner, T. Pajdla, and V. Hlavač. Efficient 3-D scene visualization by image extrapolation. In *Proceedings European Conference on Computer Vision*, pages 382–296, 1998.

[49] J. C. Xia, J. El-Sana, and A. Varshney. Adaptive real-time level-of-detail-based rendering for polygonal models. *IEEE Transactions on Visualization and Graphics*, 3(2):171–183, Apr. 1997.

[50] Z. Zhang. Determining the epipolar geometry and its uncertainty: a review. *International Journal of Computer Vision*, 27(2), March 1998.

Chapter 6

ACQUIRING RANGE IMAGES OF OBJECTS WITH NON-UNIFORM REFLECTANCE USING HIGH DYNAMIC SCALE RADIANCE MAPS

Danijel Skočaj, Aleš Leonardis

Abstract   We present a novel approach to acquisition of range images of objects with non-uniform reflectance using a structured light sensor. The main idea is to systematically vary the illumination intensity of the light projector and to form high dynamic scale radiance maps. The range images are then formed from these radiance maps. We tested the method on the objects which had surfaces of very different reflectance properties. We demonstrate that range images obtained from high dynamic scale radiance maps are of much better quality than those obtained directly from the original images of a limited dynamic scale.

1.   INTRODUCTION

Sensor systems consisting of a structured light projector and a camera are commonly used for acquiring range images. In such systems, patterns of structured light are projected onto an object. These patterns can be of different types: a laser dot or a line, grids, different stripe patterns, stripes of different colors, etc. [3, 5, 4]. 3-D coordinates of the points on the visible surfaces of the object are then calculated by a triangulation. Before the acquisition, the geometric relationship between the structured light source and the camera has to be estimated by the calibration procedure.

A major limitation of these methods is their sensitivity to reflectance properties of the object's surfaces. Most of the methods assume that the reflectance properties of the surfaces are uniform. Therefore, it is often even suggested that the objects are sprayed with a grey matte paint [4] to obtain objects with uniform albedo, thus eliminating the problems which

A. Leonardis et al. (eds.), Confluence of Computer Vision and Computer Graphics, 105–122.

may be caused by non-uniform surface reflectance properties. However, when dealing with arbitrary objects in a non-destructive manner, this is not permissible.

Most of the problems related to the acquisition of range images of objects with non-uniform reflectance properties are caused by the limited *dynamic scale*[1] of CCD cameras. Since the dynamic scale is limited, it is impossible to reliably capture both high and low reflective surfaces simultaneously. When we capture low reflective surfaces we suffer from low noise-to-signal ratio, while during acquisition of high reflective surfaces, we may face problems due to pixel saturation and blooming effect. As a consequence, the depth of some of the surfaces can not be successfully recovered.

In this work we present a novel approach to overcome this problem. The main idea is to systematically vary the illumination intensity of the light projector and to form high dynamic scale radiance maps. The range images are then formed from these radiance maps.

The paper is organized as follows. In the next section we briefly describe the acquisition technique of a coded light range sensor. In section 3 we elaborate the acquisition problem, while in the following section we explain our approach to the solution of the problem. In section 5 we present some results of the new approach and compare them with the results obtained with the original acquisition method. The last section concludes the paper and gives a short outline of a planned future work.

2.   ACQUISITION TECHNIQUE

We use a coded light range sensor based on an LCD stripe projector [7, 6]. It projects nine Gray coded stripe patterns onto the object (Fig. 6.1). The patterns allow the distinction of 2^9 different projection planes indicated by s coordinate in the projector space (see Fig. 6.2). A camera, displaced from the projector, acquires grey level images of the deformed stripe patterns, which are binarized so as to separate projector-illuminated from non-illuminated areas. For each pixel a 9-bit code is stored, which represents s coordinate of the point in the projector space. By knowing s coordinate in the projector space, u and v coordinates of the pixel in the image space, and by knowing the sensor calibration parameters, we can compute the 3-D coordinates of the point using a triangulation.

---

[1]The term *dynamic range* is commonly used in the literature, however, we rather use the term *dynamic scale* to avoid possible confusion with the term *range (i.e., depth) image*.

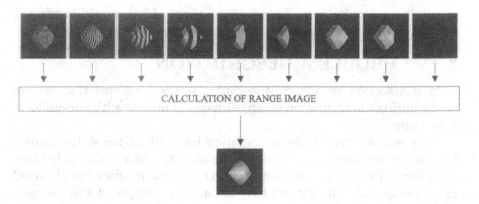

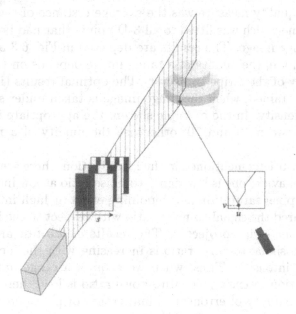

Figure 6.1 Obtaining a range image from intensity images captured under a single illumination intensity.

Figure 6.2 Acquisition principle

The most important and delicate part of this procedure is the binarization of the stripes. The accurate estimation of the *s* coordinate (and subsequently 3-D point calculation) depends on the correct binarization of the projected stripes. We use a simple space-variant thresholding, where the threshold is calculated for each pixel independently. We set the threshold at each pixel as the mean of the corresponding pixel value in the image of fully illuminated object and the pixel value in the image of non-illuminated object. Therefore the threshold at a pixel is affected by illumination and reflectance of the particular point on the object.

3.   PROBLEM DESCRIPTION

In this section we analyze the causes of the problems that we are facing during the acquisition of range images of objects with non-uniform reflectance.

Since we can control the illumination intensity of the stripe projector, we can acquire range images of the objects under different lighting conditions. How do the different lighting conditions affect the obtained range images? To find out, we have taken range images of a flat surface illuminated by several illumination intensities. We evaluated the quality of the acquired range images using two quality measures. The first measure was the number of image pixels where depth could not be obtained. The second quality measure was the average distance of the 3-D points from the plane which was fitted to all 3-D points that had been obtained from the range image. The results are depicted in Fig. 6.3 and Fig. 6.4.

As we can see, the quality of a range image depends on the illumination intensity of the stripe projector. The optimal results (i.e., minimal errors) are obtained, when the range image is taken under suitable illumination intensity. In the example shown, the appropriate illumination levels are between 40 and 70, otherwise the quality of a range image degrades.

As already briefly mentioned in the introduction, there are two reasons for such a behavior: one is low signal-to-noise ratio at low intensities and the other is pixel saturation and blooming effect at high intensities.

We measured the signal-to-noise ratio with respect to the illumination intensity of the stripe projector. The results of the test are plotted in Fig 6.5. The signal-to-noise ratio is increasing with the increase of the illumination intensity. Thus, when we acquire a range image under a low illumination intensity, signal-to-noise ratio is low, therefore there is a higher probability of erroneous binarization of pixels on the edges of projected stripes (see Fig. 6.6(b)) and, consequently wrong estimation of projector coordinates s. This is the reason why many of 3-D points are not calculated accurately if we use too low illumination intensity.

On the other hand, we face the problem of camera saturation at high illumination intensities. All the points which have radiance higher than the camera intensity scale limit yield the same intensity level which is not proportional to their radiance. This can result in incorrect threshold determination and consequently in incorrect binarization of the stripes.

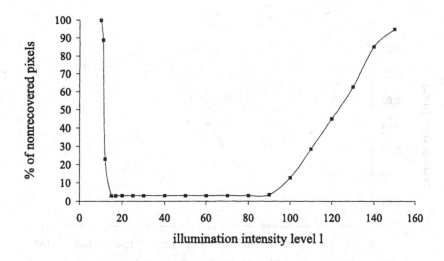

Figure 6.3 Percentage of pixels where the depth could not be recovered

In the extreme case, some highly saturated pixels spill over and affect values at the neighboring pixels. This is known as "blooming" of CCD cells. Such an example is presented in Fig. 6.6(c). Black and white stripes of the same width were projected onto the object, but in the image white stripes appear much wider than black stripes, due to the camera blooming effect. In such cases it is impossible to produce a proper binarization and consequently a correct estimation of the 3-D points.

Therefore, we should aim to use as high projector illumination intensity as possible to achieve high signal-to-noise ratio, but at the same time to avoid pixel saturation. Having a scene containing multiple surfaces of varying reflectance, it is evident that high reflective surfaces require lower illumination intensities while surfaces with lower reflectance require higher illumination intensities to achieve optimal results.

How could we satisfy both conditions simultaneously? Fig. 6.7 demonstrates that when we acquire a range image of an object with non-uniform reflectance with low illumination intensity, we can not reliably acquire the depth of surfaces with low reflectance (because of low signal-to-noise ratio), while when we acquire a range image with high illumination intensity, we can not acquire the depth of surfaces with high reflectance (because of the saturation). As a solution to this problem we propose a new method which uses a high dynamic scale radiance maps of an object instead of its intensity images.

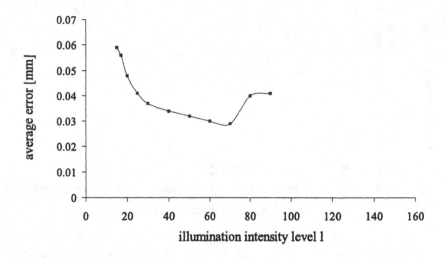

Figure 6.4 Average distance between the points and the fitted plane in the range images where almost all pixel depths were recovered.

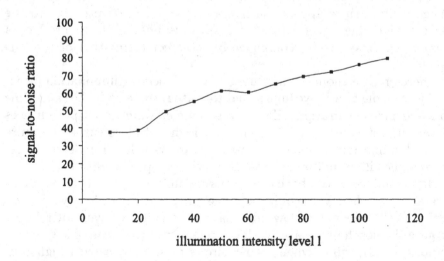

Figure 6.5 Signal-to-noise ratio depends on the illumination intensity

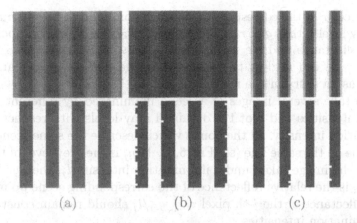

Figure 6.6 First row: intensity images, second row: binarized images of a stripe pattern taken under (a) suitable, (b) too low and (c) too high illumination intensity.

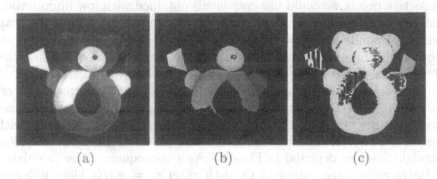

Figure 6.7 (a) The intensity image of a toy containing parts of different colors, range images taken under (b) low and (c) high illumination intensity.

4. OUR APPROACH

We obtain a high dynamic scale radiance map by taking multiple images at different illumination intensity levels of the stripe projector[2]. The question is how to combine multiple images into a single map.

Ideally, we can assume that a pixel value g is proportional to the radiance of the corresponding point in the scene (with the exception of saturated pixels). Since the stripe projector is the only light source in the system, the scene radiance is proportional to the illumination intensity of the projector. Therefore, a pixel value g should be proportional to the

---

[2] A similar effect can be achieved by varying exposure times [1] or iris settings.

reflectance[3] r of the corresponding surface point and to the illumination intensity level l, thus $g \propto r \cdot l$. Since a radiance of a point is proportional to its reflectance and we are interested only in relative values of the radiance, we can neglect the scale factor and write $g = r \cdot l$ and take value r as an entry in the radiance map.

If we take several images of a scene illuminated by different illumination intensities and plot the obtained gray levels with respect to the illumination intensity, all the points which describe the same scene point should lie on the same line (see Fig. 6.8). If g_{ij} is the grey level of the i-th pixel in the image taken under illumination intensity l_j, then $g_{ij} = r_i l_j$, where r_i is the relative reflectance of the corresponding scene point. Relative reflectance of the i-th pixel $r_i = g_{ij}/l_j$ should remain constant for all illumination intensities.

In this way we could combine the information from several images into a single radiance map. For computation of radiance map values of high reflective points we could use gray levels obtained with low illumination intensity to avoid saturation, while for computation of radiance map values of points with low reflectance we could use gray levels obtained with high illumination intensity to achieve better signal-to-noise ratio. This is illustrated in Fig. 6.9.

This simple method would yield correct results, if the strict linear relationship held. However, it turns out that the sensor system introduces nonlinearities. In Fig. 6.10 are plotted the captured gray levels with respect to the illumination intensity. The plots are far from the ideal straight lines as depicted in Fig 6.8. As a consequence, the calculated relative reflectance values of the i-th pixel $r_i = g_{ij}/l_j$ yield different values at different illumination intensities. This is plotted in Fig. 6.11. Thus, to combine the data from multiple images, we have to recover this nonlinear mapping.

To achieve this, we have adopted an approach of Debevec and Malik proposed in [1] which dealt with recovering high dynamic scale radiance maps from photographs. Let us denote an unknown nonlinear function with f:

$$g_{ij} = f(r_i l_j) \ . \tag{6.1}$$

If we assume that f is invertible, we can write (6.1):

$$f^{-1}(g_{ij}) = r_i l_j \ . \tag{6.2}$$

---

[3] We use the term *reflectance* for the product of two factors: geometric term expressing the dependence on the angles of light reflection and albedo [2].

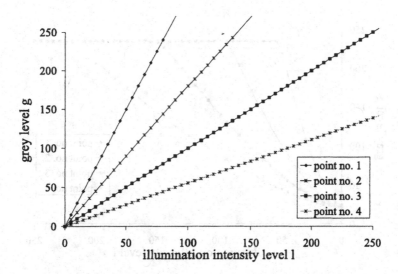

Figure 6.8 Ideal relation between the projector illumination intensity levels and pixel values for four scene points with different reflectance properties.

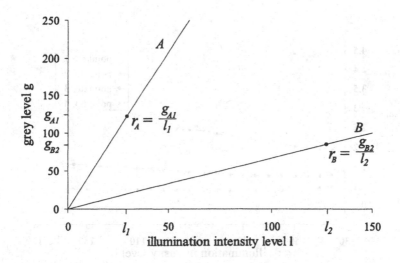

Figure 6.9 Obtaining relative reflectance values of high reflective point A, and point B with low reflectance.

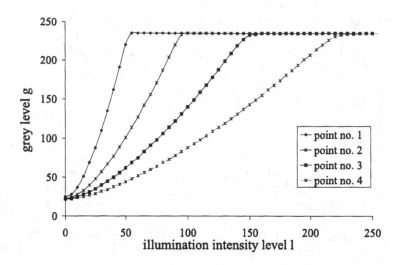

Figure 6.10 Relation between the illumination intensity levels of the projector and pixel values in our sensing system. The point no. 1 has the highest reflectance while the point no. 4 has the lowest.

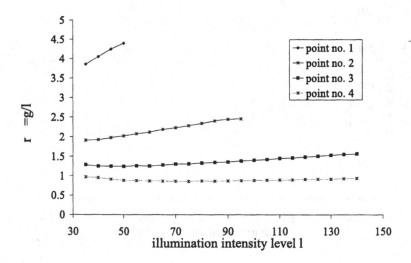

Figure 6.11 Relative reflectance values of the four points computed by $r_i = g_{ij}/l_j$

From (6.2) we can derive:

$$\ln f^{-1}(g_{ij}) = \ln r_i + \ln l_j .$$ (6.3)

Let us define $h = \ln f^{-1}$. We obtain a set of equations:

$$h(g_{ij}) = \ln r_i + \ln l_j; \quad i = 1 \ldots n, \quad j = 1 \ldots m ,$$ (6.4)

where pixel gray values g_{ij} and illumination intensity values l_j are known values while function h and reflectance values r_i are unknowns. We wish to recover these unknowns that best satisfy the set of equations arising from (6.4) in a least-squared error sense. Since the camera has a limited intensity scale, a pixel gray level g_{ij} can only be an integer number from a finite interval. Therefore we only need to recover a finite number of values of the function $h(g_{ij})$. Let us define the lower and upper bounds of the interval of grey levels as g_{min} and g_{max}. If we take m images with different illumination intensities and if we observe n pixels, then we can formulate the problem as one of finding the $(g_{max} - g_{min} + 1)$ values $h(g)$ and n values of $\ln r_i$, that minimize the following function:

$$C_1 = \sum_{i=1}^{n} \sum_{j=1}^{m} [h(g_{ij}) - \ln r_i - \ln l_j]^2 .$$ (6.5)

As an additional constraint we simultaneously minimize the function

$$C_2 = \sum_{g=g_{min}+1}^{g_{max}-1} h''(g)^2 ,$$ (6.6)

which ensures the smoothness of the function $h(g)$. For calculation of h'' we use $h''(g) = h(g-1) - 2h(g) + h(g+1)$. It turns out [1] that by enforcing the smoothness of the function $h(g)$ we assure also its monotonicity.

In addition we introduce a weighting function which puts more weight on the grey values in the middle of the grey level interval than on those near its extrema. We use a simple hat function:

$$w(g) = \begin{cases} g - g_{min} & \text{if } g \leq \frac{1}{2}(g_{min} + g_{max}) \\ \\ g_{max} - g & \text{if } g > \frac{1}{2}(g_{min} + g_{max}) \end{cases} .$$ (6.7)

The combination of Eqs. (6.5), (6.6), and (6.7) leads to the following minimization problem:

$$C = \sum_{i=1}^{n} \sum_{j=1}^{m} \{w(g_{ij})[h(g_{ij}) - \ln r_i - \ln l_j]\}^2 + \lambda \sum_{g=g_{min}+1}^{g_{max}-1} [w(g)h''(g)]^2,$$ (6.8)

where λ is the parameter which weights the smoothness term relative to the data fitting term. The minimization of the function C is a linear least squares problem. The over-determined system of linear equations is solved using the singular value decomposition method as proposed in [1].

By knowing the function $h(g)$, we can calculate a relative reflectance of every point in the scene from the image taken under an arbitrary known illumination intensity. From (6.4) we obtain:

$$\ln r_i = h(g_{ij}) - \ln l_j \ , \tag{6.9}$$

and finally:

$$r_i = \frac{e^{h(g_{ij})}}{l_j} \ . \tag{6.10}$$

Using (6.10), all images taken under the different illumination intensities yield almost the same values of r_i for a scene point. This is depicted in Fig. 6.12. Thus, nonlinearity which caused errors depicted in Fig. 6.11 is removed.

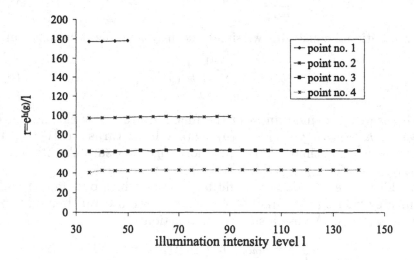

Figure 6.12 Relative reflectance values of the four points

Now we can use the idea of combining images taken under different illumination intensities into a single radiance map. Using (6.10) we can calculate radiance values of high reflective surfaces from images obtained under low illumination intensity to avoid saturation problems. Also we can calculate radiance values of surfaces with low reflectance from images obtained under high illumination intensity to take advantage of a better signal-to-noise ratio. To increase robustness we should use all gray values g_{ij} captured under various illumination intensities l_j weighted with a weighting function $w(g)$:

$$\ln r_i = \frac{\sum_{j=1}^{m} w(g_{ij})(h(g_{ij}) - \ln l_j)}{\sum_{j=1}^{m} w(g_{ij})} .\qquad (6.11)$$

We store values r_i as floating point numbers, so they are not limited to a finite number of levels any more. Thus, by calculating r_i for all pixels, we obtain a high dynamic scale radiance map.

The remaining issue is how many images are necessary to estimate r_i. Already two images are often enough to obtain a good radiance map. We take one image with low and one with high illumination intensity level of the stripe projector. If we take more images we achieve a higher robustness and noise insensitivity.

Now, we can use the benefits of high dynamic scale radiance maps for calculation of range images. The basic algorithm, as explained in Section 2, remains the same, only the input data changes. For every projected stripe pattern we have to take several images illuminated by different intensities and form a radiance map from them. These radiance maps are then used instead of ordinary intensity images as an input in the algorithm for range image formation. This procedure is illustrated in Fig. 6.13.

With high dynamic scale radiance maps we overcome the problem caused by the limited scale of intensity images and we can reliably capture range images of objects with non-uniform reflectance. This we will demonstrate in the next section.

5.   EXPERIMENTAL RESULTS

We tested the algorithm which uses the high dynamic scale radiance maps on a number of objects with non-uniform reflectance. We compared the results with those obtained with the original range image acquisition algorithm.

Fig. 6.14(a) shows an object consisting of parts in different colors. It is evident that we can not acquire the range image of the entire object under a single illumination intensity. The range image in Fig. 6.14(b) was obtained under low illumination intensity of the stripe projector, while the range image in Fig. 6.14(c) was obtained under high illumination. Only the depth of high reflective parts was successfully acquired in the first image, while the depth of some of these parts was not successfully recovered in the second range image. However, when we used the

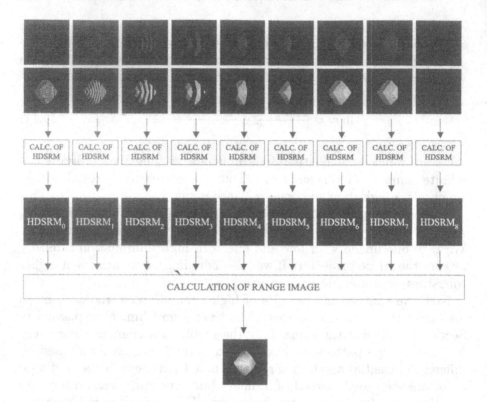

Figure 6.13 Obtaining range images from high dynamic scale radiance maps obtained from images captured under various illumination intensities.

high dynamic scale radiance maps, we reliably acquired the depth of all surfaces (Fig. 6.14(d)).

As the second example we have chosen a well-known Rubic's cube. The cube is covered with squares of six different colors. Figs. 6.15(a)–(j) show that we can not recover the depth of all squares simultaneously. However, this can be achieved using high dynamic scale radiance maps. Each radiance map was formed from three images, taken under low, medium, and high illumination intensity (Figs. 6.15(k)–(m) show images used for calculation of one high dynamic scale radiance map). These radiance maps were then used to create a range image, shown in Fig. 6.15(n). The depth of all colored squares was successfully estimated. Note that the spaces between the squares are black so it is impossible to acquire the depth of these parts with coded light range sensor.

In another experiment we took range images of a flat surface consisting of two parts of different reflectance properties. The results are depicted in Fig. 6.16. Since the difference in the reflectance properties between the

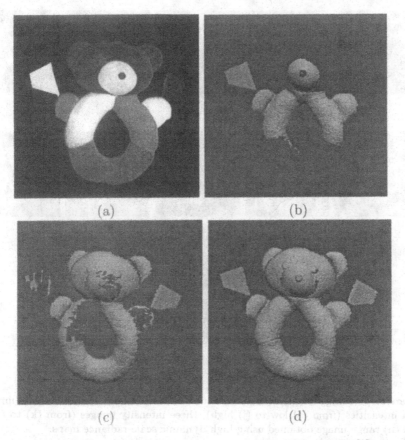

Figure 6.14 (a) The intensity image of a toy, rendered models obtained from range images taken under (b) low and (c) high illumination intensity and (d) a rendered model obtained from the range image obtained using high dynamic scale radiance maps.

two surfaces is not too large, we can obtain a complete range image also from intensity images taken under a suitable single illumination intensity (level 40–60, Figs. 6.16(d)–(f)). However, the error[4] in the range images obtained using high dynamic scale radiance maps is smaller. The error is even further reduced if we form radiance maps from a larger number of images taken under different illumination intensities.

Table 6.1 presents the percent of non-recovered pixels in range images from Figs. 6.16(d)–(f) and errors of these images with the respect to the illumination intensity of the stripe projector. Table 6.2 lists the

---

[4]The error is computed as the average distance of the 3-D points from the plane which was fitted to all 3-D points that had been obtained from the range image.

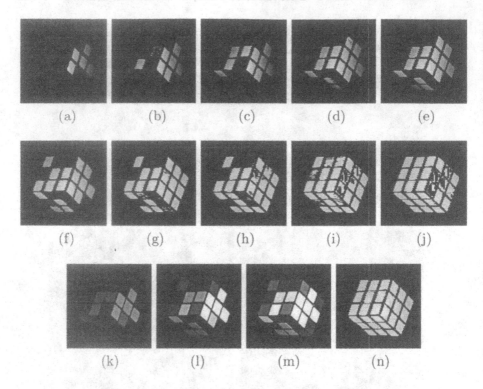

Figure 6.15 Range images of a Rubic's cube obtained under various single illumination intensities (from (a) low to (j) high), three intensity images (from (k) to (m)), and (n) range image obtained using high dynamic scale radiance maps.

errors of the range images calculated from radiance maps which were obtained from a different number of intensity images taken under various illuminations. The error in all range images obtained from radiance maps is smaller than the error in the best range image obtained under a single illumination. This improvement is even greater if the reflectances of the surfaces differ more. Therefore, this method is suitable for obtaining range images of objects consisting of surfaces with very different surface reflectances.

6.   CONCLUSION

In this paper we have presented a solution to one of the main problems which we face during acquisition of range images of objects with non-uniform reflectance. Because of the limited sensing range of the CCD sensor it is impossible to simultaneously acquire the depth of both high

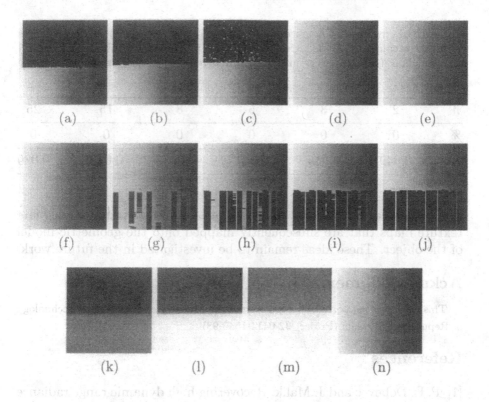

Figure 6.16 Range images obtained under various single illumination intensity levels (from (a) 10 to (j) 100), three intensity images (from (k) to (m)), and (n) range image obtained using high dynamic scale radiance maps.

Table 6.1 Percentage of nonrecovered pixels (%) and errors (E) of range images taken under different single illumination intensities (l) of the stripe projector.

l	10	20	30	40	50	60	70	80	90	100
%	55.2	51.6	47.7	0	0	0	16.9	32.6	41.4	43.0
E	0.068	0.049	0.056	0.056	0.050	0.052	0.056	0.059	0.060	0.060

and low reflective surfaces of the object with good quality. We presented a method for forming a high dynamic scale radiance maps which solves this problem.

The high dynamic scale radiance maps contain much more information about the surface properties than ordinary images taken under a

Table 6.2 Percentage of nonrecovered pixels (%) and errors (E) of range images which were calculated from high dynamic scale radiance maps obtained from different number (n) of intensity images, which were taken under various illumination intensities.

n	2	3	5	8	15	25
%	0	0	0	0	0	0
E	0.049	0.046	0.044	0.043	0.042	0.039

single illumination intensity. They can also be used to produce adequate texture maps that are subsequently mapped onto the geometric model of the object. These ideas remain to be investigated in the future work.

Acknowledgments

This work was supported by a grant from the Ministry of Science and Technology of Republic of Slovenia (Project J2-0414-1539-98).

References

[1] P. E. Debevec and J. Malik. Recovering high dynamic range radiance maps from photographs. In *SIGGRAPH'97 Conference Proceedings*, pages 369–378, August 1997.

[2] B. K. P. Horn, editor. *Robot Vision*. The MIT Press, 1986.

[3] E. Horn and N. Kiryati. Toward optimal structured light patterns. In *Proceedings of International Conference on Recent Advances in 3-D Digital Imaging and Modeling*, pages 28–35, May 1997.

[4] R. Pito. Automated surface acquisition using range cameras. Phd. thesis, University of Pennsylvania, 1996.

[5] M. Proesmans and L. Van Gool. Reading between the lines: a method for extracting dynamic 3d with texture. In *Proceedings of the ACM Symposium on Virtual Reality Software and Technology (VRST-97)*, pages 95–102, September 1997.

[6] D. Skočaj. Instructions to use range scanner. Technical report, Faculty of Computer and Information Science, Ljubljana, 1998.

[7] M. Trobina. Error model of a coded-light range sensor. Technical report, Communication Technology Laboratory, ETH Zentrum, Zürich, 1995.

Chapter 7

DYNAMIC VIEW INTERPOLATION WITHOUT AFFINE RECONSTRUCTION

Russell A. Manning, Charles R. Dyer

Abstract   This chapter presents techniques for view interpolation between two reference views of a dynamic scene captured at different times. The interpolations produced portray one possible physically-valid version of what transpired in the scene during the time between when the two reference views were taken. We show how straight-line object motion, relative to a camera-centered coordinate system, can be achieved, and how the appearance of straight-line object motion relative to the background can be created. The special case of affine cameras is also discussed. The methods presented work with widely-separated, uncalibrated cameras and sparse point correspondences. The approach does not involve finding the camera-to-camera transformation and thus does not implicitly perform affine reconstruction of the scene. For circumstances in which the camera-to-camera transformation can be found, we introduce a vector-space of possible synthetic views that follows naturally from the given reference views. It is assumed that the motion of each object in the original scene consists of a series of rigid translations.

1.   INTRODUCTION

View interpolation [5] involves creating a sequence of virtual views of a scene that, taken together, represent a continuous and physically-correct transition between two reference views. A number of techniques for view interpolation have been developed to date, but all have been restricted to static scenes. Dynamic scenes change over time and, consequently, these changes will be evident in two reference views that are captured at different times. Therefore, view interpolation for dynamic scenes must portray a continuous change in viewpoint *and* a continuous change in the scene itself in order to transition smoothly between the reference views.

A. Leonardis et al. (eds.), Confluence of Computer Vision and Computer Graphics, 123–142.
© 2000 *Kluwer Academic Publishers. Printed in the Netherlands.*

Figure 7.1 View interpolation of a dynamic scene involves creating the view for the virtual camera in the middle frame using only the two reference views from the cameras in the left and right frames.

Algorithms that can interpolate and extrapolate the motion of dynamic scenes from a set of reference views have a wide range of potential applications. Using such an algorithm, video compression and video summarization could be accomplished by the selection of a small number of key frames bracketing primitive motion events. Dynamic augmented-reality sequences could be created that place moving synthetic objects into real scenes. Video sequences could be generated from legacy photographs of dynamic scenes. Missing gaps in video sequences, arising from camera slews, could be filled in (as illustrated in Fig. 7.1). Occluding objects, both stationary and moving, could be removed from video sequences. Finally, the ability to perform temporal extrapolation of a dynamic environment could lead to a wide variety of important applications in visual servoing, navigation, and robot motion planning (where visual simulations of objects in motion could be used to anticipate the effects of actions). It is interesting to note that the human visual system is capable of generating the impression of smooth, continuous apparent motion when shown alternating images at appropriate intervals [21], further motivation for this area of research.

Our approach to view interpolation for dynamic scenes is called *dynamic view morphing* [17]. The method is based on our earlier work for static scenes called "view morphing" [22] and it retains the advantages of that earlier work. In particular, only two reference views of the scene are required, each reference camera can be different and uncalibrated, the views can be widely separated, and only a sparse set of corresponding points between the views is necessary. If more information about the reference views is available, this information can be used for added control over the output and for increased realism.

Dynamic view morphing follows a pure image-based rendering (IBR) methodology wherein the goal is to compute new views directly from the input images with minimal recovery of three-dimensional information about the cameras or scene. Such direct approaches offer several advantages over image-based methods that involve explicit scene reconstruction. For instance, pure IBR methods avoid potentially noise-producing intermediate steps such as the estimation of camera calibration. They can be computationally efficient, operating independently of scene complexity and number of input views. They can produce photorealistic results in cases where explicit reconstruction methods are not reliable (e.g., with small scene objects or noisy images). Their output can be gracefully degraded when computational efficiency is more important than exact photorealism (e.g., when creating an out-of-focus background for a movie special-effect shot). Finally, they do not amplify errors in camera calibration and conjugate point correspondences as many explicit reconstruction algorithms, by repeated reconstruction and reprojection of scene points, are prone to doing.

Methods exist for creating view interpolations of static scenes without explicit scene reconstruction [1, 5, 22, 25] or with (at most) explicit projective reconstruction [9]. Many other methods exist for performing explicit affine or metric reconstruction of static scenes (e.g., [24, 18, 23, 16]). Once explicit scene models have been recovered, view interpolations can be created via the standard graphics pipeline. Of particular recent interest in the area of scene reconstruction are a variety of "self calibration" techniques (e.g., [10, 11, 13, 19, 20]) which can perform affine or metric scene reconstruction without relying on scene knowledge to calibrate the cameras. Unfortunately, all of the techniques listed so far were developed specifically for static scenes and cannot be directly applied to the kinds of dynamic scenes considered in this chapter.

Some related work has been performed specifically for dynamic scenes. Avidan and Sashua [2] developed a method for explicitly recovering the geometry of dynamic scenes in which the objects move along straight-line trajectories. However, their algorithm does not apply to the problem discussed in this chapter because it assumes that five or more views are available and that the camera matrix for each view is known or can be recovered. Clarke and Zisserman [6] developed a related method for the problem of collision detection; they also required the computation of the camera matrix for each object and view. There are several mosaicing techniques for dynamic scenes [7, 14], but mosaicing involves compositing multiple small-field views to create a single large-field view, whereas view interpolation synthesizes new views from vantage points not in the input set. Non-reconstructive image-based rendering methods have been applied to animating facial expressions (e.g., [4, 8, 26]) and body motions [15], though these methods were not concerned with creating physically-correct new views.

The techniques of dynamic view morphing presented in this chapter apply only to scenes that satisfy the following assumption: For each object in the scene, all of the changes that the object undergoes during the missing time interval, when taken together, are equivalent to a single, rigid translation of the object.

The term *object* has a specific meaning in this chapter, defined by the condition given above: An object is a set of points in a scene for which there exists a fixed vector $\mathbf{u} \in \Re^3$ such that each point's total motion during the missing time interval is equal to $\mathbf{u}$.

When the *camera-to-camera transformation* (see Section 3) between the reference views can be determined, the synthetic view interpolations produced by dynamic view morphing will portray *linear motion*. This means the synthetic interpolation sequence will portray all objects in the scene as undergoing rigid, constant-velocity, straight-line motion as viewed from a virtual camera moving along a straight-line, constant-velocity trajectory.

Unfortunately, calculating the camera-to-camera transformation is at least as difficult as affine reconstruction of objects in the scene. Consequently, the focus of this chapter is on techniques that do *not* require knowledge of the camera-to-camera transformation. We demonstrate how a variety of conditions can be imposed on the interpolations without guaranteeing linear motion. In the special case of affine cameras, we discuss how the camera-to-camera transformation cannot be found (except in special cases) and what this means for the resulting view interpolations.

2.   DYNAMIC VIEW MORPHING

Dynamic view morphing refers to a variety of techniques whose applicability depends on what information can be extracted from the reference views. All of the techniques share the following structure:

The reference views are segmented into layers, with each layer representing an object or part of an object.

Each object layer is interpolated separately, and the resulting intermediate views of each object are combined to produce the final, complete intermediate view of the whole scene.

The second step above (interpolation of individual object layers) proceeds as follows:

A prewarp transformation is applied to make the image planes of both reference views parallel to each other and to the object's motion.

Conjugate points are linearly interpolated to produce a physically-accurate intermediate view (of the conjugate points only).

The intermediate view is completed via a morphing algorithm (e.g., Beier-Neely [3]) using the interpolated conjugate points as guides.

3.   NOTATION AND PRELIMINARY CONCEPTS

This and the following section provide the mathematical background for dynamic view morphing. In particular it is shown that, with proper prewarping of the reference views, linear interpolation of conjugate points produces a correct new view of the scene.

Assume two reference views are captured at times $t = 0$ and $t = 1$ using pinhole cameras, which are denoted *camera A* and *camera B*, respectively. A *fixed-camera formulation* is used, meaning the two reference cameras are treated as if they were at the same location and the world is moving around them; this is accomplished by subtracting the displacement between the two cameras from the motion vectors of all objects in the scene. When the scene is static, there will be a single moving object, called the background object, consisting of all points in the scene. Under the fixed-camera assumption, the camera matrices are just 3×3 and each camera is equivalent to a basis for $\Re^3$. Note that no assumption is made about the cameras other than they share the same optical center; the camera matrices can be completely different.

Let U denote the "universal" or "world" coordinate frame, and let the notation $\mathbf{H}_{UA}^{\infty}$ mean the transformation between basis U and basis A. Hence $\mathbf{H}_{UA}^{\infty}$ is the camera matrix for A. Note that boldface capital letters will always represent 3×3 matrices; in particular, $\mathbf{I}$ will be the identity matrix.

Of particular interest is the matrix $\mathbf{H}_{AB}^{\infty}$. This matrix represents a homography between the planes at infinity of the two cameras; that is, it transforms a direction as represented in one camera into the same direction represented in the other camera. The notation $\mathbf{H}^{\infty}$ signifies how the basis transformation equals the infinity homography. Under the fixed-camera formulation $\mathbf{H}_{AB}^{\infty}$ transforms the view from camera A into the view from camera B. For this reason, we refer to it as the *camera-to-camera transformation*.

A position or a direction in space exists independently of what basis is used to measure it; we will use a subscript letter when needed to denote a particular basis. For instance, if $\mathbf{e}$ is the direction between two camera's optical centers (ignoring the fixed-camera formulation momentarily), then $\mathbf{e}_A$ is $\mathbf{e}$ measured in basis A. The quantity $\mathbf{e}$ is called the *epipole*. The fundamental matrix $\mathbf{F}$ for two cameras A and B that are at different locations has the following representation [12]:

$$\mathbf{F} = [\mathbf{e}_B]_\times \mathbf{H}_{AB}^\infty , \qquad (7.1)$$

where $[\cdot]_\times$ denotes the cross product matrix. When the two cameras share the same optical center, the fundamental matrix is 0 and has no meaning. However, for each moving object Ω in the scene, we can define a new kind of fundamental matrix. If, after making the fixed-camera assumption, Ω is moving in direction $\mathbf{u}$, then the fundamental matrix *for the object* is:

$$\mathbf{F}_\Omega = [\mathbf{u}_B]_\times \mathbf{H}_{AB}^\infty . \qquad (7.2)$$

The epipoles of $\mathbf{F}_\Omega$ are the vanishing points of Ω as viewed from the two reference cameras, and the epipolar lines trace out trajectories for points on Ω.

4.   VIEW INTERPOLATION FOR A SINGLE MOVING OBJECT

Assume the two reference cameras share the same optical center and are viewing a point ω that is part of an object Ω whose translation vector is $\mathbf{u}$. Let $\mathbf{q}$ and $\mathbf{q} + \mathbf{u}$ denote the position of ω at times $t = 0$ and $t = 1$, respectively (Fig. 7.2).

Assume for this section that the image planes of the cameras are parallel to each other and to $\mathbf{u}$. The first half of this condition means that the third row of $\mathbf{H}_{UA}^\infty$ equals the third row of $\mathbf{H}_{UB}^\infty$ scaled by some constant λ. The second half means that $(\mathbf{H}_{UA}^\infty \mathbf{u}_U)_z = (\mathbf{H}_{UB}^\infty \mathbf{u}_U)_z = 0$, where $(\cdot)_z$ denotes the z-coordinate of a vector. Note that the condition of parallelism can be met retroactively by using standard rectification methods [22].

Setting $\xi = (\mathbf{H}_{UA}^\infty \mathbf{q}_U)_z = \lambda (\mathbf{H}_{UB}^\infty (\mathbf{q} + \mathbf{u})_U)_z$, the linear interpolation of the projection of ω into both cameras is

$$(1 - s)\frac{1}{\xi}\mathbf{H}_{UA}^\infty \mathbf{q}_U + s\frac{\lambda}{\xi}\mathbf{H}_{UB}^\infty (\mathbf{q} + \mathbf{u})_U . \qquad (7.3)$$

Now define a virtual camera V by the matrix

$$\mathbf{H}_{UV}^\infty = (1 - s)\mathbf{H}_{UA}^\infty + s\lambda \mathbf{H}_{UB}^\infty . \qquad (7.4)$$

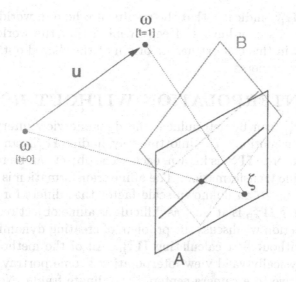

Figure 7.2 Cameras A and B share the same optical center ζ and are viewing a point on an object that translates by **u**. The image planes of the cameras are parallel to each other and to **u**, and hence interpolation will produce a physically-correct view of the object. On each image plane a line parallel to **u** is shown.

Then the linear interpolation (Eq. 7.3) is equal to the projection of scene point $\mathbf{q}(s)$ onto the image plane of camera V, where

$$\mathbf{q}(s) \;=\; \mathbf{q} + \mathbf{u}(s)\,, \tag{7.5}$$
$$\mathbf{u}(s)_V \;=\; s\lambda \mathbf{u}_B\,. \tag{7.6}$$

Notice that $\mathbf{u}(s)$ depends only on **u** and the camera matrices and not on the starting location **q**. Thus linear interpolation of conjugate object points by a factor s creates a physically-valid view of the object. The object is seen as it would appear through camera V if it had translated by $\mathbf{u}(s)$ from its starting position.

Note that in Eq. 7.6, $\mathbf{u}(s)$ is represented in basis V. Since V changes with s it is difficult in general to characterize the trajectory in world coordinates. A key result in [17] states that, if $\mathbf{u}_A = k\mathbf{u}_B$, then

$$\mathbf{u}(s)_B = \frac{s\lambda}{(1-s)k + s\lambda} \mathbf{u}_B\,. \tag{7.7}$$

Thus the virtual trajectory, given by $\mathbf{u}(s)_B$, is a straight-line in basis B; basis V no longer plays a role. If $k = \lambda$ then $\mathbf{u}(s)_B = s\mathbf{u}_B$ and the object moves at constant velocity. The results are in basis B, but multiplying by $\mathbf{H}_{BU}^{\infty}$ or $\mathbf{H}_{BA}^{\infty}$ indicates that the results also hold in world coordinates and camera A's coordinates. Keep in mind that the world coordinate system used in this context has its origin at the shared optical center of the reference cameras.

5.   INTERPOLATION WITHOUT H^{∞}

When $\mathbf{H}_{AB}^{\infty}$ can be determined, the dynamic view interpolation will portray linear motion [17]. Unfortunately, finding $\mathbf{H}_{AB}^{\infty}$ can be a difficult task. In fact, once $\mathbf{H}_{AB}^{\infty}$ is known, each scene object can be reconstructed up to an affine transformation. The affine transformation is the same for each object up to an unknown scale factor that differs for each object. Hence, finding $\mathbf{H}_{AB}^{\infty}$ is at least as difficult as affine object reconstruction.

In this section we discuss the problem of creating dynamic view interpolations without first calculating $\mathbf{H}_{AB}^{\infty}$. All of the methods presented produce physically-valid view interpolations; some portray straight-line motion relative to a camera-centered coordinate frame. None are guaranteed to portray constant-velocity motion, however.

In addition, we show how the *appearance* of straight-line motion can be produced in certain situations by correct prewarping. Finally, we discuss the benefits and drawbacks of using the methods in conjunction with affine views.

5.1   SPECIAL CASE: PARALLEL MOTION

Assume a fixed-camera formulation and let $\mathbf{u}_i$ denote the 3D displacement between the position of object i at time $t = 0$ and its position at time $t = 1$. We will say the scene consists of *parallel motion* if all the $\mathbf{u}_i$ are parallel in scene space.

Dynamic view morphing algorithm for the parallel motion case:
Segment each view into layers corresponding to objects. Apply static view morphing to each layer and recomposite the results.

The algorithm works because the fundamental matrix with respect to each object is the same, so the same prewarp works for each layer. The prewarp will make the direction of motion for each object parallel to the x-axis in both views; consequently, the objects will follow straight-line trajectories as measured in the camera frame. If we assume that the background object has no motion in world coordinates, then the virtual camera also moves parallel to the motion of all the objects and hence each object's motion is straight-line in world coordinates.

5.2   SPECIAL CASE: PLANAR PARALLEL MOTION

We now consider the case in which all the u_i are parallel to some fixed plane in space. Note that this does not mean all the objects are translating in the *same* plane. Also note that this case applies whenever there are two moving objects (i.e., the background object and one object moving in the scene).

Recall that in Section 4 the only requirement for the virtual view to be a physically-accurate portrayal of an object that translates by u is that the image planes of both reference views be parallel to u and to each other. In the planar parallel motion case, it is possible to prewarp the reference views so that their image planes are parallel to each other and to the displacements of all objects simultaneously.

Dynamic view morphing algorithm for the planar parallel motion case: *Segment each view into layers corresponding to objects. For each reference view, find a single prewarp that sends the z coordinate of the vanishing point of each object to 0. Using this prewarp, apply static view morphing to each layer and then composite the results.*

The algorithm given above only guarantees physical correctness, not straight-line or linear motion. The *appearance* of straight-line motion can be created by first making the conjugate motion vectors parallel during the prewarp step.

5.3   PRODUCING THE APPEARANCE OF STRAIGHT MOTION WITHOUT H^∞

This subsection discusses the example illustrated in Fig. 7.3. Assuming the fixed-camera formulation, let u_0 denote the direction of motion of the background object and let u_1 denote the direction the road is heading. That is, u_1 is a vector parallel to the edges of the road. Note that u_1 is not the direction of the car's motion under the fixed-camera formulation; the car's motion is the original translation of the car traveling down the road minus the translation of the camera.

Since vectors u_0 and u_1 are both parallel to the ground, they can be used to transform the two reference views to be parallel to the common plane. After this transformation, the views can be further transformed so that u_0 points in the direction of the y-axis in both views and u_1 points in the direction of the x-axis.

The car's translation at this point is the sum of two perpendicular vectors: one is the translation of the background, which is entirely along the y-axis, and the other is the original translation of the car along

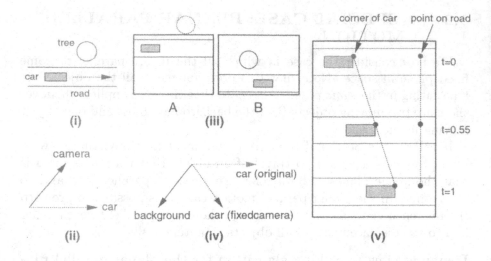

Figure 7.3 Illustration of how a car object can appear to stay traveling down a road during an interpolation sequence even when H_{AB}^{∞} is unknown. *(i)* A dynamic scene in world coordinates. *(ii)* Direction of camera and car movement in world coordinates. *(iii)* Reference views as captured by the moving camera. *(iv)* Movement of objects under the fixed-camera formulation. *(v)* Assuming the background motion is purely vertical and the road is purely horizontal, linear interpolation of conjugate points on the car will produce a motion where the car stays on the same horizontal line on the interpolated road.

the road, which is entirely along the x-axis. When the car object is interpolated, the interpolation of the y-component of the car's fixed-camera motion will exactly match the interpolation of the background object (which is interpolated entirely in the y direction). Since the road is part of the background object, this means that the car will stay on the road at every step of the interpolation, even as it translates in the x direction. In particular, the wheels of the car will stay on the correct horizontal line of the road throughout the interpolation; if the wheels had been touching one of the straight edges of the road, then they would stay touching that edge (Fig. 7.3(v)).

Producing a view interpolation in which the car appears to move straight down the road is crucial for realism. The previous observation shows that this can be accomplished in some cases even without knowledge of H_{AB}^{∞}.

Is it necessary that the road be made purely horizontal and the background motion be made purely vertical before the interpolation is performed in order for the interpolated car object to stay on the road? The answer is "no" as we now demonstrate.

Assume the two reference views have been transformed so that (1) the image planes of both cameras are parallel to the common plane of the ground, and (2) the conjugate directions $\mathbf{u}_0$ and $\mathbf{u}_1$ are aligned in the views. At this point a transformation $\mathbf{M}$ that preserves z-coordinates (i.e., a 2D affine transformation) could be applied to both views so as to make the road parallel to the x-axis and the motion of the background object parallel to the y-axis. For instance, $\mathbf{M}$ could be a rotation followed by a shear, both in the x,y-plane.

By the discussion above, after $\mathbf{M}$ is applied the interpolated car object will always stay on the interpolated road. After the interpolation, $\mathbf{M}^{-1}$ could be applied to the virtual view to bring it into agreement with the reference views. The interpolated car will, of course, still be on the road after $\mathbf{M}^{-1}$ is applied. Mathematically, this process of interpolation is described by

$$\mathbf{M}^{-1}\left[(1-s)\frac{1}{\xi}\mathbf{M}\mathbf{H}_{UA}^{\infty}\mathbf{q}_U + s\frac{\lambda}{\xi}\mathbf{M}\mathbf{H}_{UB}^{\infty}(\mathbf{q}+\mathbf{u})_U \ . \right] \tag{7.8}$$

The corresponding virtual camera is

$$\mathbf{M}^{-1}\left[(1-s)\mathbf{M}\mathbf{H}_{UA}^{\infty} + s\mathbf{M}\mathbf{H}_{UB}^{\infty}\right] \ . \tag{7.9}$$

In both equations, the matrix $\mathbf{M}$ cancels out and the resulting equations exactly match those of Section 4. The net effect is that it was not necessary to apply $\mathbf{M}$ at all; straight-forward interpolation would have kept the car on the road just as well.

Note that the previous discussion applies to any invertible $\mathbf{M}$ that preserves the z-component. This can be a powerful tool for generalizing view interpolation results. For instance, it could have been used to prove the results of Section 4.

5.4 AFFINE CAMERAS

Although the development for affine cameras is very similar to that for pinhole cameras, the underlying geometry of the two models is very different and requires a separate analysis.

The affine camera case is extremely important in practice. In addition, the algorithms for affine cameras are simpler and more robust than those for pinhole cameras.

Like a pinhole camera, an affine camera has an orientation in space and can be associated with a system of basis vectors. However, projection onto the image plane consists simply of setting the z-coordinate to 0. In effect, an affine camera has a z-axis corresponding to an infinitely long z basis vector. Using the fixed-camera formulation, in which the

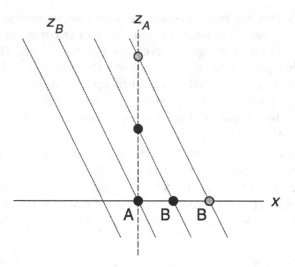

Figure 7.4 Two affine cameras share the same optical center, but not the same z-axis. The scene consists of two points lying on the z-axis of camera A. The points both project to the same location in camera A but to different locations in camera B, so no camera-to-camera transformation exists.

camera matrices are just 3×3, the third row of an affine camera is all 0's. Such a representation does not contain information about the camera's orientation and basis vectors. Hence, for the purposes of this section we will represent an affine camera A by the product of two matrices:

$$\tilde{\mathbf{H}}_{UA}^{\infty} = \begin{bmatrix} 1 & 0 & 0 \\ 0 & 1 & 0 \\ 0 & 0 & 0 \end{bmatrix} \mathbf{H}_{UA}^{\infty} . \qquad (7.10)$$

Here $\tilde{\mathbf{H}}_{UA}^{\infty}$ denotes the affine camera matrix for A while $\mathbf{H}_{UA}^{\infty}$ provides the underlying camera basis and orientation.

When cameras A and B share the same z-axis, there exists a camera-to-camera transformation. This transformation is given by the matrix

$$\tilde{\mathbf{H}}_{AB}^{\infty} = \begin{bmatrix} 1 & 0 & 0 \\ 0 & 1 & 0 \\ 0 & 0 & 0 \end{bmatrix} \mathbf{H}_{AB}^{\infty} \begin{bmatrix} 1 & 0 & 0 \\ 0 & 1 & 0 \\ 0 & 0 & 0 \end{bmatrix} . \qquad (7.11)$$

When the camera-to-camera transformation $\tilde{\mathbf{H}}_{AB}^{\infty}$ exists, resulting virtual views can be made to depict linear motion. $\tilde{\mathbf{H}}_{AB}^{\infty}$ can be determined in this case from knowledge of just two conjugate directions: one conjugate direction is aligned with the x-axis of each view, the other with the

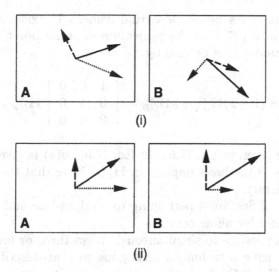

Figure 7.5 *(i)* Three conjugate directions as seen in view A and view B. *(ii)* It is possible to transform the views so that all three conjugate directions are aligned. In this case, a rotation is used to point the dotted vector along the x-axis, then a shear is used to point the dashed vector along the y-axis, and finally the x- and y-axes are scaled to align the solid vector.

y-axis, and then the x- and y-axes are scaled to place conjugate points on the same horizontal or vertical lines. Alternatively, a third conjugate direction could be used to determine scaling for the x- and y-axes (Fig. 7.5).

In general, except for when the z-axes are aligned, no camera-to-camera transformation exists for affine cameras (Fig. 7.4). The following results lead to a general-purpose algorithm for affine cameras:

Let Ω denote an object in the scene and let $\mathbf{u}$ be the associated translation vector. Let ω be a point belonging to the object and let $\mathbf{q}$ and $\mathbf{q} + \mathbf{u}$ denote the position of ω at times $t = 0$ and $t = 1$, respectively.

Projecting ω into camera A at time $t = 0$ and into camera B at time $t = 1$ and then linearly interpolating the projected image points yields

$$\begin{bmatrix} 1 & 0 & 0 \\ 0 & 1 & 0 \\ 0 & 0 & 0 \end{bmatrix} [(1 - s)\mathbf{H}_{UA}^{\infty}\mathbf{q}_U + s\mathbf{H}_{UB}^{\infty}(\mathbf{q} + \mathbf{u})_U] \ . \tag{7.12}$$

Because the x,y-projection matrix can be factored to the left, the development for affine cameras continues exactly as for pinhole cameras with one notable exception: There are no conditions on the reference views because the z-coordinates will always be 0, and consequently there is no prewarp step. As before, a virtual camera V exists such that the interpolation in Eq. 7.12 is the projection of scene point $\mathbf{q} + \mathbf{u}(s)$ into camera V. Camera V is defined by

$$\tilde{\mathbf{H}}_{UV}^{\infty} = (1 - s)\tilde{\mathbf{H}}_{UA}^{\infty} + s\tilde{\mathbf{H}}_{UB}^{\infty} = \begin{bmatrix} 1 & 0 & 0 \\ 0 & 1 & 0 \\ 0 & 0 & 0 \end{bmatrix} \mathbf{H}_{UV}^{\infty} , \qquad (7.13)$$

and $\mathbf{u}(s)$ is as given in Eq. (7.6). In Eq. (7.6), $\mathbf{u}(s)$ is given in terms of basis V, which is the basis implicit in $\mathbf{H}_{UV}^{\infty}$. Note that the z-coordinate of $\mathbf{u}(s)$ is arbitrary.

The results of Section 4 pertaining to straight-line and linear virtual motion also hold for affine cameras.

It is always possible to simultaneously align three or fewer conjugate directions by using a technique analogous to that described above for finding $\tilde{\mathbf{H}}_{AB}^{\infty}$ (Fig. 7.5). Any object whose conjugate translation direction can be aligned in both views will be portrayed as moving along a straight-line path in camera coordinates.

With pinhole cameras, the camera-to-camera transformation always exists so it is always possible to align any number of conjugate directions. With affine cameras, the camera-to-camera transformation may not exist so it is not always possible to portray straight-line motion for four or more objects.

6.   INTERPOLATION WITH H^{∞}

If $\mathbf{H}_{AB}^{\infty}$ is known or can be determined, then view interpolations can be produced in a much more controlled fashion. As discussed in Section 4, an interpolation sequence can be created that portrays linear motion. Furthermore, as we now demonstrate, the space of possible intermediate virtual views that can be created from a set of reference views has an elegant vector-space structure.

So far, we have only presented view interpolation for two reference views. When three reference views are available, view interpolation can be applied in a pairwise manner to make use of all three reference views: An interpolation can be performed on two of the views, and the resulting virtual view can be interpolated with the third reference view. This process can be continued so as to incorporate an arbitrary number of reference views.

If the camera-to-camera transformation between each pair of reference views is known, the repeated pairwise interpolation will always portray linear virtual motion (Fig. 7.6). The order in which the pairwise interpolations are performed will not matter, and the final image will represent

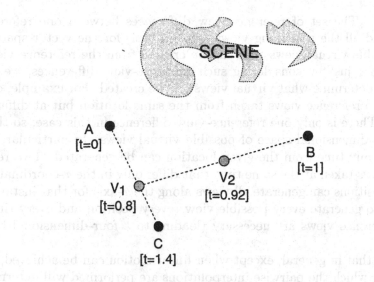

Figure 7.6 Virtual views can be created from multiple reference views by combining them in a pairwise manner. Here the reference views are A, B, and C, and the pairwise camera-to-camera transformations are known.

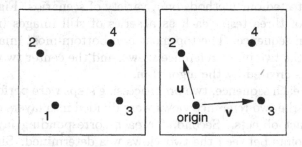

Figure 7.7 Reference view differences. The left-hand figure shows four points on a plane. By formally defining **u** to be the *difference* between point 2 and point 1, formally defining **v** to be the difference between point 3 and point 1, and formally taking point 1 to be the *origin*, point 4 can be represented as a linear combination of the quantities **u** and **v**. The same development exists if the points represent reference views acquired at various positions and times, assuming that linear motion can be achieved. Thus we can create a vector space of virtual views out of the purely formal concept of *reference view differences*. Note that each virtual view will have a time component as well as a space component.

a "weighted sum" of reference-view differences analogous to a weighted sum of Euclidean vectors (Fig. 7.7).

A reference-view difference is just an abstract concept; it does not, for instance, mean subtraction of the intensity values of one image from another. The set of reference-view differences between one reference view and all the remaining views forms a basis for the vector space of all possible virtual views that can be created from the reference views. Therefore, just by considering such reference-view differences, we can quickly determine what virtual views can be created. For example, consider two reference views taken from the same location but at different times. There is only one reference-view difference in this case, so there is a one-dimensional space of possible virtual views. In particular, the view at any time from the given location can be generated. Two reference views taken at the same time that differ only in the x-coordinate of their positions can generate all views along the x-axis for that instant in time. To generate every possible view (every position and every time), five reference views are necessary (leading to a four-dimensional basis set).

Note that in general, except when linear motion can be achieved, the order in which the pairwise interpolations are performed will determine the final virtual view (i.e., the process is not commutative).

7.   EXPERIMENTAL RESULTS

We have tested our methods on a variety of scenarios. Fig. 7.8 shows the results of three tests, each as a series of still images from a view interpolation sequence. The top-most and bottom-most images in each column are the two input reference views, and the center two images are virtual views created by the algorithm.

To create each sequence, two preprocessing steps were performed manually. First, the two reference views were divided into layers corresponding to distinct objects. Second, for each corresponding layer a set of conjugate points between the two views was determined. Since our implementation uses the Beier-Neely algorithm [3] for the morphing step, we actually determined a series of line-segment correspondences instead of point correspondences. For each sequence, between 30 and 50 line-segment correspondences were used (counting all layers).

For all the sequences, the camera calibration was completely unknown, the focal lengths were different, and the cameras were at different locations.

The first sequence is from a test involving three moving objects (including the background object). Since $\mathbf{H}_{AB}^{\infty}$ could only be approximated, the appearance of straight-line motion was achieved by aligning the conjugate directions of motion for each object during the prewarp step (Section 5.3). An object's direction of motion is given by the epipoles of the object's fundamental matrix. Instead of calculating the fundamental

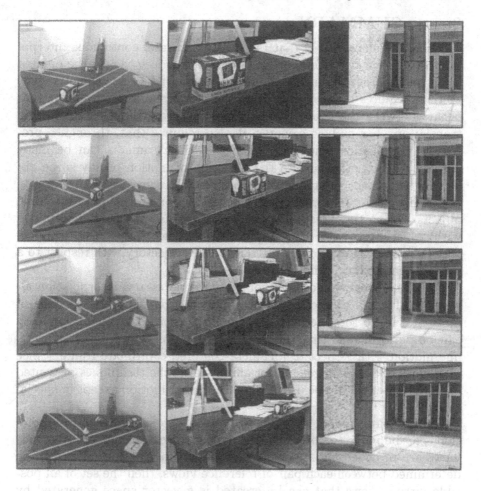

Figure 7.8 Experimental results

matrices for the small objects on the table, we used the conjugate vanishing points of the tape "roads" for the same effect.

The second sequence involves two moving objects (counting the background object) and a large change in focal length. The third sequence demonstrates the parallel motion algorithm (Section 5.1). The scene is static, but the pillar in the foreground and the remaining background points are treated as two separate objects that are moving parallel to each other.

8.   SUMMARY

We have demonstrated that physically-accurate, continuous interpolations between two reference views of a dynamic scene can be created in an image-based manner without reconstructing scene geometry. The method requires that, for each object in the scene, the movement that occurs between the two reference views must be equivalent to a rigid translation. For pinhole cameras, it also requires that, through a process of rectification, the image planes of both cameras can be made parallel to each other and to the direction of motion of any scene object for which the interpolation is desired. In some cases this can be achieved without determining the exact direction of motion of the scene objects. When the direction of motion of an object can be determined with respect to the two cameras' bases, the view interpolation will portray the object moving along a straight-line trajectory with respect to a camera-centered coordinate frame.

For affine cameras, no prewarping step is necessary; interpolation always produces a physically-correct interpolation. If the directions of motion of up to three scene objects can be determined, then a prewarp can be performed so that the view interpolation will portray straight-line motion with respect to a camera-centered coordinate frame. Since $\mathbf{H}_{AB}^{\infty}$ does not exist in general for affine views, the techniques presented in this chapter cannot be used to portray linear motion except in special cases.

For pinhole cameras, when $\mathbf{H}_{AB}^{\infty}$ can be determined, the interpolations can be made to portray linear motion. If more than two reference views are provided and if the camera-to-camera transformation can be determined between each pair of reference views, then the set of all possible virtual views that can be created is a vector space generated by reference-view differences.

Acknowledgments

The support of the National Science Foundation under Grant No. IIS-9530985, and the Defense Advanced Research Projects Agency and Rome Laboratory, Air Force Materiel Command, USAF, under Agreement No. F30602-97-1-0138 is gratefully acknowledged.

References

[1] S. Avidan and A. Shashua. Novel view synthesis in tensor space. In *Proc. Computer Vision and Pattern Recognition Conf.*, pages 1034–1040, 1997.

[2] S. Avidan and A. Shashua. Non-rigid parallax for 3D linear motion. In *Proc. Image Understanding Workshop*, pages 199–201, 1998.

[3] T. Beier and S. Neely. Feature-based image metamorphosis. In *Proc. SIGGRAPH'92*, pages 35–42, 1992.

[4] C. Bregler, M. Covell, and M. Slaney. Video rewrite: Driving visual speech with audio. In *Proc. SIGGRAPH'97*, pages 353–360, 1997.

[5] S. E. Chen and L. Williams. View interpolation for image synthesis. In *Proc. SIGGRAPH'93*, pages 279–288, 1993.

[6] J. C. Clarke and A. Zisserman. Detection and tracking of independent motion. *Image and Vision Computing*, 14:565–572, 1996.

[7] J. Davis. Mosaics of scenes with moving objects. In *Proc. Computer Vision and Pattern Recognition Conf.*, pages 354–360, 1998.

[8] G. J. Edwards, C. J. Taylor, and T. F. Cootes. Learning to identify and track faces in image sequences. In *Proc. Sixth Int. Conf. Computer Vision*, pages 317–322, 1998.

[9] O. D. Faugeras. What can be seen in three dimensions with an uncalibrated stereo rig. In *Proc. Second European Conf. Computer Vision*, volume 588 of *Lecture Notes in Computer Science*, pages 563–578. Springer, 1992.

[10] O. D. Faugeras, Q-T. Luong, and S. J. Maybank. Camera self-calibration: Theory and experiments. In *Proc. Second European Conf. Computer Vision*, volume 588 of *Lecture Notes in Computer Science*, pages 321–334. Springer, 1992.

[11] A. W. Fitzgibbon, G. Cross, and A. Zisserman. Automatic 3D model construction for turn-table sequences. In R. Koch and L. Van Gool, editors, *Proc. Workshop on 3D Structure from Multiple Images of Large-Scale Environments (SMILE '98)*, volume 1506 of *Lecture Notes in Computer Science*, pages 155–170. Springer, 1998.

[12] R. I. Hartley. Projective reconstruction and invariants from multiple images. *IEEE Trans. Pattern Analysis and Machine Intelligence*, 16(10):1036–1041, 1994.

[13] R. I. Hartley. Self-calibration from multiple views with a rotating camera. In *Proc. Third European Conf. Computer Vision*, pages 471–478, 1994.

[14] M. Irani, P. Anandan, and S. Hsu. Mosaic based representations of video sequences and their applications. In *Proc. Fifth Int. Conf. Computer Vision*, pages 605–611, 1995.

[15] M. Jagersand. Image based view synthesis of articulated agents. In *Proc. Computer Vision and Pattern Recognition Conf.*, pages 1047–1053, 1997.

[16] K. N. Kutulakos and S. M. Seitz. A theory of shape by space carving. In *Proc. Seventh Int. Conf. Computer Vision*, pages 307–314, 1999.

[17] R. A. Manning and C. R. Dyer. Interpolating view and scene motion by dynamic view morphing. In *Proc. Computer Vision and Pattern Recognition Conf.*, volume 1, pages 388–394, 1999.

[18] L. McMillan and G. Bishop. Plenoptic modeling. In *Proc. SIG-GRAPH'95*, pages 39–46, 1995.

[19] M. Pollefeys. *Self-Calibration and Metric 3D Reconstruction from Uncalibrated Image Sequences*. PhD thesis, Katholieke Universiteit Leuven, Belgium, 1999.

[20] M. Pollefeys, R. Koch, and L. Van Gool. Self-calibration and metric reconstruction in spite of varying and unknown internal camera parameters. In *Proc. Sixth Int. Conf. Computer Vision*, pages 90–95, 1998.

[21] V. S. Ramachandran. Visual perception in people and machines. In A. Blake and T. Troscianko, editors, *AI and the Eye*, pages 21–77. Wiley, 1990.

[22] S. M. Seitz and C. R. Dyer. View morphing. In *Proc. SIG-GRAPH'96*, pages 21–30, 1996.

[23] S. M. Seitz and C. R. Dyer. Photorealistic scene reconstruction by voxel coloring. *Int. J. Computer Vision*, 35(2):151–173, 1999.

[24] C. Tomasi and T. Kanade. Shape and motion from image streams under orthography: A factorization method. *Int. J. Computer Vision*, 9(2):137–154, 1992.

[25] S. Ullman. *The Interpretation of Visual Motion*. MIT Press, Cambridge, Mass., 1979.

[26] Y. Yacoob and L. Davis. Computing spatio-temporal representations of human faces. In *Proc. Computer Vision and Pattern Recognition Conf.*, pages 70–75, 1994.

Chapter 8

FACIAL MOTION CAPTURING USING AN EXPLANATION-BASED APPROACH

Hai Tao, Thomas S. Huang

Abstract   Building deformation models using the motions captured from real video sequences is becoming a popular method in facial animation. In this paper, we propose an explanation-based facial motion tracking algorithm based on a piecewise Bézier volume deformation model (PBVD). The PBVD is a suitable model both for the synthesis and the analysis of facial images. It is linear and independent of the facial mesh structure. With this model, basic facial movements, or action units, are interactively defined. By changing the magnitudes of these action units, animated facial images are generated. The magnitudes of these action units can also be computed from real video sequences using a model-based tracking algorithm. However, in order to customize the articulation model for a particular face, the predefined PBVD action units need to be adaptively modified. In this paper, we first briefly introduce the PBVD model and its application in facial animation. Then a multi-resolution PBVD-based motion tracking algorithm is presented. Finally, we describe an explanation-based tracking algorithm that takes the predefined action units as the initial articulation model and adaptively improves them during the tracking process to obtain a more realistic articulation model. Experimental results on PBVD-based animation, model-based tracking, and explanation-based tracking are shown in this paper.

1.   INTRODUCTION

Recently, great efforts have been made to integrate the computer vision and the computer graphics techniques in the areas of human computer interaction, model-based video conferencing, visually guided animation, and image-based rendering. A key element in these vision-graphics systems is the model. A model provides the information describing the geometry, the dynamics, and many other attributes of an object that represents the prior knowledge and imposes a set of con-

A. Leonardis et al. (eds.), Confluence of Computer Vision and Computer Graphics, 143–160.

straints for analysis [6]. Among many applications, the analysis and synthesis of facial images is a good example that demonstrates the close relationships between graphics and vision technologies. As shown in Figure 8.1, a model-based facial image communication system involves three major parts (a) the analyzer or the motion generator, (b) the synthesizer that renders the facial image (c) the transmission channel that efficiently communicates between (a) and (b). The system relies on an important component - the facial model.

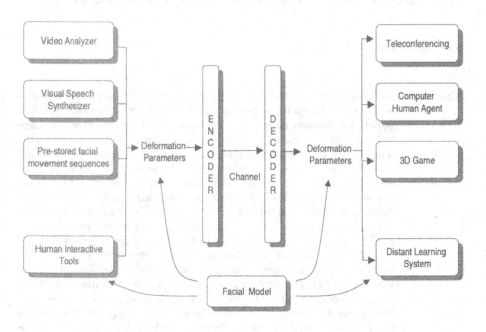

Figure 8.1   A facial image communication system

Both geometric and deformation representations are equally important components in facial modeling. We have developed system to obtain 3D mesh model of a face from 3D CyberWare scanner data (Figure 8.2). In this paper, however, our focus is the facial deformation model, which represents the dynamics of a face. Four categories of facial deformation models have been proposed. They are parameterized models [10], physical muscle models [7], free-form deformation models [5], and performance-driven animation models [12, 4]. In analysis, these models are applied as the constraints that regulate the facial movements.

In this paper, a new free-form facial deformation model called piecewise Bézier volume deformation (PBVD) is proposed. Some properties of this model such as linearity and independence of mesh structure make it a suitable choice for both realistic facial animation and robust facial motion analysis. The difference between this approach and Kalra's method [5] is twofold. By using non-parallel volumes, irregular 3D manifolds are formed. As a result, fewer deformation volumes are needed and the number of control points is reduced. This is a desired property for tracking algorithms. Further, based on facial feature points, this model is mesh independent and can be easily adopted to articulate any face model.

By using the PBVD model, a facial animation system, a model-based facial motion tracking algorithm, and an explanation-based tracking algorithm are presented. These algorithms have been successfully implemented in several applications including video-driven facial animation, lip motion tracking, and real-time facial motion tracking. The remaining sections are organized as following: Section 2 introduces the PBVD model and the PBVD-based animation system. Section 3 describes a PBVD model-based tracking algorithm. Explanation-based tracking is then described in Section 4. Some experimental results are demonstrated in Section 5, followed by discussions and concluding remarks in Section 6.

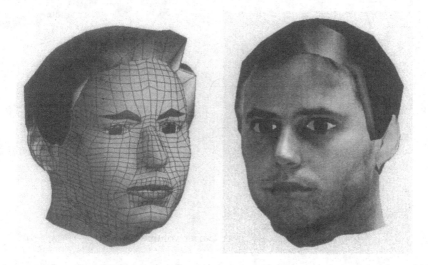

Figure 8.2 A facial mesh model derived from the CyberWare scanner data. Left: the mesh model. Right: the texture-mapped model.

2.   PBVD MODEL

2.1   PBVD - FORMULATION AND PROPERTIES

A 3D Bézier volume [11] is defined as

$$\mathbf{x}(u,v,w) = \sum_{i=0}^{n}\sum_{j=0}^{m}\sum_{k=0}^{l} \mathbf{b}_{i,j,k} B_i^n(u) B_j^m(v) B_k^l(w) , \qquad (8.1)$$

where $\mathbf{x}(u,v,w)$ is a point inside the volume, which, in our case, is a facial mesh point. Variables (u,v,w) are the parameters ranging from 0 to 1, $\mathbf{b}_{i,j,k}$ are the control points, and , $B_i^n(u)$, $B_j^m(v)$, and $B_k^l(w)$ are the Bernstein polynomials. By moving each control point $\mathbf{b}_{i,j,k}$ with a amount of $\mathbf{d}_{i,j,k}$, the displacement of the facial mesh point $\mathbf{x}(u,v,w)$ is

$$\mathbf{v}(u,v,w) = \sum_{i=0}^{n}\sum_{j=0}^{m}\sum_{k=0}^{l} \mathbf{d}_{i,j,k} B_i^n(u) B_j^m(v) B_k^l(w) . \qquad (8.2)$$

Figure 8.3 shows the deformation of a Bézier volume that contains a part of the facial mesh.

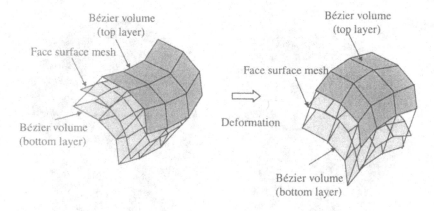

Figure 8.3   A Bézier volume

In order to deform the face, multiple Bézier volumes are formed to embed all the deformable parts. These volumes are formed based on the facial feature points such as eye corners, mouth corners, etc. Each Bézier volume contains two layers, the external layer and the internal layer. They form the volume that contains the face mesh. Norm vectors of each facial feature points are used to form these volumes. To

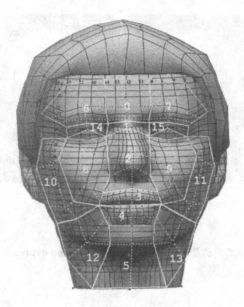

Figure 8.4 The face mesh and the 16 Bézier volumes

ensure continuity in the deformation process, neighboring Bézier volumes are of the same order along the borders. In other words, there are the same number of control points on each side of a boundary. The piecewise Bézier volume structure used in our implementation is shown in Figure 8.4. Using this model, facial regions with similar motions are controlled by a single volume and different volumes are connected so that the smoothness between regions is maintained.

Once the PBVD model is constructed, for each mesh point on the face model, its corresponding Bernstein polynomials are computed. Then the deformation can be written in a matrix form as

$$V = B\mathbf{D}, \tag{8.3}$$

where V contains the nodal displacements of the mesh points, $\mathbf{D}$ contains the displacement vectors of Bézier volume control nodes. The matrix B describes the mapping function composed of Bernstein polynomials. Manipulating the control points through an interactive tool may derive various desired expressions, visual speech, or action units. In Figure 8.5, the real control mesh and the rendered expression *smile* is illustrated. At each moment, the non-rigid motion of a face may be modeled as a linear combination of different expressions or visemes (*visual* phon*emes*), or

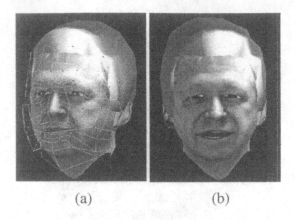

(a)   (b)

Figure 8.5   (a) The PBVD volumes (b) the expression *smile*.

formally

$$\mathbf{V} = B[\mathbf{D}_0\mathbf{D}_1 \dots \mathbf{D}_m][p_0p_1 \dots p_m]^t = BDP = LP , \qquad (8.4)$$

where $\mathbf{D}_i$ is an expression or a viseme, and p_i is its corresponding intensity. The overall motion of the face is

$$R(\mathbf{V}_0 + LP) + T , \qquad (8.5)$$

where $\mathbf{V}_0$ is the neutral facial mesh, R is the rotation decided by the three rotation angles $(\omega_x, \omega_y, \omega_z) = \Omega$, and T is the 3D translation.

2.2   PBVD-BASED FACIAL ANIMATION

Based on the PBVD model, facial action units are constructed using an interactive tool. Then various expressions and visemes are created either from combining these action units or from moving some control nodes. We have created 23 visemes manually to implement a talking head system. Six of them are shown in Figure 8.6. In addition to these visemes, six universal expressions have also been created.

Once visemes and expressions are created, animation sequences can be generated by assigning appropriate values to the magnitudes of these visemes and expressions at each time instance. In our implementation, a human subject speaks to a microphone according to a script. The phoneme segmentation is then obtained using a speech recognition tool. Based on the phoneme segmentation results, mouth shapes and expressions are computed using a coarticulation model similar to [9]. Audio and animation results are then synchronized to generate realistic talking

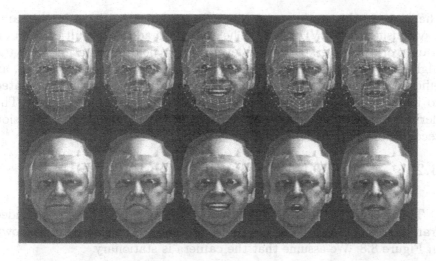

Figure 8.6 Expressions and visemes created using the PBVD model. The expressions and visemes (bottom row) and their corresponding control meshes (top row). The facial movements are, from left to right, *neutral, anger, smile, vowel_or,* and *vowel_met.*

Figure 8.7 An animation sequence with *smile* and speech *I am George McConkie.*

head sequences. Figure 8.7 shows some frames from a synthetic visual speech sequence.

3.   PBVD MODEL-BASED TRACKING ALGORITHM

3.1   VIDEO ANALYSIS OF THE FACIAL MOVEMENTS

Several algorithms for extracting face motion information from video sequences have been proposed [8, 1, 3, 2]. Most of these methods are designed to detect action-unit-level animation parameters. The assumption is that the basic deformation model is already given and will not be changed. In this section, we propose a tracking algorithm in the same flavor using the PBVD model. The algorithm adopts a multi-resolution framework to integrate the low-level motion field information with the high-level deformation constraints. Since the PBVD model is linear, an efficient optimization process using least squares estimator is formulated to incrementally track the head poses and the facial movements. The derived motion parameters can be used for facial animation, expression recognition, or bimodal speech recognition.

3.2   MODEL-BASED TRACKING USING PBVD MODEL

The changes of the motion parameters between two consecutive video frames are computed based on the motion field. The algorithm is shown in Figure 8.8. We assume that the camera is stationary.

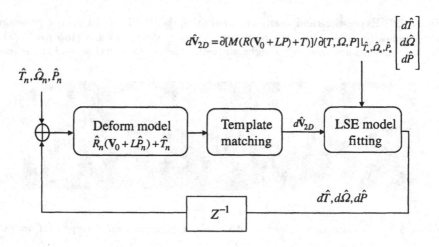

Figure 8.8   Block diagram of the model-based PBVD tracking system

At the initialization stage, the face needs to be approximately frontal view so that the generic 3D model can be fitted. The inputs to the fitting algorithms are the positions of facial feature points, which are manually picked. All motion parameters are set to zeroes (i.e., $(\hat{T}_0, \hat{\Omega}_0, \hat{P}_0,) = 0$), which means a neutral face is assumed. The camera parameters are known in our implementation. Otherwise, a small segment of the video sequence should be used to estimate these parameter using the structure from motion techniques.

Then, from the video frames n and $n + 1$, the 2D motion vectors of many mesh nodal points are estimated using the template matching method. In our implementations, the template for each node contains 11×11 pixels and the searching region for each node is an area of 17×17 pixels. To alleviate the shifting problem, the templates from the previous frame and the templates from the initial frame are used together. For example, the even nodes of a patch are tracked using the templates from the previous frame and the odd nodes are tracked using those of the initial frame. Our experiments showed that this approach is very effective.

From these motion vectors, 3D rigid motions and non-rigid motions (intensities of expressions/visemes or action units) are computed simultaneously using a least squares estimator. Since the PBVD model is linear, only the perspective projection and the rotation introduce non-linearity. This property makes the algorithm simpler and more robust. The 2D inter-frame motion for each node is

$$
d\hat{\mathbf{V}}_{2D} \approx \left. \frac{\partial [M(R(\mathbf{V}_0 + LP) + T)]}{\partial [T, \Omega, P]} \right|_{\hat{T}_n, \hat{\Omega}_n, \hat{P}_n} \begin{bmatrix} d\hat{T} \\ d\hat{\Omega} \\ d\hat{P} \end{bmatrix} =
$$

$$
= M \left[\begin{bmatrix} 1 & 0 & -\frac{x}{z} \\ 0 & 1 & -\frac{y}{z} \end{bmatrix} \begin{bmatrix} G_0 - \frac{x}{z}G_2 \\ G_1 - \frac{y}{z}G_2 \end{bmatrix} \begin{bmatrix} [RL]_0 - \frac{x}{z}[RL]_2 \\ [RL]_0 - \frac{y}{z}[RL]_2 \end{bmatrix} \right] \begin{bmatrix} d\hat{T} \\ d\hat{\Omega} \\ d\hat{P} \end{bmatrix}, (8.6)
$$

where $d\hat{\mathbf{V}}_{2D}$ is the 2D inter-frame motion, and

$$
G = \begin{bmatrix} 0 & z_1 & -y_1 \\ -z_1 & 0 & -x_1 \\ y_1 & -x_1 & 0 \end{bmatrix} . \tag{8.7}
$$

The projection matrix M is

$$
M = \begin{bmatrix} \frac{fs}{z} & 0 & 0 \\ 0 & \frac{fs}{z} & 0 \end{bmatrix}, \tag{8.8}
$$

where f is the focal length of the camera, s is the scale factor, and z is the depth of the mesh node. The vector (x, y, z) represents the 3D mesh nodal position after both rigid and non-rigid deformation, or $R(\mathbf{V}_0 + LP) + T$. The vector (x_1, y_1, z_1) represents the 3D mesh nodal position after only non-rigid deformation, but without translation and rotation (i.e., $\mathbf{V}_0 + LP$). Matrix G_i and $[RL]_i$ denote the ith row of the matrix G and the matrix RL, respectively.

An over-determined system is formed because many 2D inter-frame motion vectors are calculated. As the result, changes of the motion parameters $(d\hat{T}, d\hat{\Omega}, d\hat{P})$ can be estimated using a least squares estimator. By adding these changes to the previously estimated motion parameters $(\hat{T}_n, \hat{\Omega}_n, \hat{P}_n)$, new motion parameters $(\hat{T}_{n+1}, \hat{\Omega}_{n+1}, \hat{P}_{n+1})$, are derived.

3.3   MULTI-RESOLUTION FRAMEWORK

Two problems with the above algorithm are the expensive template matching computation and the noisy motion vectors it derives. The first problem is obvious because the computational complexity for each motion vector is $(11 \times 11)(17 \times 17) \times 3 = 104,907$ integer multiplications. The second problem is partially caused by the fact that in the above algorithm, the computation of the motion field is totally independent of the motion constraints, which makes it vulnerable to various noises. If the lower-level motion field measurements are too noisy, good estimation of motion parameters can never be achieved, even with correct constraints.

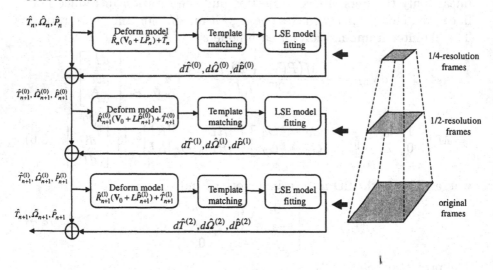

Figure 8.9   The multi-resolution PBVD tracking algorithm

A multi-resolution framework is proposed in this section to partially solve the above problems. The block diagram of this new algorithm is illustrated in Figure 8.9. An image pyramid is formed for each video frame. The algorithm proposed in the previous section is then applied to the consecutive frames sequentially from lowest resolution to the original resolution. For the diagram depicted in Figure 8.9, changes of motion parameters are computed in quarter-resolution images as

$$(d\hat{T}^{(0)}, d\hat{\Omega}^{(0)}, d\hat{P}^{(0)}).$$

By adding these changes to $(\hat{T}_n, \hat{\Omega}_n, \hat{P}_n)$, the estimated new motion parameters are derived as

$$(\hat{T}_{n+1}^{(0)}, \hat{\Omega}_{n+1}^{(0)}, \hat{P}_{n+1}^{(0)}).$$

Similarly, changes of motion parameters are computed in the half-resolution images as $(d\hat{T}^{(1)}, d\hat{\Omega}^{(1)}, d\hat{P}^{(1)})$ based on the previous motion parameter estimation

$$(\hat{T}_{n+1}^{(0)}, \hat{\Omega}_{n+1}^{(0)}, \hat{P}_{n+1}^{(0)}).$$

This process continues until the original resolution is reached.

In this coarse-to-fine algorithm, motion vector computation can be achieved with smaller searching regions and smaller templates. In our implementation, for each motion vector, the number of multiplications is $[(5 \times 5) \times (7 \times 7) \times 3] \times 4 = 14,700$, which is about seven times fewer than the model-based scheme. A more important property of this method is that, to some extent, this coarse-to-fine framework integrates motion vector computation with high-level constraints. The computation of the motion parameter changes is based on the approximated motion parameters at low-resolution images. As the result, more robust tracking results are obtained.

3.4   CONFIDENCE MEASUREMENTS

Two quantities are computed for each frame as the confidence measurements. The average normalized correlation Q_c is computed based on nodes using the templates from the initial video frame. If the tracker fails, this quantity is small. The average LSE fitting error Q_f indicates the tracking quality. When Q_f is large, it means the motion field and the fitted model are not consistent. Q_c and Q_f are closely related. When Q_c is small, which means the matching has low score, Q_f is large. However, a large Q_f does not necessarily imply a small Q_c because the problem could be that the model itself is not correct. In our implementation, we use a confidence measurement $J = Q_c/Q_f$ to monitor the status of the tracker. When J is smaller than a certain threshold, a face detection algorithm is initiated to find the approximate location of the face. The tracking algorithm will then continue.

4.   EXPLANATION-BASED MOTION TRACKING

The model-based approach is powerful because it dramatically reduces the solution searching space by imposing domain knowledge as constraints. However, if the model is oversimplified, or is not consistent with the actual dynamics, the results are prone to errors. To be able to learn new facial motion patterns while not to loose the benefits of model-based approach, a new tracking algorithm called explanation-based method is proposed in this section.

4.1   THE APPROACH

We use the term explanation-based to describe the strategy that starts from a rough domain theory and then incrementally elaborates the knowledge by learning new events. The existing domain theory provides some possible explanation of each new event, and the learning algorithm explores the new data to adjust the domain theory. For a PBVD tracking algorithm, the predefined action units provide an explanation for the computed motion vectors. The fitting error, which is the combination of the noise and error of the model, is then analyzed to adjust the model. A block diagram is shown in Figure 8.10. It is essentially the same as the block diagram for the model-based PBVD method except for the block that adjusts the non-rigid motion model L. The model L includes two parts: B and D. Both of them can be adjusted. Changing D means to change the displacement vector or control nodes for each action units so that the model fits the data better. Modifying B means to modify Bézier volumes so that descriptive power of the model is enhanced. In this paper, we discuss the learning of D.

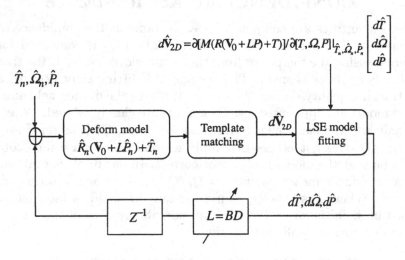

Figure 8.10 The block diagram of the explanation-based tracking algorithm

4.2   LEARNING EXPRESSIONS/VISEMES AND ACTION UNITS

The learning of D is based on the model-based analysis of a video segment. As shown in Figure 8.11, the predefined action units D are first used in a model-based method to track n frames, then the tracking error is analyzed and the deformation D is modified. The new D is then used as the model in the next segment. This process is performed during the entire tracking process.

To adjust D, for each frame, 2D motion residuals are projected back to 3D non-rigid motion according to the 3D model and in-surface motion assumption. The fitting error for any mesh nodes can be written as

$$\mathbf{V}_{res2D} = M\hat{R}\mathbf{V}_{res} = M\hat{R}(a\mathbf{u}_1 + b\mathbf{u}_2) \qquad (8.9)$$

where $\mathbf{V}_{res2D}$ is the 2D fitting error in the LSE equation, M is the perspective projection matrix, and R is the rotation matrix. Vectors $\mathbf{u}_1$ and $\mathbf{u}_2$ are the 3D vectors that span the tangent plane of the investigated facial mesh node. They can be decided from the norm vector of that mesh node. From Eq. (8.9), a and b can be solved and the 3D residual $\mathbf{V}_{res}$ is derived.

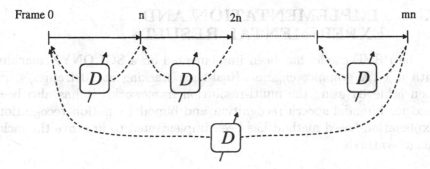

Figure 8.11 Learning of the expressions/visemes or action units (D) in a video sequence

For each frame, the projected 3D motion is

$$\mathbf{V}_{mes} = L\hat{P} + \alpha\mathbf{V}_{res} , \qquad (8.10)$$

where L is the previous PBVD model, $\hat{P}$ is the vector representing the non-rigid motion magnitudes, and α is the learning rate. The term $L\hat{P}$ means the fitted part of the motion. The vector $\mathbf{V}_{mes}$ is collected for each frame in a video segment. At the end of that segment, adjustment of the D is performed.

Adjusting D is equivalent to adjusting $\mathbf{D}_i$ (see Eq. (8.4)). An iterative algorithm is proposed in this paper. For each loop, only one $\mathbf{D}_i$ is modified; the others are fixed. For example, for the first iteration, only $\mathbf{D}_0$ is adjusted. For each frame, we derive the 3D-motion vector that equals

$$\mathbf{V}_{r0} = \mathbf{V}_{mes} - B[\mathbf{0D}_1 \ldots \mathbf{D}_m]\hat{P} . \qquad (8.11)$$

The PCA analysis of $\mathbf{V}_{r0}$ in a video segment is performed to extract the major motion patterns such as $\mathbf{V}_{e00}$, $\mathbf{V}_{e01}$, etc. The number of these patterns is decided by the energy distribution in the eigenvalues. The maximum number of these patterns can also be imposed to avoid over-fitting. We assume these motions are due to some $\mathbf{D}_{0i}$.

To find the deformation unit that causes each eigenvector, the following LSE problems are solved

$$\begin{bmatrix} \mathbf{V}_{e0k} \\ 0 \end{bmatrix} = \begin{bmatrix} B \\ C \end{bmatrix} \mathbf{D}_0 k , \qquad (8.12)$$

where C is the smoothness constraint that regulates $\mathbf{D}_{0k}$ so that the motion of PBVD control nodes are smooth.

5.   IMPLEMENTATION AND EXPERIMENTAL RESULTS

The PBVD model has been implemented on a SGI ONYX machine with a VTX graphics engine. Real-time tracking at 10 frames/s has been achieved using the multi-resolution framework. It has also been used for bimodal speech recognition and bimodal emotion recognition. Explanation-based method has been implemented to improve the facial image synthesis.

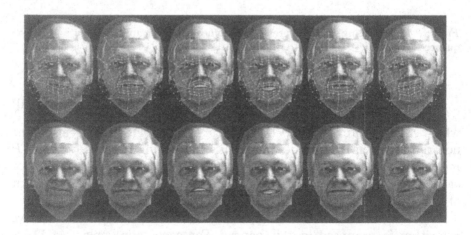

Figure 8.12 The action units in bimodal speech recognition. Top: the control nodes. Bottom: the action units.

5.1 FACIAL MODEL INITIALIZATION

The face in the first video frame needs to be approximately frontal view and with a neutral expression. From this frame, facial feature points are extracted manually. The 3D fitting algorithm is then applied to warp the generic model according to these feature points. However, since we only have 2D information, the whole warping process is performed in 2D except the initial scaling. Once the geometric facial model is fitted, a PBVD model is automatically derived from some facial feature points and their corresponding norms.

5.2 PBVD MODEL-BASED TRACKING

In PBVD tracking algorithm, the choice of deformation units D_i depends on the application. In a bimodal speech recognition application, 6 action units are used to describe the motions around the mouth. These action units are illustrated in Figure 8.12. The tracking result for each frame is twelve parameters including the rotation, the translation, and the intensities of these action units.

For the bimodal emotion recognition and the real-time demo system, 12 action units are used. Actually, users can design any set of deformation units for the tracking algorithm. These deformations can be either at expression level or at action unit level. Lip tracking results are shown in Figure 8.13. Figure 8.14 shows the results of the real-time tracker.

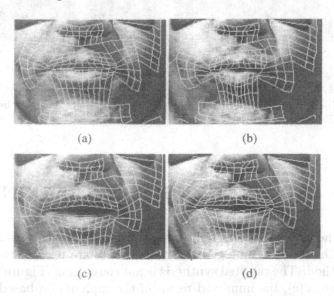

(a)   (b)

(c)   (d)

Figure 8.13 Lip tracking for bimodal speech recognition

Facial animation sequences are generated from the detected motion parameters. Figure 8.15 shows the original video frames and the synthesized results. The synthesized facial model uses the initial video frame as the texture. The texture-mapped model is then deformed according to the motion parameters.

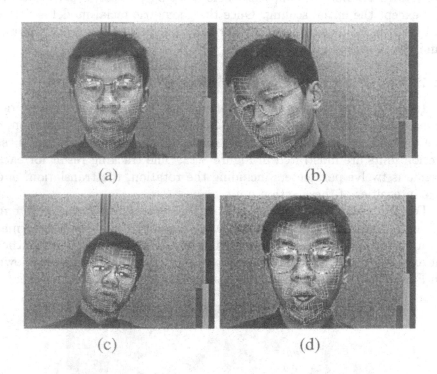

Figure 8.14 Tracking results of the real-time demo system. The two bars are Q_c (left) and Q_f (right), respectively.

5.3   EXPLANATION-BASED TRACKING

A set of predefined motion units is used as the initial deformation model. Then, these motion units are adjusted during the tracking. To compare the results, some generic motion units are used in the model-based method. The resulted synthesis is not convincing (Figure 8.16(b)). In Figure 8.16(c), the improved result of the explanation-based method is shown. In our implementation, the segment size is 20 frames, and the learning rate is $\alpha = 0.4$.

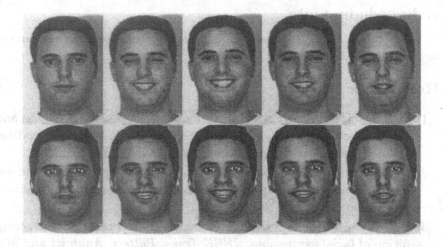

Figure 8.15 The original video frames (top) and the synthesized tracking results (bottom).

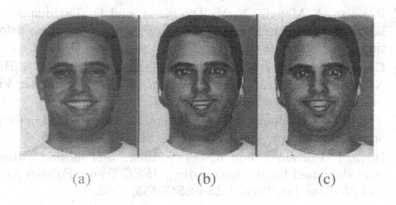

(a)   (b)   (c)

Figure 8.16 The synthesis results (a) original frame (b) model-based (c) explanation-based.

6.   DISCUSSION

In this paper, issues on generating facial articulation models from real video sequences are addressed. Three major contributions are PBVD model and facial animation, PBVD model-based tracking, and explanation-based tracking. For future research, the emphasis will be on improving low-level motion field calculation, combining the explanation-based approach with multi-resolution framework, and recognizing spatio-temporal patterns from the facial motion parameters.

Acknowledgments

This work was supported in part by the Army Research Laboratory Cooperative Agreement No. DAAL01-96-0003.

References

[1] C. S. Choi, K. Aizawa, H. Harashima, and T. Takebe. Analysis and synthesis of facial image sequences in model-based image coding. *IEEE Trans. Circuit Sys. Video Technol.*, 4(3):257–275, 1994.

[2] D. DeCarlo and D. Metaxas. The integration of optical flow and deformable models with applications to human face shape and motion estimation. In *CVPR'96*, pages 231–238, 1996.

[3] I. Essa and A. Pentland. Coding, analysis, interpretation and recognition of facial expressions. *IEEE Trans. Pattern Analysis and Machine Intelligence*, 19(7):757–763, 1997.

[4] B. Guenter, C. Grimm, D. Wood, H. Malvar, and F. Pighin. Making faces. In *SIGGRAPH 98*, pages 55–66, 1998.

[5] P. Kalra, A. Mangili, N. M. Thalmann, and D. Thalmann. Simulation of facial muscle actions based on rational free form deformations. In *Proc. EUROGRAPHICS'92*, pages 59–69, 1992.

[6] C. Kambhamettu, D. B. Goldgof, D. Terzopoulos, and T. S. Huang. Nonrigid motion analysis. In *Handbook of PRIP: Computer Vision*, pages 405–430. Academic Press, 1994.

[7] Y. Lee, D. Terzopoulos, and K. Waters. Realistic modeling for facial animation. In *Proc. SIGGRAPH 95*, pages 55–62, 1995.

[8] H. Li, P. Roivainen, and R. Forchheimer. 3-D motion estimation in model-based facial image coding. *IEEE Trans. Pattern Analysis and Machine Intelligence*, 15(6):545–555, 1993.

[9] D. W. Massaro and M. M. Cohen. Modeling coarticulation in synthetic visual speech. In *N. M. Thalmann and D. Thalmann (Eds.) Models and Techniques in Computer Animation*, pages 139–156. Springer-Verlag, 1993.

[10] F. I. Parke. Parameterized models for facial animation. *IEEE Comput. Graph. and Appl.*, 2(9):61–68, 1982.

[11] T. W. Sederberg and S. R. Parry. Free-form deformation of solid geometric models. In *SIGGRAPH 86*, pages 151–160, 1986.

[12] L. Williams. Performance-driven facial animation. In *SIGGRAPH 90*, pages 235–242, 1990.

Chapter 9

IMAGE-BASED 3D MODELING: MODELING FROM REALITY

Luc Van Gool, Filip Defoort, Johannes Hug, Gregor Kalberer, Reinhard Koch, Danny Martens, Marc Pollefeys, Marc Proesmans, Maarten Vergauwen, Alexey Zalesny

Abstract   Increasingly, realistic object, scene, and event modeling is based on image data rather than manual synthesis. The paper describes a system for visits to a virtual, 3D archeological site. One can navigate through this environment, with a virtual guide as companion. One can ask questions using natural, fluent speech. The guide will respond and will bring the visitor to the desired place. Simple answers are given as changes in the orientations of his head, by him raising his eyebrows or by head nodding. In the near future the head will speak.

The idea to model directly from images is applied in three subcomponents of this system. First, there are two systems for 3D modeling. One is a shape-from-video system, that turns multiple, uncalibrated images into realistic 3D models. This system was used to model the landscape and buildings of the site. The second projects a special pattern and was used to model smaller pieces, like statues and ornaments that often had intricate shapes. Secondly, the model of the scene is only as convincing as the texture by which it is covered. As it is impossible to keep images of the texture of a complete landscape, images of the natural surface were used to synthesize more of similar texture, starting from a very compact yet effective texture model. Thirdly, natural lip motions were learned from observed, 3D face dynamics. These will be used to animate the virtual guide in future versions of the system.

1.   INTRODUCTION

We describe preliminary results for a virtual tour operator system. The demonstrator is centered around a visit to virtual Sagalassos, an ancient city in Turkey, that is being excavated by archaeologists of the University of Leuven. This demonstrator—coined EAMOS—integrates research on speech (Univ. Leuven) and vision (Univ. Leuven and ETH

-A. Leonardis et al. (eds.), Confluence of Computer Vision and Computer Graphics, 161–178.

Zurich). The underlying, three-dimensional site model not only consists of the current landscape, ruins, and other finds, but it also contains CAD models of the original city. This helps to interpret the ruins in their original context.

One can navigate through this environment, with a virtual guide as companion. EAMOS allows a user to visually explore the scene with the assistance of this guide, which responds to spoken commands. The guiding agent presents itself as a hovering mask, and is able to communicate back to the user through head gestures and emotional expressions. The user is invited to inquire about the archeological site. The user is free to query for any interesting places to visit, or may ask for additional information about something visible in the scene. The guide takes the user on a tour, navigating from viewpoint to viewpoint in the scene. The visitors of virtual Sagalassos can formulate their queries through fluent, natural speech. The visual presence of the guide makes the interaction even more intuitive. As the mask reacts to the requests, a protocol is established that is quite similar to that of a normal person-to-person conversation. If wrongly understood, the user can soon pick up on the guide's mental state, as the facial mask frowns in anguish. Simple head nods confirm or negate questions, affirm or deny requests. In the near future the head will be animated to also let it speak, so that the guide can formulate more intelligent answers. Fig. 9.1 shows some example views during such a virtual tour.

The current line-up deployed for EAMOS consists of a single parallel processing computer (Onyx Infinite Reality), equipped with an audio interface. Different concurrently running software packages take care of rendering the scene, animating the guide, as well as processing and interpreting the speech.

This contribution focuses on the vision, not the speech aspect. In particular it describes how the EAMOS demonstrator is based on three vision tasks, that each have been approached using image-based modeling as the primary paradigm:

1. 3D modeling of the landscape, ruins, and finds,

2. modeling of the landscape texture,

3. speech-oriented animation of the virtual guide's face.

Currently, the team is integrating these techniques into a system that guides people around through virtual Sagalassos. A first version is ready, but each aspect needs improvement. Each of these aspects in now discussed in more detail, as well as our plans for the future.

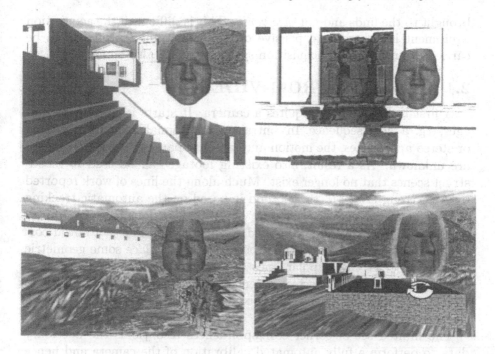

Figure 9.1 Holiday pictures from a trip to virtual Sagalassos. The guide was very helpful, but not very talkative. The weather was good: dry and room temperature throughout our stay. The figures show several of the components of which the site model is composed: a 3D landscape model, more detailed building models, CAD models that show the original shapes of the buildings and the context of the remaining ruins; the face mask of the virtual guide to whom questions can be asked in fluent speech and which reacts with emotional expressions.

2.   TWO IMAGE-BASED 3D ACQUISITION SYSTEMS

A first requirement for the EAMOS demonstrator is that visually convincing 3D models of the site be built. In the end, this will have to include a 3D model of the terrain (landscape), of the existing ruins, of the statuary (sculptures and ornaments), and of the different finds such as pottery. For now, initial models have been produced for the terrain, for some of the ruins, and for a few sculptures.

This section describes the two 3D acquisition systems that were used. They share the underlying idea of building systems that are easy to use and only require off-the-shelf hardware. This is important, as the archaeologists should be able to use the equipment *in situ* and without causing lengthy interruptions in the excavations. The systems should be brought to the finds and not *vice versa*. This is difficult if the acquisition equipment is either too expensive or too vulnerable. As it has to be carried around, the 3D acquisition systems should also be very light.

2.1   SHAPE-FROM-VIDEO

A first technique only requires a camera. It starts from multiple images, e.g. a video sequence. In contrast to traditional shape-from-motion or stereo approaches, the motion and intrinsic parameters of the camera are unknown. As a result, also existing footage can be used to reconstruct scenes that no longer exist. Much along the lines of work reported by Armstrong *et al.* [1], the method is based on the automatic tracking of image features over the different views. This is done in stages. First, a (Harris) corner detector is applied to yield a limited set of initial correspondences, which enable the process to put in place some geometric constraints (e.g. the epipolar lines as restricted search areas). These constraints support the correspondence search for a wider set of features and in the limit, for a dense, i.e. pixel-wise, field of disparities between the images [9].

The limited set of corner correspondences also yields the necessary data to perform a fully automated calibration of the camera and hence the camera projection matrices for its different, subsequent positions. Once these matrices are available, the 3D reconstruction of the observed scene can be produced. In general, to arrive at metric structure— i.e. to undo any remaining projective and affine skew from the 3D reconstruction—the camera intrinsic parameters like the focal length etc. have to remain fixed. But even if one has limited *a priori* knowledge about these parameters, like the pixel aspect ratio or the fact that rows and columns in the images are orthogonal, then also focal length can be allowed to change [7, 11, 12].

Fig. 9.2 gives an example of a historic building that has been reconstructed with this shape-from-video technique. It shows two of 6 images of an Indian temple, used for its 3D reconstruction. All images were taken from the same ground level as these two. Fig. 9.3 shows 2 views of the 3D reconstruction—a general overview and a detail—from viewpoints substantially different from those of the input images. The same method was applied to model the Sagalassos landscape. Several images were taken along the rim of a hill overlooking the excavation site. For several of the buildings (ruins) close range images were taken and also these were modeled. In all cases the intrinsic and extrinsic parameters of the camera were unknown.

Figure 9.2   Images of an Indian temple

As the method produces the list of intrinsic and extrinsic camera parameters one could also add virtual objects to the video sequences that were used as input. We have just started to explore such augmented reality work.

Our ongoing research in the shape-from-video area focuses on the following aspects:

1. to process longer image sequences fully automatically;

2. to integrate data from different sequences, e.g. for the exterior and interior of a building;

Figure 9.3   Two views of the shape-from-video reconstruction obtained for the Indian temple

3. to solve the wide baseline correspondence problem, as to ensure that the system can automatically combine information from sequences taken from very different viewpoints;

4. to better combine the texture information contained in the different frames, e.g. to arrive at super-resolution;

5. to model different excavation strata in 3D and to integrate such information to build a detailed 3D, dynamic record of the excavations;

6. to extend the use of 3D acquisition technology to the support of virtual or real restoration and anastylosis, i.e. to use the 3D shapes of building blocks, sherds, and pieces in general to see how they can fit together. If the building or the artifact to which the pieces belong is of high scientific or artistic value a real restoration can then follow.

2.2   ACTIVE, ONE-SHOT 3D ACQUISITION

The 'passive' technique outlined in the previous section cannot deal with untextured parts of a scene. This is a major problem with objects such as statues, the shape of which should be extracted with high precision, but which often do not have strongly textured surfaces. The same goes for the extraction of the shape of human faces, as is required for the animation of the guide's mask, as discussed later.

"Active" systems bypass the problem by projecting a pattern onto the scene. The 3D shape is extracted by analyzing the displacements/deformations of the pattern when observed from a different direction (see [8] and Besl [2] for an overview). Typically, such methods have relied on the projection of single points or lines and on scanning the scene to gradually build a 3D description point by point or line by line.

It is possible, however, to extract more complete 3D information from a single image by projecting a grid of lines. So far, such approaches had used additional constraints or information codes which force the grid to remain sparse [3, 13, 10]. With the technique we have developed and which has been refined and commercialised by Eyetronics [4] dense grids are projected, yielding high resolution 3D models. A single image yields the 3D shape of what is visible of the object to the camera and the projector. Fig. 9.4 shows the setup and a detail of an image from which 3D information can be extracted.

In order to also extract the surface texture, the lines of the grid are filtered out. Obviously, an alternative for static objects is to take another image without the grid. Yet, this is not an easy option if texture is to

camera

projector

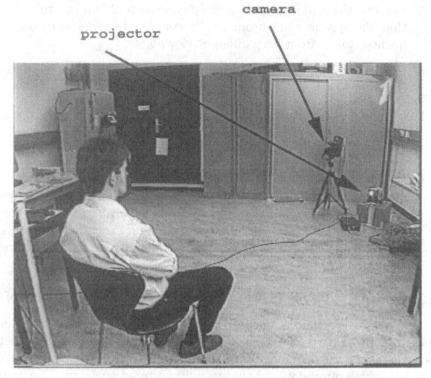

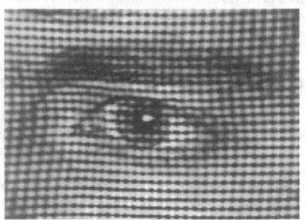

Figure 9.4 Top: The active system only consists of a normal slide projector and camera, and a computer. The camera takes an image from a direction that is slightly different from the direction of projection. Bottom: A regular square pattern is projected on the scene, as seen in this detailed view. In this case, the grid covers the complete face. 3D coordinates are calculated for all the line intersections, resulting in the simultaneous measurement for thousands of points.

Figure 9.5 Two views of the reconstructed Dionysos statue

be obtained for dynamic scenes. The elimination of the grid is based on non-linear diffusion techniques and, of course, the precise knowledge of where the grid lines are in the image, but this is known from the shape extraction step.

Fig. 9.5 shows the 3D reconstruction of a Dionysos statue, found at the archaeological site of Sagalassos. It would be difficult to put such several tons heavy statue into the working volume of a laser scanner and it is not sure that the latter would survive ...

Currently studied extensions to this technology include:

1. building a more compact, hand-held setup that is easy for use *in situ*;

2. the automatic crude registration of partial 3D patches, after which a traditional technique like ICP or mutual information is used to perform the fine-registration. Now crude registration still has to be done manually;

3. to specialize the setup also for pottery sherds, which are very important in archaeology for dating the stratigraphic layers uncovered during the excavations.

3.   IMAGE-BASED TEXTURE SYNTHESIS

Only a rather rough model of the landscape has been built. In fact, the resolution of this model is much coarser than that of some of the ruins. As one moves from building to building and crosses the bare landscape in between, there is a noticeable and disturbing difference in visual detail between the textures. On the other hand, precise modeling

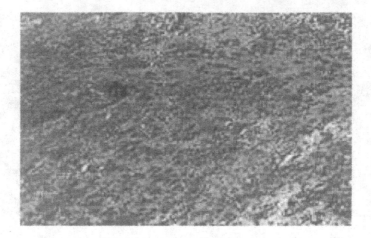

Figure 9.6   Image showing terrain texture at the Sagalassos site

of the landscape texture would cost an enormous amount of time and memory space. Also, such precise modeling is not really required. It would for most practical means suffice to cover the landscape with a texture that looks detailed and realistic, but that does not necessarily correspond to the real texture on that particular part of the site. Thus, as a compromise we model the terrain texture on the basis of a few, selected example images. Such example image is shown in Fig. 9.6. The resulting model is very compact and can be used to generate arbitrarily large patches of texture that look very similar to the exemplar texture. Emphasis so far has been on the quality of the results rather than the efficiency of the texture synthesis.

The approach builds on the cooccurrence principle: nearly all possible pairwise interactions in the example texture image are analyzed. The fact that only pairwise interactions are analyzed is in line with Julesz's observation that mainly first and second-order statistics govern our perception of textures. Yet, it is well-known that third and higher order statistics cannot be neglected just like that, mainly because of figural patterns that are not preserved. Here we are dealing with natural textures and this issue is less crucial. Nevertheless, this restriction is dictated rather by the computational complexity and not by the underlying principles.

Textures are synthesized as to mimick the pairwise statistics of the example texture. Just using all pairwise interactions in the model is not a viable approach and a good selection needs to be made [6]. We have opted for an approach that makes a selection as to keep this set minimal but on the other hand bring the statistics of the synthesized textures very close to that of the example textures [14]. Parameter selection follows an iterative approach, where pairwise interactions are added one by one, the synthetic texture is each time updated accordingly, and the statistical difference between example and synthesized texture is analyzed to decide on which further addition to make. The set of pairwise interactions selected for the model (from which textures are synthesized) is called the neighborhood system.

A sketch of the algorithm is as follows:

step 1: Collect the complete 2nd-order statistics for the example texture, i.e. the statistics of all pairwise interactions. (After this step the example texture is no longer needed). As a matter of fact, the current implementation does not start from all pairwise interactions, as it focuses on interactions between positions within a maximal distance.

step 2: Generate an image filled with independent noise and with values uniformly distributed in the range of the example texture. This noise image serves as the initial synthesized texture, to be refined in subsequent steps.

step 3: Collect the full pairwise statistics for the current synthesized image.

step 4: For each type of pairwise interaction, compare the statistics of the example texture and the synthesized texture and calculate their 'distance'. For the statistics the intensity difference distribution (normalized histograms) were used and the distance was simply Euclidean. In fact, the intensity distribution of the images was added also, where 'singletons' played the role of an additional interaction. The current implementation uses image quantization with 32 gray levels.

step 5: Select the interaction type with the maximal distance (cf. step 4). If this distance is less than some threshold go to step 8—the end of the algorithm. Otherwise add the interaction type to the current (initially empty) neighborhood system and all its statistical characteristics to the current (initially empty) texture parameter set.

step 6: Synthesize a new texture using the updated neighborhood system and texture parameter set.

step 7: Go to step 3.

step 8: End of the algorithm.

For texture synthesis the images are treated as a realization from the family of Markov random fields with the neighborhood system corresponding to the selected interaction types. The convergence of the corresponding relaxation procedure to a single stationary point has been proven [14].

After the 8-step analysis algorithm we have the final neighborhood system of the texture and its parameter set. This model is very small compared to the complete 2nd-order statistics extracted in step 1. Typically only 10 to 40 pairwise interactions are included and the model amounts from a few hundreds to a few thousands bytes. Nevertheless, it yields small statistical differences between the example and synthesized textures.

This texture synthesis approach can handle quite broad classes of textures. Nevertheless, it has problems with capturing complex semantic orderings or texels of specific shapes. The method has mainly been used for colored textures, as is also required for the Sagalassos virtual site. In the case of color images pairwise interactions are added that combine intensities of different bands. The shortest 4-neighborhood system and the vertical interband interactions were always preselected because experiments showed that they are important for the vast majority of the texture classes. Fig. 9.7 shows a synthesized texture for the example image in Fig. 9.6. Fig. 9.8 shows part of the site with the original terrain model texture (top) and with synthesized texture mapped onto the landscape (bottom).

Ongoing work is aimed at extending the results in order to

1. include the 3D nature of texture: the idea is to model textures from images taken from different views, but without a complete extraction of the neighborhood system for every view separately as this would take too much time;

2. compress the 3D texture models: this could be done by exploiting the relation between a texture's appearance for different viewing angles;

3. to achieve viewpoint consistency: if the goal is to move around in a scene, the texture at a certain location should change in a way that is consistent with the texture generated in the previous views, e.g. pattern mimicking rocks should not be shifted around. The hope is to achieve this by driving the probabilities for the generation of different color patterns not only from the model for the required viewing angle, but also from transition probabilities given the previous view.

Figure 9.7 A synthesized texture based on the example image of Fig. 9.6.

Figure 9.8 View of the old bath house and surrounding landscape at Sagalassos. Top: view with the original landscape texture. As this view strongly zooms in onto this model, the texture is of insufficient quality. Bottom: the landscape texture has been replaced by synthetic texture.

4.   FACE ANIMATION FOR SPEECH

Currently the guide only listens and answers through facial expressions, but he does not talk. Work on face animation should change this. The plan is to learn realistic 3D representations of visemes from observed 3D lip motions captured with the active system (section 2.2). As 3D can be captured from a single image, one can also take a video of a moving or deforming object and get as many 3D reconstructions as there are frames. Fig. 9.9 shows the 3D reconstructions extracted from three frames of a talking head video, each seen from three different viewpoints. From video data taken with a normal camera 25 (or 30) reconstructions can be made for every second of motion. The quality suffices to carry out detailed investigations into 3D face dynamics. Each 3D snapshot consists of 3D data for thousands of points (the full grid contains 600 × 600 lines and for every intersection a 3D coordinate can be given out by the system, so camera resolution is the limiting factor here). The 3D reconstructions can be made at the temporal resolution of the video camera, but processing is done off-line. For the moment, the reconstruction of a single frame including texture takes about 2 minutes.

At the time of writing, 3D dynamics have been captured for a basic set of 16 visemes, following conclusions by Ezzat and Poggio [5]. In a first step, a topological lip mask was fitted to the different 3D mouth positions. This mask is illustrated in Fig. 9.10.

Statistics were extracted for the mask nodes positions. These were used to generate a robust lip tracker. Apart from the 3D positions, the tracker also uses color information and 3D surface curvature. Fig. 9.11 shows the lip mask as it was automatically fitted to different mouth poses, in order to learn 3D lip dynamics for the 16 basic visemes.

The work on face animation has just started. Several issues are under investigation:

1. the set of basic visemes, including co-articulation effects, needs to be determined. Currently, there is not much agreement on this point in the literature;

2. these visemes have to be extracted with a high degree of automation from examples for different people, in order to draw the necessary statistics;

3. the step from analysis to synthesis/animation of the virtual guide has to be performed, based on speech input.

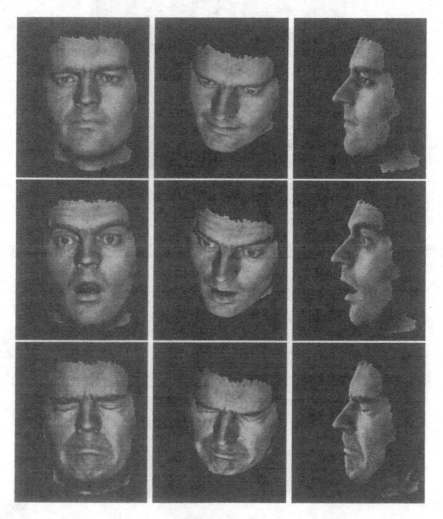

Figure 9.9   3D reconstructions of a face for three frames of a video and shown from 3 different viewpoints.

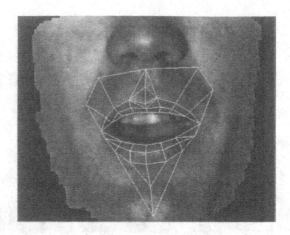

Figure 9.10   A lip topology mask is used to support tracking

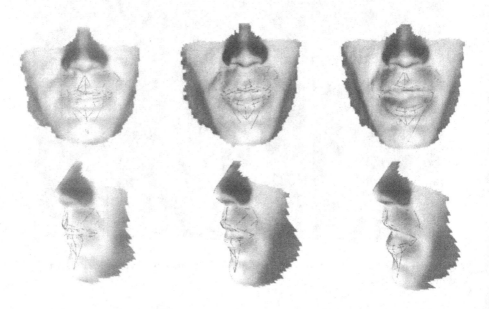

Figure 9.11   The lip topology mask is fitted automatically to the 3D data, using 3D positions, surface color, and surface curvature.

5.   CONCLUSIONS AND FUTURE WORK

In this paper we discussed ongoing work on a system that guides visitors through a virtual archæological site. The underlying 3D acquisition technology was concisely described. It plays a crucial role in making such large-scale projects possible, as it is easy to operate and yet yields realistically looking models. A similar philosophy of modeling from observations was used to synthesize textures similar to those found on site and to learn 3D mouth dynamics for a range of visemes.

Much work remains to be done also on the visualisation side. In future implementations, EAMOS will try to anticipate user requests through user modeling. Also will more 3D models be produced, of additional buildings (with the passive shape-from-video technique) and finds (with the active one-shot technique). Also will the CAD reconstructions be extended to represent different periods: from the 2nd century BC (Greek period, Sagalassos' heydays) up to the 6th century AD (Christian period, decline and shortly before its destruction by an earthquake, after which it was abandoned for good). In parallel, some of our colleagues are working on the compression of the 3D models and level-of-detail oriented compression.

Acknowledgments

The authors gratefully acknowledge support of ACTS project AC074 'VANGUARD', IUAP project 'Imechs' financed by the Belgian OSTC (Services of the Prime Minister, Belgian Federal Services for Scientific, Technical, and Cultural Affairs) and GOA project 'HVS' sponsored by the K.U.Leuven Research Council. Filip Defoort and Marc Pollefeys gratefully acknowledge support of a FWO grant (Flemish Fund for Scientific Research). Alexey Zalesny is supported as 'Akademischer Gast' by the ETH. The authors also gratefully acknowledge support by ETH through the 'Visemes' project. Finally, the authors also want to thank their colleagues from the speech group at PSI, K.U.Leuven for providing the natural speech understanding system.

References

[1] M. Armstrong, A. Zisserman, and P. Beardsley. Euclidean structure from uncalibrated images. *Proc. British Machine Vision Conf.*, 1994.

[2] P. Besl. Active Optical Range Imaging Sensors. *Machine Vision and Applications*, 1(2):127–152, 1988.

[3] K. Boyer and A. Kak. Color-encoded structured light for rapid active ranging. *IEEE Transaction on Pattern Analysis and Machine Intelligence*, 9(10):14–28, 1987.

[4] http://www.eyetronics.com

[5] T. Ezzat and T. Poggio. *Visual speech synthesis by morphing visemes.* AI Memo No. 1658, MIT, May 1999.

[6] A. Gagalowicz and S. D. Ma. Sequential synthesis of natural textures. *CVGIP*, vol. 30, pp. 289–315, 1985.

[7] A. Heyden and K. Aström. Euclidean reconstruction from image sequences with varying and unknown focal length and principal point. *Proc. Conf. on Computer Vision and Pattern Recognition*, pp. 438–443, 1997.

[8] R. A. Jarvis. A perspective on range finding techniques for computer vision. *IEEE Transaction on Pattern Analysis and Machine Intelligence*, 5(2):122–139, 1983.

[9] R. Koch, M. Pollefeys, and L. Van Gool. Multi viewpoint stereo from uncalibrated video sequences. *Proc. Eur. Conf. Computer Vision*, Vol. I, pages 55–71. LNCS, Springer, 1998.

[10] M. Maruyama, and S. Abe. Range sensing by projecting multiple slits with random cuts. *IEEE Transaction on Pattern Analysis and Machine Intelligence*, 15(6):647–650, 1993.

[11] M. Pollefeys, R. Koch, and L. Van Gool. Self-calibration and metric reconstruction in spite of varying and unknown internal camera parameters. *Int. Conf. on Computer Vision*, pages. 90–95, Bombay, India, Jan. 4–7, 1998.

[12] M. Pollefeys, R. Koch, and L. Van Gool. Self-calibration and metric reconstruction inspite of varying and in known intrinsic camera parameters. *International Journal of Computer Vision*, 32(1):7–25, 1999.

[13] P. Vuylsteke and A. Oosterlinck. Range image acquisition with a single binary-encoded light pattern. *IEEE Transaction on Pattern Analysis and Machine Intelligence*, 12(2):148–164, 1990.

[14] A. Zalesny. *Analysis and Synthesis of Textures With Pairwise Signal Interactions.* Techn. rep. KUL/ESAT/PSI/9902, Katholieke Universiteit Leuven, Belgium, 1999.

Chapter 10

COMPUTER VISION AND GRAPHICS TECHNIQUES FOR MODELING DRESSED HUMANS

Nebojša Jojić, Thomas S. Huang

Abstract   In this chapter we present techniques for building dressed human models from images. We combine computer vision based approaches such as 3-D reconstruction of a human body and analysis-by-synthesis of the behavior of cloth material with the computer graphics approaches for realistic rendering of complex objects. The experimental results include building textured 3-D models of humans from multiple images, dressing these models into virtual garment, and joint estimation of cloth draping parameters and the underlying object's geometry in range images of dressed objects.

1.   INTRODUCTION

This chapter is a study of methods for acquiring relatively detailed human models from images. We concentrate on two important components of a human model: body geometry and physics-based models of the garment, both augmented by texture mapping. Potential applications include synthetic-natural hybrid coding (SNHC), virtual reality, CAD systems for garment design, and even garment shopping over the Internet (see [12]).

In the first part of the chapter, we study the problem of 3-D reconstruction of complex multi-part objects, such as a human body, from visual cues. In the second part, we present an algorithm for vision-based analysis of the cloth draping effect that allows for estimating parameters of a physics-based cloth model jointly with the geometry of the supporting object. In one of the experiments, we also demonstrate how a dressed human model can be built from images by combining these two algorithms.

A. Leonardis et al. (eds.), Confluence of Computer Vision and Computer Graphics, 179–200.

We define the problem of the reconstruction of a human body in an arbitrary posture as the problem of 3-D shape estimation of an object consisting of several parts which may partially or completely occlude each other from some views. The algorithms that we derive here could be used for other such objects, or for multiple occluding objects.

The usual stereo or structured light methods cannot give a complete surface estimate in such cases, as either the lighting source or the cameras may not see all the parts of the object. Moreover, the correspondence problem is not a trivial task in using stereo or structured light methods.

To overcome these difficulties, we model the object with several deformable superquadrics and use occluding contours and stereo to govern part positioning, orientation and deformation. Image contours provide a crude surface estimate which guides the stereo matching process. In turn, the 3-D points provided by stereo cues can further refine the surface estimate and improve contour fitting.

Compared with related work [16, 21], we propose a faster force assignment algorithm based on chamfer images. We can reconstruct multiple objects and multipart self-occluding objects, which can be rigid or may not be capable of performing prescribed set of movements as required in [15, 14]. We can use arbitrary camera configuration, unlike the case in [24] where parallel projection and coplanar viewing directions are assumed. Moreover, the whole scheme avoids the problem of merging of reconstructed surface patches from different views as in [24].

Experimental results in this chapter include building texture-mapped 3-D models of real humans from images. These models could be used for automatic body measurements, or could be dressed into virtual clothing and animated.

The main topic of the second part of the chapter is motivated by the extensive use and advancement of CAD/CAM systems for garment design and manufacturing, as well as the ever-increasing computer speed and popularity of the Internet. These developments indicate that the clothed human models might be more on demand in the next generation of model-based video coding and telepresence software, as well as in home shopping businesses that would involve trying on virtual garments before making the order of the physical ones. Several physics-based cloth models have been developed over the last decade. A good survey of cloth modeling techniques is given in [18].

Another approach to "simulating" draping has been rather successful in the garment CAD software. Instead of physics-based simulation of the three-dimensional draping effect, this type of software uses a single image of a model wearing a garment of uniform color. The human operator places a distorted 2-D or 3-D grid over the garment in the image, and this grid is then used to apply a desired pattern by texture mapping. The shading from the original image is kept. This technique is usually referred to as re-imaging and is widely used to reduce the cost of photo shooting and sample manufacturing [17, 4].

The physics-based cloth models are used to simulate the internal and external forces that cause the cloth to drape [22, 3, 2, 6, 19]. Model parameters can be derived from mechanical measurements obtained by the Kawabata Evaluation System [2, 5]. To the best of our knowledge, a quantitative comparison between simulated and real drape has not yet been offered, except for the comparison of "drape factors" as in [5]. However, this measure is not reliable, as different materials may have the same drape factor, but exhibit visually different draping behavior.

In this chapter, we address the problem of estimating model parameters of any physics-based cloth model by comparing the simulated drape to the range data of the real drape. There are several advantages to this approach:

1. We define a measure of the model quality, the mean distance between the model and the range data, computed over the *whole* surface of the scanned cloth.

2. By minimizing this mean distance, we avoid performing mechanical measurements with expensive equipment.

3. We directly address the problem of achieving the synthetic drape as close to the real drape as the model allows. Traditional approaches concentrate only on ensuring correct mechanical properties of the model. Therefore, our algorithm could also be used in combination with mechanical measurements to compare the performance of different cloth modeling approaches.

4. We show that analysis-by-synthesis of the range data of the cloth draped over an object, also reveals the geometry of parts of the object's shape. This encourages research on utilizing physics-based cloth models in tracking humans.

We tested the cloth draping analysis algorithm both on synthetic and real data (including an analysis of a dressed doll). We concluded that even a crude cloth model with imprecise bending constants could still be used for the detection of body-garment contact points, which in turn could be used in body reconstruction. We hope that this result will inspire further work on utilizing cloth models in computer vision areas such as dressed human tracking.

The above mentioned re-imaging technique could also benefit from our algorithm, as it can be used for automatic registration of the model with the image data (though it would require more views or some other way of capturing the 3-D geometry of the dressed human).

2.   HUMAN BODY RECONSTRUCTION

2.1   DEFORMABLE SUPERQUADRICS

In this section, we describe briefly the deformable model that we use to model body parts [21].

The deformable model is represented as a sum of a reference shape

$$\mathbf{s}(u, v) = [a_1 C_u^{\epsilon_1} C_v^{\epsilon_2}, a_2 C_u^{\epsilon_1} S_v^{\epsilon_2}, a_3 S_u^{\epsilon_1}], \qquad (10.1)$$

and a displacement function $\mathbf{d}(u, v) = \mathbf{S}(u, v)\mathbf{q_d}$, where u and v are material coordinates; $S_w^{\epsilon} = \text{sign}(\sin w)|\sin w|^{\epsilon}$; $C_w^{\epsilon} = \text{sign}(\cos w)|\cos w|^{\epsilon}$; a_1, a_2, a_3, ϵ_1, ϵ_2 are global deformation parameters (stored in $\mathbf{q_s}$); $\mathbf{q_d}$ contains nodal variables (displacements at the nodes sampled over material coordinates), and $\mathbf{S}(u, v)$ is the shape matrix containing basis functions in the finite element representation of the continuous displacement function.

In addition to global and local deformations of the parts, a rigid transformation of each part is allowed. It is defined by translational and rotational degrees of freedom $\mathbf{q}_c$ and $\mathbf{q}_\theta$. Under the external forces $\mathbf{f}$ the model will move and deform according to the following equation:

$$\mathbf{C\dot{q}} + \mathbf{Kq} = \mathbf{f_q}, \qquad (10.2)$$

where $\mathbf{q} = (\mathbf{q}_c^T, \mathbf{q}_\theta^T, \mathbf{q}_s^T, \mathbf{q}_d^T)^T$ is the state of the model; $\mathbf{C}$ and $\mathbf{K}$ are the damping and stiffness matrices; and $\mathbf{f_q}$ are the generalized external forces associated with the degrees of freedom of the model. These forces are related to the external (image) forces [21].

The image forces we use in this chapter can be written as $\mathbf{f} = \mathbf{f}_{contour} + \mathbf{f}_{3D}$, where the first component of the force deforms the superquadric to have similar occluding contours as the imaged object and the second component governs fitting of the model to the range data provided by the stereo cue.

2.2   CONTOUR FORCE COMPUTATION

We first find model nodes residing on the occluding contour. With respect to camera l, such nodes $\mathbf{P}_i$ should satisfy $|\mathbf{N}_i \cdot (\mathbf{P}_i - \mathbf{O}_l)| \leq \epsilon$, where $\mathbf{O}_l$ is the optical center of the camera, $\mathbf{P}_i$ is the position vector of the model node i, and $\mathbf{N}_i$ is the surface normal at this node (refer to Fig. 10.1). Then, the $\mathbf{P}_i s$ are projected onto the image plane by the projection operator $\prod_l$ acquired by camera calibration, i.e. $\mathbf{p}_i^I = \prod_l \mathbf{P}_i$, where the superscript I denotes the image plane points.

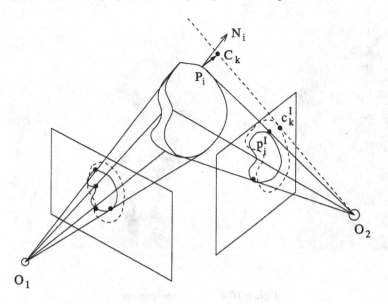

Figure 10.1   Contour forces

For each image contour point $\mathbf{c}_k^I$, the closest model projection $\mathbf{p}_i^I$ is found. Let $\mathbf{P}_i$ be its corresponding 3-D point on the model, and $\mathbf{C}_k$ be a 3-D point that is projected to $\mathbf{c}_k^I$, i.e. $\mathbf{c}_k^I = \prod_l \mathbf{C}_k$. As can be seen in Fig. 10.1, such $\mathbf{C}_k$ should lie on the line formed by $\mathbf{O}_l$ and $\mathbf{c}_k^I$. To find a single direction for the force to bring $\mathbf{p}_i^I$ to $\mathbf{c}_k^I$ we utilize the principle of minimal action and compute $\mathbf{C}_k$ as follows:

$$\mathbf{C}_k = arg\left(min_{\mathbf{C}_k}|\mathbf{C}_k - \mathbf{P}_i|\right), \quad given \quad \mathbf{c}_k^I = \prod_l \mathbf{C}_k. \tag{10.3}$$

The contour force acting on the model point $\mathbf{P}_i$ is defined as:

$$\mathbf{f}_{c_i} = k_c(\mathbf{C}_k - \mathbf{P}_i). \tag{10.4}$$

In the case of a pinhole camera, the solution to Eq. (10.3) is simply the orthogonal projection of $\mathbf{P}_i$ onto the line $\mathbf{O}_l\mathbf{c}_k^I$. In general, $\mathbf{C}_k$ could be found independently of camera model using Eq. (10.3).

A similar type of occluding contour force was used in [23].

To avoid a computationally expensive search for the closest model point for each contour point, we developed an algorithm for force assignment based on the chamfer image of the occluding contours with an additional index matrix containing the index of the closest contour point for each pixel in the image (see [9, 10, 8]).

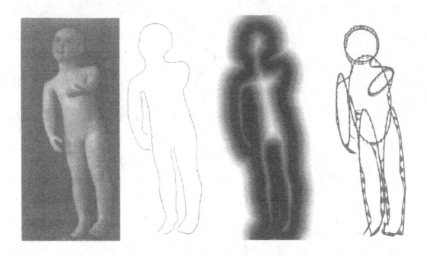

Figure 10.2   Force assignment

2.3   FORCES BASED ON STEREO AIDED BY STRUCTURED LIGHT

Providing that the correspondences between the features in two images are available, it is possible to reconstruct a number of 3-D points on the object's surface using triangulation techniques. If necessary, the feature points can be created by a structured light source.

Correspondence establishment in stereo is known to be a difficult problem. In this section, we make use of the surface estimated by occluding contours to assist feature matching (Fig. 10.3). A match between two features is considered good only if it satisfies both the epipolar constraint and a constraint on the distance from the point, which is reconstructed by the match under consideration, to the surface estimated using occluding contours.

Once the feature correspondences have been established and a number of surface points R_k have been reconstructed by triangulation, the part models can be further deformed to fit these points by applying forces:

$$\mathbf{f}_{3D_i} = k_{3D}(\mathbf{R}_k - \mathbf{P}_i), \tag{10.5}$$

where $\mathbf{P}_i$ is the model node closest to the point $\mathbf{R}_k$, and k_{3D} is a scaling constant.

These forces may reposition superquadrics slightly so that a better contour force assignment can be achieved. Therefore, the two visual cues assist each other. They also complement each other, as occluding

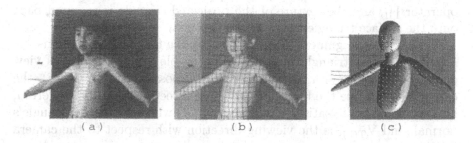

Figure 10.3 Structured light provides feature points: (a) The intensity image of a human object; (b) The object illuminated by structured light; (c) The reconstructed feature points overlapped with an estimate from contours.

contours provide constraints at the parts where stereo becomes unreliable, while stereo refines the estimate at the rest of the surface.

2.4   FORCE ASSIGNMENT BASED ON FUZZY CLUSTERING

We also experimented with weighted force assignment based on fuzzy clustering as proposed by Kakadiaris [15]. Instead of using the nearest neighbor force as in the previous sections, each data point r_i should attract points on several models with forces scaled by a weight $p_{r_{i,j}}$ equal to the probability that this point is correctly associated with the superquadric j. Among other advantages, this allows for better merging of the body parts. For more details, see [9, 10, 8].

2.5   TEXTURE MAPPING

The task of mapping the texture from all the available images onto a single 3-D model is not a trivial one. Even very small errors in the 3-D model create artifacts around the edges of the object. In addition to that, due to different camera gains, specular reflections, etc., the same 3-D point may have different intensities in different images.

We solve this problem in two steps. First, we compute the mapping $T : (i, j) \rightarrow l$, that assigns the image from the l-th camera to the j-th surface triangle on the i-th model part. This mapping is based on the triangle's position and orientation, as well as some local continuity constraints. Next, we compensate for the difference in the image intensities, by computing the scaling constants for each pixel. After this, the usual texture mapping algorithm can be applied—each triangle in the model is projected onto the appropriate image plane using the camera projection operator $\prod_l$, and the texture of the projected triangle is mapped back onto the surface triangle.

The texture assignment T should satisfy the following conditions:

1) The surface triangle (i, j) has to be visible from the point of view of the $T(i, j)$-th camera. If there are several possibilities for $T(i, j)$, the cameras which face the triangle (i, j) more directly should be preferred, i.e., we should try to satisfy $\mathbf{V}_{T(i,j)} \cdot \mathbf{N}_{ij} = -1$, where $\mathbf{N}_{ij}$ is the triangle's normal, and $\mathbf{V}_{T(i,j)}$ is the viewing direction with respect to the camera $T(i, j)$.

2) Mapping T should be as continuous as possible, i.e., the preferable assignments are the ones in which the neighboring surface triangles have the same assigned texture source as often as possible.

3) We may want some views to be preferred as texture sources to others. For example, we may want to make more use of the frontal camera views, especially for the part representing the head in the human body model.[1]

Such an assignment can be achieved by minimizing the following cost criterion:

$$c(T) = \sum_i \sum_j w_{T(i,j),i} \left[\left| N_{ij} \cdot V_{T(i,j)} + 1 \right| + p(T, i, j) \right], \qquad (10.6)$$

where $w_{T(i,j),i}$ is the weight given to the choice of texture $T(i, j)$ for the model part i, and $p(T, i, j)$ is the cost of the non-continuous texture assignment for the triangle j of the part i. For example $p(T, i, j)$ could simply be proportional to the number of the different assignments in the local neighborhood of the triangle j. Due to this constraint, the cost $c(T)$ needs to be minimized iteratively. Usually 4–5 iterations are sufficient.

In Fig. 10.9 (a) an example of the texture assignment without the term $p(T, i, j)$ is given. The surface of the body is color-coded according to the texture assignment map T. In Fig. 10.9 (b) the result after iterative minimization of the whole energy in Eq. (10.6) is shown. The small islands of texture inconsistent with the surrounding texture have been eliminated.

When this assignment is used to map the original images onto the model surface, the resulting image looks like Fig. 10.9(c). The borders along which the texture source is changed are more or less visible in the image. To compensate for that, it is necessary to re-scale the intensities

---

[1] The textured head model is bound to have artifacts, as the reconstruction algorithm presented here is suited to smooth objects such as the human body; for detailed modeling of the human head a different model should be used.

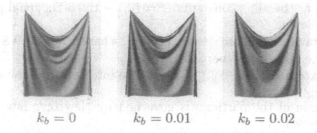

$$k_b = 0 \qquad\qquad k_b = 0.01 \qquad\qquad k_b = 0.02$$

Figure 10.4   Three 100×100 particle systems with different bending constants

in images while preserving the appearance of the texture. This results in the texture-mapped body in Fig. 10.9(d) (for details, see [10]).

3.   MODELING AND ANALYSIS OF CLOTH DRAPING

3.1   A CLOTH MODEL

In our experiments, we represent a rectangular piece of cloth as a particle system $\{\mathbf{P}_{i,j} : i = 1, M; j = 1, N\}$. Each particle (i, j) interacts with its neighbors and the supporting object:physics-based cloth model

1) Repelling and stretching are modeled using simple springs:

$$\mathbf{F}_{s_{ij}} = k_s \left[\sum_{k \in \{i-1, i+1\}} (u - d_{k,j})\mathbf{e}_{k,j} + \right.$$

$$\sum_{k \in \{j-1, j+1\}} (v - d_{i,k})\mathbf{e}_{i,k} +$$

$$r \sum_{k \in \{i-1, i+1\}} (d - d_{k,j-1})\mathbf{e}_{k,j-1} +$$

$$\left. r \sum_{k \in \{i-1, i+1\}} (d - d_{k,j+1})\mathbf{e}_{k,j+1} \right], \qquad (10.7)$$

where $\mathbf{P}_{i,j} = (x_{ij}, y_{ij}, z_{ij})$, $d_{k,l} = |\mathbf{P}_{i,j} - \mathbf{P}_{k,l}|$, $\mathbf{e}_{k,l} = (\mathbf{P}_{i,j} - \mathbf{P}_{k,l})/d_{k,l}$; u, v are nominal horizontal and vertical mesh spacings; $d = \sqrt{u^2 + v^2}$; k_s is the elasticity constant; r is the diagonal-to-axial strength ratio controlling shearing in the model [18].

2) Bending resistance in horizontal and vertical directions is modeled by the force:

$$\mathbf{F}_{b_{i,j}} = k_{bh}(Proj_{\mathbf{P}_{i-1,j}\mathbf{P}_{i+1,j}}^{\mathbf{P}_{i,j}} - \mathbf{P}_{i,j}) + k_{bv}(Proj_{\mathbf{P}_{i,j-1}\mathbf{P}_{i,j+1}}^{\mathbf{P}_{i,j}} - \mathbf{P}_{i,j}) \quad (10.8)$$

k_{bh} and k_{bv} are bending constants. $Proj_{BC}^{A}$ is the orthogonal projection of A onto the line BC.

3) The gravitational force is equal to $m\mathbf{g}$, where $\mathbf{g} = (0, -9.81, 0)[m/s^2]$ and m is the mass of the particle.

4) The external forces, $\mathbf{F}_{ext_{i,j}}$, model the interaction of the cloth with other objects.

The motion of the particles is governed by Newton's law (k_v is the damping factor):

$$\mathbf{F}_{s_{i,j}} + \mathbf{F}_{b_{i,j}} + m\mathbf{g} + \mathbf{F}_{ext_{i,j}} - k_v \frac{d\mathbf{P}_{i,j}}{dt} = m\frac{d^2\mathbf{P}_{i,j}}{dt^2}. \qquad (10.9)$$

If only the final drape is of interest, the oscillations during the model relaxation can be avoided by setting the right hand side of this equation to zero.

Other physics-based cloth models could also be used with the algorithm explained in the following section. The model and the estimation algorithm are based on the study of the internal and external forces, but it is easy to derive these forces for energy-based deformable models, such as the models described in [2, 22, 3]. Also, the algorithm is not concerned with the discretization of the model, so it can be applied to models based on continuum approximations using finite differences or finite elements.

3.2   PARAMETER ESTIMATION

The estimation algorithm is shown in Fig. 10.5. It is assumed that the cloth sample is rectangular and its size is known. M, N are chosen in advance and the spacings u, v are derived from the size of the sample. However, no assumptions are made regarding the shape of the supporting object (Fig. 10.11 a), or cloth model parameters. Of the several model parameters in Eq. (10.7)–(10.9), only a few are important. k_v does not affect the final drape, and m can be divided out from Eq. (10.9). k_s is usually set to a high value, as cloth does not stretch visibly under its own weight. The parameters of our model that affect the final drape and should be estimated are $p1 = r$, $p2 = k_{bh}/m$, $p3 = k_{bv}/m$. For example, the effect of the bending constants is demonstrated in Fig. 10.4.

The range points, obtained by any available range finder, are organized into a smooth surface over which the model of the sample can be draped. The force $\mathbf{F}_{ext}$ is derived from the range data:

$$\mathbf{F}_{ext_{i,j}} = \mathbf{F}_{c_{i,j}} + \mathbf{F}_{d_{i,j}}, \quad \mathbf{F}_{d_{i,j}} = k_d(\mathbf{r}_{i,j} - \mathbf{P}_{i,j}), \qquad (10.10)$$

where $\mathbf{r}_{i,j}$ is the range point closest to the particle (i, j). The forces $\mathbf{F}_{d_{i,j}}$ force the model to drape similarly to the scanned cloth. With a low k_d, these forces are not sufficient to prevent the model from falling through

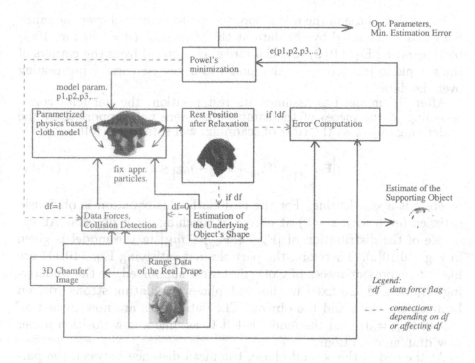

Figure 10.5 Simplified block diagram of the estimation algorithm (the case of unknown draping conditions).

the data surface, so it is prevented by our collision handling routine, symbolically represented by force $\mathbf{F}_c$ in Eq. (10.10). This force is not included into Eq. (10.9) when it is integrated. Instead, the position and speed of a particle are directly adjusted each time step according to the law of momentum conservation [3], if collision with the range data surface is detected.

To speed up the force assignment and collision detection algorithms, we use the 3-D chamfer image, the 3-D matrix containing the approximate distances to the range data for any point in a certain volume [1]. In addition to this distance map, we create a 3-D index matrix, containing indices of the closest range points for each entry [8]. To create this matrix, it is necessary to keep track of the closest point during the chamfer image computation in a standard two-pass algorithm. The distance map helps to evaluate the possibility of collision of a particle with the surface of the scanned cloth, while the index matrix allows intersection tests with the right triangles on the surface, and fast computation of the data forces $\mathbf{F}_{d_{i,j}}$.

In the first phase in the main loop, the model is draped over the range data and is attracted by the data at the same time (df=1 in Fig. 10.5) by integrating Eq. (10.9). Special forces are applied from the corners of the sample to the corners of the model to insure its correct positioning over the data.

After the model has assumed its rest position, the particles corresponding to the pieces of the sample that were not supported by the underlying object at the time of scanning, will satisfy the following:

$$\left| \mathbf{F}_{ext_{i,j}} \right| = \left| \mathbf{F}_{s_{i,j}} + \mathbf{F}_{b_{i,j}} + m\mathbf{g} \right| \leq \varepsilon, \tag{10.11}$$

where ε is a small value. For the real cloth, this equation is obviously satisfied (even with $\varepsilon = 0$) at parts not touching other objects. An example of the distribution of $|\mathbf{F}_{s_{i,j}} + \mathbf{F}_{b_{i,j}} + m\mathbf{g}|$ in the model is given in Fig. 10.10(c). Therefore, the particles not satisfying Eq. (10.11) are likely to represent pieces of cloth that were supported by the underlying object, and are fixed in the next phase, simulating strong friction between the cloth and the object. The data forces are now turned off (df=0, $\mathbf{F}_{ext} = 0$), and the model is left to assume a new position under new draping conditions.

At the end of the second phase, the mean distance between the particles and the range data is computed:

$$e(p1, p2, p3, ...) = \frac{1}{MN} \sum_{i,j} \left| \mathbf{r}_{i,j} - \mathbf{P}_{i,j} \right|, \tag{10.12}$$

and this approximation error, as a function of model parameters $p1$, $p2$, $p3$, ..., is forwarded to a multivariate minimization routine. We use Powel's direction set minimization technique [20], as it does not require gradient information. The shape estimate is updated after each change of parameters, as Eq. (10.11) is better satisfied with more accurate model parameters.

When some parts of the range data are missing, these parts are excluded from the error computation in Eq. (10.12). Missing data can be detected by a large distance $|\mathbf{r}_{i,j} - \mathbf{P}_{i,j}|$, which, at the end of the phase one, should be small due to the attracting data forces.

If the supporting object's shape is known a priori, the algorithm is slightly different [11]. Collision of the cloth model with the model of the underlying object is performed and handled in each time step ($\mathbf{F}_c$ in Eq. (10.10)) , and in the second phase, there is no need to fix the positions of the particles touching the object. Instead, only the data force component of $\mathbf{F}_{ext}$ is turned off, but collision detection and handling is continued.

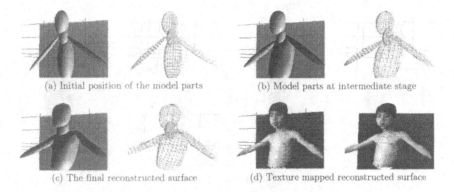

(a) Initial position of the model parts   (b) Model parts at intermediate stage

(c) The final reconstructed surface   (d) Texture mapped reconstructed surface

Figure 10.6   Reconstruction of the human upper body

4.   EXPERIMENTAL RESULTS

4.1   HUMAN BODY RECONSTRUCTION

We performed preliminary experiments on human-like objects with two CCD cameras and a structured lighting source in between to project a stripe pattern on the object surface. Both ordinary intensity images and images under structured lighting were taken.

In the first experiment, we imaged a real human (Fig. 10.3) with two cameras in the above configuration. Five deformable superquadrics (for arms, torso, neck and head) are manually positioned in the virtual 3-D space so that their projections onto image plane lie relatively near the image contours (see the rightmost figure in Fig. 10.6(a)). Fig. 10.6 illustrates several steps in integrating Eq. (10.2). In each step, the left image shows the model parts smoothly shaded or texture mapped and the right image shows the fitting of the model parts to the contours in one of the images.

In the second experiment, we tried to reconstruct a more difficult object—a doll with such a posture that the body parts occlude each other(see Fig. 10.2). The object was positioned on the turning table and a total of eight camera views were used in reconstruction. Six superquadrics were initialized and in Fig. 10.7(b) we show the final result after fitting to both contours and the 3-D points reconstructed by stereo cue. The reconstructed surface is compared to the reconstruction using only stereo correspondences obtained by manual matching (Fig. 10.7(a)) to demonstrate how efficiently our scheme deals with self-occlusion.

The experiments show that the contour based estimate of the surface, even by only two cameras can efficiently assist stereo matching. In the

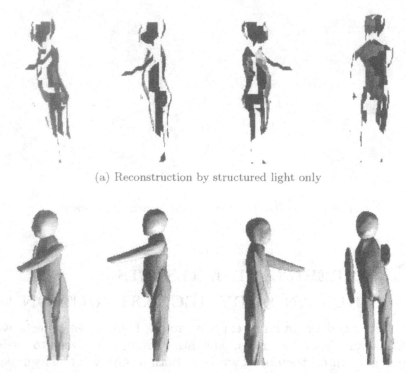

(a) Reconstruction by structured light only

(b) Reconstruction based on integration of occluding contours
and stereo aided by structured light

Figure 10.7 Reconstruction of a mannequin

first experiment, for example, for the 80 feature points detected in the image, 74 correct matches are found purely guided by the contour based estimate of 3-D surface. Usually, the remaining false matches are corrected as well during further refinement of the surface estimate using both cues. As can be seen in Fig. 10.7(a), stereo aided by structured light cannot make estimates near the occluding contours due to the absence of matched feature points there, but the two combined cues can provide a rather complete estimate of those parts that were not visible to both cameras.

An example of full body reconstruction from six views is shown in Fig. 10.8. In order to be able to use distortion-free narrow angle cameras in a limited space, we used two cameras for each view, each camera capturing approximately half of the body. In this experiment, only the contours were used in the reconstruction. The body model, consisting of 15 superquadrics, was initialized automatically using an algorithm

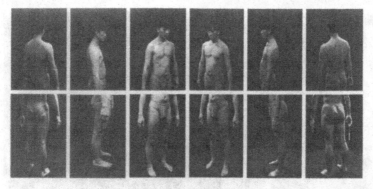

(a) Images used for reconstruction

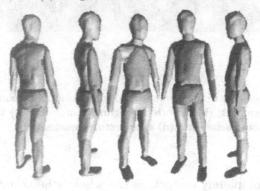

(b) Several views of the reconstructed 3-D model

Figure 10.8 Human body reconstruction from occluding contours

based on volume intersection [7], and then refined by contour-driven
deformation. Currently, due to the large number of nodes in the finite
element model of the local deformations, the full body reconstruction
takes a couple of hours on an SGI Indigo. However, the speed can
be dramatically increased using the adaptive sampling in the material
coordinate system, and the adaptive time steps.

A number of measurements necessary for tailoring have been taken
from this reconstruction and compared to the physical measurements [9].
The errors were mostly around 0.5–1%.

As a demonstration of our texture mapping algorithm, in Fig. 10.9 (d)
and (c), the texture mapping results with and without texture equalization are given. The mapping is based on the texture assignment in (b)
(see also the section on texture mapping). As can be seen in the figure,
the texture equalization leads to better images, though the resulting

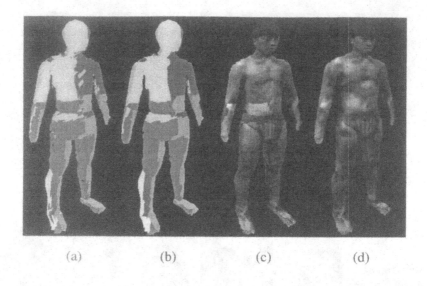

(a)   (b)   (c)   (d)

Figure 10.9 Mapping the texture from several sources onto a human body model: (a) initial texture assignment; (b) smoothed assignment map and (c) the corresponding texture mapped model before and (d) after texture equalization.

texture is not completely correct, as the whole scheme introduces artificial specularities at parts where the texture in Fig. 10.9 (c) had abrupt changes. However, if the visual effect is the main goal, the proposed scheme works fine.

4.2   ANALYSIS OF CLOTH DRAPING

Experiments were performed on both synthetic and real range data. In Fig. 10.10(a), a synthetic drape of a cloth sample 400×400mm over four spheres is given. In Fig. 10.10(b), 10.10(c), and 10.10(d), the best approximation with the 25×25 model (at the end of the parameter estimation algorithm), the distribution of forces in the model and the estimated supporting shape (the contact points between the cloth and the object) are shown. The mean distance between the model and the data was 2.77mm. A typical execution time of the estimation algorithm on an SGI Onyx is a couple of hours.

In the second experiment we used the Cyberware laser scanner to scan the drape of a 380×380mm cloth sample (Fig. 10.11(b)). The mean distances were 2.2mm for a 50×50 model (Fig. 10.11(c)) and 4.12mm for a 25×25 model (Fig. 10.11(d)). Note that even with a very crude 25×25 model, the estimate of the supporting object's shape (Fig. 10.11(f)) still

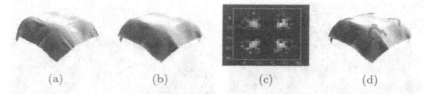

Figure 10.10 (a) Synthetic range data created with a 50×50 particle system; (b) the best approximation using a 25×25 model; (c) the distribution of forces in the model and; (d) the estimated supporting shape overlapped with the model.

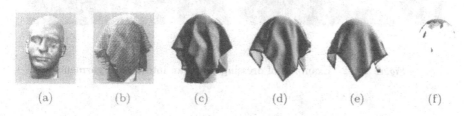

Figure 10.11 (a) The object, (b) over which a piece of cloth was draped, (c) the smooth shaded surface of the range data, (d) the result of approximation with a 50×50 model, (e) and 25×25 model; and (f) estimated shape of the supporting object, determined from the 25×25 model.

contains part of the nose of the underlying head (Fig. 10.11(a)) because the cloth sample was touching the nose at that point.

4.3 SYNTHESIS AND ANALYSIS OF DRESSED HUMANS

The rectangular cloth piece model can easily be extended to a more complex garment model [8]. Examples of dressing a real human into a virtual T-shirt are given in Fig. 10.12. The T-shirt was positioned above the body model in the virtual space and allowed to drape over it using a fast collision detection and handling algorithm [8]. Then, the seaming forces were applied to merge the front and back pieces along the seam lines. Finally, a fabric texture and textile print design were applied on the cloth model surface and combined with smooth-shading.

In the last experiment, we used the physics-based cloth model to analyze the range data of a doll dressed into a simple T-shirt-like garment. The topological model and the size of the T-shirt were known in advance. The dressed doll was imaged from several angles using a stereo pair of cameras and a structured light source. The range data was interpolated and used as an input to the cloth drape analysis algorithm in

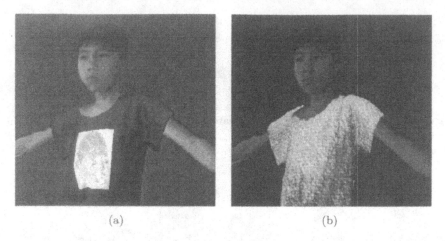

(a)   (b)

Figure 10.12   Examples of dressing a human into virtual garments

Fig. 10.5. In Fig. 10.13 we show the registered crude T-shirt model and the estimated contact points (in blue). In Fig. 10.14(a), we show the total range data available; (b) the range data that was kept after discarding the data corresponding to the non-contact points of the T-shirt model; (c) the final reconstruction using the selected range data, as well as the proper contour information. Finally, in (d) the 3-D reconstruction obtained from the images of the naked doll is given for comparison. Note that the legs of the doll were visible in all images (though not shown in the images in Fig. 10.13), and that for the reconstruction (c) the contours of all uncovered body parts were used, as well as the image contours corresponding to the parts that were estimated as contact points.

Interestingly, even crude models with sub-optimal model parameters can relatively successfully be used for detection of major cloth support points. The contact forces are usually considerably stronger than the internal bending forces, and thus, at the contact points, the equilibrium equation is violated for a wide range of parameters. This means that in the analysis algorithm, only a single iteration of model draping and contact point estimation is necessary for this purpose.

5.   CONCLUSIONS

We presented techniques for building realistic human body models from images. These models can be dressed into virtual garments, whose draping is simulated by a physics-based cloth model. Furthermore, we

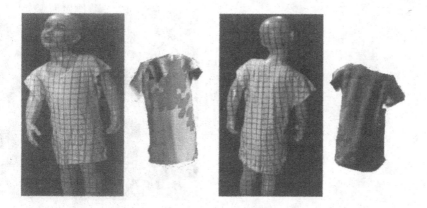

Figure 10.13   Registration of a T-shirt model and estimation of contact points

demonstrate how such cloth models can be used to analyze the draping behavior of real cloth, and even for analysis of images of dressed humans.

In the first part of this chapter we have developed a method for reconstructing multiple occluding objects or multi-part self-occluding objects by integrating occluding contours and stereo (possibly aided by structured light) within the deformable bodies framework. We applied the algorithm on 3-D reconstruction of human bodies. The reconstructed models can be texture-mapped using the texture from all available images.

Our method does not require a particular camera configuration and makes no assumptions about the type of the projected patterns, as long as the feature detectors are available. Stereo matching is guided by the surface estimate from occluding contours, so the grid does not need to be labeled, and in fact, if there is a sufficient number of features on the object, structured light is not even necessary. We are also working on making the purely passive stereo applicable for body reconstruction using our camera configurations with very wide baselines.

In the future, we plan to address the problem of "gluing" the object parts together where necessary. Fuzzy force assignment already helps by allowing partial overlaps, which can be seen in the case of legs in Fig. 10.7 , and the arms in Fig. 10.6. However, the parts may not always connect to each other (as in the case of the arms in lower right figure in Fig. 10.7). In such cases, to make the reconstruction complete, it may be necessary to include additional superquadrics, for example the 'shoulders' superquadric in Fig. 10.14 (d).

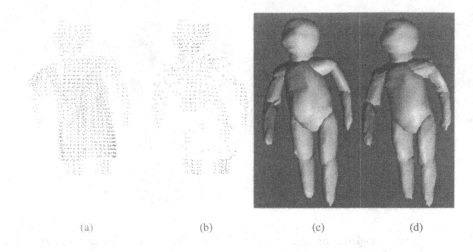

(a)   (b)   (c)   (d)

Figure 10.14   Segmentation of the range data and the 3-D reconstruction of the doll

Our vision-based algorithm for analysis of cloth draping offers an alternative to using the expensive Kawabata Evaluation System for estimating cloth model parameters. Furthermore, the algorithm is model independent and it offers a way to evaluate the quality of a cloth model for simulating draping behavior, which could be useful for design and testing cloth modeling techniques.

The last experiment demonstrates the feasibility of utilizing cloth models for dressed human analysis. While this technique is not necessary for automatic body measurements, as a subject can be imaged without unnecessary clothing, it can be very useful for automatization of the re-imaging technique mentioned in the introduction, or for combining natural and synthetic content in special effects in movies. Since the detection of the garment-body contact points helps reveal the geometry of the body underneath the clothing, we believe that the methods described in this chapter can be extended to analysis of the dressed human motion, and we hope to inspire further research in this direction.

Other research in our laboratory has focused on vision-based tracking of articulated human motion [13] as well as face and hands modeling and tracking in images (visit our web site www.ifp.uiuc.edu) which should eventually result in detailed human models animated by the output of a vision-based motion capture system. Potential applications of our research include realistic avatars in telepresence applications, virtual garment shops, virtual battleground, and more natural human-computer interfaces.

Acknowledgments

The authors were supported by the National Science Foundation (grant IRI-9634618) and the Army Research Laboratory under Cooperative Agreement No. DAAL01-96-2-0003. A part of this project was performed in collaboration with Helen Shen's group at the Hong Kong University of Science and Technology.

References

[1] G. Borgefors. Distance transformations in arbitrary dimensions. *Computer Vision, Graphics, and Image Processing*, 27:321–345, 1984.

[2] D. E. Breen, D. H. House, and M. J. Wozny. Predicting the drape of woven cloth using interacting particles. In *Proceedings of SIGGRAPH'94*, pages 365–372, 1994.

[3] M. Carignan, Y. Yang, N. Magnenat Thalmann, and D. Thalmann. Dressing animated synthetic actors with complex deformable clothes. In *Proceedings of SIGGRAPH'92*, pages 99–104, 1992.

[4] http://www.cdi-u4ia.com/cdifiles/u4prem.html.

[5] J. R. Collier, B. J. Collier, G. O'Toole, and S. M. Sargand. Drape prediction by means of finite element analysis. *Journal of the Textile Institute*, 82(1):96–107, 1991.

[6] B. Eberhardt, A. Weber, and W. Strasser. A fast, flexible particle-system model for cloth draping. *IEEE Computer Graphics and Applications*, 16(5):52–59, 1996.

[7] J. Gu. *3D reconstruction of sculptured objects*. PhD thesis, Hong Kong University of Science and Technology, 1998.

[8] N. Jojić. Computer modeling, analysis and synthesis of dressed humans. Master's thesis, University of Illinois at Urbana-Champaign, 1997.

[9] N. Jojić, J. Gu, I. Mak, H. Shen, and T. S. Huang. Computer modeling, analysis and synthesis of dressed humans. In *Proc. IEEE Conf. on Computer Vision and Pattern Recognition (CVPR'98)*, pages 528–534, June 1998.

[10] N. Jojić, J. Gu, H. Shen, and T. S. Huang. Computer modeling, analysis and synthesis of dressed humans. *IEEE Transactions on Circuits and Systems for Video Technology*, 9(2):378–388, 1999.

[11] N. Jojić and T. S. Huang. On analysis of the range data of cloth drapes. In *Proceedings of 3rd Asian Conference on Computer Vision (ACCV'98)*, pages 463–470, Jan. 1998.

[12] N. Jojić, Y. Rui, Y. Zhuang, and T. S. Huang. A framework for garment shopping over the Internet. In M. Shaw et al., editors, *Handbook on Electronic Commerce*, pages 249–270. Springer Verlag, 2000.

[13] N. Jojić, M. Turk, and T. S. Huang. Tracking articulated objects in dense disparity maps. In *Proc. Intl. Conference on Computer Vision (ICCV'99)*, pages 123–130, June 1998.

[14] I. Kakadiaris and D. Metaxas. Model-based estimation of 3D human motion with occlusion based on active multi-viewpoint selection. In *Proceedings 1996 IEEE Computer Society Conference on Computer Vision and Pattern Recognition*, pages 81–7, 1996.

[15] I. A. Kakadiaris. *Motion-based part segmentation, shape and motion estimation of complex multi-part objects: Application to human body tracking*. PhD thesis, University of Pennsylvania, Philadelphia, PA, 1996.

[16] D. Metaxas and D. Terzopoulos. Shape and nonrigid motion estimation through physics-based synthesis. *IEEE Transaction on Pattern Analysis and Machine Intelligence*, 15(6):580–91, 1993.

[17] http://www.monarchcad.com/rend.htm.

[18] H. N. Ng and R. L. Grimsdale. Computer graphics techniques for modeling cloth. *IEEE Computer Graphics and Applications*, 16(5):28–41, 1996.

[19] H. N. Ng, R. L. Grimsdale, and W. G. Allen. A system for modeling and visualization of cloth material. *Computer Graphics*, 19(3):423–430, 1995.

[20] W. H. Press, S. A. Teukolsky, W. T. Vetterling, and B. P. Flannery. *Numerical Recipes in C: The Art of Scientific Computation*. Cambridge University Press, 1995.

[21] D. Terzopoulos and D. Metaxas. Dynamic 3D models with local and global deformations: Deformable superquadrics. *IEEE Transactions on Pattern Analysis and Machine Intelligence*, 13(7):703–14, 1991.

[22] D. Terzopoulos, J. Platt, A. Barr, and K. Fleischer. Elastically deformable models. In *Proceedings of SIGGRAPH'87*, pages 205–214, 1987.

[23] D. Terzopoulos, A. Witkin, and M. Kass. Constraints on deformable models: Recovering 3D shape and nonrigid motion. *Artificial Intelligence*, 36(1):91–123, 1988.

[24] Y. F. Wang and J. K. Aggarwal. Integration of active and passive sensing techniques for representing three-dimensional objects. *IEEE Transactions on Robotics and Automation*, 5(4):460–71, 1989.

Chapter 11

URBAN SITE MODELS: ACCURATE, DETAILED, RAPID AND INEXPENSIVE

Franz W. Leberl, Konrad Karner, Markus Maresch

Abstract

Three-dimensional computer models of urban areas have become the latest topic of discussion in photogrammetric circles, although the production of such models has long been a standard offering of photogrammetric data providers. Initial "killer applications" of such data have been in defense organizations to support military operations in urban terrain (MOUT), and in the Telecom industry in their optimization of certain communications networks that depend on line-of-sight analyses in urban environments. Other applications are trailing behind these trailblazing needs.

The issues today are cost, accuracy, detail, throughput and manageability of data. This paper therefore ignores the discussion of principles of image information extraction. Instead we are concerned with work flow in the production of such data as they concern the actual creation of data sets with perhaps half a million buildings of one metropolitan area. The challenge is to create this at modest budgets, at tight schedules, and with verified accuracy and detail.

1. INTRODUCTION

The primary role of terrain data and maps of the land have not changed with the transition from the strictly 2-dimensional representation on paper maps and in the initial digital geographic data bases to the 3-dimensional renderings on computer monitors. The primary purpose was and is the support of the human navigator, planner, user of the land and explorer of its riches.

The creation of such maps and data has always included the third dimension; had it not, the maps and data would have been distorted by the effect of the vertical dimension on the planimetric representation and positioning of objects. Photogrammetry has, since its inception at the

A. Leonardis et al. (eds.), Confluence of Computer Vision and Computer Graphics, 201–214.

turn of this century, seen the world with its 3 dimensions, and always modeled, to this day, its objects in their 3, sometimes even 4 dimensions. The most radical effect of the transition from the 2-D maps and GIS to 3-D data has not been in the modeling of the objects or the creation of the data, but in the storing and rendering of such data.

The idea of 3-D models of urban areas was initially discussed in the context of Military Operations in Urban Terrain (also denoted as "MOUT", see publications in the context of the Image Understanding Workshops, for example [16,25], and in academic environments [2,4,10,13]. Very recent telecommunications developments in Broadband Wireless Access need line-of-sight analyses from one building top to another, and this has created a market for 3-D building models (Fig. 11.1; see [14,22]).

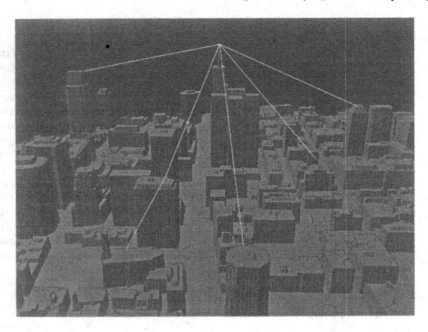

Figure 11.1 Example of a telecom-type urban site model for line-of-sight analyses for the so-called Local Multipoint Distribution System (LMDS). The example is from downtown Montreal, showing Place-Ville-Marie. The suggested "lines-of-sight" represent broadband wireless access communications.

From a consideration of photogrammetric technology it is self-evident that urban 3-D data have been produced since a long time, using traditional photogrammetric means. In fact, architectural applications were at the root of the creation of the field of photogrammetry, and even the word "photogrammetry" was coined by M. Meydenbauer, an architect at the end of the 1800s and user of 3-D building data in Berlin.

New are thus the computer graphics aspects that have created innovations which now support the use and application of vast quantities of 3-dimensional urban building data (see for example [5,11]). As a result, the focus of discussions may preferably be on dealing with, and creating an application for, large quantities of such data. Key concepts are work flow, quality control, efficiency and automation to achieve cost advantages, data retrieval and visualization using varying levels of detail and organizational concepts, and trade-offs between geometric detail versus information contained in photographic textures.

2.   SOURCE DATA

2.1   AERIAL PHOTOGRAPHY

Aerial photography is the overwhelmingly used source of urban site models [6,7,15]. This is the straight forward extension of traditional photogrammetry. The scales of standard photography, its overlaps, the use and role of color versus black & white material are at times items for discussions. However, it is the traditional standard of 60% forward and 30% sidelap photography that serve as primary input to urban modeling.

2.2   SCANNING LASER

Laser scanning is currently considered as an alternative to aerial photography [8,17]. There is no other consideration than that of cost that leads one to deviate from photos and propose the use of lasers. A scanning laser and video camera combine into a single pass 3-dimensional data collection and photo texturing system. Generally, however, the advantages of this approach have not yet been demonstrated with sufficient clarity to make it replace the use of imagery. And as soon as aerial photography needs to be collected anyway, one may question the added value received in return for the added cost for the scanning laser data.

2.3   INTERFEROMETRIC SYNTHETIC APERTURE RADAR

Interferometric radar imagery has begun to get consideration as a primary source for building models. At image resolutions of 30 cm to 10 cm per radar image pixel, and with the benefits of the single pass, autonomous measurements of 3-D shape by means of interferometry, radar may gain in importance for this application (Fig. 11.2). At this time, however, there is hardly any research to develop such autonomous modeling and texturing systems.

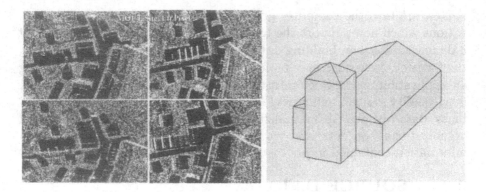

Figure 11.2 Example of a building reconstruction based on high-resolution, taken from 4 flight lines (left). Shown is the church in the village, as marked in the four images. The SAR images are at a resolution of 30 cm per pixel, and the reconstruction (right) has an uncertainty of about 1 meter.

2.4   DATA COLLECTION FROM THE GROUND AND INSIDE A BUILDING

At issue is of course also the detail of buildings both concerning their outside features such as skylights, chimneys, windows, doors or other structures, as well as their inside. This has led to various ideas for efficient source data collections with linear array and digital frame cameras, with indoor imaging and laser scanning systems, again combined with video cameras for autonomous 3D and phototexturing.

3.   WORK FLOW ISSUES

3.1   THREE MAJOR PROCESSING FUNCTION BLOCKS

A system to build urban site models consists of three major components, each of which consumes about an equal part of the overall resources required:

1. Aerial photogrammetry subsystem;

2. Bulk processing for digital canopy elevation modeling;

3. Manual refinements for building geometry extraction.

All three components are very well established capabilities with a high degree of technological maturity. Many hundreds of commercial companies are currently able technologically to apply these components to create urban site models. At issue is thus not whether one can create such data, but how inexpensively, how accurately, how reliably. This is where automation is at issue.

However, automation is already a standard in many of the work flow elements. Aerial photography gets scanned and submitted to aerial triangulation, producing the geometric foundation on which the urban site models are built. Stereo matching then follows as a mature technology, and very little gain is being expected from additional automation in the creation of canopy Digital Elevation Models (DEMs).

3.2   REFINEMENT OF BUILDING MODELS

The aspects of actually producing the geometric building models are the "last frontier" at which the opportunity exists for significant gains in productivity and thus in a reduction of cost. However, this still addresses no more than a third of the entire work flow. Manual interaction with the digital sources addresses both the initial creation of building polygons as well as the control of the quality of the resulting data. Many authors have consistently argued that the human operator just be in the loop in this data extraction and quality assurance component of the work flow, and as a result have developed strategies for data extraction that have the computer support the human, instead of having a fully autonomous data processing strategy followed by a manual editing effort.

3.3   BUILDING DETAILS

Modeling the insides of buildings and the architectural details on the outside of buildings have their separate technological challenges. Ground based imagery is much less well structured in comparison to aerial imagery, and there is no photogrammetric tradition to deal with such ground based data sources. As a result the work flow for the use of such images is less well developed and more opportunities exist to develop and study new methods for data extraction from such images, as will be discussed later.

3.4   HUMAN STEREO VERSUS MONOPLOTTING

Traditionally, photogrammetry has made a strong case in favor of consistent stereoscopic viewing and measuring on specialized stereo equipment. Recently this view has been challenged, for example by Englert and Gülch [1] or Spradley and Welch [24]. A much more "scalable" interactive process results when it is based on monocular viewing, but a machine supports the augmentation of the monocularly collected 2-D data into the 3-D domain. Interesting work flow issues result: what really is the human contribution to the image analysis task? Is the man-machine system capable of creating an equally effective product without regard to the way the human operator works—monocularly or in stereo?

These questions currently have no clear answer, however, in the Urban Site Modeling debate, monocular human interaction has found a valuable role that reduces cost, creates scalability of procedures, and in the process does not compromise the result.

4.   THE USE OF IMAGE MATCHING

4.1   CANOPY DEM

Matching is the classical approach to create a so-called "canopy DEM". The reflective surface as seen in aerial photography will be modeled by simply finding as dense a set of surface points as is reasonable, and using for that either regular stereo overlaps, or exploiting multiple overlaps involving more than 2 stereo photographs.

4.2   MONOCULAR MAN-MACHINE SYSTEM

Matching has a second role to play by assigning a third dimension to the 2-dimensional data collected by a human in a monocularly interactive man-machine environment.

By identifying the buildings in one image (2-D polygons), one of the most critical parts of computer vision, the segmentation, is solved by the human operator. This information combines with a rough bald Earth or so-called canopy DEM and the exterior orientation of the aerial images to calculate the 3-D roof line of buildings in the following way:

- Assuming that the roof line of a building lies in the horizontal plane, we can calculate a mask (see Fig. 11.3), to show the areas used for image matching in white areas. The mask is calculated by using the outline of the building and a given inflation and deflation factor. By employing several tests on different data sets, we optimized the inflation and deflation factors, separately for large and small polygons.

- Using the position of a currently considered building in the image in which it was monocularly defined (thus still a 2-D polygon) and the DEM we get an estimate of the elevation of a building. Furthermore, we use the information of a maximum building height in an area of interest or in a town—which is easy to find out—and

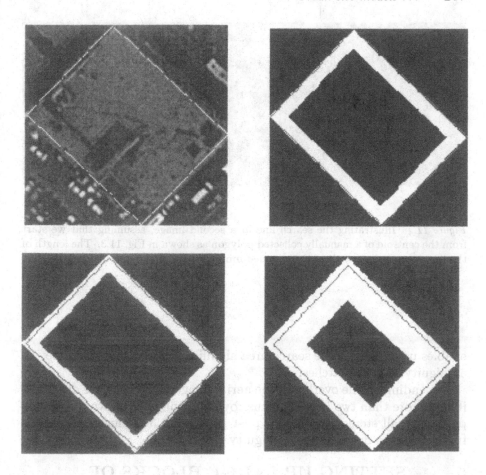

Figure 11.3 Illustrating the matching areas to assign an elevation to a polygon collected in one image, and the role of inflation and deflation parameters. The manually collected input is shown in the upper left image; the upper right image presents one assumed parameter set for the inflation and deflation values, and other parameters are shown in the two lower images.

a tolerance depending on the quality of the DEM. We can restrict the search area for a stereo match by means of the minimum and maximum height and thus the search areas are limited in all images that cover a building (see Fig. 11.4).

The process starts with the largest polygons and proceeds down to the smallest ones, using inside/outside tests to decide whether we are considering polygons in an urban or downtown area. This knowledge

Figure 11.4 Illustrating the search line in a second image, assuming that we start from the centroid of a manually collected polygon as shown in Fig. 11.3. The length of the line segment is a result of the assumed minimum and maximum building heights.

enables us to restrict the search area significantly and thus decrease the ambiguity of false matches.

Depending on the overlap of the aerial images, polygons are often visible in more than two images. Thus, by employing the above mentioned process to all stereo pairs and a post processing 3-D clustering, one is further able to decrease the ambiguity.

5.   SETTING UP LARGE BLOCKS OF IMAGERY

5.1   CLASSICAL AERIAL PHOTOGRAMMETRY

Mature procedures exist to deal with many 1,000 aerial photographs and set them up geometrically so that individual overlaps can then be exploited for optimum accuracy. Since such images taken from the air follow some very strict rules of flight lines and standardized overlaps, it has become a standard to set up such blocks of images with a great degree of automation.

The determination of relative orientations between aerial images, the identification of common points and finally the calculation of the exterior orientation is a well-known process for aerial images. Furthermore a fairly simple geometry and global positioning systems support these procedures.

5.2 INSIDES OF BUILDINGS AND GROUND BASED IMAGES

Modeling the insides of a building may be based on 10,000 digital images that need to be geometrically linked together and put into a consistent geometric framework. Because ground based imaging, and the insides of buildings, are subject to vagaries absent in aerial imaging, the task is harder to automate.

An approach has to be chosen for ground based images which are used for facade modeling and extraction of detailed features not visible by aerial images. A generally higher depth variance in images, oblique views, repetitive patterns (windows, man-made structures) and therefore ambiguity make it a more challenging task for automation than is the case in aerial photogrammetry.

We have developed procedures to automate the analytic phase for ground based facade images and are able to reduce human effort to about 5%, compared with the prior fully manual process. Our method is based on "video-like" image sequences with high overlap ($\leq 75\%$, see also Maresch [18]). This requirement seems to be justified with the recent dramatic drop in camera and disc storage prices. Some of the frames are used for point transfer only.

The process is based on standard cross correlation based image matching as described in standard texts on image processing, for example by Gonzalez and Woods [3], and supported by high and low level feature extraction [19,23], and relative orientation algorithms to verify and qualify match candidates [9,12].

The simultaneous employment of completely different strategies in most sub-tasks of this process and the use of matching and the calculation of the relative orientation yield a reliable tool. Human effort is reduced to quality control and the throughput for the analytic phase was increased by a factor of 10 to 20 using this method over a purely manual process. About 1 minute of processing time is budgeted per image pair.

6. EXTRACTING DETAILS OF BUILDING FACADES

So far, building models were simply understood to be "lego-boxes". This, of course, is entirely satisfactory for many applications that deal with line-of-sight issues such as those in Telecom. However, when buildings themselves are the object of interest, then one is concerned with doors, windows, escape routes, chimneys and so forth. Such details are costly to collect by hand and efforts are being made to produce such building details with machine support.

Figure 11.5 Example of an automatic relative orientation of a pair of overlapping terrestrial photographs using a large number of candidate points in each of two images, and pruning the candidates for correspondence to fit a legitimate relative orientation.

The source of such information is ground-based imagery. We are using an approach for modeling 3-D building facades that is similar to the one explained in sub-section 4.2. The human operator again is working monoscopically in one image only and the 3-D information is calculated automatically by image matching employing geometry-based restrictions (e.g. conics) using other images, showing the same part of the object. In the modeling process pre-calculated features like corners, lines, conics and splines are used. The user is able to select and edit these features as well as to define new features, which might not be found in the pre-processing due to weak edges or peculiarities. Thus again, the critical part is the segmentation and it is solved by the human operator by only selecting different kinds of features and combining them to surface facets.

We use well known matching techniques for different kinds of features. The point matching algorithm works similarly to the one explained in sub-section 4.2. For line features we are using a slightly modified approach of Schmid and Zisserman [21]. Conics are calculated without calculating cross correlation. We use the approach of Quam [20], with an additional 3-D clustering, however only if more than 2 images are available, so that one reduces ambiguities. A result is illustrated in Figs. 11.6 and 11.7.

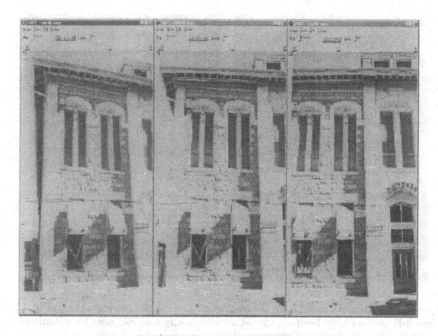

Figure 11.6 Example of a facade shown in three photographs, in which various features have been found.

7.   WHERE WILL THIS LEAD?

The Telecom industry has charged ahead with its requirement for line-of sight-analyses, and has embarked on massive projects to model all major metropolitan areas on the globe. Specifications vary, and such data may not be reusable unless they satisfy specifications for applications other than the planning for hubs of broadband wireless access systems. In Canada, Telecom employs data of all buildings, elsewhere the focus is on business and commercial buildings only. The Canadian concept leads to data sets, say for Montreal, with up to 1,000 buildings per km^2, and about 0.5 million for the area of interest. Unfortunately, Telecom's interest is only for the densest regions of any city, and therefore its data sets may have large holes in the less densely populated segments of urban areas. As a result, the Telecom-inspired efforts may have to be augmented to be useful for other applications.

There is little doubt that at the current cost of producing such data, the 3-dimensional building data will become as ubiquitous as the 2-D GIS currently is. There are no cost reasons not to go forward with this. A large city like Montreal may have 400,000 buildings scattered over a core area of 400 km^2. At a cost of US\$ 200 per km^2, it would be a

Figure 11.7 Lines extracted from the overlapping terrestrial photographs in Fig. 11.6. These 3-D vectors have been computed automatically and can now be submitted to a machine-supported manual editing and clean-up procedure.

modest expense of US$ 80,000 to model all of the buildings of Montreal in 3-D!

The texturing of the buildings is another issue. While the aerial photography will automatically, and almost at no additional cost, produce a texture for all horizontal or near-horizontal surfaces, this is not true for the vertical walls of buildings. These textures will need to be separately produced. Once this has been accomplished, the issue may arise concerning the geometric detail of each building versus the information contained in the photographic texture. These issues will move into the foreground once the basic data sets have come into existence.

References

[1] R. Englert and E. Gülch. One Eye Stereo System for the Acquisition of Complex 3D Building Description. *GIS*, 4:16–21, 1996.

[2] C. Fuchs. *OEEPE Survey on 3D City Models*. Inst. für Photogrammetrie, University of Bonn, Bonn, 1997.

[3] R. Gonzalez and R. Woods. *Digital Image Processing*, Chapter: Matching by correlation, pp. 583, Addison Wesley, 1993.

[4] M. Gruber, S. Meissl and R. Böhm Das dreidimensionale digitale Stadtmodell Wien. Erfahrungen aus einer Vorstudie. *VGI (Austrian J. of Surveying and Geoinformation)*, pp. 29–36, 1995.

[5] M. Gruber, M. Kofler and F. Leberl. Managing large 3D Urban Data Base Contents supporting Phototexture and Levels of Detail. *Proceedings of the Ascona Workshop 97, Automatic Extraction of Man-Made Objects from Aerial and Space Images*, pages 377–386, Birkhäuser Verlag, Basel, 1997.

[6] A. Grün. Generierung und Visualisierung von 3D Stadtmodellen. *Proc. IAPR TC 7 Workshop, Graz*, OCG-Schriftenreihe, R. Oldenburg Verlag, Wien-München, pages 183–196, 1996.

[7] A. Grün , O. Kübler, and P. Agouris. Extraction of Man-Made Objects from Aerial and Space Images. *Proc. of two meetings held at Ascona, Switzerland.* Published by Birkhäuser-Verlag, Basel, 1995 and 1997 (393 pages).

[8] N. Haala. *Building Detection by Fusion of Range and Image Data*, ZPF, 5/1994, Karlsruhe, 1994.

[9] R. I. Hartley, I. Richard. In Defense of the Eight-Point Algorithm. *IEEE Transactions on Pattern Analysis and Machine Intelligence*, 19(6):580–593, 1997.

[10] O. Henricsson, A. Streilein,and A. Grün. Automated 3D Reconstruction of Buildings and Visualization of City Models. *Proceedings of the OEEPE Workshop on 3D-City Models, Inst. für Photogrammetrie, Univ. Bonn, Germany*, paper No. 16 (16 pages), 1996.

[11] M. Kofler, H. Rehatschek, and M. Gruber. A Database for a 3D GIS for Urban Environments Supporting Photo-Realistic Visualization. *Intl. Archives of ISPRS*, Vol. XXXI, Part B2, Comm. III, pp. 198–202, 1996.

[12] K. Kraus. *Photogrammetry*, Vol I, Dümmler, Bonn, Chapter: "Common orientation of the two photographs", pp. 121, 1993.

[13] F. Lang and W. Förstner. *Surface Reconstruction of Man-Made Objects Using Polymorphic Mid Level Features and Generic Scene Knowledge*, ZPF 6/96, Karlsruhe, pages 193–201, 1996.

[14] A. Loffet. 3D-Models for Telecommunication – Methods and Experiences. *Proceedings of the OEEPE Workshop on 3D-City Models*, Inst. für Photogrammetrie, Univ. Bonn, Germany, paper No. 7 (9 pages), 1996.

[15] F. Leberl, R. Kalliany, and M. Gruber (editors). Man-Made Objects from Aerial and Space Imagery. *Special Issue, ISPRS J. on Photogrammetry and Remote Sensing*, 53(2), 1998.

[16] G. Lukes (editor). *Proc. Image Understanding Workshop, 20-23 November 1998, Monterey, California.* Morgan Kaufmann Publishers Inc., San Francisco, 1999.

[17] H. Maitre. Fusion and Optimization. In A. Pinz (Ed.), *Proceedings of the 20th Workshop of the ÖAGM/AAPR, Leibnitz, Austria,* pages 11-26, 1996.

[18] M. Maresch. *The FotoG matcher.* Internal publication of Vexcel Corp. Boulder, CO, 1998.

[19] M. Maresch. *The FotoG Feature Extraction.* Memorandum, Vexcel Corp. Boulder, Colorado, 1998.

[20] L. Quam. Conic Reconstruction and Correspondence from two Views. *IEEE Transactions on Pattern Analysis and Machine Intelligence,* 18(2):151–160, 1996.

[21] C. Schmid and A. Zisserman. *Automatic Line Matching across Views.* Technical Report, University of Oxford, 1997.

[22] E. Siebe. Requirements of 3D-City Structure Data from the View Point of a Radio Network Service. *Proceedings of the OEEPE Workshop on 3D-City Models,* Institut für Photogrammetrie, Univ. Bonn, Germany, paper No. 5 (6 pages), 1996.

[23] S. M. Smith and J. M. Brady. SUSAN—A New Approach to Low Level Image Processing. *International Journal of Computer Vision,* 23(1):45–78, 1997.

[24] H. Spradley and R. Welch. PC-Based Construction and Visualization of 3D Urban Databases (oral presentation). *ASPRS Annual Convention, Portland, Oregon, May 17-21,* 1999.

[25] T. Strat (ed.). *Proc. Image Understanding Workshop, 11-14 May 1997 in New Orleans,* Morgan Kaufmann Publishers Inc., San Francisco, 1997.

Chapter 12

MEDICAL VISUALISATION, BIOMECHANICS, FIGURE ANIMATION AND ROBOT TELEOPERATION: THEMES AND LINKS

Gordon J. Clapworthy, Igor R. Belousov, Alexander Savenko, Wei Sun, JiaCheng Tan, Serge L. Van Sint Jan

Abstract   The relatively-unconnected areas of medical visualisation, biomechanics, figure animation and robot teleoperation are considered, and relationships between the fields are identified. Influences of computer imaging on the computer graphics content are described, as is assistance provided in the opposite direction.

1.   INTRODUCTION

In its early days, what constituted computer graphics was relatively clear. An image was generated by the use of software, and at that point the process stopped. Over the years, as a variety of technologies merged with computer graphics and computer animation, so what was computer graphics and what not became much less distinct. For example, it is not uncommon to find papers on sound or haptic interfaces and tactile feedback [2, 28, 32] being presented at computer graphics conferences. With the advent of image-based rendering [7, 13, 19, 27], existing two-dimensional images, from whatever source, were used to create a three-dimensional scene. Motion capture has matured considerably and is now the major means of animating faces and articulated figures [11, 16]. Laser-based capture of objects has reduced the need for a graphics-based approach to modelling three-dimensional objects. And there are many other examples of how advances in other technologies have had a major impact on the way in which computer graphics images are created.

The Computer Graphics & Modelling Group at De Montfort University has interests in a number of areas. Although the focus is firmly

A. Leonardis et al. (eds.), Confluence of Computer Vision and Computer Graphics, 215–228.

on computer graphics, the use of images is central to a number of the projects and, although at first sight, they appear to be radically different, several areas of overlap can be identified.

2.   MEDICAL VISUALISATION AND BIOMECHANICS

For many years, the two-dimensional images produced for radiologists by Computed Tomography (CT) and Magnetic Resonance Imaging (MRI) have been used to create three-dimensional scenes for viewing either by surface or, more recently, volume visualisation. Surfaces rendering normally uses the Marching Cubes Algorithm [25] or one of its variants. Segmentation, in which the various components of the structure are separated, can be a problem for complex anatomical structures.

The combination of rapidly-decreasing hardware costs and improving rendering techniques has increased the demand for volumetric rendering [23, 24] which, though computationally more demanding than surface-based methods, is also much more versatile.

One of the problems with CT and MRI images is that they are static data. The installations that collect them are expensive, large and immobile. This makes it difficult to use the available data for cases in which movement is important, for example, orthopaedics. So, while joint kinematics and joint disease are frequently closely related, it can be difficult to identify the problems by non-invasive diagnostic techniques.

Some researchers have created models of the bones in the joint of an individual from radiological data and attempted to animate the model using what they felt was appropriate kinematic data. The difficulty in employing this approach in a clinical situation is that knowledge of the precise individual characteristics of that person's movement and their effect on the joint are important to the clinician in making his diagnosis.

Van Sint Jan et al [21] have recently developed a system for combining radiological and kinematic data of the same patient, so that accurate demonstrations of the joint movement for that patient can be viewed.

Standard reconstruction techniques produce a 3D surface model of the bones of the joint from the radiological data. The user positions virtual markers on the surface of each bone in this model, wherever suitable anatomical markers are found. This is performed on the image of the model using the mouse-driven screen cursor.

The landmarks are any bony features that can be repeatedly localised in all the datasets analysed. During this process, the bones can have standard 3D transformations applied to allow viewing from any direction so that the best landmarks are identified.

An electrogoniometer is attached to the joint in question to record its full (six-degrees-of-freedom) movement in three-dimensions. This is fed into the joint model built from radiological scans of the joint. The reference frame for the goniometer is aligned with the reference frame for the joint.

Thus, an accurate animation of the bones of the joint can take place, reasons for the discomfort experienced by the patient can be identified, and suitable remedial treatment can be diagnosed.

In certain joints, combined motion is highly significant. During joint rotation, one bone moves around the surface of the other. The surfaces of the bones are not regular or symmetric, and the bones are constrained in their movements by the actions of ligaments and the synovial capsule. Thus, the concept of a simple hinge joint is, for many applications, a gross oversimplification; nevertheless, it is one that is almost universally used outside clinical biomechanics.

The results obtained in the current work concerning the functional anatomy of the knee are already challenging classical thinking. The way in which the instant axis of rotation of the joint changes during motion is illustrated in Figure 12.1.

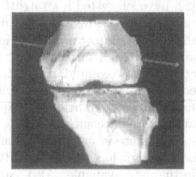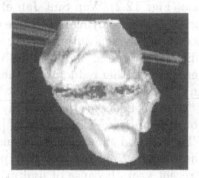

Figure 12.1 Frames from the animation of a human knee. The lines indicate the positions of the instant axes of rotations at previous frames.

For the first time we have accurate kinematics data together with accurate morphological data of the same joint. More examples from a range of subjects have to be analysed before we can judge how general the current findings are.

By pre-processing the radiological images, it is also possible to use knowledge of the morphological structure of bones to simplify the models produced by segmentation without losing information. Conventional segmentation techniques employed on the radiological slices of a bone in order to create a three-dimensional model of its surface produce an excessive number of polygons. These are conventionally reduced to manageable numbers by decimation [34], though this is a process that loses some surface detail.

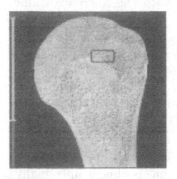 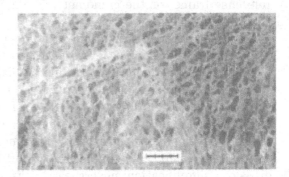

Figure 12.2 Spongy bone contains trabeculea which are small cavities within the spongy bone. On the enlarged image, a 4mm scale is shown.

Many of these polygons are interior to the bone because of its morphology—they are associated with the trabeculea which exists within spongy bone (Fig. 12.2). Van Sint Jan et al. [22] have suggested a straightforward way of employing knowledge of bone structure, to remove these unnecessary polygons automatically and thus create simpler models which, unlike decimated models, still fully retain the required surface detail. If, thereafter, further reduction in the polygon count is required, decimation can still take place but it will not be necessary to apply it as vigorously.

"Lean" models are particularly useful in Internet transfer [8], rapid prototyping [10], Virtual Reality [12] and telepresence surgery [31].

The method shows great promise for clinical use in orthopaedics and other areas. It is thought that prosthesis design has progressed little in recent years because of limitations in the data available. Also, early prosthesis failure is probably caused by poor modelling, again usually the result of insufficient or inexact data. The availability of good morphological and kinematic data of the same patient will address this fundamental problem.

However, the method has the drawback that it is dependent upon the use of the three-dimensional goniometer, which is somewhat intrusive, but it is vital that the recording of the patient's movements is accurate, as clinical decisions will be based upon it.

The extension of the model to deal with whole-limb data is seen to be an urgent priority. It is impractical to use the goniometer on several joints of the same limb. However, current motion-capture techniques, as employed in the animation industry, do not have sufficient accuracy as they are associated with capturing external data and the skin can stretch considerably during the motion of a joint. The development of a highly-accurate, non-intrusive motion capture system for use in this context is a challenge for the future.

3.   FIGURE ANIMATION

The biomechanics results concerning joint motion have implications about the form of joints adopted within the models conventionally used in figure animation. Figure animation has inherited joint models from robotics that are mathematically convenient but not anatomically correct.

Robotics normally assumes a single-degree-of-freedom (sdof) joint, which is well suited to precision-machined parts. Multiple-degree-of-freedom joints are constructed from several sdof joints joined by dimensionless and mass-less links. Thus, motion of the joint is represented by successive rotations about the orthogonal axis system associated with the proximal link. This is the fundamental model used throughout figure animation, [1, 14, 37]. It is not clear that it is well suited to the anatomical characteristics of most real-life joints.

Combined motions [20] are functionally important and they provide the smooth aspect of most joint motions. They have two main characteristics:

- they have limited amplitude (in general),

- they occur subconsciously.

In some joints, combined motion is not highly significant. However, that is not the case with the knee; here, the bones are complex and asymmetric and there is a system of ligaments which produces quite complicated motion (Fig. 12.3). In full flexion, the secondary motion of the knee is about $15°$.

The axis of knee flexion is inclined at an angle to that which the simplified model would use, and changes throughout the movement. This may explain why knee movement in computer-generated figures often appears inaccurate.

Given the critical position of the knee in the kinematic chain of a moving figure, it is clear that accurate modelling of the knee is important to the "look" of any animation. Savenko et al. [33] have created a model for knee motion using biomechanical principles and will be extending this to a full figure in order to address these problems.

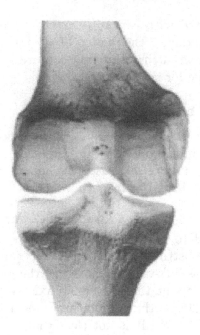

Figure 12.3   The articulating surfaces of the knee

The complications in such an approach are clear: the joint rotation no longer takes place about pre-configured orthogonal axes, and it changes as the movement progresses.

The knee is also capable of abduction/adduction, but these are not currently being investigated. For atypical gaits (bow-legged or knock-kneed), it is likely that the biomechanical model will be even more beneficial than in a "standard" gait.

A number of researchers have attempted to use dynamics [18, 35, 36] as a basis for figure animation. The joint model used for these figures is based upon the types of joints used in robotics and the dynamical equations employed are precisely those developed in that area. The biomechanical analysis above demonstrates that this model is flawed. It is unclear how deleterious an effect this has on the performance of the model because other factors, such as the inaccuracies in the calculation of ground reaction forces, may also contribute to the problems. However, it is fair to say that even the most advanced applications of dynamics to figure modelling are still far from producing results which are sufficiently versatile and convincing for general use.

The most commonly-used form of input to a figure animation system currently is motion-captured data. However, there is, as yet, no accepted method by which the individual (or idiosyncratic) characteristics of captured motion can be changed in a structured and predictable way in order that, for example, the mood of the character performing the action is changed, or that the character to whom the motion is transferred imbues the movement with qualities more suited to his own "personality" rather than that of the "donor".

Hodgins and Pollard [17] and Gleicher [15] have developed systems which enable data captured from individuals to be edited and re-used on other figures having different physical characteristics. While this appears to work well and makes captured data much more versatile, it fulfills only part of the requirements. The data that is changed still has the same overall qualities, in terms of emotion and subtle secondary messages, as the original.

The eye is extremely sensitive to individual characteristics associated with people with whom we are familiar. We are often able to recognise someone at a distance simply by the manner in which they are holding themselves or small idiosyncrasies in their locomotion. If figures in a Virtual Environment are to provide with individualism, their complete range of motions must exhibit similar, and distinguishable, characteristics.

An early attempt at developing a model to support this was made by Unuma et al. [26] using Fourier analysis, and the problem was revisited by Clapworthy and Sun [9] using wavelets. An attractive feature about wavelets is that they can be used to separate localised detail from general trends. Wavelets also supply a common underlying mathematical framework to the models and thus allow data from different gaits to be compared and blended. By identifying a "signature" in a set of motion-captured data for one person, it may be possible to transfer personal characteristics on to the general trend of data for a different set of movements that have been captured from another individual.

Until this, or some other method, provides a versatile tool for modelling personal traits, the only way to providing inhabitants on virtual environments with individual characteristics will be to model them all, separately and in detail.

4. TELECONTROL OF ROBOTS

Tele-operation of robots has great promise for its potential applications such as remote surgery and operation in hazardous conditions such as in subterranean, underwater or nuclear environments, or in outer space. Communication delays in such systems clearly present technical difficulties, and other unresolved problems in this area include insufficient visual information, slow system reaction and tedious task description. A combination of computer vision, computer graphics and Virtual Reality techniques holds the promise of overcoming many of the current obstacles to successful deployment.

In a project currently being undertaken, a PUMA robot (of standard industrial design) has been connected to the Internet at a remote site (in fact at the Keldysh Institute of Applied Mathematics in Moscow) and a virtual environment has been created at DMU with which to control the robot. The dynamics of the robot can be amended so that reacts as if it is working in a gravity-free environment, if required [5].

Apart from the hardware installed, the major factor influencing the efficiency and acceptability of a teleoperation system is a flexible and informative user interface. As users are separated from the physical robot, an effective visual interface is vital for the system to be used effectively. It is often desirable to have a live video picture of the remote site, but low bandwidth and communication delays often make this difficult, particularly if the connection is via the Internet. The Internet connection in the current set-up has been found to have an operating transmission rate within the range 0.1–3.0 KB/sec.

One approach to the problem is the immersion of a graphic robot model into TV images transmitted from the remote work site [3, 30]. Minimum knowledge of the remote site is required; the TV images are not updated except for changes in the camera view. In such a model, the graphics is more suited to simulation of the task, preliminary planning or autonomous repetition of the tasks. The real robot is not visually available to the operator who sees only the final status of the robot and the work site between control sessions.

The system described by Belousov et al. [6] uses a graphical display of an accurate virtual environment for the robot, Figure 12.4, and the visual display of the robot performance is updated by numerical data transmitted by the actual robot as it performs the task. The volume of this data is considerably less than that of video images, so the state of the local virtual robot more closely resembles the physical situation at the remote site than would a transmitted image.

The operator's control environment contains a sophisticated graphic control panel and a tool for remote robot programming. Using this, the operator can conduct sophisticated actions such as pick-and-place or assembly in manual and automatic regimes.

The system architecture is illustrated in Figure 12.5. The client part of the system consists of independent applets running: the robot graphical visualisation module (Java3D), the robot control panel, a module for remote robot programming and two "live" video images from the remote site (if required). The control system can operate on-line (the operator

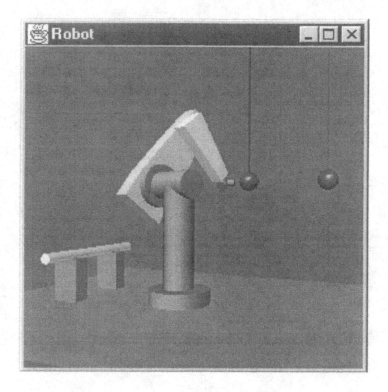

Figure 12.4   Java3D model of the robot

controls the real robot) or off-line (the operator controls the graphical model—useful for preliminary testing). In the programming module, the operator can execute individual commands or arbitrary sequences of commands (programs). A robot-control language has been developed to support this [4].

In operation, small data parcels (6 joint and 6 Cartesian coordinates) are transmitted to the visualisation module several times a second. A path-planning module at the operator's site can choose to use linear interpolation or an interpolated trajectory in joint space to smooth the trajectory between the robot positions received.

The system can operate in world space, joint space or in the robot grip reference frame. Moves are made incrementally, with the user controlling the size of the increment.

Experiments in which a rod is collected from a support and transported to another support, and the robot strikes one of two balls suspended on string in such a way that it collides with the other, are currently being conducted. The next phase will be to use methods, based

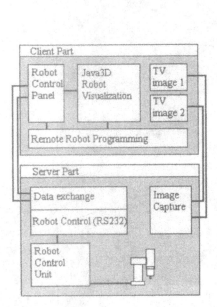
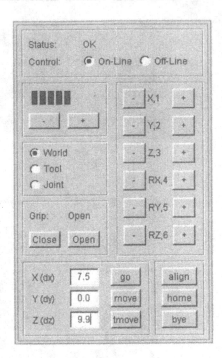

Figure 12.5   The system architecture and robot control panel

on computer vision, which have been developed for trajectory prediction by Okhotsimsky et al. [29] to work in the virtual environment with dynamic scenes.

This work will be adapted in the future to control of figures in a virtual environment. The control of figures is computationally intensive; if this is combined with the rendering calculations, frame rates will be excessively slow. By decoupling the control calculations on the server from the rendering calculations on the client and defining control mechanisms for the figures which reduce communications overheads, sophisticated real-time control of complex inhabited virtual environments should be possible on relatively low-specification computers.

5.   SUMMARY

Computer graphics is no longer the pure, "standalone" discipline it was at the outset, it is now influenced by many forms of technology. Several projects were identified which appeared to bear little relation to each other, but which did, in fact, gain greatly from cross-fertilisation. A common thread through them was the use of images (taken in its broadest sense).

As research in graphics becomes more diversified, often more interdisciplinary, so the teams involved will have to call on a greater variety of knowledge and skills.

As the power of visualisation spreads the influence of computer graphics into other disciplines, so they, in turn, influence the way in which computer-generated images are produced.

However, the use of vision is not necessarily the complete answer. For example, motion capture is often used for figure animation with considerable success. But it is not very versatile and the development of, for example, motion-editing tools, will enable data to be widely re-used and, therefore, much cheaper to acquire. Likewise, retaining the individuality of the figure is very important and without a rigorous underlying model, identifying the characteristics associated with a particular figure is very difficult.

Thus, while computer vision and computer graphics are continuing to combine to produce effective solutions to many problems, these solutions are not necessarily complete. It should not be overlooked, therefore, that a sound underlying model can provide improved solutions and broaden the applicability of the techniques developed.

References

[1] W. W. Armstrong, M. W. Green, and R. Lake. Near real-time control of human figure models. *IEEE Computer Graphics & Applications*, 7(6), 1987.

[2] N. Asamura, N. Yokoyama, and H. Shinoda. Selectively stimulating skin receptors for tactile display. *IEEE Computer Graphics & Applications*, 18(6):32–37, Nov–Dec 1998.

[3] A. K. Bejczy. Virtual reality in telerobotics. In *Proc. International Conference on Advanced Robotics ICAR-95, Sant Feliu de Guixols, Spain*, 1995.

[4] I. Belousov. Rcl/Rci: Multiplatform Tcl/Tk-based robot control language and robot control interface. In *Proc. International Conference on Adaptive Robots and General System Logical Theory, St Petersburg (Russia)*, July 1998.

[5] I. Belousov, V. Kartashev, and D. Okhotsimsky. Real-time simulation of space robots on the virtual robotic testbed. In *Proc. 7th International Conference on Advanced Robotics ICAR-95, Sant Feliu de Guixols, Spain*, pages 195–201, 1995.

[6] I. Belousov, J. C. Tan, and G. J. Clapworthy. Teleoperation and Java3D visualization of a robot manipulator over the World Wide

Web. In *Proc. Information Visualisation 99*, pages 543–548. IEEE Press, 1999.

[7] S. E. Chen. Quicktime VR — an image-based approach to virtual environment navigation. In *Proc. SIGGRAPH 95*, pages 29–38. ACM Press, 1995.

[8] G. J. Clapworthy and M. Krokos. The graphical demands on medical visualisation systems using the WWW. In *Information Visualisation '97*, pages 296–305. IEEE Press, 1997.

[9] G. J. Clapworthy and W. Sun. Giving individuality to inhabitants of virtual worlds. In *Proc. IEE Computer Vision for Human Modelling*, pages 11/1–11/4, July 1998.

[10] A. Dolenc. Rapid recipes for parametric surface models. *Computers & Graphics*, 19(2):225–236, 1995.

[11] S. Dyer, editor. *Motion Capture in Practice*. ACM Press, 1997. Course Notes SIGGRAPH 97.

[12] J. M. Rosen et al. Evolution of virtual reality. *IEEE Engineering in Medicine & Biology*, 15(2):16–22, 1996.

[13] H. Gagnon, M. Soucy, R. Bergevin, and D. Lauendeau. Registration of multiple-range views for automatic 3D model building. In *Proc. IEEE Conference on Computer Vision & Pattern Recognition*, pages 581–586, June 1994.

[14] M. Girard and A. A. Maciejewski. Computational modeling for the computer animation of legged figures. *Computer Graphics*, 19(3):263–270, 1985.

[15] M. Gleicher. Retargetting motion to new characters. In *Proc. Siggraph 98*, pages 33–42. ACM Press, 1998.

[16] B. Guenter, C. Grimm, D. Wood, H. Malvar, and F. Pighin. Making faces. In *Proc. SIGGRAPH 98*, pages 55–66. ACM Press, 1998.

[17] J. Hodgins and N. Pollard. Adapting simulated behaviours for new characters. In *Proc. Siggraph 97*, pages 153–162. ACM Press, 1997.

[18] J. K. Hodgins, W. L. Wooten, D. C. Brogan, and J. F. O'Brien. Animating human athletics. In *Proc. Siggraph 95*, pages 71–78. ACM Press, 1995.

[19] Y. Horry, K.-I. Anjyon, and K. Arai. Tour into the picture: Using a spidery mesh interface to make animation from a single image. In *Proc. SIGGRAPH 97*, pages 225–232. ACM Press, 1997.

[20] S. L. Van Sint Jan, G. J. Clapworthy, and M. Rooze. Visualization of combined motions in human joints. *IEEE Computer Graphics & Applications*, 18(6):10–14, Nov-Dec 1998.

[21] S. L. Van Sint Jan, G. J. Clapworthy, and M. Rooze. A computer graphics system for the analysis of joint kinematics. *Machine Graphics & Vision*, 8(1):55–62, 1999.

[22] S. L. Van Sint Jan, G. J. Clapworthy, and M. Rooze. Morphology-based data elimination for joint modeling from medical-image data. *IEEE Computer Graphics & Applications*, 20(2):46–52, 2000.

[23] P. Lacroute and M. Levoy. Fast volume rendering using a shear-warp factorization of the viewing transformation. In *Proc. SIGGRAPH 94*, pages 451–458. ACM Press, 1994.

[24] L. Lippert, M. Gross, and C. Kurmann. Compression domain volume rendering for distributed environments. *Computer Graphics Forum*, 16(3):125–135, 1998.

[25] W. E. Lorensen and H. E. Cline. Marching cubes: A high-resolution 3D surface-construction algorithm. *Computer Graphics*, 21(4):163–169, 1987.

[26] K. Anjyo M. Unuma and R. Takeuchi. Fourier principles for emotion-based human figure animation. In *Proc. Siggraph 95*, pages 91–96. ACM Press, 1995.

[27] L. McMillan and G. Bishop. Plenoptic modeling: An image-based rendering system. In *Proc. SIGGRAPH 95*, pages 39–46. ACM Press, 1995.

[28] R. Minghim and A. R. Forrest. Sound mapping for surface visualisation. In *Proc. WSSG 95, Plzen (Czech Rep)*, pages 410–420, 1995.

[29] D. Okhotsimsky, A. Platonov, I. Belousov, G. Borovin, S. Yemelianov, M. Komarov, and V. Sazonov. Vision system for automatic capturing a moving object by the robot manipulator. In *Proc. IEEE/RSJ Int'l Conf on Intelligent Robots & Systems (IROS '97), Grenoble (France)*, pages 1073–1079, 1997.

[30] A. Rastogi, P. Milgram, and J. Grodski. Augmented telerobotic conrol: a visual interface for unstructured environments. In *Proc. KBS/Robotics Conference*, pages 133–138, October 1995.

[31] R. A. Robb. VR-assisted surgery planning. *IEEE Engineering in Medicine & Biology*, 15(2):60–69, 1996.

[32] D. C. Ruspini, K. Kolarov, and O. Khatib. The haptic display of complex graphical environments. In *Proc. SIGGRAPH 97*, pages 345–352. ACM Press, 1997.

[33] A. Savenko, S. L. Van Sint Jan, and G. J. Clapworthy. A biomechanics-based model for the animation of human locomotion. In *Proc. GraphiCon 99, Moscow*, pages 82–87, August 1999.

[34] G. Turk.   Re-tiling polygonal surfaces.   *Computer Graphics*, 26(2):55–64, 1992.

[35] N. Vasilonikolidakis and G. J. Clapworthy.   Design of realistic gaits for the purpose of animation.   In N. Magnenat-Thalmann and D. Thalmann, editors, *Computer Animation'91*, pages 101–114. Springer Verlag, 1991.

[36] J. Wilhelms. Dynamic experiences. In N. Badler, B. Barsky, and D. Zeltzer, editors, *Making Them Move*, pages 265–279. Morgan Kaufmann, 1990.

[37] W. L. Wooten and J. K. Hodgins.   Animation of human diving. *Computer Graphics Forum*, 15(1):3–13, 1996.

Chapter 13

CAN VIRTUAL LOOK REAL?
A REVIEW OF VIRTUAL STUDIO
TECHNIQUES

Andrew Wojdala

Abstract

Five years since its introduction to television world, Virtual Studio has proven that it can be successfully used. More and more broadcasters are using this technology, even for complex, live-to-air productions.

The goal of this paper is to address the most basic issue raised by this relatively new technology: how realistic virtual sets can appear? Has the technology reached the level high enough to create a convincing illusion?

Virtual Studio is a very interdisciplinary technology. To answer these questions, we need to discuss techniques related to computer graphics, today's graphics workstations, chroma keying, video camera behavior, camera tracking and interaction between real and virtual worlds.

1. INTRODUCTION

Virtual Studio evolved from traditional blue-box technique, where actors and real objects are shot in front of a blue screen. The camera signal (foreground) is then fed to the chroma keyer, where it is mixed with another video signal (background), coming from a VTR or a computer (Fig. 13.1). This technique, used for years for weather forecasts, has one major drawback: the camera cannot move, because the background video is static. If the camera moved or zoomed, then only foreground would change, while the background would remain the same, which of course is not what we expect.

There is no "official" definition of the Virtual Studio. In fact, new developments and products obscure the matter even more. Virtual studios can be "3D", "2D" or even "still", "live" or "post", "SGI-based" or "NT-based", "standalone" or "plug-in", "low-end" or "high-end".

229

A. Leonardis et al. (eds.), Confluence of Computer Vision and Computer Graphics, 229–252.
© 2000 *Kluwer Academic Publishers. Printed in the Netherlands.*

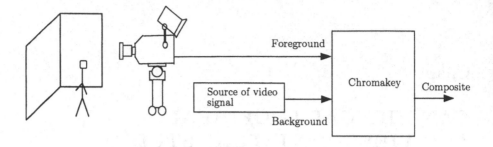

Figure 13.1   Traditional blue-box technique

But in fact, there is one major feature that defines Virtual Studio: camera motion. Virtual Studio is a technology, which allows cameras to move, and which changes background video in such a way, that it matches the foreground when camera moves. To change the background according to the camera motion, the graphics computer is needed. This computer should be connected to the camera tracking system, in order to get the real-time information about current camera position. The presence of a camera tracking system and the computer constitutes the main difference between traditional blue-box and Virtual Studio (Fig. 13.2).

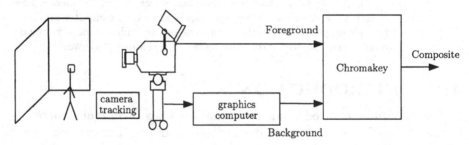

Figure 13.2   The presence of a camera tracking system and the computer constitutes the main difference between traditional blue-box and Virtual Studio.

There are many reasons to use Virtual Studio. The most important of them are:

- Shorter production cycle: virtual sets can be created quicker than real ones.

- Better studio utilization: the same studio can be used for different productions; the change of a virtual set is a matter of seconds.

- Easy changes: since virtual set is not a real thing, some modifications are possible even in the last moment.

- Unleashed imagination: sets can be created, that in reality would be too difficult, too expensive, or even physically impossible to build.

- Bigger sizes: virtual sets can be much more spacious than studios that host them, and tricks like rotating platforms, can further enhance the impression of spaciousness.

- Live graphics effects: computer allows to enrich the set with special effects and graphics in real time, significantly enhancing the look and making viewer's perception easier.

- No storage problems: virtual sets do not occupy expensive storage space.

Most television programs can benefit from using virtual sets. The types of programs that are obvious candidates for this technology are: news programs, weather forecasts, sportscasts, talk-shows, music programs and video clips, programs for kids, educational programs, ads, game shows, soap operas, corporate presentations.

Since they replace real sets, the primary function of virtual sets is to look convincing. There is no point in using the technology, which generates sets that look worse than cheap cartoon decorations. To create a convincing illusion that actors are immersed in a computer-generated set, issues of various areas must be addressed:

- real-time performance of all virtual studio components, in particular of camera tracking and computer graphics display,

- realism of computer-generated sets,

- proper lighting of the virtual and real stage and good chroma keying,

- proper interaction of virtual and real shadows,

- precise camera tracking and in consequence—matching motion of real and virtual cameras,

- precise lens calibration,

- simulation of lens behavior, such as depth of field and distortion,

- display of virtual objects in front of real ones.

In the following sections we will discuss these issues in detail.

2.   REAL-TIME PERFORMANCE

The term "real-time" is frequently treated as an equivalent to "interactive". This is partially the result of the confusion between Virtual Studio and Virtual Reality (VR). Although there are many similarities between them, there are also notable differences. The goal of the Virtual Reality is for the actor (i.e., the person being the subject of the experiment) to have an impression of being immersed in the virtual environment, by using such attributes as Head Mounted Displays. In Virtual Studio only the audience is "cheated" by looking at the composite image; the actor remains perfectly aware of his real environment. But perhaps the most important difference stems from the area of application: while it is still acceptable for VR images to be crude and motion to be jerky, Virtual Studio demands absolutely flawless and smooth motion as well as good-quality images, because they are eventually broadcast in TV. This condition imposes strict requirements on the equipment and software used in the Virtual Studio:

- The display frame rate has to be equal to the video frame rate (50Hz in PAL, 59,94Hz in NTSC). Consequently, in Virtual Studio the term "real-time" means 20/16.6 milliseconds per frame. Within that time, the virtual scene must be displayed, and all special effects applied.

- In consequence, computers used to generate the virtual scene must be high-performance graphic workstations. Until recently, the only computer regarded as capable of handling this demanding task was Silicon Graphics Onyx.

- Both camera tracking and the computer must use studio genlock as a reference for sending data reports and redrawing the scene with new perspective.

- Finally, the computer must support broadcast-quality graphics-to-video conversion.

3.   REALISM OF COMPUTER-GENERATED SCENES

Sets can be generally classified into two categories: recreated real sets, where as much realism as possible is needed, and unreal, impossible worlds. It is important to realize however, that to look convincing even unrealistic sets need realistic lighting.

At present, the most advanced commercially available methods to simulate lighting are mutations and combinations of radiosity (Cohen et al. [2] and further works) and ray tracing (Whitted [17] and further works). Although they are able to produce very good results, they are far from being real-time.

On the other hand, computer graphics hardware of even most powerful among today's workstations is limited to simple rendering methods using z-buffer and Gouraud shading. The main bottlenecks are the number of polygons that can be displayed within video frame rate, the number of light sources and the texture space. Certainly, more realistic scenes are bigger challenge for graphics hardware, because they are composed of more polygons and use more textures and light sources. A number of methods can be employed to simplify the geometry of the set while retaining the same look. Apart from polygon reduction algorithms, techniques such as replacing flat complex shapes by textures with an alpha channel can be used. Those techniques usually eliminate superfluous polygons while retaining the visual complexity at the expense of texture memory space.

Light sources supported by hardware are usually the weakest point: there is a limited number of them (typically 8) and the lighting model they employ is very simple. Therefore, the typical solution is to trade light sources for increased number of polygons, which have lighting preprocessed and converted into vertices' color, which is then interpolated by the graphics hardware. Unfortunately, methods such as radiosity subdivide the original geometry, generating a lot of polygons (frequently hundreds of thousands) which makes real-time performance unreachable. Such subdivision can be converted into textures; at present the technique of preprocessing lighting and combining it with original texture patterns, known as "texture rendering" (Figs. 13.3, 13.4), is the only efficient way to achieve high level of realism while maintaining the requirement of real-time performance (Fig. 13.5) [5,10,18]. Of course, texture space is also limited, and exceeding the limit results in texture swapping, which kills the real-time performance, but this seems to be the most acceptable trade-off.

The discussion above concerns mainly diffuse lighting. Specular lighting effects (e.g., mirror reflections) usually cannot be preprocessed, because they are inherently view-dependent, but can be simulated using capabilities of the graphics hardware, although not without certain performance penalties [18,7]. On the other hand, the usability of specular reflections in a virtual set is somewhat limited, because it is naturally expected that real objects would be reflected in virtual mirrors as well. Such effect can be accomplished to the certain extent, by placing sheets of glossy material on the floor or walls (Fig. 13.6) or by employing ded-

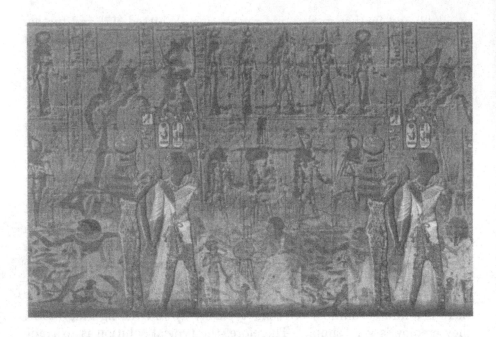

Figure 13.3   Texture rendering

Figure 13.4   Texture rendering

Figure 13.5 Texture rendering

icated hardware to process foreground video, as was recently demonstrated by Orad.

While simulation of interiors reached quite convincing level of realism (Fig. 13.7), outdoor scenes are still beyond computer simulation, unless they are limited to a "look through the window", photographed and mapped onto the background.

4. LIGHTING AND CHROMA KEYING

Proper, even lighting of the blue-box is essential to eliminate unwanted shadows and to ensure quality keying. While the lighting plays a key role in building the mood of every production, because of the chroma key limitations the virtual set lighting director's freedom is limited, especially if colored lights are desired. Moreover, unless the blue-box walls coincide with the walls of the virtual set, the light effects must be limited to the floor only. Setting flat and very bright lighting for the whole stage, including actors and foreground objects precludes the possibility of dramatic lighting, which—contrary to the popular belief—can be achieved in a blue screen. This is especially true when replacing the paint with retro-reflective material (HoloSet from Play, Inc., developed by BBC and formerly known as Truematte; Fig. 13.10). Illuminated by a ring of blue

Figure 13.6   Specular reflections in a virtual set

Figure 13.7   Simulation of interiors

LEDs mounted around the lens (Fig. 13.11), the material reflects almost all incident light back in the direction of the camera, which "sees" the whole background stage as blue. This gives the lighting director much more freedom in lighting actors and the stage, and even allows to work in almost complete darkness (Fig. 13.12).

Good quality keying is critical to create the convincing illusion. The color and shape of the blue-box, the lighting, cameras, and the quality of the chroma keyer all play their roles, and setting the entire environment is still more an art than a science. But even technically perfect keying will not help, if the lighting of a real stage does not match the lighting of a virtual scene. Unfortunately, this is usually the case, because the lighting of the actor is white and even (as a result of even lighting of a blue-box), unlike the lighting of the scene. Only recently the new Ultimatte-9 keyer addressed the critical issue of ambiance, adding an automatic adjustment of the foreground image color to match the influence of the virtual background. This way, when the background is red, the foreground (e.g., the actor) gets the subtle reddish coloring, which is exactly' what the human visual system expects.

Matching lighting levels between virtual scene and real foreground is a separate problem. The latter stems from the technical requirements, while the former is an artistic issue. Ultimatte keyers enable the software to control the foreground brightness in real-time, thus allowing lighting levels to be matched within certain limitations (Figs. 13.8, 13.9). Any dynamic lighting changes make the things even more difficult, whether they occur in the virtual set (possibilities are limited, because of performance issues) or in the real environment (here possibilities are limited due to the chroma keying considerations). With the techniques of lighting preprocessing discussed in previous chapter, it is reasonable to design certain number of lighting situations and dissolve between them, simultaneously with the transition between foreground brightness levels (Figs. 13.8, 13.9). To really synchronize the changes of the real and virtual lighting, the studio lights should be computerized. This allows the lighting situations to be recorded and repeatedly recalled. Ideally, any changes of the real lights should be detected by the computer generating the background to trigger an appropriate change of the virtual lighting (and vice versa). Of course, the keyer should also synchronously recall the settings appropriate for the new lighting conditions.

5.   SHADOWS

Shadows were always recognized as an important element responsible for proper understanding of computer-generated images. Generation of

Figure 13.8 Ultimatte keyer: The foreground brightness is matched to the bright subject in real-time.

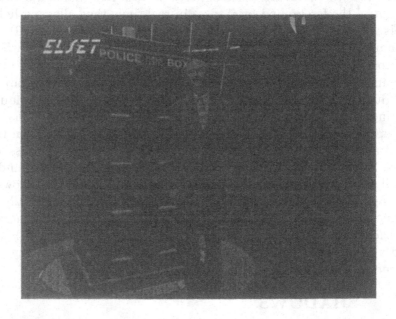

Figure 13.9 Ultimatte keyer: The foreground brightness is matched to the dark subject in real-time.

Figure 13.10   Dramatic lighting can be achieved in a "Truematte".

Figure 13.11   Blue LEDs mounted around the camera lens

Figure 13.12 Using the illumination by a ring of blue LEDs mounted around the camera lens allows the lighting director to work in almost complete darkness.

shadows is an integral part of realistic image synthesis methods, but it was always more difficult in real-time rendering algorithms. Application in Virtual Studio makes it even more difficult, because it imposes the requirement of sustained display rate equal to the video frame rate. If the textures are rendered, they already contain static shadows. But if virtual objects that cast shadows move, the shadows do not move with them. To allow dynamic lighting and animated objects, it is necessary to employ hardware-assisted shadowing techniques [1]. Of these, most are multi-pass rendering methods, which usually significantly degrade the performance, thus requiring the scene complexity to be reduced several times. In practical cases only *projection shadow (fake shadows)* and *shadow object* methods, being the most efficient, can be used in Virtual Studio. Unfortunately, these methods have limitations; primarily shapes of shadowed objects need to be planar.

But the biggest challenge is to address the problem created by and specific to Virtual Studio: casting shadows of real elements (especially

Figure 13.13 Casting shadows of real people on virtual objects

an actor) on virtual ones and vice versa. For real-to-virtual shadow casting the solution is to use another camera, which emulates the light source. The camera signal is run through the chroma keyer to obtain the black-and-white mask, which is then input to the computer, as was demonstrated by some virtual studio vendors, most notably by RT Set. Multi-pass projected texture method [14] is then used to map the shadow onto virtual objects in the scene (Fig. 13.13). Casting shadows of virtual objects on real objects is also technically possible. One of the simple solutions is to cover the studio lights with masks of the proper shapes.

It can be concluded, that while proper shadowing is really important for realistic look of virtual sets, it was not yet resolved in a satisfactory manner, so that aspect of interaction of the real and virtual worlds still requires better solutions.

6.   CAMERA TRACKING

To properly match perspectives of the real foreground and virtual background, the precision and stability of the camera tracking system is crucial. If the information about camera motion delivered to the computer does not reflect the real change of its position and orientation, then real objects will "swim" with respect to the virtual ones, and most visibly to the virtual floor. Camera tracking systems available today use the following techniques:

- sensors (encoders),

- pattern recognition,

- position detection.

Encoders-based camera tracking is the most accurate and proven technology. Encoders are mounted on the pan and tilt axes of camera heads. This way, the precise information about camera orientation in space can be passed to the computer. Zoom and focus rings have special brackets and separate encoders, necessary to calculate the view angle of the camera. To allow camera motion, it can be put on a dolly with the height sensor. Using the rail with additional sensor allows a movement on the floor. Mounting the camera on a crane with encoders, and even mounting such crane on a rail usually gives all the freedom and precision of movement that might be desired, except for hand-held cameras. Also, large studios can be a problem. The leaders in sensor tracking are Thoma Filmtechnik (Germany), Radamec EPO (Great Britain) and Hybrid MC (France).

Pattern recognition tracking systems use fixed pattern, that the camera must "see" all the time. Pattern's construction makes it possible to calculate the position and orientation of the observing camera based on what it sees. The biggest advantage of pattern recognition systems is their ability to track even hand-held cameras. The drawback is that when the pattern falls out of view (big tilt or roll, obscuring objects), the tracking stops to work. Although this type of tracking is less precise than sensor-based solutions (because it is limited by the resolution of a video image seen be a tracking camera), it is possible to reach the satisfactory level of accuracy (positional accuracy of the order of 0.1 mm and angular accuracy of 0.01 degree is considered good). Two mature solutions are available on the market.

Orad Hi-Tec Systems, one of Virtual Studio vendors, has a proprietary system, in which the same camera that is used for shooting also watches the pattern, a non-uniform grid painted in two shades of blue on a flat wall of a blue-box [15]. In its theory, it is an ideal tracking system, because it calculates the camera parameters directly from the foreground image, to which the background will be matched. In particular, the advantage of this solution is that no zoom/focus sensors are needed, because the view angle is determined from the pattern along with positional information. The drawback is that if the camera looks away from the blue-box the tracking no longer works. The same can happen in big zooms, because the pattern can get obscured or defocused. To reduce these negative effects, additional sensors and infra-red position detection elements usually complement Orad's pattern-recognition tracking. Another problem with Orad's tracking is that it makes chroma keying more difficult than in normal environments painted with one shade of the keying color. This is particularly true when keying with green. British company Radamec EPO offers the system licensed from BBC, where a small progressive-scan camera, mounted to the body of the shooting camera is used to determine the position and orientation, by looking at the grid of targets usually mounted under the ceiling (Fig. 13.14); zoom and focus information is received from encoders [16]. This way the tracking still works even if the shooting camera points away from the blue-box. The big advantage of this system is its ability to cover large studios. Interestingly, it has rather problems with studios, where the ceiling is not high enough.

In position detection tracking, fixed elements of the system are mounted in the studio and detect the position and orientation of the camera in space, by tracking special construction or active elements mounted to the camera body. Zoom and focus information is derived from encoders. This technology comes from motion capture systems and is opposite to what pattern recognition systems are doing, but the precision is similar. Two mature solutions available on the market are Walkfinder from Thoma Filmtechnik and X-pecto from Xync (both from Germany).

Walkfinder uses intelligent, infra-red cameras that track the antenna-like construction mounted to the video camera body. The ring of diodes around the lens of the tracking cameras emits IR flashes, which are reflected back from the five balls mounted on the "antenna" and coated with the retro-reflective material. As long as this construction is "seen" by at least two IR cameras, the tracking is possible. The advantage of this solution is practically unlimited pan, tilt and roll, which gives the full freedom of camera motion. The two main problems are interference from shining objects and strong light sources, and the precision of tracking at bigger distances between IR cameras and the tracked construction, which makes it difficult to use this system in high studios without the additional supporting construction.

Figure 13.14   Camera determines the position and orientation by looking at the grid of targets usually mounted under the ceiling.

X-pecto is also based on infra-red technology, although it uses the reverse process: it is the circular construction mounted to the camera body that contains IR light sources, which are detected by the high-resolution surveillance cameras overlooking the tracked area. The main advantage of X-pecto is its high precision.

Recently, American company InterSense demonstrated camera tracking system based on its Constellation technology [4]. IS-900 Studio Camera Tracker uses inertial and ultrasonic components to track the construction attached to the camera body. While the results of the first tests are promising, extensive tests in the real studio environments are still needed. What should be certainly attractive about this system is a potentially very competitive price.

Aside from the prices, the main difference between tracking systems presented above is their robustness and ease of use in different conditions. Certainly, there is no universal tracking system suitable for every studio, but today the selection is wide enough to satisfy most environments, thus fulfilling the goal of matching background and foreground with enough precision.

7. SIMULATION OF LENS BEHAVIOR

An important observation is that it is not enough for computer-generated sets to look real—they also need to behave in a realistic way. Proper simulation of the lens behavior is the key element to achieve the convincing illusion.

7.1 LENS CALIBRATION

The information delivered by the camera tracking system is used by the computer to adjust the virtual camera, so that the perspectives of the real foreground and virtual background match. Unfortunately, the graphics hardware of today's computers uses the simple camera model that does not consider the optics of the lens. The only parameters that can be specified are: viewpoint, target point, roll angle, view angle and aspect ratio, and the projection screen is flat. To match perspectives, we have to find the virtual camera parameters which are the best approximation of the information about the real camera, obtained from the tracking system. The position and orientation of the camera can be directly used, but the lens causes problems, because:

- the lens' nodal point, representing the virtual camera viewpoint, travels when zoom and focus change, and its behavior is non-linear,

- the view angle depends on both zoom and focus, and the relation is non-linear,

- the center of the CCD can be off the optical axis of the lens,

- the lens has the depth of field, which does not have its counterpart in the virtual camera model at all,

- the lens produces non-linear distortions on the edges, which are also not considered because of flat projection screen,

- the lighting on the edges depends on the iris (which usually is not reported anyway).

The nodal point travel, view angle dependency on the zoom and focus and CCD centering offset have undoubtedly the biggest influence on matching of the virtual "pinhole" camera with real perspective. Lens calibration is the process of finding these relations, by matching virtual and real objects of the known size. Usually, specialized equipment is used for that purpose by either the virtual set software vendor or tracking system vendor. If the calibration is poor, then real objects do not keep their position on the floor and seem to "float" during panning, tilting and zooming. Calibration procedures used by today's Virtual Studio and tracking systems vendors are sufficiently accurate to assure good matching of real and virtual perspectives; usually, it is enough to calibrate one lens to obtain the relations satisfactory for all lenses of that type. Visible artifacts can occur only on the edges for lenses with relatively big distortions (see below).

7.2   DEPTH OF FIELD

To address the issues of depth of field and lens distortions, a more realistic camera model would be needed. Such model was created for computer graphics by Kolb [9], but it is non-real time. Therefore, the only way to deal with these effects is to simulate them with hardware-supported techniques.

Defocus due to the depth of field is one of the key effects responsible for realistic look of the virtual scenes. Proper simulation of this effect is time consuming [11]. The algorithm works as a post-processing stage after rendering an image in sharp focus, and requires both RGB and depth information to be stored for an image. The advantage of that approach is its physical foundation, and consequently, convincing results. Several methods have been developed to simulate this effect in real time.

Texel magnification method assumes, that the resolution of the texture is such that zooming at it causes texel (texture pixel) to occupy more than one pixel on the screen. Graphics hardware extrapolation makes such texture blurred, which visually looks like defocusing. Of course, the effect is far from being natural and is very difficult to control.

Better results can be achieved by the method using texture's Level of Detail (LOD). By switching between levels of different resolution in real time, the blurring effect can be better controlled.

Hardware accumulation buffer allows a multi-pass solution that gives results of better quality, but only under the condition that the number of passes is relatively big [6], which makes it practically unusable in real-time application such as Virtual Studio.

As was shown by Rokita [12], a convolution filter can be used to approximate physically based simulation. Dudkiewicz [3] modified Rokita's method to use multi-pass display with hardware-supported convolution on the Silicon Graphics Onyx computers. Unfortunately, the rate was at best several frames per second on SGI's RealityEngine2. Although faster on InfiniteReality graphics, it still remains an expensive method.

In 1996, in its ELSET virtual set software Accom implemented real-time, physically-based and visually convincing depth-of-field algorithm. The algorithm has preprocessing stage based on Potmesil's algorithm

Figure 13.15 Multilayer textures are used to control the defocusing level

and assumed ranges of camera movements. Multilayer textures are used to control the defocusing level in real-time during shooting [19]. Such effects as rack- or back-focus are easy to achieve, because the algorithm is driven by both zoom and focus information coming from the camera head, and can also take iris into account, if available (Figs. 13.15).

Methods presented above use computer's graphic hardware to achieve the effect of real-time depth of field. Some of these methods impose performance penalties, others reduce available texture space. Another approach was taken by BBC and Radamec. In their solution, background generated by the computer is routed through D•focus—a specialized hardware, which applies special blurring filters in real time, effectively simulating the depth of field effect. Unfortunately, D•focus requires depth information for every pixel of the virtual background delivered as the digital video signal, while currently available graphics workstations do not output z-buffer in a natural way, which makes this solution difficult to efficiently use.

7.3   LENS DISTORTION

Lenses with significant distortion clearly reveal that virtual and real worlds do not match on the edges of the composite video. Two techniques can be used to simulate the distortion.

If the scene is tessellated into relatively small polygons, the position of each vertex can be transformed, so that vertices on the edges of the view frustum are visibly displaced, while centrally-located vertices stay unchanged. Unfortunately, the general tendency is to avoid high tessellation, and also the cost of transforming every vertex in every field of display is non-negligible.

Another approach is to use spherical image warping, applied to the background image rendered with ordinary, planar projection. This can be done by reading the rendered frame from the frame buffer and mapping it as a texture on the sphere in the second display pass. Of course, this technique degrades the performance; an alternative approach is to use another, low-cost computer to execute the second pass.

8.   DISTANCE KEYING

Having virtual objects in the background is obvious, but there is also a need to place them in front of real objects, and actors in particular. This allows, for example, putting newscaster behind the virtual desk. First attempts to place virtual objects in front of real ones were made by German company DVS, which developed a digital keyer with additional video input, fed with 8-bit values representing the distance between the virtual objects and the camera. At the same time, the cutting distance (usually the distance between the camera and the talent) was sent through the serial line [13]. Similar solution was implemented by BBC and Radamec in their D•focus unit. Unfortunately, as already noticed, today's graphics workstations do not output z-buffer in a natural way, which makes these techniques difficult to employ. However, similar result can be achieved using graphics hardware feeding the chroma key with external matte signal, at a certain expense of performance.

Two solutions are in use in virtual sets: object- and distance-based. The former assigns one of two priorities (foreground or background) to every object. Foreground objects are additionally drawn in alpha channel, which goes to the matte input of the chroma keyer. Consequently, they appear in front of real objects on the composite image (Fig. 13.16). Distance-based solution is also technically simple: in this case, all pixels that display virtual set points closer to the camera than the cutting distance get white alpha. The advantage of this approach is the possibility to put real objects inside virtual ones. On the other hand, object-based approach allows to put one actor behind one pillar and second actor behind another pillar, as long as pillars do not overlap. In other words, the only issue is not to assign contradicting priorities to the same object. In distance-based technique it usually cannot be done, because of one cutting distance. Solutions for automatic determination of the cutting distance are offered by Orad and Xync. Orad uses overhead camera and IR sensor located on the talent; Xync's X-ploro talent tracking system uses multiple surveillance cameras overlooking the blue stage.

The biggest problem of the distance-key techniques is that while computer "knows" the depth of each pixel of the virtual scene, there is no depth data available for the foreground, other than the cutting distance representing the distance of real objects (usually the talent) from the camera. This makes it impossible for the actor to embrace the virtual column, for example. The hope for solution came with the Zcam, the first z-buffer camera based on infrared technology and introduced by the Israeli company 3DV Systems at NAB'99 convention [8].

Virtual blue-box is in a way an extension of the distance keying. This technique allows to mask out areas past the physical boundaries of the real blue-box, and to display the virtual set instead. It is achieved by feeding alpha channel generated by the computer simultaneously with the background, as a video matte signal to the chroma key. This technique is especially useful in masking out the ceiling and the studio lights mounted there. Of course, chroma keying of actors and real objects in masked areas is not possible.

Figure 13.16   Distance keying

9.   CONCLUSIONS

The goal of all the techniques presented above is to combine two separate images: camera foreground and computer-generated background so well, that the composite looks as if it was shot together, in one environment. This is not an easy task, since human visual system is very picky in detecting all incorrect subtleties, even though the nature of an error need not be consciously recognized.

In the light of the discussions presented in this paper we can say, that reaching such level of realism is very difficult, and even impossible in general case. Technologies associated with the Virtual Studio still face many challenges, but they are constantly improved [20] and every year brings new, exciting developments. But at the same time we can risk the statement, that under certain conditions (for certain types of virtual environments), it is possible to successfully create an illusion that will be convincing to most viewers, maybe except for TV professionals. Perhaps the best conclusion of this paper is the situation that really happened during one of the TV productions using Virtual Studio technology. During the rehearsal, one of the managers passing by the control room and seeing only the composite video, commented that the virtual set looks really good, but complained that the model of one of the chairs was incorrectly constructed and looks artificial. As it happened, this was a real chair.

References

[1] D. Blythe and T. McReynolds. *Advanced graphics programming techniques using OpenGL.* Siggraph Course Notes, 1999.

[2] M. F. Cohen and D. P. Greenberg. The hemi-cube: A radiosity solution for complex environments. *ACM Computer Graphics*, 19(3):31–40, 1985.

[3] K. Dudkiewicz. Real-time depth of field algorithm, Image Processing for Broadcast and Video Production. In Y. Paker and S. Wilbur (Eds.), *Proceedings of the European Workshop, Hamburg 23-24 Nov. 1994*, pages 255–268, Springer/British Computer Society, 1995.

[4] E. Foxlin, M. Harrington, and G. Pfeifer. Constellation ^{TM}: A wide-range wireless motion tracking system for Augmented Reality and Virtual Set applications. *Computer Graphics Proceedings, Annual Conference Series*, pages 371-378, 1998.

[5] M. Goslin. *Illumination as texture maps for faster rendering*, Technical Report 95-042, Dept. Of Computer Science, Univ. Of North Carolina, Chapel Hill, 1995.

[6] P. Haeberli and K. Akeley. The accumulation buffer: hardware support for high-quality rendering. *ACM Comput Graph*, 24(4):309–318, 1990.

[7] M. Kilgard. Rendering Fast reflections with OpenGL. http://reality.sgi.com/opengl/tips/, Dec. update, 1997.

[8] D. Kirk, K. Ross, and D. Woolfson. NAB'99 Innovation. *International Broadcast Engineer*, May/June 1999; see also the web site www.3dvsystems.com, 1999.

[9] C. Kolb, D. Mitchell, and P. Hanrahan. A realistic camera model for computer graphics. *ACM Computer Graphics Proceedings*, pages 317-324, 1995.

[10] K. Myszkowski and T. L. Kunii. Texture mapping as an alternative for meshing during walkthrough animation. *Proceedings of 5th Eurographics Workshop on Rendering, Darmstadt, Germany*, pages 375–388, 1994.

[11] M. Potmesil and I. Chakravarty. A lens and aperture camera model for synthetic image generation. *ACM Computer Graphics*, 15(3):297–306, 1981.

[12] P. Rokita. Fast generation of depth of field effects in computer graphics. *C & G*, 17:593–595, 1993.

[13] W. Schmidt. Real-time mixing of live action and synthetic backgrounds based on depth values. In Y. Paker and S. Wilbur (Eds), *Image Processing for Broadcast and Video Production, Proceedings of the European Workshop, Hamburg 23-24 Nov. 1994*, pages 26–34, Springer/British Computer Society, 1994.

[14] M. Segal and C. Korobkin. Fast shadows and lighting effects using texture mapping. *ACM Computer Graphics*, 26(2):249–252, 1992.

[15] M. Tamir. The Orad Virtual Set. *Broadcast Origination*, March 16–18, 1996.

[16] G. A. Thomas, J. Jin, T. Niblett, and C. Urquhart. A versatile camera position measurement system for virtual reality TV production. *International Broadcasting Convention'97 Proceedings*, pages 284–289, IEE Conference Publication, 1997.

[17] T. Whitted. An improved illumination model for shaded display. *Communications of the ACM*, 23(6):343–349, 1980.

[18] A. Wojdala, M. Gruszewski, and K. Dudkiewicz. Using hardware texture mapping for efficient image synthesis and walkthrough with specular effects. *Machine Graphics & Vision*, 3(1/2):139–151, 1994.

[19] A. Wojdala. Challenges of Virtual Set technology. *IEEE Multimedia*, 5(1):50–57, 1998.

[20] A. Wojdala, M. Gruszewski, K. Dudkiewicz, and M. Donotek. Real-time depth of field algorithm for Virtual Studio. *Machine Graphics & Vision*, 7(1/2):5–14, 1998.

Chapter 14

REAL-TIME 3D-TELEIMMERSION

Kostas Daniilidis, Jane Mulligan, Raymond McKendall, David Schmid,
Gerda Kamberova, Ruzena Bajcsy

Abstract

In this paper we present the first implementation of a new medium for telecollaboration. The realized testbed consists of two tele-cubicles at two Internet nodes. At each telecubicle a stereo-rig is used to provide an accurate dense 3D-reconstruction of a person in action. The two real dynamic worlds are transmitted over the network and visualized stereoscopically. The full-3D information facilitates interaction with any virtual object, demonstrating in an optimal way the confluence of graphics, vision, and communication.

In particular, the remote communication and the dynamic nature of telecollaboration put the challenge of optimal representation for graphics and vision. We treat the issues of limited bandwidth, latency, and processing power with a tunable 3D-representation where the user can choose the trade-off between delay and 3D-resolution by tuning the spatial resolution, the size of the working volume, and the uncertainty of reconstruction. Due to the limited number of cameras and displays our system can not provide the user with a surround-immersive feeling. However, it is the first system that uses *3D-real-data* that are reconstructed *online* at another site. The system has been implemented with low-cost off-the-shelf hardware and has been successfully demonstrated in a local area network.

1. INTRODUCTION

Advances in networking and processor performance open challenging new directions for remote collaboration via immersive environments. With the continuing progress in bandwidth and protocols for the information highway, new education and business structures become feasible. The incorporation of graphical models in remote training is already a reality: Two astronauts from two different continents can already train together in a virtual space-shuttle [9]. However, nothing that they see is

253

A. Leonardis et al. (eds.), Confluence of Computer Vision and Computer Graphics, 253–265.

real: they see each other as their graphical avatars and the space shuttle is a virtual model. The demand for collaboration among physicians, for a common medical consultation during an operation, or between engineers for virtual prototyping, is increasing.

The purpose of this paper is to show, in the context of teleimmersion, the utility of an integrated approach coming from two fields: Computer Vision and Computer Graphics. The problem of teleimmersion requires two different technologies: data acquisition/reconstruction (the typical domain of Computer Vision) and fast realistic and interactive data display (the typical domain of Computer Graphics). Further, it requires rethinking some of the basic representations of the data in view of the constraints coming from the real time, low latency, high spatiotemporal resolution, and low cost demands.

While the Computer Vision community is mainly concerned with scene reconstruction to be used in different tasks such as navigation/manipulation or recognition, here the goal is different. In teleimmersion applications, the goal is *communication* amongst people who are geographically distributed but are meeting in the space of each local user augmented by the dynamic, lifelike avatar of the remote partner. This is quite different from the conventional virtual reality. What is most important is not the realism but the usefulness with respect to the task in hand, for example, collaboration or entertainment. It is also different from traditional off-line versions of image-based rendering which just replace virtual with static image worlds. Therefore, the challenging issue for computer vision beside the representation is the real-time processing - which has long been a focus for the visualization and the graphics community.

What will follow is a description of a fully integrated dynamic 3D telepresence system working over the network. The highlights of the system are:

1. Full reconstruction and transmission of dynamic *real* 3D-data which can be combined with any *virtual* object or world.

2. Real-time performance using off-the-shelf components.

3. Optimal balance between several quality factors (spatial resolution, depth resolution, work volume).

Why is 2D not enough. Nowadays, most advanced teleconferencing and telepresence systems transmit 2D-images. In order to get additional views, the systems use either panoramic systems and/or interpolate between a set of views [3, 16, 15]. We argue here, that for collaboration purposes 3D-reconstruction can not be avoided. First, view morphing approaches are able to interpolate views over a very restricted range of weakly calibrated viewpoints. Second, even if a system is fully calibrated [15] we need a calibration between the observer tracker and the cameras. In a collaboration scenario, where multiple persons discuss real 3D properties of mechanical objects or even give instructions requiring 6DOF movements, there is no camera placement constellation which can produce the required variability of viewpoints resulting from the head movements of a user. Therefore, we pursue a 3D image based rendering which is viewpoint independent based on stereo reconstruction.

2. RELATED WORK

Here we are not going to review the huge number of existing papers (refer to the annual bibliographies by Azriel Rosenfeld) on all aspects of stereo (the reader is referred to a standard review [5]). Application of stereo to image based rendering is very well reviewed in the recent paper by Narayanan and Kanade [13]. Although terms like virtualized reality and augmented reality are used in many reconstruction papers, it should be emphasized that we address a reactive telepresence problem, whereas most image based rendering approaches try to replace a graphic model with a real one *off-line*.

Stereo approaches may be classified with respect to the matching as well as with respect to the reconstruction scheme. Regarding matching we differentiate between sparse feature based reconstructions (see the treatise in [6]) and dense depth reconstructions [14, 13]. Approaches such as [2, 17] address the probabilistic nature of matching with particular emphasis on the occlusion problem. Area-based approaches [10] are based on correlation and like our approach emphasize the real-time issue.

An approach with emphasis on virtualized reality is [13]. This system captures the action of a person from a dome of 51 cameras. The processing is off-line and in this sense there is no indication how it could be used in telepresence beside the off-line reconstruction of static structures.

With respect to reconstruction, recent approaches can be classified as strongly or weakly (or self-calibrated) approaches. Self-calibration approaches [11] provide a metric reconstruction from multiple views with an accuracy which is suitable only for restricted augmented reality applications like video manipulation where the quality of depth is not relevant. Weakly calibrated approaches [8] provide real time performance and are suitable for augmenting scenes only with synthetic objects. Our approach is the first that provides an optimal balance between depth accuracy and speed and therefore can be applied in teleimmersion.

3.   SYSTEM DESCRIPTION AND SCENARIO

The teleimmersion testbed we work with is a continuously evolving system. Before delving into the individual algorithms we describe below the first hardware configuration realized in spring 1999 (See Fig. 14.1). Each side consists of

1. a stereo rig of two CCD-cameras,

2. a PC with a frame grabber,

3. a PC with an accelerated graphics card capable of driving stereo-glasses.

The spring-99 version has an Intel Pentium-II 450 MHz and a Matrox-Genesis Frame Grabber at the local site. The latter includes the TI C80 processor as a component. The CCD-cameras are the Sony XC-77. For visualization we use the Diamond FireGL-4000 board and CrystalEyes stereo-glasses. Both sites are connected to the network and send their data using the TCP/IP protocol. Implementation of networking is for the local area network used now and will be extended to include compression and to compensate for lossy transmission protocols in a wide area Internet2 connection.

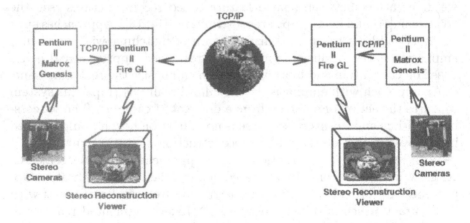

Figure 14.1   First set-up for teleimmersion hardware

The next generation of the system will integrate rendering and display technology by Henry Fuchs and his co-workers at the University of North Carolina, Chapel Hill. The difference in the 3D scene acquisition will be a new surround configuration of seven cameras arranged in an arc of 120 deg. These seven cameras yield five overlapping stereo triples each of them connected to a four-Pentium-III multi-processor workstation. The cameras will be digital and connected to the workstations via an IEEE 1394 interface.

The display system will be in a remote geographic location consisting of a polarized stereo projector system and a wall as a display. The user's head will be magnetically tracked and the received 3D-scene will be rendered in an SGI engine. Projection of the remote scene in life size will maximize spatial augmentation and thus the feeling of sharing the same room.

Our innovation in this system will be a new trinocular stereo reconstruction algorithm. Our surround camera configuration produces image planes which cannot be warped into a common rectified plane. We describe in a later section a new algorithm and results based on such a non-rectifiable stereo configuration.

To minimize processing and transmission time the background is assumed to be stationary, reconstructed once initially, and then permanently subtracted from every incoming scene.

4.   BINOCULAR STEREO RECONSTRUCTION

We elaborate next the main steps of the reconstruction algorithm with emphasis on the factors that affect the quality of reconstruction and the processing time. Our reconstruction uses two images but it is easily extensible to a polynocular configuration. We rely on the well known stereo processing steps of matching and triangulation given that the cameras are calibrated.

Filtering. It is well known that two image patches can be matched if they contain sufficient gray-value variation. Since most of the matching steps are time consuming we want to avoid them if we know a-priori that there is not sufficient image structure to match. Therefore, we compute the image gradient at each position by convolving the image with a Gaussian derivative. A subsequent thresholding extracts the image areas with a high gradient.

If the background is stationary we would like to avoid its reconstruction at each time-frame. A change detection method detects only the moving area on the image by thresholding the quotient of temporal derivative and spatial gradient.

Rectification. When a 3D-point is projected onto the left and the right image plane of a fixating stereo-rig the difference in the image positions is both in horizontal and vertical directions. Given a point in the first image we can reduce the 2D search to 1D if we know the so called *epipolar geometry* of the camera which is given from calibration. Because the subsequent step of correlation is area based, and for reduction of time complexity, we first perform a warping of the image that makes every epipolar line horizontal [1]. This image transformation is called *rectification* and results in corresponding points having coordinates (u, v) and $(u - d, v)$, in left and right rectified images, respectively, where d is the horizontal disparity.

Matching: disparity map computation. The degree of correspondence is measured by a modified normalized cross-correlation (MNCC) [12],

$$c(I_L, I_R) = \frac{2\,cov(I_L, I_R)}{var(I_L) + var(I_R)} , \tag{14.1}$$

where I_L and I_R are the left and right rectified images over the selected correlation windows. For each pixel (u, v) in the left image, the matching produces a correlation profile $c(u, v, d)$ where d ranges over a disparity range. The definition domain is the so called *disparity range* and depends on the depth of *working volume*, i.e. the range of possible depths we want to reconstruct. The time complexity of matching is linearly proportional to the size of the correlation window as well as to the disparity range.

We consider *all* peaks of the correlation profile as possible disparity hypotheses. This is different from other matching approaches which decide early on the maximum of the matching criterion. We call the resulting list of hypotheses for all positions a *disparity volume*. The hypotheses in the disparity volume are pruned out by a *selection procedure* that is based on the constraints imposed by

- Visibility: If a spatial point is visible then there can not be any other point in the viewing rays through this point and the left or right camera.

- Ordering: Depth ordering constrains the image positions in the rectified images. Both constraints can be formulated in terms of disparities without reconstructing the considered 3D-point [20, 5].

The output of this procedure is an integer *disparity map*. To refine the 3-D position estimates, a *subpixel correction* of the integer disparity map is computed which results in a subpixel disparity map. The subpixel disparity can be obtained either using a simple interpolation of the scores or using a more general approach as described in [4] which takes into account the distortion between left and right correlation windows, induced by the perspective projection, assuming that the surface can be locally approximated with a plane. The first approach is faster while the second gives a more reliable estimate of the subpixel disparity. We chose an extended version of the former which assumes preservation of the intensity value left and right. To achieve fast subpixel estimation and satisfactory accuracy we proceed as follows.

Let ϵ be the unknown subpixel correction. For corresponding pixels in the left and right images,

$$I_L(u,v) = \alpha I_R(u - d + \epsilon, v) = \alpha(I_R(u - d, v) + \epsilon \nabla I_R(u - d, v)), \quad (14.2)$$

where the coefficient α takes into account possible differences in camera gains. By taking a first order linear approximation of Eq. (14.2) over the correlation window we obtain the equivalent of a differential method for computing the optical flow. We use an FIR-filter-approximation of the image gradient appearing in the above formula. The disparity map is the input to the reconstruction procedure.

3D-reconstruction. Each of the stereo rigs is calibrated before the experiment using a standard "strong" calibration technique [18]. The calibration estimates the two 3x4 projection matrices for the left and the right camera. Given the disparity at each point and the calibration matrix the coordinates of a 3D-point can be computed.

From the disparity maps and the camera projection matrices the spatial positions of the 3D points are computed based on triangulation [6]. The result of the reconstruction (from a single stereo pair of images) is a list of spatial points.

The error in the reconstruction depends on the error in the disparity and the error in the calibration matrices. Since the action to be reconstructed is close to the origin of the world coordinate system the depth error due to calibration is negligible in comparison to the error in the disparities. What is mainly of concern is the number of outliers in the depth estimates resulting in invalid depth points usually appearing near occlusion or texture-less areas.

Once we have extracted the depth of the remote user, we augment the local user's world by putting the extracted real avatar of the remote user in it. We can further augment the environment with a synthetic object like a teapot by placing it in the local user's world.

5.   A NOVEL TRINOCULAR STEREO ALGORITHM

Reconstructions from a single stereo pair often have errors and extreme outliers due to ambiguity in matches along the epipolar line. For applications such as building detailed object models or creating models of humans for virtual environments, identifying and eliminating such points or patches is critical, but often difficult and expensive. One well known constraint for reducing these ambiguities is to add a third camera to verify hypothesized matches. The trinocular epipolar constraint in stereo vision is based on the fact that for a hypothesized match $[u, v, d]$ in a pair of images, there is a unique location we can predict in the third camera image, where we expect to find evidence of the same world point [5]. A hypothesis is correct if the epipolar lines in the third camera image for the original point $[u, v]$ and the hypothesized match $[u - d, v]$, intersect.

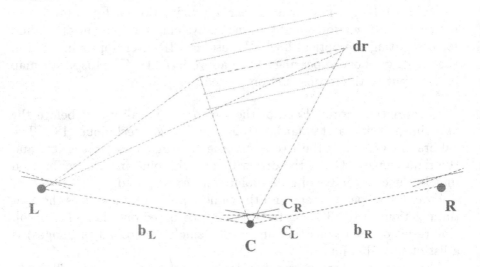

Figure 14.2   Trinocular camera triple

The configurations we are interested in are similar to that depicted in Figure 14.2, where a sequence of cameras surrounds an object to be modeled or a user interacting with an augmented reality system.

We begin by independently rectifying the left and center cameras (L and C_L) and the center and right cameras (C_R and R), so that their epipolar lines are parallel respectively. For the right rectified camera pair every disparity d_R to be searched represents a plane with constant Z, which can be projected into the L and C_L images to compute the corresponding $[u_L, v_L, d_L]$ for each $[u_R, v_R, d_R]$. This straightforward application of the trinocular constraint is illustrated in Figure 14.2.

Of course for any Z-plane constructed from d_R, a range of d_L will be required to match points in the left pair. For example for the im-

Figure 14.3 Three camera views

ages used later, the right range $D_R = [-90, 10]$ corresponds to a left range $D_L = [-74, 67]$. Also because the two pairs are independently rectified, corresponding points in the left pair will not necessarily have $v_L = v_R$, thus all of u_L, v_L, and d_L depend on $[u_R, v_R, d_R]$. The calculation is simplified slightly by the fact that C_L and C_R are derived from the same image C and are related by the a priori rectification rotations R_{CL} and R_{CR}. We can thus precompute a lookup table of locations in C_L equivalent to those in C_R by precalculating $[u_{CL}, v_{CL}, s] = R_{CL}R_{CR}^{-1}[u_{CR}, v_{CR}, 1]^T$, for all image locations.

Our underlying matching measure is modified normalized cross correlation (MNCC) as defined above. Borrowing from [14] the insight that we need to select matches based on minima (or maxima in the case of correlation) of the combined matching measure with respect to depth, we sum the MNCC values for corresponding $[u_R, v_R, d_R]$ and $[u_L, v_L, d_L]$ to obtain a correlation measure which now varies between -2 and $+2$.

Given the intrinsic and extrinsic camera parameters, and rectification matrices we can precalculate D_L, the range of d_L generated by the plane implied by the current d_R. We calculate and store the right to left (C_L to L) correlation for the left pair, for all $d_L \in D_L$. This gives us a set c_L of $k = |D_L|$ planes of correlation values for the left center image. To evaluate a match at $[u_R, v_R, d_R]$, we calculate $c_r = \text{MNCC}(C_R, R, d_R)$ first. For the left pair we calculate the location (u_{LL}, v_{LL}) of points on the depth plane in the left rectified image L. Using the precomputed lookup table we find the coordinates (u_{CL}, v_{CL}) and finally we can calculate the disparity $d_L = u_{LL} - u_{CL}$ for each point. Given the corresponding $[u_{CL}, v_{CL}, d_L]$ for each point in the center right image, we can look up the correlation value c_L at the specified location in the computed left correlation planes. We can now calculate our overall correspondence by $S_{corr} = c_L + c_R$.

In Fig. 14.4 we show results of binocular and trinocular reconstruction of the stereo triple in Fig. 14.3.

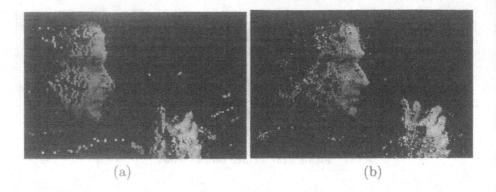

(a)   (b)

Figure 14.4   (a) Reconstructed views for binocular and (b) trinocular matching.

6.   PERFORMANCE

We next present a listing of the timing of every algorithmic step for two exemplary parameter set-ups resulting in a frame-rate of 2Hz and 0.5Hz, respectively. The fast set-up has a quarter of the resolution of the original slow set-up as well as half of the working volume. The working volume in the slow set-up is 50cm at a distance of 1m of the camera. We do not mention the effective bandwidth of our network connection and the display speed because both of them are orders of magnitude faster than the reconstruction processing (for a local network application) and depend on the coding of the transmitted data.

Table 14.1   Timings of each processing step in two different qualities

Step	Fast setup	Slow setup
Total time	506ms	2080ms
Rectification	26ms	110ms
Filtering	32ms	90ms
Correlation and Selection	358ms	1460ms
Subpixel disparity	42ms	270ms
Reconstr. and Coloring	48ms	150ms

The real power of the system lies in the accuracy of the depth estimation without sacrificing time. We achieve a relative depth error of less than 0.1% at a distance of 1m (less than 1mm). The comparison to the performance of other stereo algorithms is difficult since we have to consider both depth accuracy and speed. Furthermore, depth accuracy is measurable only on objects with known ground-truth which are difficult to compare with human figures.

There exist considerably faster systems all of them based on rougher depth estimates. The Stereo Vision Machine II from SRI [7] and the Interval stereo processor [19] use a DSP C60 and an FPGA array, respectively, achieving a video frame rate (30Hz) of processing. However, their depth accuracy is not useful for close range systems because it is based on integer disparity estimation. Pentium-II based machines are the SRI-SVM-I [7] and the Point-Grey Triclops trinocular systems which achieve 12 and 3 frames per second, respectively, but also provide only integer-valued disparities. It should be emphasized that the Genesis frame grabber board used in our approach may have a DSP on board but still has to be considered as off-the-shelf hardware, first due to its low price and second due to the convenience of its programming.

7. CONCLUSIONS AND THE FUTURE

We have presented a first real-time implementation of 3D-teleimmersion based on view-point independent scene acquisition. The current stereo-reconstruction uses state of the art stereo matching. We also introduced a novel trinocular algorithm which will be part of the next system release. The fusion of the two 3D worlds is asynchronous which facilitates higher flexibility in the display site. The implementation enables the tuning of quality and working volume vs. speed. The user can choose an acceptable balance among size of working volume, depth quality, and spatial resolution.

As with many other prototypes in the history of technology, ours opens numerous challenges for all disciplines of graphics, vision, and communication. Teleimmersion is already recognized as one of the key-applications for Internet-2. The main challenge for the vision as well as the graphics community is the issue of representation. Like the explosion of coding techniques for transmission of 2D images after the introduction of WWW we anticipate breakthroughs in problems related to representation.

The wide use of 3D-data from reconstruction raises demand for a higher quality of shape representation. We are working on the critical problems of occluding contours and specularities arising in stereo reconstruction. The dynamics of the scene necessitate shape representations that will be easily updatable using some simple assumptions on temporal coherence. Even if we use multiple cameras to obtain a surround capture we need surface parameterizations that can be also spatially registered in a simple and robust way. Last but not least, the 3D-data have to be transmitted over the network. The challenge for progressive 3D wavelet-like representations which simultaneously address the critical issues above, remains open.

Acknowledgments

This work has been supported by Advanced Network and Services (National Teleimmersion Initiative), ARO/MURI DAAH04-96-1-0007, and NSF CDS-97-03220. The authors gratefully acknowledge the exciting collaboration with the leading scientist of the National Teleimmersion Initiative Jaron Lanier, as well as with Henry Fuchs and the other colleagues at the University of North Carolina, Chapel Hill.

References

[1] N. Ayache and C. Hansen. Rectification of images for binocular and trinocular stereovision. In *Proc. of 9th International Conference on Pattern Recognition*, volume 1, pages 11–16, 1988.

[2] P. Belhumeur. A bayesian approach to binocular stereopsis. *Intl. J. of Computer Vision*, 19(3):237–260, 1996.

[3] E. Chen and L. Williams. View interpolation for image synthesis. In *ACM SIGGRAPH*, pages 279–288, 1993.

[4] F. Devernay. Computing differential properties of 3-D shapes from stereoscopic images without 3-D models. Technical Report RR-2304, INRIA, Sophia Antipolis, 1994.

[5] U. Dhond and J. Aggrawal. Structure from stereo: a review. *IEEE Transactions on Systems, Man, and Cybernetics*, 19(6):1489–1510, 1989.

[6] O. Faugeras. *Three-dimensional Computer Vision*. MIT Press, Cambridge, MA, 1993.

[7] K. Konolige. Small vision system: Hardware and implementation. In *Eighth International Symposium on Robotics Research, Hayama, Japan*, pages 203–212, 1997.

[8] K. Kutulakos and J. Vallino. Calibration-free augmented reality. *IEEE Trans. on Visualization and Computer Graphics*, 4(1):1–20, 1998.

[9] M. Macedonia and S. Noll. Real-time 60hz distortion correction on a silicon graphics IG. *IEEE Computer Graphics and Applications*, 5:76–82, 1998.

[10] L. Matthies. Stereo vision for planetary rovers: Stochastic modeling to near real-time implementation. *Intl. J. of Computer Vision*, 8:71–91, 1992.

[11] S. Maybank and O. Faugeras. A theory of self-calibration of a moving camera. *Intl. J. of Computer Vision*, 8(2):123–151, 1992.

[12] H. Moravec. Robot rover visual navigation. *Computer Science: Artificial Intelligence*, pages 105–108, 1980/1981.

[13] P. Narayanan, P. Rander, and T. Kanade. Constructing virtual worlds using dense stereo. In *Proc, Intl. Conf. Computer Vision ICCV98*, pages 3–10, 1998.

[14] M. Okutomi and T. Kanade. A multiple-baseline stereo. *IEEE Trans. on Pattern Analysis and Machine Intelligence*, 15(4):353–363, 1993.

[15] D. Scharstein and R. Szeliski. Stereo matching with non-linear diffusion. In *Proc. Int. Conf. Computer Vision and Pattern Recognition*, pages 343–350. IEEE Computer Society, 1996.

[16] S. M. Seitz and C. R. Dyer. View morphing. In *ACM SIGGRAPH*, pages 21–30, 1996.

[17] C. Tomasi and R. Manduchi. Stereo without search. In *Proc. European Conf. Computer Vision*, pages 452–465, Cambridge, UK, 1996.

[18] R. Tsai. A versatile camera calibration technique for high accuracy 3D machine vision metrology using off-the-shelf TV cameras and lenses. *IEEE Trans. Robotics and Automation*, 3:323–344, 1987.

[19] J. Woodfill and B. Von Herzen. Real time stereo vision on the PARTS reconfigurable computer. In *IEEE Workshop on FPGAs for Custom Computing Machines*, pages 201–210, 1997.

[20] A. Yuille and T. Poggio. A generalized ordering constraint for stereo correspondence. AI Lab Memo 777, MIT, 1984.

Chapter 15

AUGMENTED REALITY: A PROBLEM IN NEED OF MANY COMPUTER VISION– BASED SOLUTIONS

Gudrun Klinker

Abstract   Augmented reality (AR) is a technology by which a user's view of the real world is augmented with additional information from a computer model. It constitutes a very promising new user interface concept for many applications. Yet, AR applications require fast and accurate solutions to several very complex problems, such as user and real object tracking, occlusion and reflection handling, as well as virtual user motion. Currently, computer vision based solutions are considered to be among the most promising approaches towards solving these issues. This paper discusses several such AR issues and potential solutions.

1.   INTRODUCTION

Augmented reality (AR) is a technology by which a user's view of the real world is augmented with additional information from a computer model [4, 26]. Users can work with and examine real 3D objects while receiving additional information about those objects or the task at hand. Rather than pulling the user into the computer's virtual world, AR brings information into the user's real world, thereby building upon people's visual and spatial skills.

AR constitutes a very promising new user interface concept for many applications, e.g., in medicine [6, 13, 15, 34], exterior construction [22], interior design [1, 32], the assembly, maintenance and repair of complex technical objects [8, 11, 28], and games [21, 32] (Fig. 15.1). With the increasing availability of virtual prototypes, industries can benefit from AR during all phases of the life cycle of a product, integrating the computer- generated information with the physical environment.

267

A. Leonardis et al. (eds.), Confluence of Computer Vision and Computer Graphics, 267–284.

Figure 15.1   Manipulation of real objects within an augmented world [20, 21].

Yet, AR applications require fast and accurate solutions to several very complex problems, such as user and real object tracking, occlusion and reflection handling, as well as virtual user motion. Currently, computer vision based solutions are considered to be among the most promising approaches towards solving these issues. This paper discusses several such AR issues and potential solutions.

2.   TYPICAL AR CONFIGURATIONS

Several different arrangements of display and tracking devices are currently in use depending on the purposes and constraints of different applications.

- *Head-mounted see-through AR*
  Head-mounted, see-through displays are the prototypical setup that people envision first when talking about AR [20]. Users wear a head-mounted semi-transparent display through which they can see the world like through a set of sunglasses. Shown inside the glasses are three-dimensional objects. They are rendered according to the current vantage point of the user such that the virtual objects seem to co-exist side-by-side with real objects in the scene. When users move their heads, the virtual objects maintain their position in the world. Magnetic or acoustical trackers, gyroscopes, or mini-cameras [20] are attached to the HMD in order to track its position in the scene.

- *Head-mounted video-feed-through AR*
  Video-feed-through HMDs are used in a fashion very similar to see-through displays, except that the display is opaque in this case.

The real scene is recorded by one or two (stereo) video cameras attached to the HMD. The video signal is displayed inside the HMD, thereby showing users the real world around them. Compared to the see-through solution, precise augmentations of such video-based reality are easier to achieve since the augmentations can be inserted into a suitable recent video image whenever the results become available. Yet, implementations tend to lack the immediacy of a truely immersive see-through setup due to the offset between the cameras and the user's eyes, the limited resolution of the video signal, and the time lag between recording, processing, augmenting and displaying the video signal. Nevertheless, if the geometric offset and time lag can be kept small, video-feed-through AR is very successful. It is thus a very common setup in demonstrations.

- *Monitor-based AR*
  In monitor-based setups [20], users view video-based augmentations on a monitor rather than in an opaque HMD. The video images are recorded by a mobile camera which could be anywhere – on the user's head, in his hands, on a tripod, on a wall, on a moving robot, or with a collaborator. By decoupling the display coordinate system from the camera coordinate system, AR can thus be related to collaborative and telepresence concepts.

- *Portable monitors*
  Flat, portable AR monitors [29], provide hand-held video augmentations. A camera on the back of the device records the scene behind the screen. The picture is augmented and displayed on the monitor, generating the illusion of a picture frame inside which the real world is augmented with virtual objects.

- *Combinations of various wearable devices*
  In realistic AR applications, it is likely that no one display modality will be used by itself. Rather, users will prefer having a choice between several display devices each for its own purpose. Feiner et al. [11] are combining the immersive 3D display qualities of a HMD with better 2D resolutions of a portable monitor, allowing users to drag pieces of information involving extended amounts of text from the HMD to a Netscape-based browser in their hand.

3.   USER TRACKING

Precise user tracking is one of the key issues in AR since it determines the immersive quality and credibility of the augmentations. Virtual objects have to be rendered from a virtual camera perspective that is identical with the current vantage point of the user.

Various carefully calibrated sensing devices have been used for this purpose in the past [2, 5, 33]. Commercial tracking devices such as magnetic trackers and active LED-systems can be used [11, 33]. But the precision and the working range of such devices are insufficient for most AR applications. Thus, research is now focusing on computer vision based methods which promise untethered, higher-precision applicability of AR.

However, the vision-based approaches cannot be arbitrarily sophisticated and complex. They have to perform in real-time and they have to be very robust, degrading gracefully and recovering fast when they fail. Users wearing a HMD cannot be expected to restrain their natural head motions severely while interacting with the system, neither can they be expected to stay motionless while the system is trying to recover from failures. Thus, vision-based approaches have started from very simple, limited setups. They are now progressing towards more sophisticated approaches.

3.1   TRACKING OPTICAL MARKERS AT KNOWN 3D POSITIONS

Currently, the most successful vision-based approaches track optical markers in indoor laboratory demonstrations (Fig. 15.1) [23, 24, 27, 30, 31, 34] sometimes combined with information from other tracking modalities [22, 27, 30]. Optical markers provide enough simplifying assumptions to achieve real-time tracking performance. Typically, the markers are specially designed to be easily recognizable. Examples are polka dots of varying sizes placed in pre-designed patterns on large form boards for Boeing's wire harness assembly application [8], large dark rectangles with unique identification labels at Fraunhofer-IGD's doorlock installation demonstration [20, 28, 31], and concentric, multi-colored rings at Neumann's lab at USC [27] and in Fuchs's lab at UNC [30]. The placement of such markers is quite a severe restriction to the overall applicability of the system. It is tedious to install a significant number of them necessary to warrant a robust operation of the system. In some applications (especially outdoors), such an approach is completely impractical.

Yet, the current demonstrators are a good starting point to begin experimenting with more general concepts.

3.2   TRACKING NATURAL FEATURES AT KNOWN 3D POSITIONS

As a first step towards generalizing vision-based, real-time user tracking setups, several approaches are now tracking features that occur naturally at known positions in the scene [27, 31]. Stricker et al. [28, 31] track three-dimensional lines, such as the edges of doors and walls as well as strongly bent edges on car bodies which tend to show up as slim bright lines due to specular reflections . The 3D positions and orientations of these lines are measured ahead of time and provided to the tracker in a data file. After initialization, the system predicts the position of such known lines in each image according to the most recently known camera position and searches for them in a local image area. From several non-collinear lines, it then computes the new camera position. The approach works very well when provided with an initial calibration. Yet, it requires more detailed information at startup time, such as black squares with unique identification marks.

For outdoor exterior construction applications, Klinker et al. [19, 20] use a different approach. It is not possible to install special markers ubiquitously in vast outdoor environments. Besides, the markers would have to be huge to be visible from long distances. Instead, natural landmarks must be used as calibration marks. Klinker et al. currently select easily visible landmarks (such as church steeples, tips of power line poles, bridge pillars and river banks) off-line and determine their three-dimensional position from other sources. When calibrating and augmenting a video sequence of the area, they interactively indicate the location of such landmarks in the initial image. The landmarks are then tracked in subsequent images using normalized correlation such that the video sequence can be calibrated with minimal user intervention.

Although these approaches don't require scene modifications, they still depend on complicated setup procedures involving the three-dimensional measurement of natural landmarks and their initial identification in an initial image. Model-based computer vision approaches are needed in order to automatically associate large sets of known 3D landmarks with currently visible image features using suitable feature properties. Such object recognition has to work in real-time since the initialization phase of an AR system cannot require the user to remain motionless for extended periods of time whenever the system looses track and requires a re-initialization. Alternatively, several hybrid approaches address the initialization problem by combining optical trackers with other technology, such as magnetic trackers [30], GPS [22], or gyroscopes [27].

3.3   TRACKING NATURAL FEATURES AT UNKNOWN 3D POSITIONS

The logical next step involves striving for optical tracking solutions that do not require the off-line three-dimensional measurement of landmarks. Mendelsohn et al. [25] use an uncalibrated stereo vision approach for indoor applications. They do place special, easily identifiable targets (black pentagons) in the scene, but they do not determine their 3D location. Using the constraint that each target pentagon lies in a plane, they are able to compute a highly accurate, metric scene reconstruction after tracking the targets for a few images, gaining increasingly precise estimates the longer the tracking proceeds. The system currently runs off-line on prerecorded sequences involving up to 1200 images (40 seconds).

Neumann et al. [27] are presenting first steps towards tracking unknown landmarks outdoors . They track both interesting feature points and entire regions using differential-based local optical flow estimation. A multi-scale estimation strategy iteratively fits region and point motion estimates to an affine motion model until they agree. The approach is able to dramatically improve the precision of a hybrid inertial (3 DOF) and vision tracker. Treating the fusion of inertial and image tracks as a 2D image stabilization problem, the hybrid tracker is able to annotate three-dimensional objects such as cars and entrance gates to parking lots very reliably after the intrinsic camera parameters and an initial camera position have been determined off-line. So far, the algorithm is used off-line since it does not yet operate in real-time.

3.4   MODELING OF USER MOTION

Due to numerical instabilities of the camera calibration involving a large number of parameters in a system of non-linear equations, it is not advisable to calibrate incoming pictures independently of each other one at a time. Calibrations are likely to jump back and forth between solutions at different local maxima of the parameter space. To introduce a temporal constraint, physical motion models have to be added to the system.

It is very customary in computer vision applications to use Newtonian motion models which describe the velocity and acceleration of a point in space over time. Such models have been applied to the problem of tracking user head motions [3, 23]. Yet, due to the randomness of user head motion, it is hard to predict future head motion from history looking merely at velocity and acceleration. Impulse seems to play a significant role. Sophisticated motion prediction models [23] so far have encountered serious problems tracking a user-held or user-worn camera. The prediction of 3D user motion is too slow on today's computers to quickly react to a user's head rotations (e.g., during a quick glance to the side or a head shaking motion), generating an effect of "swimming" off track. If the head motion is very abrupt, the system never recovers from its "detour".

Thus, current approaches tend to be much more pragmatic, ignoring 3D motion constraints alltogether and simplifying motion analysis down to a 2D, image-based analysis of local pixel motion coupled with numerical initialization heuristics to ensure that calibrations of consecutive images are likely to settle at that same local extremum of the parameter space. Such approaches are surprisingly successful since they are able to perform at close-to-real-time speeds on current computer systems [20, 31].

4.   3D SCENE MODELING FOR OCCLUSION AND REFLECTION HANDLING

In order to augment real worlds with virtual objects, the virtual objects need to be integrated seamlessly into the environment. They have to behave in physically plausible manners: they occlude or are occluded by real objects, they are not able to move through other objects, and they cast shadows on other objects. To this end, AR applications require a very accurate model of the real environment (a reality model).

4.1   OCCLUSION HANDLING BETWEEN REAL AND VIRTUAL OBJECTS

Occlusion relationships between real and virtual objects can be computed efficiently by the geometric rendering hardware of today's graphics workstations. By first rendering the AR reality model transparently, the z-buffer of the rendering engine is initialized to account for the distances of real objects from the user. Since the model is drawn transparently, it remains invisible and thus does not obstruct the view onto the real world (or its video picture). When the virtual objects are rendered subsequently, only those are drawn that are closer than any real objects to the user.

4.2   GEOMETRIC REALITY MODELS

Occlusion handling in AR applications requires geometrically precise descriptions of the real world. Similar descriptions are also used in Virtual Reality (VR) applications. Yet, for AR, such reality models generally don't need to be as complex as those used for VR. VR models are expected to synthetically provide a realistic immersive impression of the simulated environment. Thus, the descriptions of surface textures are crucial. AR, on the other hand, can rely on live optical input (or a live view of the real world) to provide a very high sense of realism. For occlusion handling, the AR reality model only needs to describe the surface shape.

However, AR reality models have to be much more precise than VR models. Since an immersive VR system cuts users off from reality, users can only gain a qualitative impression whether or not the objects are modeled correctly. In AR, on the other hand, users have an immediate quantitative appreciation of the extent of disagreements between the reality model and the real world, since virtual objects then won't integrate into it seamlessly.

Reality models for AR applications are currently acquired in many different ways depending on the requirements and data sources of a particular application. In many cases, 3D scene information is provided manually by the user, e.g., in simple text files describing the locations of markers on planar laboratory walls. In other cases, pre-existing CAD models of man-made objects can be used [28]. Sometimes, maps and geodesic measurements of landscapes and cityscapes are available [19]. Most of the time, however, current AR systems ignore issues related to occlusion handling alltogether because appropriate models of cluttered scenes are hard to generate. The automatic construction of scene models by computer vision techniques is a promising way to help alleviate this problem.

The construction of 3D scene descriptions is a long-standing issue in computer vision research. Its application to AR applications is being demonstrated increasingly. Semi-automatic approaches towards generating architectural models from images have been reported by Debevec et al. [9] and by Faugeras [10]. Kanade et al. [17] have built a setup at Carnegie Mellon involving 51 calibrated video cameras that are arranged on the periphery of a "3D Dome". Dynamic scenes inside the dome such as multi-person ballgames are recorded by all cameras. Applying a trinocular vision approach to each group of three cameras, the system then computes, off-line, a fairly accurate dynamic 3D model of the game, a "virtualized reality". Hirose and Tanikawa [14] are using a van with 8 cameras, a GPS sensor, a terrestrial magnetism sensor and a 3-axis angle sensor on its roof to drive through the streets of Tokyo, recording image sequences and positional data. Back in the laboratory, they invite visitors to a virtual walk through the recorded parts of the city using image-based rendering techniques.

4.3 REFLECTION HANDLING BETWEEN REAL AND VIRTUAL OBJECTS

In addition to handling occlusions between virtual and real objects, AR-systems also need to be able to handle photometric relationships. If the positions of all light sources and the reflective material properties of all real objects are known, inter-reflections and shadows from real objects onto virtual objects can be taken into account when rendering the virtual ones. Furthermore, the video pixels showing the real objects can be modified to simulate the influence of virtual light sources as well as inter-reflections and shadows from virtual objects [12, 30].

4.4 PHOTOMETRIC REALITY MODELS

Quintessential to reflection handling in AR applications is the availability of photometric reality models. The models need to indicate the location of all direct and indirect light sources in the real scene. To this end, Ikeuchi et al. [16] have developed a photometric model-based rendering method. From calibrated input images of real objects and a previously obtained geometric reality model, it obtains reflectance parameters of the real objects by tracking individual small spots on the 3D surface through the image sequence and relating their color changes to user motion: in principle, pixels related to a particular surface area of a 3D object should remain constant when the user moves through the scene. Using a color histogram analysis, Ikeuchi et al. attribute color variations to sensor noise and to occasional specular reflections. After discounting such effects, they can attribute an intrinsic reflective color property to each small surface area of real objects.

4.5 PHYSICAL INTERACTIONS BETWEEN REAL AND VIRTUAL OBJECTS

For an augmented world to be realistic the virtual objects not only have to interact optically with the real world, but also mechanically. This applies to virtual objects when animated or manipulated by the user. For example, a virtual chair shouldn't go through walls when it is moved, and it should exhibit gravitational forces [7]. Given a reality model, this behavior can be achieved using collision detection and avoidance systems that are known from Virtual Reality systems [36].

These two laws make up the most important physical constraints. A full physical simulation including more aspects of the interaction between real and virtual objects, such as elastic behavior and friction, would be desirable. For off-line applications this is possible if enough information about the virtual objects and a complete enough reality model is available. For real-time applications most simulation systems are not fast enough. Yet, even simple implementations of the above rules will make the system much more realistic.

5.   DIMINISHED REALITY

Many AR applications require that existing structures be removed before new objects are added to the scene. For example, interior design or refurbishment typically doesn't start from an empty room. Rather, the area is cluttered with all kinds of furniture or structure that needs to be moved or removed. Similarly, many exterior construction projects require the removal of old buildings before new ones are put into their place. Medical and machine repair applications as well typically require x-ray vision skills, allowing the user to ignore current structures in the foreground to focus on what is behind it. Thus, just as important as augmenting reality is technology to diminish it.

The removal of foreground objects requires a model of the objects behind them, i.e., a three-dimensional reality model of the entire area. Modeling currently unseen parts of the scene is a very complex issue. There is no general solution to this problem since we cannot know what a dynamically changing world looks like behind an object at any specific instant in time—unless another camera can see the occluded area. Yet, some heuristics can be used to solve the problem for various realistic scenarios. We can use morphological operators to extrapolate properties from surrounding "intact" areas into the occluded region (e.g: in a cloudy sky) [22]. Furthermore, when a building is to be removed from a densely populated area in a city, particular static snapshots of the buildings behind it could be taken and integrated into the reality model to be mapped as textures into the appropriate spaces of the current image.

For video sequences, computer vision techniques can be used to suitably merge older image data with the new image. Faugeras et al. [37] have shown that soccer players can be erased from video footage when they occlude advertisement banners: For a static camera, changes of individual pixels can be analyzed over time, determining their statistical dependence on camera noise. When significant changes (due to a mobile person occluding the static background) are detected, "historic" pixel data can replace the current values.

In more general schemes involving mobile cameras, such techniques can lead towards incremental techniques to diminish reality. While moving about in the scene, users and cameras see parts of the background objects. When properly remembered and integrated into a three-dimensional model of the scene, such "old" image data can be reused to diminish newer images, thus increasingly effacing outdated objects from the scene as the user moves about. Stricker uses geometric constraints to compute pixelwise correspondences between regions in several images that outline a particular object [19]. From such correspondences, he traces specific points on the object across all images and then decides in which images it is visible or occluded. Accordingly, occluded pixels can be replaced by visible ones, effectively removing the occluding object from the image.

6.   MOBILE OBJECT TRACKING

In realistic AR applications, real objects in the scene cannot be expected to remain stationary throughout the entire course of running the application. Actions or instructions issued by the computer as augmentations in the HMD or on the monitor cause the user to perform actions changing the real world - which, in turn, prompt the computer to generate new, different augmentations. For example, a machine repair task typically includes a partial disassembly of the machine, followed by a replacement of some parts and a subsequent reassembly.

To maintain correct virtual-real occlusion relationships, the AR application has to keep track of all moving objects in real-time and update the reality model accordingly. Furthermore, the AR-system has to understand the meaning of the user's actions such that it can react and propose the next step of a repair procedure or indicate that a mistake has been made.

Several prototypes of two-way human-computer interaction involving limited degrees of reality tracking with non-optical means have been demonstrated. In Feiner et al.'s space frame construction system [11], selected new struts are recognized via a bar code reader, triggering the computer to update its visualizations. In a mechanical repair demonstration system, Breen et al. [7] use a magnetically tracked pointing device to ask for specific augmentations regarding information on specific components of a motor.

6.1   DETECTION AND TRACKING OF OBJECTS WITH SPECIAL MARKERS

Klinker et al. [21] currently use rather pragmatic, simple solutions towards reality tracking that can be run approximately in real-time. In a "mixed mockup" demonstration involving the insertion of virtual buildings in a miniaturized scene they attach special markers to mobile objects, such as toy buildings. Both virtual and real buildings can be moved to experiment with different house arrangements.

The current approach assumes that unique markers are attached to all mobile real and virtual objects and that they are manipulated on a set of known surfaces. The marks can then automatically be identified and their 3D position and orientation can be determined by intersecting the rays defined by the positions of the squares in the image with the three-dimensional surfaces on which they lie. If the markers are manipulated in mid-air rather than on a known surface, more sophisticated approaches are needed, such as stereo vision or the computation of the 3D target location from its projected size and shape. The current system does not apply the latter concepts due to real-time and robustness considerations.

Attaching markers to a few real objects is an elegant way of keeping track of objects even when both the camera and the objects move. The objects can have arbitrary textures that don't even have to contrast well against the background - as long as the markers can be easily detected. Yet, the markers take up space in the scene; they must not be occluded by other objects unless the attached object becomes invisible as well. Furthermore, this approach requires a planned modification of the scene which generally cannot be arranged for arbitrarily many objects. Thus it works best when only a few, well-defined objects are expected to move.

6.2   DETECTION OF OBJECTS USING OBJECT MODELS

Klinker et al. [21] show more general reality tracking schemes in the context of an augmented Tic Tac Toe game. The user and the computer alternate placing real and virtual stones on the board. When the user has finished a move, he waves his hand past a 3D "Go" button. The computer then scans the image area containing the board. If it finds a new stone, it plans its own move and places a new virtual cross on the board. If it could not find a new stone or if it found more than one, it asks the user to correct his placement of stones.

The Tic Tac Toe system uses model-based object recognition princi-ples to find new pieces on the board. Due to the image calibration the location of the game board in the image is known, as well as all nine valid positions for pieces to be placed. Furthermore, the system has maintained a history of the game. It thus knows which positions have already been filled by the user or by its own virtual pieces. It also knows that the game is played on a white board and that the user's stones are red. It thus can check very quickly and robustly which tiles of the board are covered with a stone, i.e. which tiles have a significant number of pixels that are red rather than white. Error handling can consider cases in which users have placed no new stone or more than one new stone—or whether they have placed their stones on top of one of the computer's virtual stones.

Using a model-based object recognition approach is a more general approach than the one based on special markers since it does not require scene modifications. Yet, the detection of sophisticated objects with complex shape and texture has been a long standing research problem in computer vision, consuming significant amounts of processing power. Real-time solutions for arbitrarily complex scenes still need to be developed.

Thus, the appropriate choice of algorithm depends on the requirements of an application scenario. In many cases, hybrid approaches including further information sources such as stationary overhead surveillance cameras that track mobile objects are most likely to succeed.

6.3   PEOPLE AND HAND TRACKING

During a repair procedure, the user typically manipulates real objects with his hands or with special tools. Potentially, he is also assisted by coworkers. Thus, for large parts of an AR application, moving hands and people will be visible within the scene. Human hand-eye coordination requires that the user's hands are integrated particularly well into the augmented world: when the user touches a virtual object or some virtual positioning aid like a pointer or a virtual yard stick on the floor, users have to receive immediate and precise feedback as to where their hands are in relationship to the virtual objects. Thus occlusion handling has to work well. To this end, hands and people have to be tracked in real-time.

Yokoya et al. [35] have developed a stereo-based vision system which uses two cameras on an HMD. From optical markers at unknown scene locations, the system tracks user head motion. In addition, it also tracks the motion of the user's hands, determining their current position by stereo triangulation on an SGI Onyx2 IR. The system is able to perform the stereo approximately in real-time due to its heuristics for quickly detecting skin color in each image and thereby pruning the time-consuming stereo matching process significantly. Kanade et al. [18] have reported real-time stereo vision performance for arbitrary objects using a stereo vision machine based upon special-purpose hardware. Kanade's "3D Dome" demonstrations of constructing a dynamic 3D model of a several people playing a ball game together is another example of a reality tracking system [17]—yet, it currently still has to rely on 51 prerecorded video sequences and doesn't run in real-time yet.

7.   VIRTUAL USER MOTION AND TELEPRESENCE

In addition to analyzing real user motion and real and virtual object motion, AR applications are likely to also be confronted with requirements of virtual user motion. While looking at an augmented scene and working in it in a reality-based coordinate frame, users may want to temporarily take a side-step from reality to look at the world from a different perspective. For example, while discussing a planned new building at a construction site, users might be interested in getting a bird's-eye view of the location. Similarly, a mechanic may want to temporarily step into his colleague's shoes (or HMD) during a complex repair effort of a big machine or look at details of the machine through a magnifying glass.

In this sense, augmented reality and virtual reality are not two discrete alternatives but rather part of a spectrum of mixed realities [26] with full virtual reality on one end and full physical reality on the other. Augmented Reality is in the middle, combining the best of both worlds. But sometimes it might be desirable to lean more in one direction or the other.

To leave reality behind without getting lost, users need a smooth transition path from their current position to virtual places and back. Whenever possible, available real data should be integrated into the virtual presentations. To this end, 3D scene descriptions are essential. As discussed in the previous sections, computer vision techniques lend themselves to generating and dynamically updating such descriptions from the live image data being obtained while the user moves about.

8.   SUMMARY

Augmented reality is an exciting new technology with the potential of becoming a "killer application", combining many aspects of computer science into well-designed and well-tuned systems. One of the most essential ingredients of such a system is intelligent sensor analysis technology, such as provided by computer vision research. This paper has listed many areas in which augmented reality systems can benefit greatly from concepts and approaches that are common within the computer vision community.

Acknowledgments

Most of this work was conceived and developed while the author was at the Fraunhofer Project Group for Augmented Reality at ZGDV. Close collaborators were Didier Stricker, Dirk Reiners, Eric Rose, and Dieter Koller.

References

[1] K. H. Ahlers, A. Kramer, D. E. Breen, P.-Y. Chevalier, C. Crampton, E. Rose, M. Tuceryan, R. T. Whitaker, and D. Greer. Distributed augmented reality for collaborative design applications. In *Proceedings of Eurographics '95*, 1995. Also available as technical report ECRC-95-03 (http://www.ecrc.de).

[2] R. Azuma and G. Bishop. Improving static and dynamic registration in an optical see-through HMD. In *Proc. Siggraph'94*, pages 197–204, Orlando, FL, July 1994. ACM.

[3] R. Azuma and G. Bishop. A frequency-domain analysis of head-motion prediction. In *Proc. Siggraph'95*, pages 401–408, Los Angeles, CA, August 1995. ACM.

[4] R.T. Azuma. A survey of augmented reality. *Presence, Special Issue on Augmented Reality*, 6(4):355–385, August 1997.

[5] R.T. Azuma. The challenge of making augmented reality work outdoors. In *Proc. ISMR'99 (1. International Symposium on Mixed Reality)*, pages 379–390, Yokohama, Japan, March 1999.

[6] J.W. Berger and D.S. Shin. Computer-vision-enabled ophtalmic augmented reality: A PC-based prototype. In *Proc. IEEE and ACM IWAR'98 (1. International Workshop on Augmented Reality)*, pages 19–30, San Francisco, November 1998. AK Peters.

[7] D.E. Breen, E. Rose, and R.T. Whitaker. Interactive occlusion and collision of real and virtual objects in augmented reality. Technical Report ECRC-95-02, ECRC, Arabellastr. 17, D-81925 Munich, http://www.ecrc.de, 1995.

[8] D. Curtis, D. Mizell, P. Gruenbaum, and A. Janin. Several devils in the details: Making an AR App work in the airplane factory. In *Proc. IEEE and ACM IWAR'98 (1. International Workshop on Augmented Reality)*, pages 47–60, San Francisco, November 1998. AK Peters.

[9] P. E. Debevec, C. J. Taylor, and J. Malik. Modeling and rendering architecture from photographs: A hybrid geometry- and image-based approach. In *Proc. SIGGRAPH*, pages 11–20, New Orleans, August 4-9 1996. ACM.

[10] O. Faugeras, S. Laveau, L. Robert, G. Csurka, and C. Zeller. 3D reconstruction of urban scenes from sequences of images. In A. Gruen, O. Kuebler, and P. Agouris, editors, *Automatic Extraction of Man-Made Objects from Aerial and Space Images*. Birkhauser, 1995.

[11] S. Feiner, B. MacIntyre, and T. Hoellerer. Wearing it out: First steps toward mobile augmented reality systems. In *Proc. ISMR'99 (1.*

International Symposium on Mixed Reality), pages 363–377, Yokohama, Japan, March 1999.

[12] A. Fournier. Illumination problems in Computer Augmented Reality. *Journee Analyse/Synthese d'Images (JASI)*, pages 1–21, January 1994.

[13] W. E. L. Grimson, G. J. Ettinger, S. J. White, P. L. Gleason, T. Lozano-Perez, W. M Wells III, and R. Kikinis. Evaluating and validating an automated registration system for enhanced reality visualization in surgery. In *Proc. of Computer Vision, Virtual Reality and Robotics in Medicine (CVRMed '95)*, pages 3–12, Nice, France, April 1995. IEEE.

[14] M. Hirose, T. Tanikawa, and T. Endo. Building a virtual world from the real world. In *Proc. ISMR'99 (1. International Symposium on Mixed Reality)*, pages 183–197, Yokohama, Japan, March 1999.

[15] W. A. Hoff. Fusion of data from head-mounted and fixed sensors. In *Proc. IEEE and ACM IWAR'98 (1. International Workshop on Augmented Reality)*, pages 167–182, San Francisco, November 1998. AK Peters.

[16] K. Ikeuchi, Y. Sato, K. Nishino, and I. Sato. Photometric modeling for mixed reality. In *Proc. ISMR'99 (1. International Symposium on Mixed Reality)*, pages 147–163, Yokohama, Japan, March 1999.

[17] T. Kanade, P. Rander, S. Vedula, and H. Saito. Virtualized reality: Digitizing a 3D time varying event as is and in real time. In *Proc. ISMR'99 (1. International Symposium on Mixed Reality)*, pages 41–57, Yokohama, Japan, March 1999.

[18] T. Kanade, A. Yoshida, K. Oda, H. Kano, and M. Tanaka. A stereo machine for video-rate dense depth mapping and its new applications. In *Proc. 15th Computer Vision and Pattern Recognition Conference (CVPR'96)*, San Francisco, June 18-20 1996. IEEE.

[19] G. Klinker, D. Stricker, and D. Reiners. The use of reality models in augmented reality applications. In *European Workshop on 3D Structure from Multiple Images of Large-scale Environments (SMILE)*, Freiburg, Germany, June 6-7 1998.

[20] G. Klinker, D. Stricker, and D. Reiners. Augmented reality: A balancing act between high quality and real-time constraints. In *Proc. ISMR'99 (1. International Symposium on Mixed Reality)*, pages 325–346, Yokohama, Japan, March 1999.

[21] G. Klinker, D. Stricker, and D. Reiners. An optically based direct manipulation interface for human-computer interaction in an

augmented world. In *Proc. Eurographics Workshop on Virtual Environments (EGVE)*, Vienna, Austria, June 1999.

[22] G. Klinker, D. Stricker, and D. Reiners. Augmented reality for exterior construction applications. In W. Barfield and T. Caudell, editors, *Augmented Reality and Wearable Computers*. Lawrence Erlbaum Press, 2000.

[23] D. Koller, G. Klinker, E. Rose, D. Breen, R. Whitaker, and M. Tuceryan. Automated camera calibration and 3D egomotion estimation for augmented reality applications. In *7th Int'l Conf. on Computer Analysis of Images and Patterns (CAIP-97)*, Kiel, Germany, September 10–12, 1997, G. Sommer, K. Daniilidis, and J. Pauli (eds.), Lecture Notes in Computer Science 1296, Springer-Verlag, Berlin, Heidelberg, New York, 1997.

[24] J. P. Mellor. Enhanced reality visualization in a surgical environment. Master's thesis, Dept. of Electrical Engineering, MIT, 1995.

[25] J. Mendelsohn, K. Daniilidis, and R. Bajcsy. Constrained self-calibration for augmented reality registration. In *Proc. IEEE and ACM IWAR'98 (1. International Workshop on Augmented Reality)*, pages 201–208, San Francisco, November 1998. AK Peters.

[26] P. Milgram and Jr H. Colquhoun. A taxonomy of real and virtual world display integration. In *Proc. 1st International Symposium on Mixed Reality (ISMR'99)*, pages 5–30, Yokohama, Japan, March 1999.

[27] U. Neumann, S. You, Y. Cho, J. Lee, and J. Park. Augmented reality tracking in natural environments. In *Proc. 1st International Symposium on Mixed Reality (ISMR'99)*, pages 101–130, Yokohama, Japan, March 1999.

[28] D. Reiners, D. Stricker, G. Klinker, and S. Mueller. Augmented reality for construction tasks: Doorlock assembly. In *Proc. IEEE and ACM IWAR'98 (1. International Workshop on Augmented Reality)*, pages 31–46, San Francisco, November 1998. AK Peters.

[29] J. Rekimoto. Navicam: A magnifying glass approach to augmented reality. *Presence, Special Issue on Augmented Reality*, 6(4):399–412, August 1997.

[30] A. State, G. Hirota, D. T. Chen, W. F. Garrett, and M. A. Livingston. Superior augmented reality registration by integrating landmark tracking and magnetic tracking. In *Proc. SIGGRAPH*, pages 429–438, New Orleans, Aug 4-9 1996. ACM.

[31] D. Stricker, G. Klinker, and D. Reiners. A fast and robust line-based optical tracker for augmented reality applications. In *1. Interna-*

tional Workshop on Augmented Reality (IWAR'98), pages 129–145, San Francisco, November 1998. AK Peters.

[32] H. Tamura, H. Yamamoto, and A. Katayama. Steps toward seamless mixed reality. In *Proc. ISMR'99 (1. International Symposium on Mixed Reality)*, pages 59–59, Yokohama, Japan, March 1999.

[33] M. Tuceryan, D. Greer, R. Whitaker, D. Breen, C. Crampton, E. Rose, and K. Ahlers. Calibration requirements and procedures for a monitor-based augmented reality system. *IEEE Transactions on Visualization and Computer Graphics*, 1, September 1995.

[34] M. Uenohara and T. Kanade. Vision-based object registration for real-time image overlay. In *Proc. of Computer Vision, Virtual Reality and Robotics in Medicine (CVRMed '95)*, pages 13–22, Nice, France, April 1995. IEEE.

[35] N. Yokoya, H. Takemura, T. Okuma, and M. Kanbara. Stereo vision based video see-through mixed reality. In *Proc. ISMR'99 (1. International Symposium on Mixed Reality)*, pages 131–145, Yokohama, Japan, March 1999.

[36] G. Zachmann. Real-time and exact collision detection for interactive virtual prototyping. In *Proc. of the 1997 ASME Design Engineering Technical Conferences*, Sacramento, CA, Sept 14–17 1997. ASME. CIE-4306.

[37] I. Zoghlami, O. Faugeras, and R. Deriche. Traitement des occlusions pour la modification d'objet plan dans une sequence d'image. Private communication; see also http://www.inria.fr/robotvis/ personnel/zimad/Orasis6/Orasis6/html, 1996.

Chapter 16

REGISTRATION METHODS FOR HARMONIOUS INTEGRATION OF REAL WORLD AND COMPUTER GENERATED OBJECTS

Gilles Simon, Vincent Lepetit, Marie-Odile Berger

Abstract We focus in this chapter on the problem of adding computer-generated objects in video sequences. A two-stage robust statistical method is used for computing the pose from model-image correspondences of tracked curves. This method is able to give a correct estimate of the pose even when tracking errors occur. However, if we want to add virtual objects in a scene area which does not contain (or contains few) model features, the reprojection error in this area is likely to be large. In order to improve the accuracy of the viewpoint, we use 2D keypoints that can be easily matched in two consecutive images. As the relationship between two matched points is a function of the camera motion, the viewpoint can be improved by minimizing a cost function which encompasses the reprojection error as well as the matching error between two frames. The reliability of the system is shown on the encrustation of a virtual car in a sequence of the Stanislas square.

The interested reader can look at the video sequences of our results[1].

1.   INTRODUCTION

Augmented Reality (AR) is an effective means for utilizing and exploiting the potential of computer-based information and databases. In augmented reality, the computer provides additional information that enhances or augments the real world, rather than replacing it with a completely virtual environment. In contrast to virtual reality, where the user is immersed in a completely computer-generated world, AR allows

---

[1]http://www.loria.fr/~gsimon/videos.html

A. Leonardis et al. (eds.), Confluence of Computer Vision and Computer Graphics, 285–306.

the user to interact with the real world in a natural way. This explains why interest in AR has substantially increased in the past few years and medical, manufacturing or urban planning applications have been developed [3, 5, 17].

We focus in this paper on the problem of adding computer-generated objects (also called virtual objects) in video sequences. This is one of the key points for numerous AR applications: for instance, suppose we want to assess the potential impact of a new construction in its final setting; visualizing the architectural project on a video of the environment allows designers to test several architectural projects on computer simulations alone. Special effects in movies also require such a composition process.

In order to make AR systems effective, the computer generated objects and the real scene must be combined seamlessly so that the virtual objects align well with the real ones. It is therefore essential to determine accurately the location and the optical properties of the cameras. The registration task must be achieved with special care because the human visual system is very good at detecting even small mis-registrations. Realistic merging of virtual and real objects also requires that objects behave in a physically plausible manner in the environment: they can be occluded by objects in the scene, they are shadowed by other objects etc.

In this paper, we only focus on the registration problem because it is one of the most basic challenges in augmented reality. But we have proposed some preliminary solutions to the occlusion problem in [2].

Registration problems can be solved by using either algorithmic solutions or sensor-based solutions. For instance, position sensors (as Polhemus sensors) can be used to locate the camera (or the viewer) [15]. Easily detectable landmarks placed in the scene can also be used to make the registration process easier [5]. However, instrumenting the real world is not always possible, especially for vast or outdoor environments. Thus, vision-based object registration is an interesting and cheaper approach that leaves the environment unmodified.

2.   CONTRIBUTIONS

Since 1996, we have proposed methods to make the registration task easier, especially for complex outdoor scenes [3, 14]. For outdoor urban scenes, some 3D knowledge is often available: dimensions and localization of the main buildings for instance. These 3D data can be used to compute the viewpoint provided that their corresponding 2D features can be identified in the images. In the following, this 3D knowledge of the scene is also called *model features*.

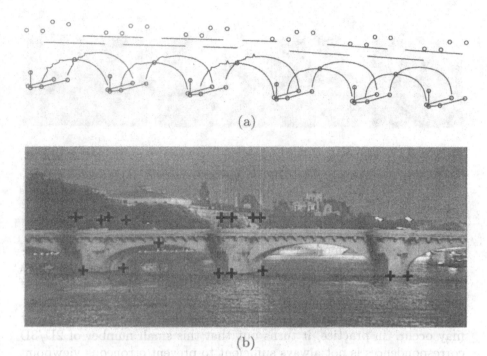

Figure 16.1 (a) The complete wire-frame model and the 3D points used for registration. (b) The corresponding 2D points extracted in an image.

First, we developed in [3] a registration method which is based on 2D/3D point correspondences: in the first frame of the sequence the user marks the 2D points which correspond to the 3D model points. Then these points are automatically tracked from frame to frame and the viewpoint is automatically computed. The points used are characteristic points in the model that correspond to corners or junctions. Hence, only a small number of interest 3D points is generally available in the images.

As an example, let us consider the application of the illumination of the Paris bridges (Fig. 16.1) . Our motivation came from the encrustation of a model illuminated synthetically in its real environment. The aim was to test several candidate illumination projects for a number of bridges in Paris, and be able to choose on computer simulations alone which project was the best. The complete wire-frame model of the bridge is shown in Fig. 16.1(a) as well as the 3D points used for registration: the light bulbs on the bridge and some junction points of the bridge. The corresponding points extracted in one image of the sequence are shown in Fig. 16.1(b).

(a)   (b)   (c)

Figure 16.2 Shortcomings of the 2D/3D registration method. (a) Incrustation in the calibration area is quit good. (b,c) Away from the calibration area, incrustation is not realistic.

As the complete model is not visible in each frame of the image sequence, we are only able to extract between 10 and 20 points which correspond to the 3D model points. In addition, due to the darkness of the scene, the localization accuracy of the 2D extracted points is poor. Moreover, false matching between the 2D point and the 3D model point may occur. In practice, it turns out that this small number of 2D/3D correspondences is not always sufficient to prevent erroneous viewpoint computation.

To overcome these problems we recently proposed in [14] a registration method which is based on 2D/3D correspondences of various features: points, lines, and free form curves. This allows us to exploit all the 3D information on the model rather than only sparse 3D points. We sketch out in section 4 our original approach. Our method minimizes the reprojection error of the model features in the image. However, one of the limitations of this method originates in the spatial distribution of the model features: the reprojection error is likely to be large far from the 3D features used for the viewpoint computation. Consider for instance the video of the *Stanislas square* shown in figure 16.2. The viewpoint has been computed using 3D knowledge of the building Opera in the background of the scene (see the eight white curves in Fig. 16.2(a)). We add in the scene a computer generated car which is coming on the square from the background along the y axis. When the car is in the area containing the 3D features used for the viewpoint computation (Fig. 16.2(a)), the overall impression is quite satisfactory. As the car moves away from the Opera, the car seems to hover. Indeed, the reprojection error of the 3D model features is small but the reprojection error is very large in the foreground of the scene.

In order to improve viewpoint computation, we now resort to 2D/2D point correspondences between consecutive frames. Unlike other approaches which attempt to recover the viewpoint from 2D/2D corre-spondences alone [6, 16], point correspondences between frames are here used to provide additional constraints on the viewpoint computation.

We present in this paper an efficient approach which encompasses the strengths of these two methods: the viewpoint is defined as the minimum of a cost function which incorporates 2D/3D correspondences between the image and the model as well as 2D/2D correspondences of key points that are automatically extracted and matched in two consecutive frames. This way, the 2D points which are automatically extracted and matched in consecutive frames are likely to appear in areas where the 3D knowl-edge available of the scene is missing. We show in the following that this method dramatically improves the viewpoint computation. As a result, our method allows us to perform efficiently registration over time without human interaction.

The paper begins with an overview of our method. Section 4 gives the explanation of our robust algorithm for viewpoint computation from 3D-2D correspondences, including results on various augmented reality applications. Section 5 describes how the viewpoint computation can be dramatically improved using key-point correspondences. Finally, we show results demonstrating the accuracy of pose estimation.

3. OVERVIEW

Fig. 16.3 gives an overview of our registration system. The knowl-edge that must be brought to the system is represented with shaded areas. Our system is initialized with known camera parameters and a user specified set of four 2D points along with their 3D counterparts. The 2D features corresponding to the visible model features are then automatically determined (see [14] for further details). The model of the object to be added as well as its trajectory in the scene must also be given to the system.

Once initialized, the system follows a four step loop:

Step 1: Tracking assessment and pose computation.

The set of features is tracked in the current image using a curve-based tracker that we have previously developed [1]. Unfortunately the tracking may sometimes fail (Fig 16.6). As a single tracking error can have a large effect on the resulting pose, it is necessary to devise a robust algorithm capable of extracting the parts of the features that match the 3D model. The interest of our algorithm is two-fold: first it computes the pose in a robust manner, second it allows us to detect and discard matching errors (see section 4).

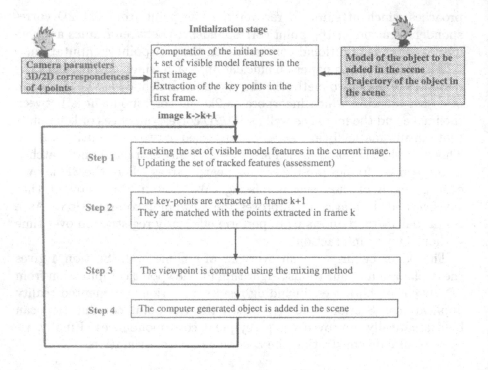

Figure 16.3 Overview of the system

Step 2: Accounting for 2D/2D correspondences

Key-points are then extracted in the current frame and they are matched with the ones extracted in the previous frame. Section 5 describes how to automatically extract these points. These matched points can be used to improve the viewpoint computation: given a point n_1 in frame I_k, the corresponding point in I_{k+1} must belong to a line. This epipolar line is the intersection of the image plane I_{k+1} with the plane (n_1, C_1, C_2) (Fig. 16.4(a)). The matching of two key points n_1 and n_2 can therefore be assessed by measuring the distance v between n_2 and the epipolar line of n_1 (Fig. 16.4(b)).

Step 3: Mixing method for viewpoint computation

We define a cost function which encompasses the strengths of the two approaches. We minimize a weighted sum of the residuals r_i obtained by the correspondences with the model and the residuals v_i between the matched key points in two consecutive images (Fig. 16.4(c)). This method is described in section 5. The computer generated object can then be added in the scene using the computed viewpoint.

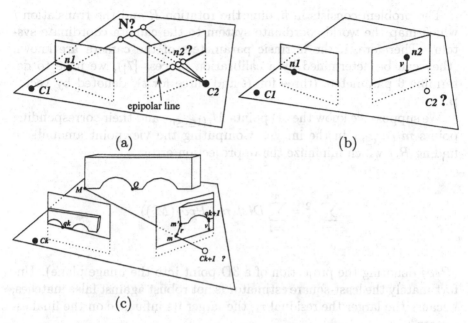

Figure 16.4 (a,b) Constraints between matched points. (c) The residuals used in the mixing method.

4. ROBUST POSE COMPUTATION FROM VARIOUS FEATURES (RPC ALGORITHM)

Once the model/image correspondences have been established in the first frame, they are generally maintained during tracking. Unfortunately, tracking errors will sometimes result in a model feature being matched to an erroneous image feature. Even a single such outlier can have a large effect on the resulting pose. For point features, robust approaches allow the point to be categorized as outlier or not [8]. When curved features are considered, the problem is not so simple, as some parts of the 2D curves can perfectly match the 3D model whereas other parts can be erroneously matched (Fig. 16.6). While numerous papers are dedicated to pose estimation from points or lines [4, 10], only few papers have been devoted to the 2D/3D registration of curves. The details of our robust pose computation algorithm (RPC) are given in this section. First we address the problem of point correspondences; a much more difficult case of curve correspondences is then considered.

4.1   POSE COMPUTATION FROM POINT CORRESPONDENCES

The problem consists in finding the rotation R and the translation t which map the world coordinate system to the camera coordinate system. Therefore, if the intrinsic parameters of the camera are known (they can be determined by a calibration process [7]), we have to determine 6 parameters (three for R and three for t), denoted by vector $\mathbf{p}$.

We suppose we know the 3D points $M_{i\{1\leq i\leq n\}}$ and their corresponding points $m_{i\{1\leq i\leq n\}}$ in the image. Computing the viewpoint amounts to finding R, t which minimize the re-projection error:

$$\sum_{i=1}^{n} r_i^2 = \sum_{i=1}^{n} Dist(m_i, Proj(M_i)) \, ,$$

(*Proj* denoting the projection of a 3D point into the image plane). Unfortunately the least-square estimator is not robust against false matches, because the larger the residual r_i, the larger its influence on the final estimate.

In order to reduce the influence of the feature outliers, statisticians have suggested many different robust estimators. Among them, one popular robust technique is the *M-estimator*. The underlying idea is to reduce the effect of outliers by replacing the squared residual $\sum r_i^2$ by another function of the residuals

$$\min_{\mathbf{P}} \sum_{i=1}^{n} \rho(r_i), \tag{16.1}$$

where ρ is a continuous, symmetric function with minimum value at zero and is chosen to be less increasing than square. Its derivative $\psi(x)$ is called the *influence function* because it acts as a weighting function in optimization of Eq. (16.1). An example of such a ρ function (Tukey function) along with its influence function is drawn in Table 16.1.

Minimizing (16.1) can be performed by standard techniques using an initial estimate of p: a very simple approach like Powell's method [12] proved to be sufficient in our case, and relatively fast to compute (for temporal registration, the initial estimate of p is the pose computed for the previous frame).

Table 16.1   The mean square estimator and the Tukey M-estimator

Type	$\rho(x)$	*Graph of $\psi(x)$*
Mean squares	$x^2/2$	
Tukey $\left\{ \begin{array}{l} \text{if } |x| \leq c \\ \text{if } |x| > c \end{array} \right.$	$\left\{ \begin{array}{l} \frac{c^2}{6}\left[1 - \left(1 - \left(\frac{x}{c}\right)^2\right)^3\right] \\ c^2/6 \end{array} \right.$	

4.2   COMPUTING VIEWPOINT FROM CURVE CORRESPONDENCES

This problem is much more difficult because point-to-point correspondences between the 3D curves and the corresponding 2D curves are not available. Let (Fig.16.5):

- C_i be a 3D model curve, described by the chain of 3D points $\{M_{i,j}\}_{1 \leq j \leq l_i}$ (note that C_i can be any 3D feature, including points and lines),

- c_i be the projection of C_i in the image plane, described by the chain of 2D points $\{m_{i,j}\}_{1 \leq j \leq l_i}$, where $m_{i,j} = Proj(RM_{i,j} + t)$,

- c'_i be the detected curve (tracked curve) corresponding to C_i, described by the chain of 2D points $\{m'_{i,j}\}_{1 \leq j \leq l'_i}$.

A simple solution would be to perform a one-stage minimization

$$\min_p \sum_{i,j} \rho(d_{i,j}), \qquad (16.2)$$

where $d_{i,j} = Dist(m'_{i,j}, c_i)$ (*Dist* being a function which approximates the Euclidean distance from a point to a contour) and ρ is a M-estimator function, as Tukey function.

Unfortunately, this method is unsatisfactory because it mixes all the features into a set of points, and makes no distinction between local

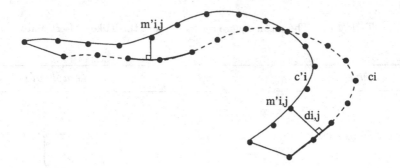

Figure 16.5 Computing the distance between the projection of the 3D model and the 2D feature extracted in the image.

errors (when a feature is only partially well localized), and gross errors (when the position of a feature is completely erroneous). However, these two kinds of errors are not identical, and not treating them separately induces a great loss of robustness and accuracy.

Therefore, we propose to perform a robust estimation in a two-stage process: a *local stage*, which computes a robust residual for each feature, and a *global stage* which minimizes a robust function of these residuals. The local stage reduces the influence of erroneous sections of the contours (features 1 and 4 on Figure 16.6(c)), whereas the global stage discards the *feature outliers*, *i.e.* contours which are completely erroneous, or which contain too large a portion of erroneous points (feature 5 on Fig. 16.6(c)).

The local stage

The aim of this stage is to reduce the influence of erroneous sections of the features: to perform this task, the residual error r_i of curve C_i is computed by a robust function of the distances $\{d_{i,j}\}_{1 \leq j \leq l'_i}$:

$$r_i^2 = \frac{1}{l'_i} \sum_{j=1}^{l'_i} \rho(d_{i,j}). \qquad (16.3)$$

The global stage

Once a robust residual has been computed for each feature, the viewpoint is computed in a robust way by minimizing

$$\min_p \sum_{i=1}^{n} \rho(r_i).$$

This way, completely erroneous features will be discarded because they have a large residual.

Discarding feature outliers

The detection of feature outliers can now be performed easily: as they should not have influenced the estimation, their residual must be much larger than the other ones. We therefore only have to compare them with the standard deviation of all the residuals: if $r_i > 2.5 \hat{\sigma}$ (where $\hat{\sigma}$ is computed in a robust way [10]), then the feature is discarded. The set of visible features is updated accordingly.

Results of the RPC method are shown in Fig. 16.6 in the *Paris bridges illumination project*. Note that the reprojection of the model using the computed viewpoint is very good. Furthermore, the algorithm is able to detect and to discard the tracked features which do not match the 3D model. These features are drawn in black.

Other results are shown on the *Stanislas square application*. Once again, the reprojection error on the 3D model features is very good. We also compare in Fig. 16.10 the computed viewpoint with the expected one. Indeed, the video was shot from a car which is passing on the opposite side of the square along the x-axis. The actual viewpoint was used as an initial guess in the first frame. The obtained curves proved that the algorithm failed to recover the expected viewpoint (the t_y and t_z coordinates should be constant over the sequence). Another way to assess the viewpoint is to consider the epipolar line for some given points (Fig. 16.9(a,b)). We can notice that the epipolar lines pass far from the corresponding points. This proves that the viewpoint is not computed with sufficient accuracy.

5.   IMPROVING THE VIEWPOINT COMPUTATION

In order to improve the accuracy of the viewpoint, we use key-points that can be easily matched in two consecutive images. As the relationship between two matched points is a function of the camera motion and of the intrinsic parameters, the viewpoint can be improved by minimizing a cost function which encompasses the reprojection error as well as the matching error between two frames. Since the key-points do not generally correspond to the model points, the viewpoint computation will be improved through these 2D correspondences.

Section 5.1 describes the way to extract key-points. Section 5.2 presents the cost function we use to improve the viewpoint. Significant results are shown in section 6.

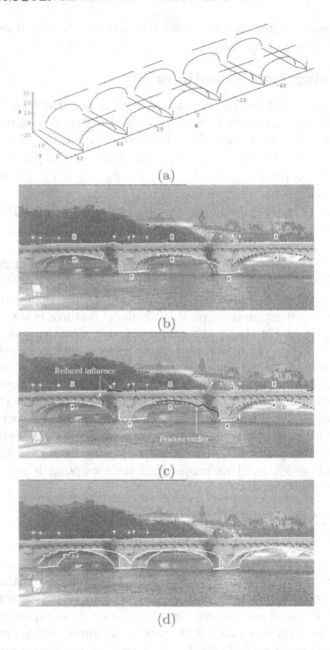

Figure 16.6 Temporal registration. (a) Wireframe model of the object to be registered (the bridge). (b) Tracking of image features. White lines correspond to the tracked features, white dashed lines to the projection of their 3D correspondents in the previous frame and black dashed lines to the features not (yet) used. (c) Robust pose computation. Sections for which residuals are greater than c and feature outliers are drawn in black. (d) Re-projection of the model.

5.1   EXTRACTING AND MATCHING KEY-POINTS

Key-points (or interest points) are locations in the image where the signal changes two dimensionally: corners, T-junctions, locations where the texture varies significantly etc. Approaches for detecting key-points can be broadly divided in two groups: the first group involves first extracting edges and then searching for points having maximum curvature; the second group consists of approaches that work directly on the grey-level image. As the edges are already used in the viewpoint computation, we resort to the second approach that provides us with interesting texture points which are not yet used. We use the approach developed by Harris and Stephens [9]. They use the autocorrelation function of the image to compute a measure which indicates the presence of an interest point. More precisely, the eigenvalues of the matrix

$$\left[\begin{array}{cc} I_x^2 & I_x I_y \\ I_x I_y & I_y^2 \end{array} \right] \; \left(I_x = \frac{\partial I}{\partial x}, I_y = \frac{\partial I}{\partial y} \right),$$

are the principal curvatures of the auto-correlation function. If these values are high, a key-point is declared.

We still have to match these key-points between two consecutive images. Numerous works use correlation techniques to achieve this task [18]. These methods are well-suited when the motion in the image is roughly a translation but they are unable to cope with rotations and scale changes. That is the reason why we prefer to use the matching approach developed in [13]; each key-point is characterized locally by a vector of differential invariants under the group of displacements. For example, the vector of differential invariants up to second order is

$$\left[\begin{array}{c} I \\ I_x^2 + I_y^2 \\ I_{xx} I_x^2 + 2 I_{xy} I_x I_y + I_{yy} I_y^2 \\ I_{xx} + I_{yy} \\ I_{xx}^2 + 2 I_{xy} I_{yx} + I_{yy}^2 \end{array} \right].$$

The invariance of the vector makes the matching stage easier even in case of important geometric transformations. Moderated scale changes can also be considered. The interested reader can find further details on the computation of the local invariants in [13]. The key-points are then matched according to a measure of similarity between the invariant vectors. Neighbouring constraints are also used to make the matching easier (close key-points must have a similar disparity).

Fig. 16.7(a,b) exhibits the key-points which have been automatically extracted in two successive images in the scene. For the sake of clarity, only a small part of the image is shown. The matched key-points are represented with an arrow in Fig. 16.7(c). These points bring depth information in areas which do not contain 3D model features: in the foreground of the scene, near the statue, and in the background of the scene (the street behind the square). Around 1000 key-points have been detected. Among them, 600 points are matched.

(a)   (b)

(c)

Figure 16.7   (a,b) Key-points extracted in two consecutive frames. (c) The matched key-points.

5.2   MIXING 3D KNOWLEDGE AND POINTS CORRESPONDENCES

Given the viewpoint $[R_k, t_k]$ computed in a given frame k, we now explain how we compute the viewpoint in the next frame $k + 1$ using the 3D model as well as the matched key-points $(q_1^i, q_2^i)_{1 \leq i \leq m}$. Before describing the cost function to be minimized, we first recall in a little detail the relationships between two matched key-points q_1, q_2 and the two viewpoints $[R_k, t_k]$ and $[R_{k+1}, t_{k+1}]$. Let $\Delta R, \Delta t$ be the relative displacement of the camera between the frames k and $k + 1$. Let A be the intrinsic matrix of the camera:

$$A = \begin{bmatrix} k_u f & 0 & u_0 \\ 0 & k_v f & v_0 \\ 0 & 0 & 1 \end{bmatrix}.$$

Let q_1 and q_2 be the images of a 3D point M from the cameras. Their homogeneous coordinates are denoted $\tilde{q}_1$ and $\tilde{q}_2$. We then have the fundamental equation (see Appendix for a proof of this result)

$$\tilde{q}_2{}^t A^{-1}{}^t \Delta T \Delta R A^{-1} \tilde{q}_1 = 0,$$

where ΔT is an antisymmetric matrix such that $\Delta T x = \Delta t \wedge x$ for all x. $F = A^{-1}{}^t \Delta T \Delta R A^{-1}$ is called the fundamental matrix.

Then, a simple way to improve the viewpoint computation using the interest points is to minimize

$$\min_{R_{k+1}, t_{k+1}} \left(\frac{1}{n} \sum_{i=1}^n \rho_1(r_i) + \frac{\lambda}{m} \sum_{i=1}^m \rho_2(v_i) \right), \qquad (16.4)$$

where

- r_i is the distance in frame $k + 1$ between the tracked features and the projection of the model features,

- $v_i = \sqrt{\frac{1}{(F\tilde{q}_1^i)_1^2 + (F\tilde{q}_1^i)_2^2} + \frac{1}{(F^t\tilde{q}_2^i)_1^2 + (F^t\tilde{q}_2^i)_2^2}} |\tilde{q}_2^i{}^t F \tilde{q}_1^i|$ measures the quality of the matching between q_1^i and q_2^i [11],

- ρ_1 and ρ_2 are M-estimators. Note that the use of an M-estimator for the key-point correspondences is not essential: as the key-points are significant points in the image, false matches are unusual.

Parameter λ controls the compromise between the closeness to the available 3D data and the quality of the 2D correspondences between the key-points. We use $\lambda = 1$ in our practical experiments.

The minimum of Eq. (16.4) is computed by using an iterative algorithm for minimization such as Powell's algorithm.

6.   RESULTS

Fig. 16.8 shows the result of using the mixing algorithm to incrust a virtual car in a video sequence. A video of the Stanislas Square, city of Nancy, France, has been shot from a car driving around the square. Our aim is to incrust a virtual car passing on the square. It is worth noting here that the 3D data available from the scene only concern the Opera. On the other hand, the 3D model of the statue is not available.

First, the importance and the working of the mixing algorithm can be visually assessed. We have compared the results obtained with the mixing algorithm (Fig. 16.8) to the ones obtained with the RPC algorithm (Fig. 16.2). These results clearly prove that the mixing algorithm dramatically improves the viewpoint computation. The car and the scene are combined seamlessly and the realism of the composition is very good.

Figure 16.8 Composition with the mixing algorithm

The quality of the viewpoint can also be assessed by looking at the epipolar lines (Fig. 16.9). The epipolar lines of five given points randomly chosen in the images have been drawn using the RPC algorithm and the mixing algorithm. The reader can note that the epipolar lines computed from the mixing algorithm pass very closely to the corresponding points.

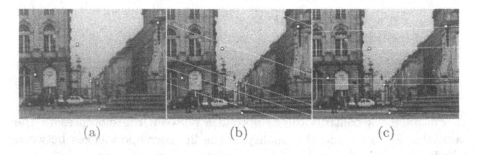

(a)   (b)   (c)

Figure 16.9 (a) Five points and (b) their epipolar lines computed with the RPC algorithm and (c) the mixing algorithm.

Table 16.2 Computation time for the three steps of the algorithm

	Machine instruction cycles	*Elapsed time (in seconds)*
Tracking	233623865	.78 s
2D/2D matching	565359817	1.88s
Mixing	370003480	1.23 s

Fig. 16.10 exhibits the viewpoint evolution for the RPC algorithm and the mixing method. In the considered sequence, the camera is passing on the opposite side of the Opera. The motion of the camera is then a translation along the x-axis. Fig. 16.10 proves the efficiency of the mixing method: the t_y and t_z coordinates are nearly constant whereas the t_x, α, β and γ parameters evolve slowly.

Finally, the computation time of our algorithm is shown in Table 16.2 for the *Stanislas square application*. The computation time of the algorithm depends on numerous factors:

- number of 3D features,

- size and motion of the 2D features that are tracked: if the motion of the feature is large, the tracking algorithm converges slowly. The rate also depend on the number of points used to discretize the curve feature.

- camera velocity: as the pose computed in the previous frame is used as initial guess in the mixing algorithm, the convergence rate of the minimum finding routine depends on the distance between two consecutive viewpoints.

- number of key-points: a key-point is declared if the principal curvatures of the auto-correlation function are high. The number of key-points can therefore be adapted. However, selecting a high threshold can lead to detect only very prominent key-points. This can suppress key-points which bring depth information.

The elapsed time has been computed for each of the three steps of the algorithm on an Ultra-sparc 300 Mhz. They are expressed in machine instruction cycles and in seconds.

Currently, the time needed to process one frame is around 3.9s in this application for eight curves and 600 key-points. However we can

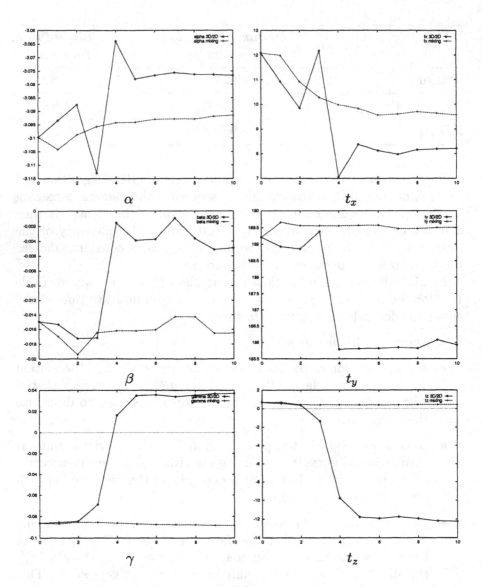

Figure 16.10 Evolution of the motion parameters for the RPC (solid lines) and the mixing algorithm (dotted lines). The Euler angles are expressed in radians and the translation is expressed in meters.

greatly improve the speed of our algorithm by processing both the pose computation and the key-points extraction in a parallel way. In this way, we think that our algorithm is likely to be amenable to real time. In any case, our registration methods can be very useful to perform post production tasks: visual assessment of new projects in their final settings, special effects in movies etc.

Other significant results on video image sequences can be seen at URL http://www.loria.fr/~gsimon/videos.html.

7.   CONCLUSION

To conclude, we have presented a robust and accurate registration method which allows us to combine the real and the virtual worlds seamlessly. One of the main advantages of our approach is to perform pose computation over the sequence in a completely autonomous manner. The accuracy of the pose computation is due to the combined use of 3D-2D correspondences in an image and 2D-2D correspondences in two consecutive frames: indeed the use of 2D-2D correspondences allows us to bring some kind of spatial information on the scene in areas where 3D model features are missing. As a result, our method only requires a limited number of 3D features to be effective.

Future works will concern the automatic determination of the intrinsic camera parameters. Indeed, these parameters are currently computed off-line before shooting the sequence. As the zoom of the camera may change during shooting, it would be interesting to compute dynamically the intrinsic camera parameters.

Appendix: The fundamental matrix

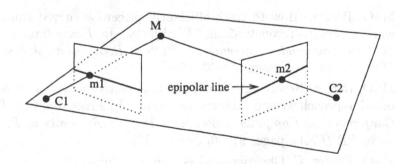

Figure 16.11   Geometry of two cameras

Consider the case of two cameras as shown in Fig. 16.11 where C_1 and C_2 are the optical centres of the cameras. Let the displacement from the first to the second be $[R, t]$. Let m_1 and m_2 be the image of a 3D point M. The three vectors $\mathbf{C_1 m_1}$, $\mathbf{C_2 m_2}$ and t are coplanar. Without loss of generality, we assume that M is expressed in the coordinate frame of the first camera. As the coordinates of $C_2 m_2$ in the first frame are $RC_2 m_2$, the coplanarity of the three vectors can be expressed by

$$(t \wedge \mathbf{C_1 m_1}).\mathbf{C_2 m_2} = 0. \tag{16.5}$$

As $t \wedge x = Tx$ with $T = \begin{bmatrix} 0 & -t_z & t_y \\ t_z & 0 & -t_x \\ -t_y & t_x & 0 \end{bmatrix}$, we can write Eq. (16.5) as

$$\mathbf{C_2 m_2}^t T R \mathbf{C_1 m_1} = 0.$$

The mapping between the pixel coordinates $m(u, v)$ and the metric coordinates (X, Y, Z) in the camera frame is given by

$$\tilde{m} = \begin{bmatrix} su \\ sv \\ s \end{bmatrix} = \begin{bmatrix} k_u f & 0 & u_0 \\ 0 & k_v f & v_0 \\ 0 & 0 & 1 \end{bmatrix} \begin{bmatrix} X \\ Y \\ Z \end{bmatrix} = A \begin{bmatrix} X \\ Y \\ Z \end{bmatrix},$$

where k_u, k_v are the pixel sizes, f is the focal length, and u_0, v_0 are the coordinates of intersection of the optical axis with the image plane.

Hence, we have

$$\tilde{m}_2^t (A^{-1})^t T R A^{-1} \tilde{m}_1 = 0.$$

Let F be $F = (A^{-1})^t T R A^{-1}$; then two corresponding points m_1, m_2 satisfy the equation

$$\tilde{m}_2^t F \tilde{m}_1 = 0.$$

References

[1] M.-O. Berger. How to track efficiently piecewise curved contours with a view to reconstructing 3D objects. In *Proceedings of the 12th International Conference on Pattern Recognition, Jerusalem (Israel)*, volume 1, pages 32–36, 1994.

[2] M.-O. Berger. Resolving occlusion in augmented reality: a contour-based approach without 3D reconstruction. In *Proceedings of IEEE Conference on Computer Vision and Pattern Recognition, Puerto Rico, PR (USA)*, pages 91–96, June 1997.

[3] M.-O. Berger, C. Chevrier, and G. Simon. Compositing computer and video image sequences: Robust algorithms for the reconstruction of the camera parameters. *Computer Graphics Forum, Conference Issue Eurographics'96, Poitiers, France*, 15(3):23–32, August 1996.

[4] D. Dementhon and L. Davis. Model based object pose in 25 lines of code. *International Journal of Computer Vision*, 15:123–141, 1995.

[5] G. Ertl, H. Müller-Seelich, and B. Tabatabai. MOVE-X: a system for combining video films and computer animation. In *Eurographics*, pages 305–313, 1991.

[6] O. Faugeras. *Three-Dimensional Computer Vision: A Geometric Viewpoint*. Artificial Intelligence. MIT Press, 1993.

[7] O. D. Faugeras and G. Toscani. The Calibration Problem for Stereo. In *Proceedings of IEEE Conference on Computer Vision and Pattern Recognition, Miami, FL (USA)*, pages 15–20, 1986.

[8] R. M. Haralick, H. Joo, C. N. Lee, X. Zhuang, V.G. Vaidya, and M. B. Kim. Pose estimation from corresponding point data. *IEEE Transactions on Systems, Man, and Cybernetics*, 19(6), 1989.

[9] C. Harris and M. Stephens. A combined corner and edge detector. In *Proceedings of 4th Alvey Conference*, Cambridge, August 1988.

[10] R. Kumar and A. Hanson. Robust methods for estimating pose and a sensitivity analysis. *CVGIP: Image Understanding*, 60(3):313–342, 1994.

[11] Q.-T. Luong, R. Deriche, O. Faugeras, and T. Papadopoulo. On determining the fundamental matrix: Analysis of different methods and experimental results. Technical Report 1894, INRIA, 1993.

[12] W. H. Press, B. P. Flannery, S. A. Teukolsky, and W. T. Vetterling. *Numerical Recipes in C, The Art of Scientific Computing*. Cambridge University Press, 1988.

[13] C. Schmid and R. Mohr. Local grayvalue invariants for image retrieval. *IEEE Transactions on PAMI*, 19(5):530–535, August 1997.

[14] G. Simon and M.-O. Berger. A two-stage robust statistical method for temporal registration from features of various type. In *Proceedings of 6th International Conference on Computer Vision, Bombay (India)*, pages 261–266, January 1998.

[15] A. State, G. Hirota, D. Chen, W. Garett, and M. Livingston. Superior augmented reality registration by integrating landmark tracking and magnetic tracking. In *Computer Graphics (Proceedings Siggraph New Orleans)*, pages 429–438, 1996.

[16] C. Tomasi and T. Kanade. Shape and motion from image streams under orthography: A factorization method. *International Journal of Computer Vision*, 9(2):137–154, 1992.

[17] M. Uenohara and T. Kanade. Vision based object registration for real time image overlay. *Journal of Computers in Biology and Medicine*, 25(2):249–260, 1996.

[18] Z. Zhang, R. Deriche, O. Faugeras, and Q. Luong. A robust technique for matching two uncalibrated images through the recovery of the unknown epipolar geometry. *Artificial Intelligence*, 78:87–119, October 1995.

Chapter 17

3D OBJECT TRACKING USING ANALYSIS/SYNTHESIS TECHNIQUES

André Gagalowicz, Philippe Gérard

Abstract   In post-production, a traditional method for creating some special effects is named "rotoscopy". This technique consists of segmenting a video sequence by hand and for every frame. Our method is a new tool designed to reduce considerably the cost of this operation by making it almost automatic and quick. In our case, we track a rigid object whose geometry is known, in a sequence of video images. This new approach is based upon a two-steps process: first, one or several "keyframes" are used in a preliminary interactive calibration session, so that a 3D model of this object is positioned correctly on these images (its projection fits to the object in the image). We use this match to texture the 3D model with its image data. Then, a 3D predictor gives a position of the object model in the next image and the fine tuning of this position is obtained by simply minimizing the error between the textured model in this position and the real image of the object. Minimization is performed with respect to the 6 DOF (Degrees of Freedom) of the model position (3 translation parameters and 3 rotation ones). This procedure is iterated at each frame. Test sequences show how robust the method is.

1.   INTRODUCTION

Tracking objects in a video sequence is a very popular topic. Possible applications are: teledetection, security, traffic control, animations, special effects, video compression. In special effects and augmented reality applications, which are the applications we are interested in, tracking accuracy must be high. The retrieved position of the object should not be beyond 1 or 2 pixels off from its real projection in the video sequence. Moreover, in order not to disturb the human eye, the residual position error should be consistent all over the video sequence in order to avoid jittering effects. Up to now, in special effects and postproduction applications (such as adding synthetic objects to a real scene) the traditional

A. Leonardis et al. (eds.), Confluence of Computer Vision and Computer Graphics, 307–329.
© 2000 *Kluwer Academic Publishers. Printed in the Netherlands.*

rotoscopy method is still used. But such a method is cumbersome, tedious and highly interactive, which is why an automated 3D tracking is direly desired.

1.1   STATE OF THE ART

The tracking research activity can be classified in two different fields:

- **2D tracking**: a significant amount of work has been done on locating salient image features. Image processing is often used to detect moving regions [1], contours [12], textures [9], oriented points, optical flows. Different kind of transformations are applied to the images such as Gabor filters or wavelets [18, 2].

- **Model-based tracking**: a model might be more or less sophisticated: it might consist of any information given to the algorithm before or during the process like the snake model used by Raveda et al. in [15] for segmentation purposes. The model used by Jang et al. [8] is a simple bounding rectangle where the object is supposed to lie. One might notice that any 2D tracking is very sensitive to noise, cluttered environment, occlusion, and object rotations. For robustness purposes, we considered the use of an explicit 3D model of the object to track. In [11] and [10], Nagel et al. got some good tracking results using a parameterized 3D car model. This type of model can be adjusted to different types of car. Complicated motions such as turn about, backing and parking manoeuvres have been correctly tracked, but their model included modeling of shadows in order to perform it properly. Gavrila et al. [7] got some really accurate results too while tracking two dancers where self-occlusions occurred. However, the background is clean and actors wore some special black and white clothes used as markers to recognize the right leg and arm from the left ones. The matching process is quite similar for every method: first, image features (gradients, edges, velocity map etc.) are extracted from the original video sequence and secondly, the 3D model is projected using a more or less sophisticated camera calibration process. For traffic control purposes and human tracking, some assumptions are made and some constraints are added: for instance, the objects can only slide above a surface. This diminishes the number of degrees of freedom and simplifies the task. The match between the projected 3D model and the images is often made comparing simple primitives such as lines or corners, then a matching function is defined and an error has to be minimized. One might notice that comput-

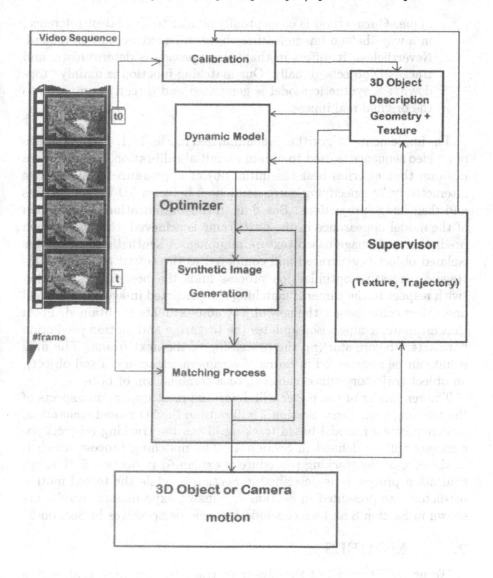

Figure 17.1 Overview of the tracking method

ing image features induces a lack of robustness in object tracking: many factors such as lighting condition variations, shadows, or cluttered environment might spoil the image feature computation. Another approach has been implemented in [6, 5, 4], where planar surface patches have been tracked over time. Their approach is stochastic using a Gaussian assumption and a Markov-type technique. Our method is conceptually similar to this latest reference, in a way that no image features have to be extracted beforehand. Nevertheless, it differs in that our approach is deterministic and tracks 3D objects globally. Our matching function is mainly "top-down": a synthetic model is generated and directly compared to the original real image.

The implemented algorithm is summarized in Fig. 17.1: the first image of a video sequence is used to obtain an initial calibration, i.e., a camera position that matches best the initial object appearance. This is done interactively, by specifying correspondences between 3D model vertices and their image projections. Based upon this initialization, a prediction of the model appearance in the next frame is achieved, through motion prediction and image-based texture mapping. A synthetic image of the isolated object is generated and compared to the actual frame. At this stage an iterative optimization process finds the best object position (with respect to the camera) matching the predicted image with the real one. After convergence, the new object pose estimate is obtained. From that estimate, a supervisor updates the texturing and motion prediction parameters before starting the processing of the next frame. The final result can be interpreted in terms of a camera trajectory (fixed object), an object trajectory (fixed camera), or a combination of both.

The remainder of the paper will detail the most important aspects of the tracking tool. First, Section 2 will outline the 3D model generation, a prerequisite for model-based tracking. Then the tracking (object) parameters will be defined in Section 4. The matching process which is at the core of the tracking procedure is explained in Section 5. The optimization procedure is described in Section 6, while the tested motion predictors are presented in Section 7. Finally, experimental results are shown in Section 8 and we conclude by some perspectives in Section 9.

2.   MODELS

We use a 3D model of the object to track by assuming that such a model can be built with a photogrammetry tool (available on the market), scanned with an active sensor, built from scratch with a computer graphics modeling software, or using a 3D reconstruction method such as [13]. The accuracy of the tracking process is related to the quality of this 3D description. The tracking algorithm was applied to 3 sequences in which the model corresponded to the real object with varying accuracy. Figure 17.2 shows the 3D models used to track the "Arche de la Défense" (building in Paris), and a minitel (telecommunication terminal). Figure 17.3 shows a car (2 accuracy levels).

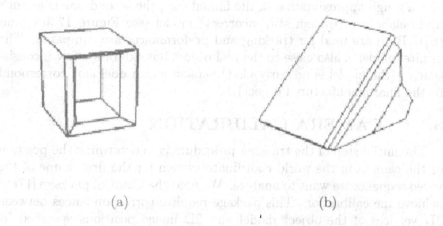

Figure 17.2 3D Models: (a) Arche de la Défense, (b) a minitel. With respect to the image data, the model (a) is excellent but (b) has some inconsistencies.

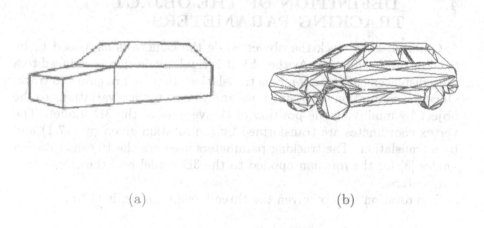

Figure 17.3 3D models: (a) A simple model of a car, (b) a more elaborate model of the same car. With respect to the image data, the model (a) has no details and (b) has some inconsistencies.

Our goal is to study the complexity of the 3D model which has to be used in order to satisfy the accuracy performance (pixelwise 3D object positioning) required by the rotoscopy application. A tradeoff between the object complexity and the computation overhead (coupled with modeling precision) has to be analysed. The "Arche de la Défense" is made of 16 faces and is really close to the real model. We have also studied two versions of a car model: One is made of only several trapezoids and is just a rough approximation of the filmed car , the second one is a much more elaborate (though still incorrect) model (see Figure 17.3(a) and (b)). Both are used for tracking and performances are compared. The minitel model is also close to the real object but exhibits a few inconsistencies (the model is an early CAD version which does not correspond to the final manufactured object).

3.   CAMERA CALIBRATION

The initial step of the tracking procedure is to determine the position of the camera in the world coordinate system for the first frame of the video sequence we want to analyze. We used the CamCal package [17] to achieve the calibration. This package requires correspondences between 3D vertices of the object model and 2D image positions specified by the user to compute the extrinsic (rotation matrix, translation vector) and intrinsic (pixel size and image center) camera parameters. Camera calibration is performed directly on the object.

4.   DEFINITION OF THE OBJECT TRACKING PARAMETERS

Our goal is to track the object while the camera is supposed to be fixed or can itself move. As the object is rigid, its motion is reduced to a pure displacement (rotation plus translation) that we are going to track. Once the calibration is obtained, we apply some motion variations to the object by modifying the position of the vertices of the 3D model. The vertex coordinates are transformed by the rotation given by (17.1) and by a translation. The tracking parameters used are the Bryant rotation angles [3] for the rotation applied to the 3D model and the translation parameters.

The rotation matrix, given the three Bryant angles, is (17.1)

$$R = \begin{bmatrix} c_2c_3 & c_1s_3 + s_1s_2c_3 & s_1s_3 - c_1s_2c_3 \\ -c_2s_3 & c_1c_3 - s_1s_2s_3 & s_1c_3 + c_1s_2s_3 \\ s_2 & -s_1c_2 & c_1c_2 \end{bmatrix},$$

where c_1, s_1, c_2, s_2, c_3, and s_3 are respectively the three Bryant angles cosine and sine values.

The camera position is given by the calibration and at the first frame the model is positioned at the origin of this coordinate system. We have to track its position with respect to the camera. For example, the minitel motion is mainly a rotation about an axis while the camera is fixed, so we only need to track the object itself. The car sequence is more tricky since both the camera and the object move, but our procedure copes with it without any problem by directly tracking the composed movement.

5.   MATCHING PROCESS

5.1   TEXTURE MAPPING

Once the model is calibrated with respect to the first image frame, we project the 3D coordinates of the complete geometry by using the transformation (17.2) given by the calibration process

$$
\begin{pmatrix} S_X \\ S_Y \\ S \end{pmatrix} =
$$

$$
\begin{pmatrix} f & 0 & u_0 \\ 0 & f*r & v_0 \\ 0 & 0 & 1 \end{pmatrix}
\begin{pmatrix} 1 & 0 & 0 & 0 \\ 0 & 1 & 0 & 0 \\ 0 & 0 & 1 & 0 \end{pmatrix}
\begin{pmatrix} \mathbf{R} & \mathbf{T} \\ \mathbf{0} & 1 \end{pmatrix}
\begin{pmatrix} X_w \\ Y_w \\ Z_w \\ 1 \end{pmatrix}, \quad (17.2)
$$

where X_w, Y_w, and Z_w are the 3D vertex coordinates and (S_X, S_Y, S) the corresponding homogeneous image coordinates. $\mathbf{R}$ and $\mathbf{T}$ are the viewing transformation matrices. They can be derived from the extrinsic parameters $(\mathbf{R}_c, \mathbf{T}_c)$ by applying a coordinate frame transformation to get the model position with respect to the camera:

$$
\mathbf{R} = \mathbf{R}_c^t
$$
$$
\mathbf{T} = -\mathbf{R}_c^t * \mathbf{T}_c \quad (17.3)
$$

In Eq. (17.2), f is the focal length, r the pixel ratio, and (u_0, v_0) the image center, which are all supposed to be known in our current implementation (obtained from the camera calibration on the object).

The computed projection coordinates are then used as texture coordinates to texture the model with the first image of the sequence. We also defined a flag associated with each face indicating their visibility in the first frame. Visible faces learn the texture, while the others do not. If a geometrical transformation is applied to the textured model (or if it is seen from another viewpoint), only the faces which learned a texture and are visible in the current viewpoint are drawn, the others are ignored.

The use of a fast standard texturing library, such as OpenGL greatly speeds up the tracking process, because this mapping has to be done at every step of the image/model matching.

5.2   TEXTURE LEARNING

At the calibration stage, texture may be learned only on the visible faces of the model. Along the sequence, if we only draw the faces that learned texture at the calibration time and are visible at the current frame and if the object under scrutiny is submitted to a rotation, the number of faces rendered by the algorithm thus decreases over time and the comparison between a synthetic view and a real image becomes increasingly difficult. It is quite obvious that we need to learn texture while tracking.

Running the algorithm, the user is able to choose the timestep for texture learning. One might learn the texture at every frame: this might be the only way to track a fast rotating object (i.e the minitel sequence) or an object getting varying illumination. But when the motion is mainly a translation, we still get a really robust algorithm learning the texture only once (i.e., the "Arche de la Défense" sequence). However, in a complicated case such as the car sequence, it might be difficult to guess the texture learning timestep, because the apparent object motion is a mixture of camera motion and object motion, because the illumination of the car varies and because the model used is not exact. The strength of this method is related to the fact that only the pixels belonging to the object are compared with the real image. Unfortunately, when the texture is not learned properly (i.e., case of the use of a non exact model), pixels from the background are mapped and used to compute the matching error (see next section).

The texture learning timestep is a parameter related to the residual matching error values. If the residual matching error between the synthetic image and a particular frame from the sequence is high (i.e., the object model was not properly positioned in that frame) it would be ill-advised to learn the texture at that time. In that case, restarting a new calibration process to initiate a proper tracking is necessary.

We used constant learning rates on the test sequences. For example, for the car sequence, the texture learning timestep was set to 4 frames. In later developments we plan to have the algorithm choose the learning rate automatically based upon the matching data.

5.3   MODEL MATCHING

The main interest of the method comes from its matching process. Once the texture learning process has been performed at the calibration frame, we go to the next frame and apply some variations to the six position parameters of the object and generate a synthetic view of this object with an OpenGL-based renderer. Meanwhile we also generate a boolean alpha image where zero and one values indicate for every pixel their ownership to the object projection on the new frame. Only the pixels from the synthetic view corresponding to a non zero value in the alpha image are computed in Eq. (17.4). Using this method, only very few pixels (ideally belonging to the object) are compared to the background.

$$Error = \frac{1}{N} \sum_{i=1}^{N} |(P_{real}(i) - P_{synt}(i))| , \qquad (17.4)$$

where N is the number of matched pixels, $P_{real}(i)$ denotes R, G, B values for the ith pixel of the real image (between 0 and 255), and $P_{synt}(i)$ denotes R, G, B values for the ith pixel of the synthetic model.

The matching method is quite simple and does not rely on computation of image features which are very often the cause of instability, unless one is working under specific conditions such as in [16] for traffic control purposes.

Finding the optimal 3D object position means finding optimum values in six dimensional space. The matching function is computed for every parameter variation, comparing the synthetic image (generated at each parameter variation) with its counterpart in the video frame. Because of the number of possible parameter values, and the number of pixel comparisons, this process might be quite computationally expensive. We reduced this computation cost by using a multiresolution matching process and an optimization algorithm, as explained below.

5.4   MULTIRESOLUTION MATCHING

A natural idea consists in first running the matching procedure at a low image resolution, which provides a good initial guess for a higher resolution search. The matching process does not behave properly without blurring the images before reducing their sizes (which avoids aliasing effects). To reduce the image size by half, we used a simple 3×3 blurring filter, while we used a 5×5 blurring filter before reducing the image size by 4. We still got some really accurate results using low resolution images. Figure 17.4(a) shows an example of the Y variation parameter evolution along the video sequence using different image resolutions. The algorithm running on smaller resolution images exhibits only a slight degradation in minimum localization but takes great advantage of the smoothness of the error function when compared to the full resolution experiment (Fig. 17.4(b)). This multiresolution approach has been taken into account for all results presented later.

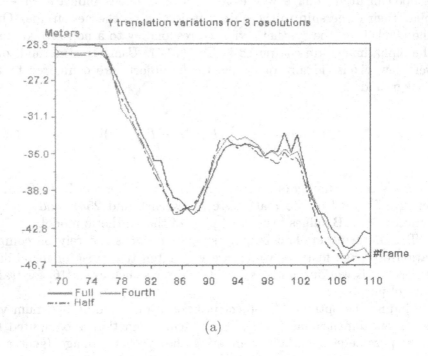

(a)

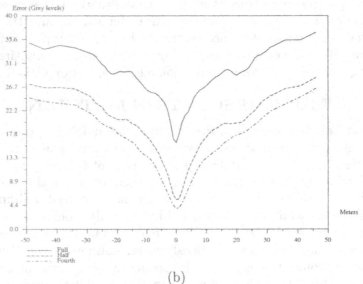

(b)

Figure 17.4 (a) Best translation parameter about the *y*-axis using different image resolutions for the Arche sequence. (b) Matching error when the translation parameter about the *z*-axis is varying around its optimal value (located at zero in the figure). This computation has been done for 3 different image resolutions.

6.   OPTIMIZATION

To avoid brute-force matching (finding the parameters that provide the smallest matching error by an exhaustive search) which would require several hundred thousands iterations in a 6-dimensional space, we tried several optimization algorithms.

- **Levenberg-Marquardt method:** This method requires the estimation of the first and second derivatives of an unknown matching error function for each parameter. This computation proved to be highly sensitive to the scale used for parameter variations: too large a variation could give a wrong estimate for slope or curvature, while too small a step could get the algorithm stuck in a local error minimum. Finding an acceptable trade-off was infeasible on the test sequences.

  As the global error function contains many local minima, the Levenberg-Marquardt method was not suitable. This led us to choose a method based upon simulated annealing.

- **Simulated annealing algorithm:** The method described in [14] is a combination of a standard simulated annealing algorithm and a simplex implementation. The procedure is started by defining a set of six λ_i values used to build the first simplex, consisting of six matching error computations around the calibration position P_0

$$P_i = P_0 + \lambda * e_i , \tag{17.5}$$

  where e_i are the six unit vectors.

  The simplex procedure deforms the shape defined by the P_is according to simple expansion, contraction, and reflection operations on the vertices until no such operation can find a better matching error. This deterministic procedure is coupled with a standard Metropolis approach, so that after a scaling operation, a stochastic search is performed on the vertex points to overcome possible local minima. See [14] for details.

  The λ_i are determined experimentally. They have to be large enough to enable the optimizer to jump over local minima. One might set these values using any a priori knowledge of the global object motion. For instance, in the car sequence, it seems obvious that the motion is mainly a rotation about the axis perpendicular to the road combined with a translation on the ground plane: thus we chose higher values for λ_i corresponding to these parameters. Exact values are not critical to achieve convergence. Finding the right scale for λ_i helps the optimizer to converge faster, however, one might impose a certain number of optimization iterations which guarantee a convergence when using smaller λ values. The annealing algorithm is relatively efficient since 600 iterations always gave a correct result for all frames of the analyzed sequences.

7.   DYNAMIC TRACKING

7.1   ZERO ORDER PREDICTOR

The first improvement of our method was to re-inject the parameter values obtained at the frame (t-1) as initial values for the optimization process at frame (t). This model is just assuming that the position parameters at time (t-1) are close to the new ones to be found for the frame (t) in Eq. (17.6).

$$\hat{X}_t = X_{t-1} , \qquad (17.6)$$

where X stands for the position vector (three Bryant angles and three translation values) and $\hat{X}$ is the predicted position vector. This improved significantly the tracking for the Arche sequence. Using only the first frame to texture the model and computing the correlation product with 1/4 image resolution were sufficient conditions to track properly the entire Arche sequence.

7.2   FIRST-ORDER MODEL

This model assumes that the object is moving at a constant speed: The optimizer initialization at time (t) is given by Eq. (17.7).

$$\hat{X}_t = 2 * X_{t-1} - X_{t-2} . \qquad (17.7)$$

For the first timestep we utilize the zero order model. This first order model forced the object to keep on turning once it started the U-Turn manoeuvre in the car sequence.

7.3   SECOND-ORDER MODEL

This model assumes that the object is moving with a constant acceleration: The prediction at time (t) is given by Eq. (17.8).

$$\hat{X}_t = 3 * X_{t-1} - 3 * X_{t-2} + X_{t-3} . \qquad (17.8)$$

For the first two timesteps we use the zero-order model and the the first-order model, respectively.

We compared the three predictors on the test sequences and found out that the zero-order one is the most stable. All presented experiments are restricted to the first-order case.

8.   EXPERIMENTS AND RESULTS

We processed three test sequences ("Arche, "Car", and "Minitel") and their corresponding 3D models according to the algorithm detailed above. The first frame of each video sequence was used to provide the tracking process with a 3D textured model. This initialization included an interactive camera calibration and a texture learning scheme. Then, a simulated annealing algorithm was used to search for the 6 DOF values providing the smallest residual matching error between the synthetic (predicted) images and the actual video sequence. The various optimizations presented in the previous sections (multiresolution matching, texture learning, dynamic prediction) were implemented to improve both computation time and robustness.

8.1   "ARCHE DE LA DÉFENSE"

We first studied the "Arche de la Défense" sequence to test the stability of the proposed tracking. We chose this sequence because we have a perfect model of the Arche to track and the sequence contains very noisy and erratic movements (pictures were taken from a helicopter). The part of the Arche seen on the sequence was nevertheless always the same. Our first goal was to study if we were able to track very noisy movements with a perfect model and viewing conditions. Figures 17.5(a), (b) and (c) present the results obtained for this sequence.

The position of the 3D model is represented by its wireframe projection overlaid on the real image. Tracking as it can be seen on the pictures was always perfect at a pixel precision level in all experience conditions tried (even with low resolution images). We studied the robustness of this method by learning texture only once at the calibration time, and then computing the residual matching errors for the best match found at each frame. In figure 17.6, parameter variations were added to the calibration position (at frame#0). The matching errors shown in this figure correspond to the best matches found using an optimization algorithm which was initialized with the initial calibration parameter values at each frame.

According to Fig. 17.6, one can conclude that tracking is pretty stable up to the end of the sequence which means that the entire "arche" sequence has been tracked properly using the same texture image. The residual matching error never went above 12 grey levels, which is a pretty low error. For this sequence, no texture learning was necessary. Evidently, being able to recover the correct object position over more than eighty frames without texture update is a good proof of robustness. Furthermore, the residual error value might be monitored to detect tracking

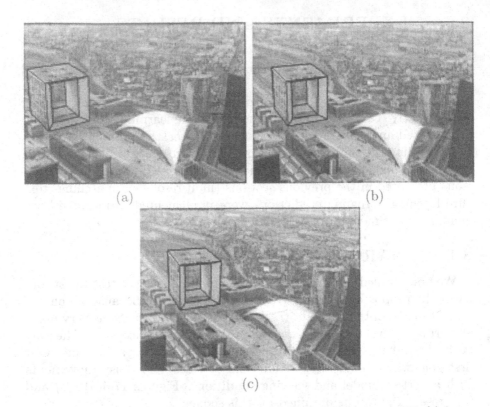

(a)   (b)

(c)

Figure 17.5   "Arche de la Défense" tracking: (a) frame #0, (b) frame #70, (c) frame #100.

failure. We found out that above an error of 40 grey levels, the algorithm is not performing properly.

We also tested the robustness of the matching process by trying to retrieve the correct parameters after applying some image modifications such as occlusion or low contrast to the video sequence (see Fig. 17.7). The synthetic model is textured with the correct image (Fig. 17.7(a)). In Figs. 17.7(c) and (d), some pixels of the arche have been replaced by pixels from the background.

The object appearance has to be severely distorted to mislead the matching process: the correct pose is computed for the cases (b), (c), (e) and (f), and fails only for extreme occlusion in case (d), all in Fig. 17.7.

The first conclusion is that tracking is very stable when we dispose of a correct model and when the view of the object does not change.

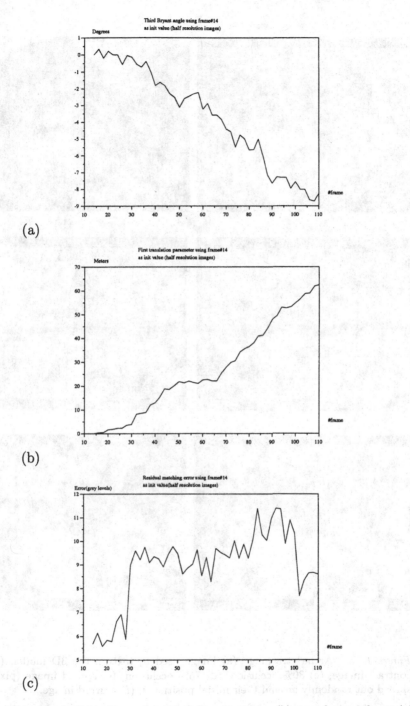

Figure 17.6 "Arche" tracking: (a) third Bryant angle, (b) translation about (x) world axis, (c) residual matching error.

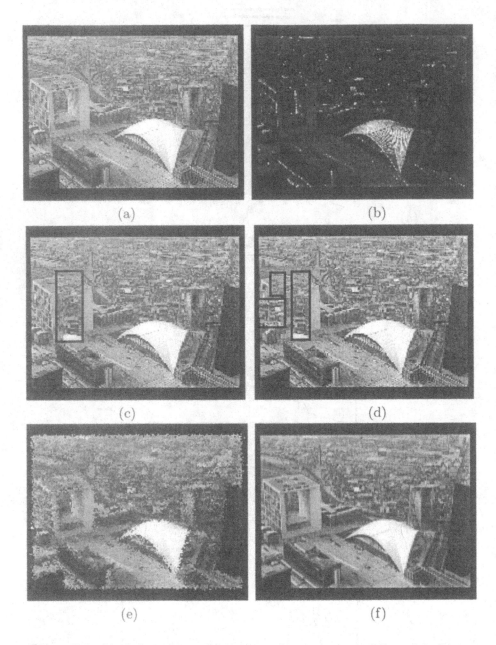

Figure 17.7 "Arche" tracking: (a) image used to texture the 3D model, (b) low contrast image, (c) 30% occlusion, (d) 75% occlusion, (e) spread image (pixels are spread out randomly around their initial positions), (f) blurred image.

Figure 17.8 "Minitel" tracking (a) frame #0, (b) frame #6, (c) frame #12.

8.2   MINITEL

In the next experiment, we studied the performance of tracking when the model used was no longer exact.

In this case of a non-exact model use, we studied first the minitel sequence. This sequence is such that the minitel is moving quickly (pure rotational motion), the camera is fixed, and the background is very different from the minitel texture. So, tracking errors will come mainly from the lack of precision of the model. Figs. 17.8(a), (b), and (c) show the tracking results.

As the object presents various aspects, tracking using only texture learning at initialization time happened to be unstable (the part of the object seen at initialization time disappears even completely after a while). In order to cope with the quick object aspect change, we implemented an adaptive tracking version where texture is learned at each frame. As the 3D model does not exactly correspond to the real object, the tracking is not correct: the 3D movement of the minitel is very poor, but the projection of this movement on the image sequence remains very good and is without jittering effect. So, as a conclusion, model errors bring 3D position errors but tracking remains stable in the sense that the projection of the 3D positions still fits well with the 2D data. The second point is that when the object aspect changes in the sequence, texture learning at the initialization time is no longer sufficient and frame by frame refreshment is a good way to alleviate this problem.

8.3   CAR

We decided to study a more realistic case, where camera and object are both moving which implies cluttered background movements. Illumination variations on the car are also very important (110 grey level differences between the two extreme frames on the object). In order to study the influence of model deficiencies in this more realistic case, we used two versions of the car model: one model is very crude (9 faces:

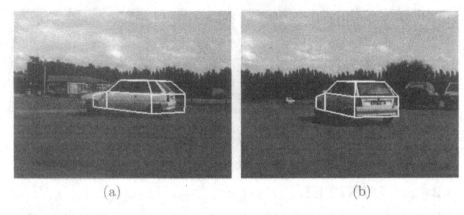

(a)   (b)

Figure 17.9   Car tracking using a simple 3D model; (a) frame #150, (b) frame #201.

(a)   (b)

Figure 17.10   Car tracking using a more detailed 3D model; (a) frame #150, (b) frame #201.

(a)   (b)

Figure 17.11   Car tracking; (a) using only one keyframe and texture learning at each frame, (b) tracking results using 4 keyframes.

Figure 17.9), the other one is more detailed but still with modeling errors (828 faces: Figure 17.10).

As the car movement is significant and the lighting conditions vary a lot, tracking needs to use adaptive texture learning. In the case when the object model is poor, such as the minitel or the car, texture learning may induce some texture error since the model does not fit properly during the learning phase. Some background pixels are then used to texture the new model. This problem implies some deviations in the tracking results. We found out that a model error produces a cumulative matching error when we process the successive frame. This matching error grows faster when the model error is greater. The matching error grows very steadily due to the feedback produced by the error function which infers stability to the positioning process. So displacement grows slowly from frame to frame and only in a more significant manner when the model error is itself greater. Compare Fig. 17.9(a) and Fig. 17.10(a). The initial positioning at frame #150 was roughly the same but the tracking error is much more significant in Fig. 17.9(b) than in Fig. 17.10(b) at the same time step. This effect might be reduced by adding a texture learning controller and, of course, by using a better 3D model. The use of the best car model, though it improves considerably the tracking performance, produces as poor results as with the more primitive model but after a longer sequence. See Fig. 17.11(a) where the positioning error becomes very pronounced after 160 time steps due to the cumulative effect of adaptive model matching.

Another source of tracking error is due to transparent or semi-transparent faces. Texture on objects such as windows, varies in an unpredictable way, because transparency implies that background pixels become part of the 3D model texture. Specular reflections create some uncontrolled texture artefacts. In order to avoid these problems one has to exclude these faces from the 3D model, so that we do not use them in the error matching function. The elimination of the windows in the car model allowed us to obtain smaller jittering effects (animation artefacts) than with the global car model.

An important problem of 3D object tracking occurs when new facets of the object appear in the sequence. They were not learned before so that tracking cannot incorporate them. Thus, tracking has the tendency to block such rotations of the object. To solve this problem, the idea consists of treating the image sequence in the reverse time sequencing. As in post-production applications, one does not care about real time computation and the order in which the sequence is computed, then we can let the user define by hand, several keyframes instead of one. In this case several calibration processes are performed and for each keyframe

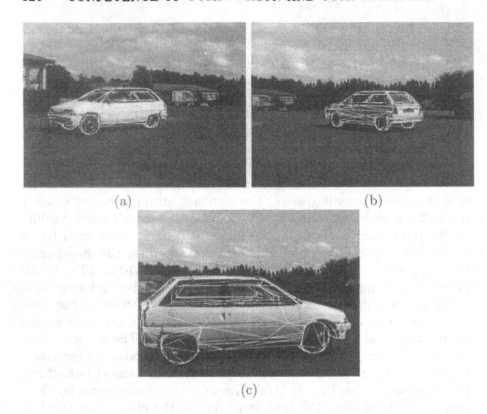

(a)   (b)

(c)

Figure 17.12   Car tracking; (a) frame #0, (b) frame #120, (c)frame #220.

two trackings (backward and forward) are computed. This allows the tracker to be able to track a sequence properly for a large number of frames (220 frames). Fig. 17.11 shows the difference when tracking the car by using one keyframe and using four keyframes.

Figs. 17.12(a), (b) and (c) show tracking results for a complicated car motion where both the camera and the car are moving. Nevertheless, the tracking is performed correctly. Another tracking difficulty is due to the fact that the visible faces at the frame #0 are completely different from the ones visible in the last frame. To obtain such results, texture learning option was enabled: the texture was refreshed every frame, and the dynamic model used the first-order predictor.

9.   CONCLUSION AND FUTURE WORK

Comparing the obtained results with the ones produced with other methods, the tracking algorithm presented appears to be more robust even for complicated motions such as 3D rotations. Using line matching like in [10] inevitably leads to model position instabilities in cluttered environment. In their paper, Nagel et al. [10] filmed a car from a high viewpoint, so that some faces were always visible during the entire sequence. In minitel and car sequences, the faces shown on the first frame are completely different from the ones shown in the last frame. Nagel et al. also had to add a shadow model to help tracking (which is not necessary in our case). Another important advantage of this method is that the model matching is consistent over time, which is important for animation and special effect purposes where getting correct (e.g., smooth) kinematics is compulsory. In other works, the overlaid model projection appears jerky, and some trajectory post-filtering is necessary. We found out that little or even no post-filtering was needed with this method.

Of course, tracking accuracy is closely related to the quality of the object geometrical description given by the 3D model. A trade-off has to be made between modeling complexity and desired accuracy. Too complex a model may slow down the tracker unnecessarily, and may not match the observed object contours any better. However if the 3D model used is too simple, not only the tracker is less accurate but it might fail completely. The exact trade-off depends on the application, but we found that even a very rough polygonal object approximation gave at least a reliable initial estimate of the 3D object motion relative to the camera.

In future work, we need to study a better dynamic model in order to force the model to follow a constrained trajectory. Also, simple texture matching is impossible when cast shadows occur: in that case, a more elaborate texture comparison scheme could be beneficial.

Further refinements can also be added to our current matching procedure, which remains very simple. For example, we could associate a confidence flag to each face of the model according to its transparency feature: this flag would modulate the matching error computation, e.g. in the car sequence the transparency of the windows implies that the model is improperly textured with pixels from the background seen through the windows. Finally, we need to extend this tracking algorithm to cameras with varying focal length by adding a zoom factor to the projection parameters to be optimized, and to more complex objects.

10.   SUMMARY

In this paper we presented a new model-based approach for object tracking. The first step is to define some keyframes for which the 3D model of the tracked object is positioned by hand. This interactive process initializes the algorithm which automatically learns the textures

Figure 17.13   A frame from an augmented reality sequence

to map them on the visible faces of the sequence. For the rest of the sequence a simulated annealing is used in order to find the new best position of the model, corresponding to its six degrees of freedom for each frame. This trajectory might be used to create an augmented reality sequence, such as in Fig. 17.13, where a 3D animated and synthetic animal has been placed on top of the car.

References

[1] R. Basri and D.W. Jacobs. Recognition using region correspondences. *International Journal of Computer Vision*, 25(2):145–166, 1997.

[2] R. N. Braithwaite and B. Bhanu. Hierarchical Gabor filters for object detection in infrared images. In *CVPR*, pages 628–631, 1994.

[3] P. Coiffet. *La Robotique, principes et applications*, pages 189–190. Editions Hermes, 1986.

[4] F. Dellaert, D. Pomerleau, and C. Thorpe. Model-based car tracking integrated with a road-follower. In *International Conference on Robotics and Automation, Leuven, Belgium, May 16-20*, 1998.

[5] F. Dellaert, C. Thorpe, and S. Thrun. Super-resolved texture tracking of planar surface patches. In *IEEE/RSJ International Conference on Intelligent Robotic Systems, Victoria, October 13-17*, 1998.

[6] F. Dellaert, S. Thrun, and C. Thorpe. Jacobian images of super-resolved texture maps for model-based motion estimation and tracking. *IEEE Workshop on Applications of Computer Vision (WACV'98), Princeton, New Jersey, October 19-21*, pages 2–7, 1998.

[7] D. M. Gavrila and L. S. Davis. 3D model-based tracking of humans in action: A multiview approach. *IEEE Intl. Symp. On Computer Vision, Coral Gables, FL*, pages 253–258, 1995.

[8] D. S. Jang, K. Gye-Young, and K. H. Choi. Model-based tracking of moving object. *Pattern Recognition*, 30(6):999–1008, 1997.

[9] T. Jebara, K. Russell, and A. Pentland. Mixtures of eigenfeatures for real-time structure from texture. In *Proceedings ICCV*, pages 128–135, 1998.

[10] D. Koller, K. Daniilidis, and H. H. Nagel. Model-based object tracking in monocular image sequences of road traffic scenes. *International Journal of Computer Vision*, 10(3):257–281, 1993.

[11] H. Kollnig and H. H. Nagel. 3D pose estimation by fitting image gradients directly to polyhedral models. In *ICCV'95*, pages 569–574, 1995.

[12] R. Mehrotra, K. R. Namuduri, and N. Ranganathan. Gabor filter-based edge detection. *Pattern Recognition*, 25(12):1479–1494, 1992.

[13] S. Moezzi, L. Tai, and P. Gerard. Virtual view generation for 3D digital video. *IEEE Multimedia*, 4(1):18–26, 1997.

[14] W. H. Press, S. A. Teukolsky, and W. T. Vetterling. *Numerical Recipes in C, the Art of Scientific Computing*. Second edition, Cambridge University Press, 1992.

[15] P. Raveda, J. Serrat, and E. Marti. A snake for model-based segmentation. In *ICCV95*, pages 816–821, 1995.

[16] T. N. Tan, G. D. Sullivan, and K. D. Baker. Pose determination and recognition of vehicles in traffic scenes. In *ECCV'94*, volume 800, pages 501–506, 1994.

[17] J. P. Tarel and J. M. Vezien. Camcal v1.0 manual. a complete software solution for camera calibration. Rapport de recherche, INRIA, 1996.

[18] X. Wu and B. Bhanu. Gabor wavelets for 3-D object recognition. In *ICCV'95*, pages 537–542, 1995.

Chapter 18

AUGMENTED REALITY BY INTEGRATING MULTIPLE SENSORY MODALITIES FOR UNDERWATER SCENE UNDERSTANDING

Vittorio Murino, Andrea Fusiello

Abstract   This chapter proposes a method for the integration of acoustic and optical data to enhance the perception of an underwater environment in teleoperation tasks. Off-shore applications are addressed, in which an underwater remotely operated vehicle is approaching an oil rig for inspection, maintenance and repairing tasks. A technique is presented which takes advantage of optical features to segment an acoustic three-dimensional (3-D) image. Cylindrical surfaces are than extracted from 3-D points, and complete cylinders are reconstructed. The final step is to present useful information to the human operator, by displaying the superposition of measured acoustic data and geometric primitives fitted to parts of it, i.e., an augmented reality view. Experimental results with real data are reported showing the effectiveness of the proposed approach.

1.   INTRODUCTION

This paper is devoted to the construction of an augmented reality view that can help a human operator of an underwater remotely operated vehicle (ROV) to better perceive and understand the surrounding environment. Two sensing channels are available, optical and acoustic. The former gives an image easier to read by a human, but visibility is very limited due to low illumination and clutter. On the other hand, acoustic data are not affected by illumination and provide inherently 3-D information, but are more complicated to understand for a human operator. From these considerations it arises the need to integrate, whenever possible, the two channels in order to exploit the best of both, so as to compensate their disadvantages. Moreover, presenting a synthetic model

331

A. Leonardis et al. (eds.), Confluence of Computer Vision and Computer Graphics, 331–349.
© 2000 Kluwer Academic Publishers. Printed in the Netherlands.

Figure 18.1 Rendering of the VRML model of an oil rig with the ROV.

of the scene superimposed on data, i.e., generating an augmented reality image, is much more useful and readable for a human operator.

The scenario for the applications consists of an ROV approaching an oil rig made up of connected pipes (see Fig. 18.1). The ROV is equipped with an optical and an acoustic camera. The optical camera provides classical gray-level images and the acoustic one provides range and intensity images associated with a set of 3-D points [18].

A virtual reality view is obtained by displaying the superposition of measured 3-D points and a synthetic model automatically constructed from the data. The key issue for automatic modeling is the segmentation of the range data into subsets of points corresponding to the desired primitives, cylinders in our case. Due to the noisy and low-density nature of the acoustic range data, segmentation using differential geometry or step-edges is infeasible. Therefore, we propose to integrate acoustic and optical images, and to use optical edges to segment the acoustic data.

First we extract pipe-boundaries in the optical image. Then, assuming that the mutual position of the two cameras is known, acoustic (3-D) points are projected onto to the image plane. The points falling inside the pipe-boundaries are segmented. The pipe direction and radius are then estimated and a synthetic model is generated by fitting cylinders.

Fusion and integration of different kinds of data is actually a matter of active research. When available information sources are of different nature, probabilistic, heuristic, or fuzzy methods are typically used [16, 3]. In case of visual data, a straightforward approach consists in recovering symbolic information separately from the several types of data, and then performing data fusion at the highest (symbolic) level. Classical symbolic Artificial Intelligence techniques [1] are applied in this case. In our case, due to the similarity of the data at hand (they are both images), we would like to integrate them at a lower processing level, possibly to improve or facilitate the recognition procedure on either sensorial channel.

Some works are present in the literature on data fusion and integration of the different sensor functionalities. Among these, some interesting papers can be considered concerning the fusion of intensity and range data, mainly derived by a laser range finder [10, 24, 23].

In [10], a Markov Random Field (MRF) model is proposed for the fusion of registered range and intensity images aimed at image segmentation. An extended weak membrane model is utilized as prior knowledge devoted to enforce the line process, thus improving edge detection. The fusion occurred by means of a coupled term in the energy function that penalized different edge configurations in the two kinds of images. A similar method for the fusion of range and intensity images was followed in [24] by integrating in a single framework edge detection, semantic labeling and surface reconstruction. Initial edge labeling and classification is based on a physical analysis of the local behavior of intensity and range data. Then, an MRF model is used to relax the edge configuration while performing concurrently the reconstruction of the surfaces. In [23], an intensity-guided range sensing technique is presented.

Concerning specifically 3-D scene modeling, there are several works on robotic applications mainly devoted to decontamination and decommissioning tasks in hazardous environments [13, 17]. The closest to our work are [9, 12, 14]. In [9], segmentation of range data of pipes and torii is proposed by using a procedure estimating local centers of curvature. Locally fitting a bi-quadratic function, the locus of centers of curvature is estimated using a robust least squares method. Then, these centers of curvatures are used to discriminate between straight and curved cylinders, thereby allowing the accurate reconstruction of these parts for CAD modeling. A-priori information is utilized to set some algorithms' parameters in order to increase the precision of the segmentation. In [12], quadric surface parameters (representing cylinders) are used to estimate radius, axis and position, so that the resulting cylinders are displayed to an operator, without performing an actual recognition phase. Generalized cylinders are fitted to range data in [14]. The extraction of axis points is done by computing the midpoints between two contour points, then the axis curve is represented as a third degree polynomial.

In our work the acoustic range data and the optical intensity image are used in a cooperative way to extract useful (topological and geometrical) information, to be used in the construction of a virtual environment. Our goal is to automatically model significant objects present in a cluttered scene and facilitate human interpretation by displaying such objects in an augmented reality view. The only a-priori information that we exploit is that the rig consists of connected pipes. No high level (CAD) description of the visible portion of the rig is available. In another work [6] we deal with the problem of fitting (a portion of) a known model of the rig to the sensed data.

The rest of the paper is organized as follows. Section 2 describes the processing of intensity and range data and their integration, in order to obtain a segmentation of the range data. In Section 3 the extraction of cylinders from range data is outlined and in Section 4 the augmented reality view is obtained. Finally, Section 5 shows some results of the method applied on real data and, in Section 6, conclusions are drawn.

2.   SEGMENTATION

The first processing step consists of filtering and segmenting both acoustic and optical data.

2.1   ACOUSTIC DATA PROCESSING

Three-dimensional data are obtained by a high resolution acoustic camera, the *Echoscope* [11]. The scene is insonified by a high-frequency acoustic pulse and a two-dimensional array of transducer gathers the backscattered signals. The whole set of raw signals is then processed in order to enhance those coming from the fixed steering directions (called *beamsignals*) and to attenuate those coming from the other directions. The distance of a 3-D point can be measured by detecting the time instant at which the maximum peak occurs in the beamsignal (see Fig 18.2). A range image is formed by 64×64 points ordered according to an angular relation, as adjacent points correspond to adjacent beamsignals. Moreover, the intensity of the maximum peak can be used to generate another image, representing the reliability of the associated 3-D measures: the higher the intensity, the more confident the associated measure.

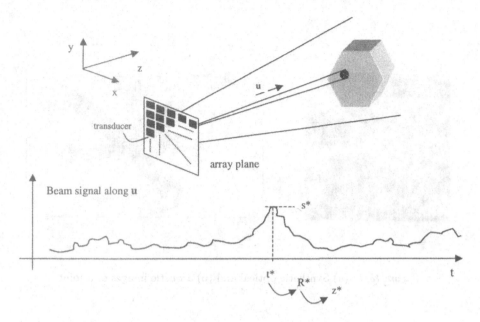

Figure 18.2   Acoustic camera

The acoustic image is affected by false reflections, caused by secondary lobes, and by acquisition noise, which is modeled as speckle noise. The intensity image turns out to provide very useful information to discriminate between "good data" and noise. A dramatic improvement of the image quality is obtained by discarding points whose associated intensity is lower than a threshold. Then, the connected components are extracted by a percolation technique: a sphere of radius R is drawn around each point, and two points are considered to be connected if their spheres intersect. Finally, a size filter eliminates the small blobs caused by noise and clutter. The radius R, the threshold on the intensity, and the threshold on the blob size are chosen based on *a priori* knowledge of the spatial resolution and direction characteristics of the sensor [8].

2.2   OPTICAL DATA PROCESSING

The image, obtained by a conventional optical camera is first filtered with an edge preserving anisotropic smoothing [19], that is a smoothing operator whose strength depends on the local gray-level gradient.

Straight lines are extracted by combining Canny's edge detector [5] and Burn's *Plane Fit Algorithm* [4]. First edge points are extracted with the Canny edge detector, that allows to find very sharp edges (often

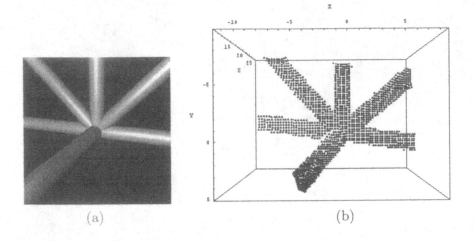

(a)   (b)

Figure 18.3   (a) Synthetic optical and (b) acoustic images of a joint.

one pixel large) thanks to the non-maxima suppression. Then, pixels are clustered in support regions if they are spatially adjacent and if their gradient orientation is roughly the same. The line parameters are computed using the intersections of the weighted plane fit to the intensity values and the horizontal average pixel intensity plane, within a support region. The weight favors the intensity values of pixels with high gradient magnitude. Taking mainly the gradient orientation as the evidence for a line and using the plane fit method, the algorithm extracts long, straight lines as well as shorter lines and is effective in finding low-contrast lines.

Each extracted segment is then labeled, and its attributes (midpoint, length, etc.) are computed. In order to find pipes in the image, pairs of segments are grouped together, which are possibly the projection of the boundaries of a pipe. Grouping is based on proximity and parallelism criteria: two segments are paired if the distance between their midpoints is less than a threshold (that is related to the expected distance of pipes boundaries in the image), and if their angle is in the range of $180° \pm 30°$. Finally, the convex hulls of all the paired segments are computed.

2.3   INTEGRATION

Optical and acoustic data are integrated by projecting 3-D points obtained by the acoustic camera onto the image plane of the optical camera. Points falling inside a convex hull are deemed to belong to a candidate pipe. Points that lie outside any convex hull are discarded. In such a way a segmentation of the acoustic image is obtained.

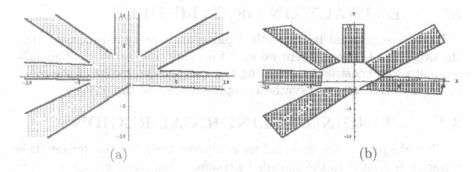

Figure 18.4 (a) Projection of the acoustic points onto the image plane, where the optical edges are also depicted. (b) Segmented points after computing the convex hulls.

In order to project 3-D points onto the image plane, the relative pose (i.e., position and orientation) between the optical and the acoustic camera is needed. This information is obtained *off-line*, once and for all, by means of a semi-automatic calibration procedure. Both acoustic and optical data are registered to the same known model of a given object in the scene, thereby obtaining the relative pose between the optical and the acoustic camera.

In our approach, we used the oil rig itself as a calibration object. It must be stressed that this is the only point in this work where we use the CAD model of the oil rig. In the rest of the paper, describing the *on-line* functioning, only generic assumptions will be made (namely, knowing that the rig consists of pipes). The procedure can be summarized as follows (for more details refer to [7]):

- calibrate camera intrinsic parameters, using Robert's algorithm [20] and a suitable calibration rig;

- register 3-D data points to the model by using the Iterative Closest Point algorithm [2], thereby obtaining the pose of the acoustic camera;

- match image segments and model segments in the image, using an algorithm due to Scott and Longuett-Higgins [22];

- register optical segments to the model, using Lowe's algorithm [15] to find the pose of the camera.

Figure 18.4 shows an example of segmentation of synthetic data.

3.   EXTRACTION OF CYLINDERS

Regions segmented in the optical plane are now back-projected into the original 3-D frame where we look for cylindrical surfaces. The subsequent phase consists of estimating the axis and the radius of the pipes in order to reconstruct a synthetic representation of the objects.

3.1   FINDING CYLINDRICAL REGIONS

Pipe-like regions are detected by analyzing their *inertial tensor* (this criterion is related to the so-called *principal component analysis* as discussed in [8]). The inertial tensor I of a set of 3-D points $\{x_i\}$ of unit mass is defined as:

$$J = \sum_i (\mathbf{x}_i - \mathbf{o}) \sqcap (\mathbf{x}_i - \mathbf{o}) , \qquad (18.1)$$

where $\mathbf{o}$ is the center of mass of the distribution, and the symbol $\sqcap$ denotes the following operator

$$\mathbf{a} \sqcap \mathbf{b} \equiv \begin{pmatrix} (a_y b_y + a_z b_z) & -a_x b_y & -a_x b_z \\ -a_y b_x & (a_x b_x + a_z b_z) & -a_y b_z \\ -a_z b_x & -a_z b_y & (a_x b_x + a_y b_y) \end{pmatrix}. \qquad (18.2)$$

We denote with $\{\lambda_i\}$ $i = 1, 2, 3$ the eigenvalues of J ordered by increasing magnitude and with $\mathbf{e}_i$ the respective eigenvectors. For a cylindrical distribution of points, it can be shown that the eigenvector $\mathbf{e}_1$ points in the axis direction and the following relations hold for the eigenvalues

$$\lambda_1 \ll \lambda_2, \qquad \lambda_2 \simeq \lambda_3. \qquad (18.3)$$

Therefore, if one eigenvalue is much smaller with respect to the others, the region is classified as a cylinder, otherwise it is discarded. This algorithm needs a threshold to decide to what extent λ_1 has to be smaller with respect to the other two eigenvalues. If this threshold is too small, elongated regions can be misclassified as cylinders. On the other hand, if it is too high, some pipes could be lost.

3.2   FITTING CYLINDERS

In order to fit a cylinder to the cylindrical regions extracted in the previous step, we need to find the axis and the radius. The axis direction is given by $\mathbf{e}_1 / \|\mathbf{e}_1\|$. The axis length is obtained by projecting the points belonging to the cylinder onto a plane parallel to the axis and computing the height of the bounding box of the points.

In order to find the radius of the pipe, we project the points belonging to the cylinder onto a plane perpendicular to its axis. 3-D points are not distributed on a cylindrical surface, but only on a portion of it, as only the sector of the pipe facing the camera backscatters the sonar signal. Hence, their projections lie approximately on a circular sector. The center of the circle fixes the position of the cylinder and the radius gives the radius of the cylinder. The problem of fitting a circle to the points is a classical parametric regression problem that we solved using the robust Least Median of Squares (LMedS) technique [21]. The principle behind LMedS is the following:

1. given a regression problem, in which d is the minimum number of points determining a solution (three, in our case)

2. compute a candidate model based on a randomly chosen d-tuple from the data;

3. estimate the fit of this model to *all* the data, measured by the median of the squared *residuals*;

4. if the current fit is better than the previous one update the model;

5. repeat from step 2.

The optimal model represents the majority of data. Data points that do not fit into this model are *outliers*. The *breakdown point*, i.e., the smallest fraction of outliers that can yield arbitrary estimate values, is 50%. Although, in principle, all the d-tuples should be evaluated, in practice a Monte Carlo technique is applied, in which only a random sample of size m is considered. Assuming that the whole set of points may contain up to a fraction $\epsilon = 0.5$ of outliers, and requiring that the probability of missing the optimal solution be $P = 0.1$, the sample size m is [25]:

$$m = \frac{\log(P)}{\log(1 - (1 - \epsilon)^d)} = 17. \qquad (18.4)$$

Although LMedS is usually a computationally intensive method, it is practicable in our case, due to the low dimensionality of the problem. Moreover, the following observation helps in reducing the number of evaluations. When the three points in the sample are very close to each other, the estimation of the circle from such points is instable, and it is a waste of time to evaluate such a sample. In order to achieve better efficiency we used a bucketing technique, analogous to the one developed in [25], which works as follows. The rectangle containing the n points is partitioned in three regions (buckets) along the major dimension, each of them containing $n/3$ points. Each triple to be fitted with a circle is built by taking one random point from each bucket. This technique does not change the probability of a point to be selected, since each bucket has the same number of points.

An example of robust circle fitting is shown in Figure 18.5, where some of the circles that have been fitted in the LMedS process are depicted, and the selected one is drawn in bold line.

3.3   FINDING INTERSECTIONS

In general, the axis of pipes belonging to a joint will not intersect exactly in one point or may not intersect at all. To extract an approximate intersection we use the following simple algorithm: for every axes pair i, we compute the midpoint $\mathbf{m}_i$ of the unique segment that connects the two lines defined by the axes and that is perpendicular to both of them.

If the number of axes is n, the number of possible pairs is $n(n-1)/2$. We define the centre of the joint as the center of mass of these midpoints, i.e.

$$\frac{\sum_{i=1}^{n(n-1)/2} \mathbf{m}_i}{n(n-1)/2} . \tag{18.5}$$

Since we consider the *line* containing the axis, we retain only the intersections that are close enough to the axis endpoints.

This method works straightforward if there is only one joint in the scene. If this is not the case, it is necessary to preliminary subdivide the set of extracted pipes in subsets containing pipes that belong to the same joint. To do this, it is sufficient to group pipes whose distance, defined as the distance between the lines passing through the axis, is below a threshold that depends on the radius of the pipes. This can be done by building the *incidence graph G* of the pipes, i.e. a graph whose nodes are the pipes and in which two nodes are connected if the distance between

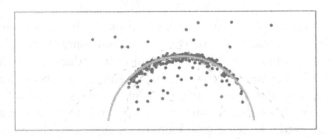

Figure 18.5 Some circles fitted during the LMedS process (the bold circle was selected).

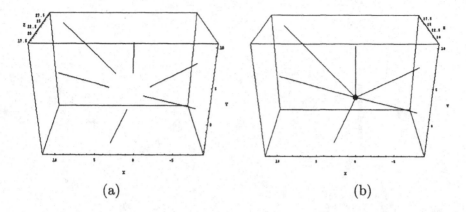

(a)   (b)

Figure 18.6 (a) Cylinder axes as extracted from data and (b) after computing the intersection.

the corresponding pipes is below the given threshold. A joint correspond to a maximal complete subgraph of G, i.e., a complete subgraph that is not contained in any larger complete subgraph. Two distinct joints can have no more than one node in common, corresponding to the pipe that connects them. The algorithm can be summarized as follows:

1. start with the graph G of order n (the total number of pipes) and with an empty list of joints;

2. while $n > 1$ repeat the following steps:

3. search for a complete subgraph of G of order n that is not contained in a subgraph of the list of joints.

4. if the latter exists, add it to the list of joints. Otherwise decrement n.

A complete subgraph of order three may not represent a real joint, but a triangle formed by three pipes (see Fig. 18.7). This a degenerate case which is easily handled. It is sufficient to calculate the three midpoints m_i defined above for the three pairs of pipes and discard those for which the distance is greater than a threshold.

For each of the remaining joints, the center is computed using Eq. (18.5).

4.   AUGMENTED REALITY

Once the pipe axes have been estimated together with their radii and their reciprocal intersections, it is possible to build a VRML (Virtual Reality Modeling Language) representation of the scene observed

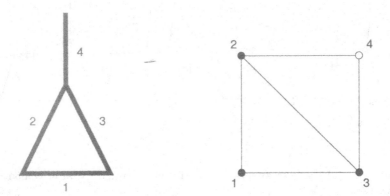

Figure 18.7 Example of a degenerate case. The rig depicted on the left has a proper joint and a false one, as its graph (right) has two complete subgraph of order three. The proper joint (2,3,4) shares two pipes with the false one (1,2,3).

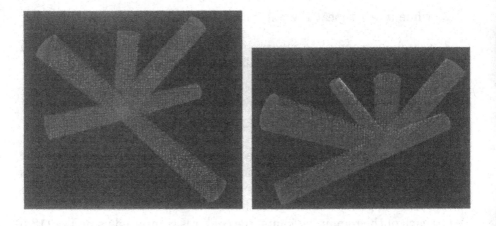

Figure 18.8 Augmented reality: virtual reconstruction of the joint with 3-D points superimposed, from two different viewpoints.

(Fig 18.8). Owing to the registration of optical and acoustic data to the model, the synthetic representation can be superimposed on actual data to support the ROV operator.

5.   EXPERIMENTAL RESULTS

We performed experiments with real and synthetic images. Figs. 18.3, 18.4, 18.6, 18.8 show an example of our technique applied to a synthetic case. Due to the nature of the data, this case is not particularly interesting. In this section we describe results obtained in a real case.

(a)   (b)

Figure 18.9   (a) Real image from the underwater camera of a joint and (b) the processed image with extracted segments.

Figure 18.9 shows a real image of a joint between four pipes, and the segments extracted from the image as described previously. Note that, due to the low quality of the image, only some segments have been detected.

Figure 18.10 shows the corresponding 3-D data, as returned by the Echoscope and the result of pre-processing.

Using the algorithm illustrated in Section 3., cylinders are fitted to 3-D data. As one might expect, the axis direction is estimated with far better accuracy than the radius. Indeed, we obtain, on the average, a relative error of 1% on the axis direction and of 20% on the radius. Figure 18.11 shows the projection onto the image plane of the 3-D points together with the boundaries of the extracted cylinders.

Finally, the reconstructed joint along with the original 3-D data are shown in Figure 18.12. Note that some pipes are missing in this joint, namely, the ones corresponding to the missing segments in the image. We are *not* assuming here that a high level description of the imaged

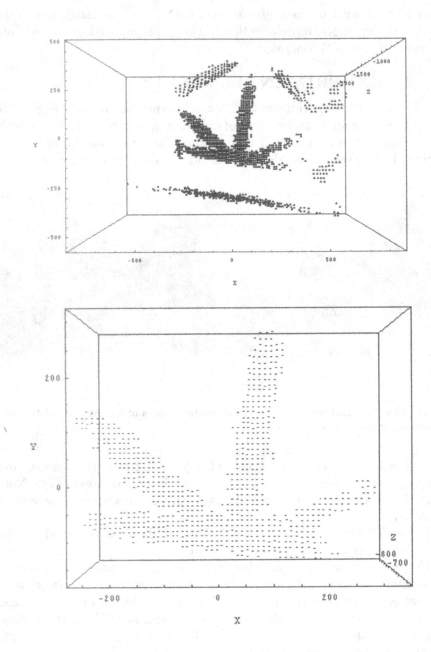

Figure 18.10 Acoustic 3-D data. Raw, from the Echoscope (top) and processed (bottom). Please note that the scale is different in the two images.

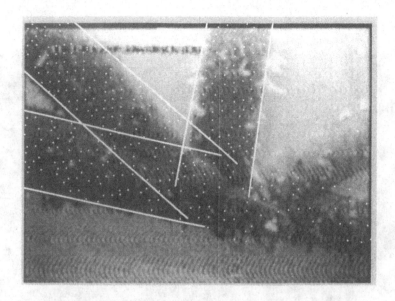

Figure 18.11   3-D points and pipe boundaries in the image plane

portion of the rig is available. *The number, position and radius of the cylinders are obtained from the data only.*

6.   SUMMARY

In this paper, the integration of optical and 3-D acoustic data for virtual scene reconstruction is addressed.

This work, carried out within the VENICE project (http://www.disi. unige.it/project/venice/), is aimed at presenting an integrated and informative view of the working environment to an underwater ROV operator. The ROV is equipped with an acoustic camera and an optical camera, and its task is the inspection, maintenance and repair of an oil rig. The only a-priori information that we exploit is that the rig consists of connected pipes. No high level (CAD) description of the portion of the rig in the view frustum is available.

Our method can be summarized as follows:

1. extract pipe boundaries in the optical image;

2. project 3-D acoustic points onto the optical image plane;

3. segment points using pipe boundaries in the image and back-project them onto the 3-D frame;

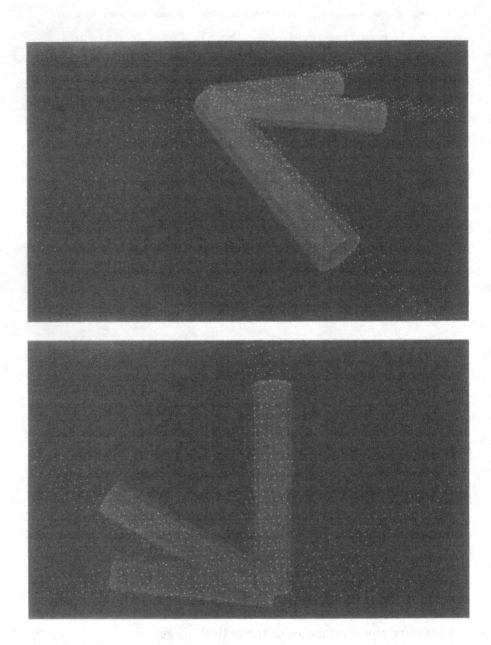

Figure 18.12   Augmented reality: virtual reconstruction of the joint with 3-D points superimposed, from two different viewpoints.

4. build a virtual reconstruction by fitting cylinders to the segmented data.

This is one of the few attempts to integrate different sensor modalities and actually fuse data having different nature and physical characteristics.

Presently, there is only a one-way influence of optical features on the analysis of 3-D acoustic data. We plan to investigate other schemes incorporating backtracking and mutual influence.

Acknowledgments

This work is supported by the European Commission under the BRITE-EURAM III project no. BE-2013 VENICE (Virtual Environment Interface by Sensor Integration for Inspection and Manipulation Control in Multifunctional Underwater Vehicles). The authors would like to thank Dr. R. K. Hansen of Omnitech A/S[1] for kindly providing the images acquired by the Echoscope acoustic camera, Riccardo Giannitrapani for the fruitful discussions, and Claudio Miatto, who wrote part of the code used in the experiments.

References

[1] D. H. Ballard and Brown C. M. *Computer Vision*. Prentice-Hall Inc., 1982.

[2] P. Besl and N. McKay. A method for registration of 3-D shapes. *IEEE Transactions on Pattern Analysis and Machine Intelligence*, 14(2):239–256, February 1992.

[3] R. R. Brooks and S. S. Iyengar. *Multi-Sensor Fusion*. Prentice Hall, Upper Saddle River, USA, 1998.

[4] J. B. Burns, A. R. Hanson, and E. M. Riseman. Extracting straight lines. *IEEE Transactions on Pattern Analysis and Machine Intelligence*, 8(4):425–456, 1986.

[5] J. F. Canny. A computational approach to edge detection. *IEEE Transactions on Pattern Analysis and Machine Intelligence*, 8(6):679–698, November 1986.

[6] A. Fusiello, R. Giannitrapani, V. Isaia, and V. Murino. Virtual environment modeling by integrated optical and acoustic sensing. In *Second International Conference on 3-D Digital Imaging and Modeling (3DIM99)*, pages 437–446, Ottawa, Canada, 4-8 October 1999. IEEE Computer Society Press.

---

[1]http://www.omnitech.no

[7] A. Fusiello and V. Murino. Calibration of an optical/acoustic sensor. In *6th International Conference on Computer Graphics and Image Processing (GKPO2000)*, 2000. To appear.

[8] R. Giannitrapani, A. Trucco, and V. Murino. Segmentation of underwater 3-D acoustical images for augmented and virtual reality applications. In *Proceedings of the OCEANS'99 Conference*, pages 459–465, Seattle (USA), September 1999. MTS/IEEE.

[9] F. Goulette. Automatic CAD modeling of industrial pipes from range images. In *International Conference on Recent Advances in 3-D Digital Imaging and Modeling*, pages 229–233, May 1997.

[10] B. Gunsel, A. K. Jain, and E. Panayirci. Reconstruction and boundary detection of range and intensity images using multiscale MRF representations. *CVGIP: Image Understanding*, 63(2):353–366, March 1996.

[11] R. K. Hansen and P. A. Andersen. A 3-D underwater acoustic camera—properties and applications. In P. Tortoli and L. Masotti, editors, *Acoustical Imaging*, pages 607–611. Plenum Press, 1996.

[12] M. Hebert, R. Hoffman, A. Johnson, and J. Osborn. Sensor based interior modeling. In *American Nuclear Society 6th Topical Meeting on Robotics and Remote Systems (ANS '95)*, pages 731 – 737, February 1995.

[13] A. Johnson, P. Leger, R. Hoffman, M. Hebert, and J. Osborn. 3-D object modeling and recognition for telerobotic manipulation. In *Proc. IEEE Intelligent Robots and Systems*, volume 1, pages 103 – 110, August 1995.

[14] D. Dion Jr. and D. Laurendeau. Generalized cylinders extraction in a range image. In *International Conference on Recent Advances in 3-D Digital Imaging and Modeling*, pages 141–147, May 1997.

[15] D. G. Lowe. Fitting parameterized three-dimensional models to images. *IEEE Transactions on Pattern Analysis and Machine Intelligence*, 13(5):441–450, May 1991.

[16] R. C. Luo and M. G. Kay. Multisensor integration and fusion in intelligent systems. *IEEE Transactions on Systems, Man and Cybernetics*, 19(5):901–931, September-October 1989.

[17] M. Maimone, L. Matthies, J. Osborn, E. Rollins, J. Teza, and S. Thayer. A photo-realistic 3-D mapping system for extreme nuclear environments: Chornobyl. In *Proceedings of the 1998 IEEE/RSJ International Conference on Intelligent Robotic Systems (IROS '98)*. IEEE, 1998.

[18] V. Murino, A. Trucco, and C. Regazzoni. A probabilistic approach to the coupled reconstruction and restoration of underwater acoustic images. *IEEE Transactions on Pattern Analysis and Machine Intelligence*, 20(1):9–22, January 1998.

[19] P. Perona and J. Malik. Scale-space and edge detection using anisotropic diffusion. *IEEE Transactions on Pattern Analysis and Machine Intelligence*, 12(7):629–639, 1990.

[20] L. Robert. Camera calibration without feature extraction. *Computer Vision, Graphics, and Image Processing*, 63(2):314–325, March 1996.

[21] P. J. Rousseeuw and A. M. Leroy. *Robust regression & outlier detection*. Wiley, 1987.

[22] G. Scott and H. Longuet-Higgins. An algorithm for associating the features of two images. In *Proceedings of the Royal Society of London B*, volume 244, pages 21–26, 1991.

[23] C. Yu W. Lie and Y. Chen. Model-based recognition and positioning of polyhedra using intensity-guided range sensing and interpretation in 3-D space. *Pattern Recognition*, 23:983–997, 1990.

[24] G. H. Zhang and A. Wallace. Physical modeling and combination of range and intensity edge data. *CVGIP: Image Understanding*, 58(2):191–220, September 1993.

[25] Z. Zhang, R. Deriche, O. Faugeras, and Q.-T. Luong. A robust technique for matching two uncalibrated images through the recovery of the unknown epipolar geometry. *Artificial Intelligence*, 78(1-2):87–119, 1995.

Index